VOLUME 1:
NORTH AND
SOUTH AMERICA

ECHOES of ARARAT

A COLLECTION OF OVER 300 FLOOD LEGENDS FROM NORTH AND SOUTH AMERICA

Nick Liguori

First printing: February 2021

Master Books®, P.O. Box 726, Green Forest, AR 72638

Master Books® is a division of
the New Leaf Publishing Group, Inc.

ISBN: 978-1-68344-271-4
ISBN: 978-1-61458-771-2 (digital)

Library of Congress Number: 2020950097

Cover design: Diana Bogardus

Interior Design: Terry White

Please consider requesting that a copy of this volume be purchased by your local library system.

Printed in the United States of America

Please visit our website for other great titles:
www.masterbooks.com

For information regarding author interviews,
please contact the publicity department
at (870) 438-5288.

Contact details: The author can be reached at
nicholasliguori@gmail.com.

Master
Books®
A Division of New Leaf Publishing Group
www.masterbooks.com

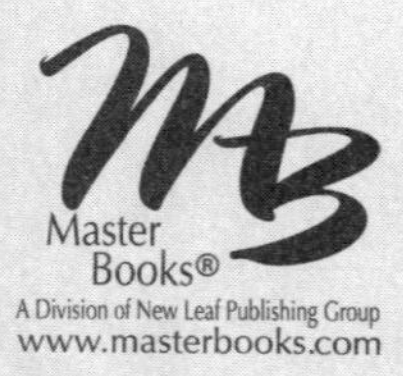

TABLE OF CONTENTS

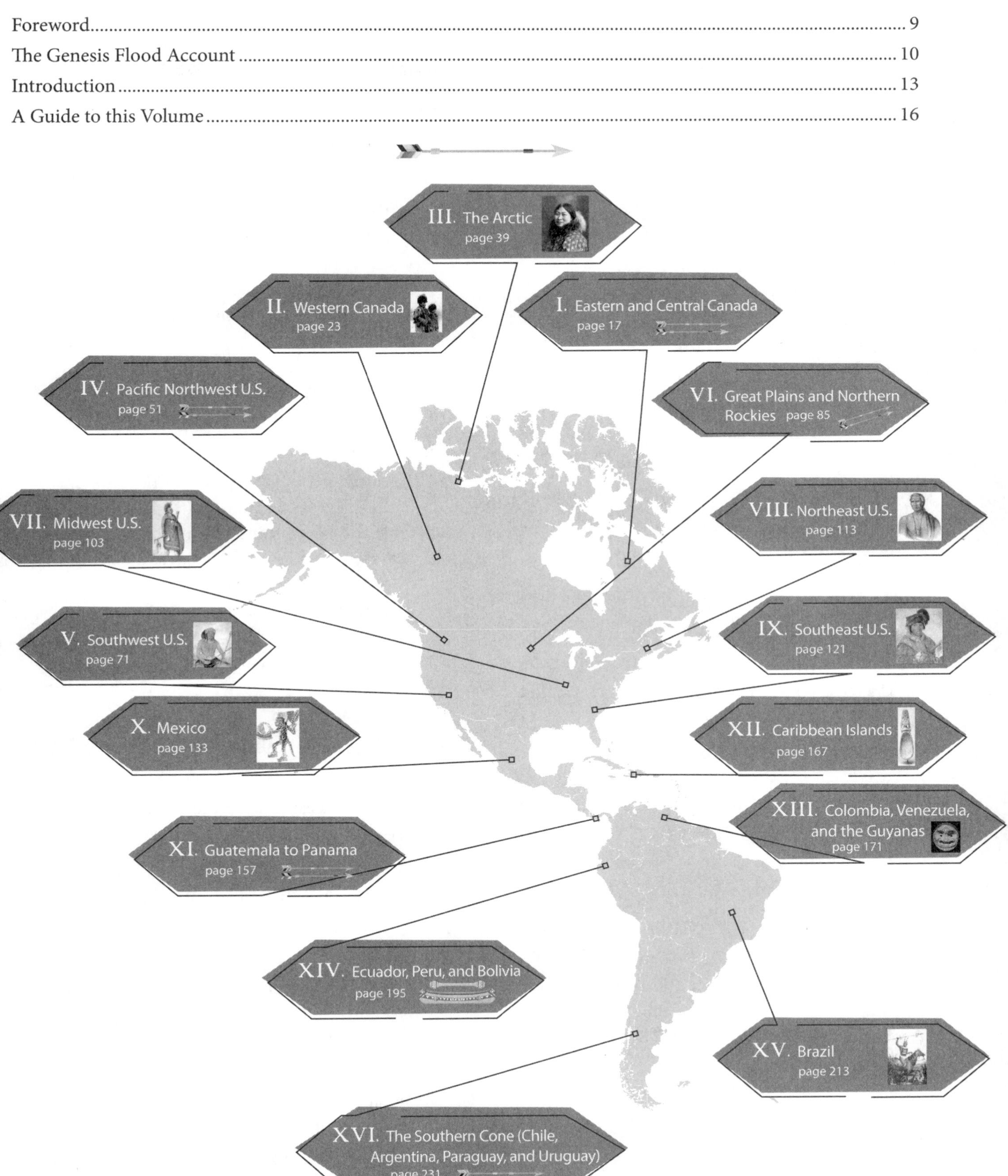
III. The Arctic
page 39
II. Western Canada
page 23
I. Eastern and Central Canada
page 17
IV. Pacific Northwest U.S.
page 51
VI. Great Plains and Northern Rockies
page 85
VII. Midwest U.S.
page 103
VIII. Northeast U.S.
page 113
V. Southwest U.S.
page 71
IX. Southeast U.S.
page 121
X. Mexico
page 133
XII. Caribbean Islands
page 167
XIII. Colombia, Venezuela, and the Guyanas
page 171
XI. Guatemala to Panama
page 157
XIV. Ecuador, Peru, and Bolivia
page 195
XV. Brazil
page 213
XVI. The Southern Cone (Chile, Argentina, Paraguay, and Uruguay)
page 231

TABLE OF CONTENTS (continued)

XIV. Ecuador, Peru, and Bolivia.................. 195

XV. Brazil... 213

FOREWORD

KEN HAM
AND
BODIE HODGE

Nick Liguori has systematically undertaken a remarkable amount of research on the First Nations peoples of North and South America. From original sources, he has masterfully documented Flood legends and even several Tower of Babel-like stories from various tribes across North and South America.

It is truly eye-opening to learn how natives were able to preserve so much of the early history of the world as it was passed down through their ancestors. This discovery is nothing less than extraordinary.

As Noah's descendants scattered from Babel to the far reaches of the globe, they took their history with them. We would anticipate that some of the historical accounts would be lost to time, embellished, mis-transmitted, incorporated local geography and fauna, etc. Naturally, there were deviations in many accounts — as we would expect.

Some of these deviations related to incorporating their local mountains, animals, boat types, and terrain into their accounts. But overall, we were very impressed with the number details they recorded, based on the true (inspired by God) Genesis account that they managed to retain. Seeing how elders of many tribes continued the knowledge of a global flood, including such things as doves and ravens being sent forth from the ship and so on, the reader is given a powerful testimony to the true account of Noah's Flood recorded in the Bible.

As a point of note, since we are all descendants of Noah, all of us are thus related — we are all one race — the human race. We have all sinned and need Jesus Christ as our Savior to save us from sin and death — which originated in the Garden of Eden recorded in Genesis, with our mutual grandparent, Adam.

Whether we live in Europe, Africa, the Americas, Asia, the Middle East and other places, we are all blood relatives — cousins if you will—and as Christians, we need to look after one another. It is a good exercise to understand and honor our heritage going back to Noah and Adam.

Reading this book should be eye-opening as it powerfully confirms the historicity of the Scriptures. Our hope is that Mr. Liguori's book helps you realize that the history recorded in the Bible is true and that the gospel (the good news of Jesus's once-for-all death, burial, and resurrection) founded in the same book is also true.

Now, it's time to dive into the Flood legends!

THE GENESIS FLOOD ACCOUNT

The following is the account of the Flood from the Book of Genesis, 6:1 through 9:19. Genesis 11:1–9, which contains the history of the Tower of Babel, is also presented.[1]

Chapter 6:

Now it came about, when men began to multiply on the face of the land, and daughters were born to them, that the sons of God saw that the daughters of men were beautiful; and they took wives for themselves, whomever they chose. Then the Lord said, "My Spirit shall not strive with man forever, because he also is flesh; nevertheless his days shall be one hundred and twenty years." The Nephilim were on the earth in those days, and also afterward, when the sons of God came in to the daughters of men, and they bore children to them. Those were the mighty men who were of old, men of renown.

Then the Lord saw that the wickedness of man was great on the earth, and that every intent of the thoughts of his heart was only evil continually. The Lord was sorry that He had made man on the earth, and He was grieved in His heart. The Lord said, "I will blot out man whom I have created from the face of the land, from man to animals to creeping things and to birds of the sky; for I am sorry that I have made them." But Noah found favor in the eyes of the Lord.

These are the records of the generations of Noah. Noah was a righteous man, blameless in his time; Noah walked with God. Noah became the father of three sons: Shem, Ham, and Japheth.

Now the earth was corrupt in the sight of God, and the earth was filled with violence. God looked on the earth, and behold, it was

Key Points in the Genesis Flood Account

1. Takes place in ancient past
2. Divine judgment upon human evil and violence
3. A prophet (an old man) is warned by God to prepare for the coming Flood
4. He warns the people, but is not believed (2 Peter 2:5)
5. He survives in a massive, enclosed wooden ship
6. Pairs of animals are brought on board, along with many foods
7. Global Flood covers all the earth, even high mountains
8. Water bursts forth from subterranean springs below, and from sky above
9. Rains for 40 days and Noah remains inside ark one year and ten days
10. All land-dwelling, air-breathing life drowns except for a few survivors
11. The ark comes to rest on a high mountain in Ararat
12. A raven and a dove are released to search for land. The second time the dove is sent, it returns with a fresh olive leaf in its beak
13. The survivors wait for the earth to dry, then return to repopulate the world
14. Many nephilim ("fallen ones," possibly giants) were present in pre-Flood world
15. Rainbow is given as a sign of promise that God will never again destroy the entire world with a flood
16. The multiplying and confusion of languages (Tower of Babel) takes place not long after Flood

1. Scripture quotations taken from the New American Standard Bible® (NASB), copyright © 1960, 1962, 1963, 1968, 1971, 1972, 1973, 1975, 1977, 1995 by The Lockman Foundation. Used by permission. www.Lockman.org.

corrupt; for all flesh had corrupted their way upon the earth.

Then God said to Noah, "The end of all flesh has come before Me; for the earth is filled with violence because of them; and behold, I am about to destroy them with the earth. Make for yourself an ark of gopher wood; you shall make the ark with rooms, and shall cover it inside and out with pitch. This is how you shall make it: the length of the ark three hundred cubits, its breadth fifty cubits, and its height thirty cubits. You shall make a window for the ark, and finish it to a cubit from the top; and set the door of the ark in the side of it; you shall make it with lower, second, and third decks. Behold, I, even I am bringing the flood of water upon the earth, to destroy all flesh in which is the breath of life, from under heaven; everything that is on the earth shall perish. But I will establish My covenant with you; and you shall enter the ark — you and your sons and your wife, and your sons' wives with you. And of every living thing of all flesh, you shall bring two of every kind into the ark, to keep them alive with you; they shall be male and female. Of the birds after their kind, and of the animals after their kind, of every creeping thing of the ground after its kind, two of every kind will come to you to keep them alive. As for you, take for yourself some of all food which is edible, and gather it to yourself; and it shall be for food for you and for them." Thus Noah did; according to all that God had commanded him, so he did.

Chapter 7:

Then the Lord said to Noah, "Enter the ark, you and all your household, for you alone I have seen to be righteous before Me in this time. You shall take with you of every clean animal by sevens, a male and his female; and of the animals that are not clean two, a male and his female; also of the birds of the sky, by sevens, male and female, to keep offspring alive on the face of all the earth. For after seven more days, I will send rain on the earth forty days and forty nights; and I will blot out from the face of the land every living thing that I have made." Noah did according to all that the Lord had commanded him.

Now Noah was six hundred years old when the flood of water came upon the earth. Then Noah and his sons and his wife and his sons' wives with him entered the ark because of the water of the flood. Of clean animals and animals that are not clean and birds and everything that creeps on the ground, there went into the ark to Noah by twos, male and female, as God had commanded Noah. It came about after the seven days, that the water of the flood came upon the earth. In the six hundredth year of Noah's life, in the second month, on the seventeenth day of the month, on the same day all the fountains of the great deep burst open, and the floodgates of the sky were opened. The rain fell upon the earth for forty days and forty nights.

On the very same day Noah and Shem and Ham and Japheth, the sons of Noah, and Noah's wife and the three wives of his sons with them, entered the ark, they and every beast after its kind, and all the cattle after their kind, and every creeping thing that creeps on the earth after its kind, and every bird after its kind, all sorts of birds. So they went into the ark to Noah, by twos of all flesh in which was the breath of life. Those that entered, male and female of all flesh, entered as God had commanded him; and the Lord closed it behind him.

Then the flood came upon the earth for forty days, and the water increased and lifted up the ark, so that it rose above the earth. The water prevailed and increased greatly upon the earth, and the ark floated on the surface of the water. The water prevailed more and more upon the earth, so that all the high mountains everywhere under the heavens were covered. The water prevailed fifteen cubits higher, and the mountains were covered. All flesh that moved on the earth perished, birds and cattle and beasts and every swarming thing that swarms upon the earth, and all mankind; of all that was on the dry land, all in whose nostrils was the breath of the spirit of life, died. Thus He blotted out every living thing that was upon the face of the land, from man to animals to creeping things and to birds of the sky, and they were blotted out from the earth; and only Noah was left, together with those that were with him in the ark. The water prevailed upon the earth one hundred and fifty days.

Chapter 8:

But God remembered Noah and all the beasts and all the cattle that were with him in the ark; and God caused a wind to pass over the earth, and the water subsided. Also the fountains of the deep and the floodgates of the sky were closed, and the rain from the sky was restrained; and the water receded steadily from the earth, and at the end of one hundred and fifty days the water decreased. In the seventh month, on the seventeenth day of the month, the ark rested upon the mountains of Ararat. The water decreased steadily until the tenth month; in the tenth month, on the first day of the month, the tops of the mountains became visible.

Then it came about at the end of forty days, that Noah opened the window of the ark which he had made; and he sent out a raven, and it flew here and there until the water was dried up from the earth. Then he sent out a dove from him, to see if the water was abated from the face of the land; but the dove found no resting place for the sole of her foot, so she returned to him into the ark, for the water was on the surface of all the earth. Then he put out his hand and took her, and brought her into the ark to himself. So he waited yet another seven days; and again he sent out the dove from the ark. The dove came to him toward evening, and behold, in her beak was a freshly picked olive leaf. So Noah knew that the water was abated from the earth. Then he waited yet another seven days, and sent out the dove; but she did not return to him again.

Now it came about in the six hundred and first year, in the first month, on the first of the month, the water was dried up from the earth. Then Noah removed the covering of the ark, and looked, and behold, the surface of the ground was dried up. In the second month, on the twenty-seventh day of the month, the earth was dry. Then God spoke to Noah, saying, "Go out of the ark, you and your wife and your sons and your sons' wives with you. Bring out with you every living thing of all flesh that is with you, birds and animals and every creeping thing that creeps on the earth, that they may breed abundantly on the earth, and be fruitful and multiply on the earth." So Noah went out, and his sons and his wife and his sons' wives with him. Every beast, every creeping thing, and every bird, everything that moves on the earth, went out by their families from the ark.

Then Noah built an altar to the Lord, and took of every clean animal and of every clean bird and offered burnt offerings on the altar. The Lord smelled the soothing aroma; and the Lord said to Himself, "I will never again curse the ground on account of man, for the intent of man's heart is evil from his youth; and I will never again destroy every living thing, as I have done. "While the earth remains, seedtime and harvest, And cold and heat, and summer and winter, and day and night shall not cease."

Chapter 9:

And God blessed Noah and his sons and said to them, "Be fruitful and multiply, and fill the earth. The fear of you and the terror of you will be on every beast of the earth and on every bird of the sky; with everything that creeps on the ground, and all the fish of the sea, into your hand they are given. Every moving thing that is alive shall be food for you; I give all to you, as I gave the green plant.,Only you shall not eat flesh with its life, that is, its blood. Surely I will require your lifeblood; from every beast I will require it. And from every man, from every man's brother I will require the life of man. "Whoever sheds man's blood, By man his blood shall be shed, For in the image of God He made man.

"As for you, be fruitful and multiply; Populate the earth abundantly and multiply in it."

Then God spoke to Noah and to his sons with him, saying, "Now behold, I Myself do establish My covenant with you, and with your descendants after you; and with every living creature that is with you, the birds, the cattle, and every beast of the earth with you; of all that comes out of the ark, even every beast of the earth. I establish My covenant with you; and all flesh shall never again be cut off by the water of the flood, neither shall there again be a flood to destroy the earth." God said, "This is the sign of the covenant which I am making between Me and you and every living creature that is with you, for all successive generations; I set My bow in the cloud, and it shall be for a sign of a covenant between Me and the earth. It shall come about, when I bring a cloud over the earth, that the bow will be seen in the cloud, and I will remember My covenant, which is between Me and you and every living creature of all flesh; and never again shall the water become a flood to destroy all flesh. When the bow is in the cloud, then I will look upon it, to remember the everlasting covenant between God and every living creature of all flesh that is on the earth." And God said to Noah, "This is the sign of the covenant which I have established between Me and all flesh that is on the earth."

Now the sons of Noah who came out of the ark were Shem and Ham and Japheth; and Ham was the father of Canaan. These three were the sons of Noah, and from these the whole earth was populated.

Chapter 11:

Now the whole earth used the same language and the same words. It came about as they journeyed east, that they found a plain in the land of Shinar and settled there. They said to one another, "Come, let us make bricks and burn them thoroughly." And they used brick for stone, and they used tar for mortar. They said, "Come, let us build for ourselves a city, and a tower whose top will reach into heaven, and let us make for ourselves a name, otherwise we will be scattered abroad over the face of the whole earth." The Lord came down to see the city and the tower which the sons of men had built. The Lord said, "Behold, they are one people, and they all have the same language. And this is what they began to do, and now nothing which they purpose to do will be impossible for them. Come, let Us go down and there confuse their language, so that they will not understand one another's speech." So the Lord scattered them abroad from there over the face of the whole earth; and they stopped building the city. Therefore its name was called Babel, because there the Lord confused the language of the whole earth; and from there the Lord scattered them abroad over the face of the whole earth.

INTRODUCTION

In tribe after tribe across the world, we find oral traditions of a great flood that happened in ancient times. These tell that a man was forewarned by God, or the Great Spirit, of a coming flood. This man prepared a large wooden vessel for the salvation of his family and the animals. The flood came and destroyed all life that was on the earth, except for those saved in the boat. Finally, the boat landed on a high mountain. The waters began to recede, and the man sent forth a raven and a dove to discern whether there was dry land. The dove returned, carrying a fresh leaf in its beak. The man took this as a sign that the flood was coming to an end. Then they came down and inhabited the land again, and repopulated the world.

In this volume, I have documented over 300 flood traditions from the First Nations peoples of North and South America, similar to the Genesis account both in general outline and specific details. Overall, it can be said that nearly every tribe—at least those whose stories we have access to—possess a memory of the Flood.

This universal testimony to the Flood must somehow be accounted for. It can no longer be ignored. I submit that the only satisfactory explanation, in light of this augmented body of evidence, is that the Flood actually happened, just as Genesis says it did.

And if that is true, then that radically changes everything. It changes our understanding of ancient history, and it changes how we study archaeology and geology. It also changes how we think of God, ourselves, the meaning of life, and what kind of lives we live.

"Amongst one hundred and twenty different tribes that I have visited in North and South and Central America, not a tribe exists that has not related to me distinct or vague traditions of such a calamity, in which one, or three, or eight persons were saved above the waters, on the top of a high mountain.[1] (George Catlin, early 19th century explorer and painter)

Who Cares?

Someone will say, "I'm a Christian. Who cares if the Flood happened? Who cares if Genesis is literal history? We just need to focus on Jesus."

My response to that is, I agree that we need to focus on Jesus. He is the Savior and the source of eternal life. Jesus is what it's all about. In fact, Jesus is why I have written this book.

What do I mean by that? I mean that if we as Christians really love Jesus, then we have to live out the faith. And if we live out the faith, then we have to interact with reality. And if we interact with reality, then we will meet and interact with real people. And then we will quickly realize that many people do not take Jesus seriously at all, and do not take the Gospel seriously.

One reason they do not take Jesus and Christianity seriously is because they subscribe to a Darwinian view of history and science, which they were taught in school. According to this, evolution over billions of years is true, man is only a material being, with no soul, the book of Genesis is myth, miracles do not happen, the Bible is false, and Jesus is irrelevant.

You see, many non-Christians understand the Bible better than Christians do, which is a shame. They understand that if you destroy the foundation—which is the book of Genesis—then the entire building collapses, Christianity is meaningless, and Jesus is irrelevant.

If the basic claims of Genesis are not true—that God created, that it was good in the beginning, that death came after sin and not before, that man is more than a material being, that God is active in the world, that God is a personal God who judges sin—then there is nothing for Jesus to save us from! If the Genesis worldview is false, then Jesus died in vain, and His death is meaningless. But if Genesis is true, then Jesus' death means everything!

We Christians need to wake up. We need to stop bringing a knife to a gunfight. We need to stop retreating and surrendering when skeptics and university professors raise objections about science and history. To retreat there is to invalidate Christianity itself.

But we don't have to retreat. The truth is on our side. All the evidence is on our side. It's about time we used it. So we need to start realizing that an assault on Genesis, Exodus, or any other book of the Bible is an assault on Jesus and the good news of Christianity itself.

Therefore, I have written this book, to show that the book of Genesis is true. To remove intellectual barriers that are blocking people from taking the claims of Jesus

1. George Catlin, O-Kee-Pa: A Religious Ceremony and other Customs of the Mandans (Philadelpha: J.B. Lippincott and Co., 1867), p. 1–2.

seriously. Even if this book is but one small piece in that puzzle, I hope it will help promote an environment where people take the claims of Jesus seriously.

A Theory in Crisis

Darwinian evolution is a theory in crisis. It is now more vulnerable than ever, as scientific advances have failed to offer the support that Charles Darwin hoped for, when he expressed hope that future discoveries would confirm his theory. Recent discoveries have damaged Darwin's theory, rather than supporting it. Today, the theory is haunted by new discoveries, impossible barriers, and a world of evidence that supports the opposite side. Billions more fossils have been found, but there is still no fossil evidence of complex life arising from primitive lifeforms, and no evidence of transitions having occurred from one type of animal to another. Worse yet, we have no mechanism for evolution to occur. The discovery of DNA and genetic information has shown that macroevolution cannot happen.

And so, while evolution continues to be inculcated to the nation's youth by teachers speaking confidently, and while textbooks trot out the same old arguments in favor of evolution—like peppered moths, fruit flies, the Miller-Urey experiment, and Australopithecus—the scientists performing the research are far less confident, and all these "icons" of evolution have been refuted.

In fact, an increasing number of scientists and scholars are breaking away from the Darwinian, evolutionary paradigm. Many scientists such as Michael Behe, Robert Carter, and Kurt Wise are performing groundbreaking research, which confirms intelligent design, and initial creation by God. Today, a powerful and persuasive body of scientific evidence exists in favor of intelligent design and the biblical view. In fact, creationism is not only proving to be defensible, but it is showing predictive value—unlocking further insights in microbiology and genetics.

A similar thing is unfolding in the field of geology. The uniformitarian view of Charles Lyell has seen its best days long ago. There is a growing recognition that slow and gradual processes are insufficient, and that catastrophic processes are necessary to account for many of the earth's features and formations. In fact, the conventional view of earth's history has difficulty explaining many aspects of the earth's surface and the geologic column—things ranging from the Grand Canyon, water gaps and wind gaps, knife-edge boundaries between flat sedimentary layers that stretch for hundreds of miles horizontally, to folded rock layers and the formation of coal beds. Creation scientists and geologists such as Andrew Snelling and Steven Austin are making revolutionary discoveries which show that a biblical history—one which acknowledges the Genesis Flood, with its enormous geologic impacts—is the only one that can explain the rocks beneath our feet.

The same can be said about the minimalist or skeptical view of the Bible's accuracy. Discoveries of the last 75 years have confirmed, time after time, the historical accuracy of the books of the Bible. New archaeological discoveries, manuscripts, and historical insights continue to pour in. Today, biblical scholars and archeologists such as Stephen Collins, Joseph Holden, and Douglas Petrovich are making important discoveries which confirm the accuracy of the Bible, from Genesis to the books of the New Testament. Every new discovery confirms the Bible's historical accuracy, rather than contradicting it.

It is an exciting time to be alive, for the Christian scholar or scientist. Indeed, for any person interested in science or history, it is an exciting time to be alive.

Global Traditions of the Flood

It is in the context of the above-mentioned growing body of evidence, which supports the Bible, that I humbly offer this book. The Noahic Flood is a subject of enormous importance to the book of Genesis, and to the Bible in general. And so we must ask: Is the Genesis Flood account true and accurate? The answer to that question will go a long way to determine whether the Bible can be trusted, whether a secular or biblical worldview is true, whether God exists and intervenes in the world, whether God judges, and whether Christianity is true.

There is, in fact, very strong evidence to confirm the truth of the Noahic Flood, and the truth of the book of Genesis. That's because it happens to be true. We are living in God's world. We did not create ourselves. One of those lines of evidence—besides scientific and historical evidence—involves Flood legends. Nearly every tribe or nation has a legend, a historical tradition, or even a written history claiming that a great Flood took place in the ancient past. And these traditions usually sound very similar to the Genesis Flood account. That is the main point of my book. And that is the sort of thing that defies an explanation—unless the Genesis account is true.[2]

> Some Christian leaders and teachers are ashamed of the book of Genesis, especially the first 11 chapters. They water down, ignore, and marginalize Genesis in favor of the world's view about history. That is a mistake.

I have not yet told you why I chose to write a book on the subject of Flood traditions. Well, I was always interested in Christian apologetics. I love exploring evidence, and learning about all of the scientific,

2. For my responses to naturalistic attempts to explain the existence of Flood traditions, see Appendix D.

historical, and experiential evidence which confirms the truth of the Bible, the existence of God, and the truth of Jesus Christ. My experience on a very liberal college campus probably had something to do with it. There was much skepticism, atheistic evolutionary teaching, and hostility to Christianity, which heightened my interest in studying apologetics.

However, it was several years after graduating college that I became interested in Flood legends. I was studying it, like any other area of biblical research, by finding the best books on the subject and reading them. It began to dawn on me that I had stumbled upon an area of much unfinished work. There were Flood traditions here and there, in various books, in various articles, but it was piecemeal. It was fragmentary. In other places there was a lot of anecdotes and second-hand sourcing. I felt that this was a very potent area of evidence for the Bible, just waiting to be tapped.

So it seemed to me that there was a need for this project. Many people reading this are already aware of the existence of Flood stories from different parts of the world. However, I believe the full weight and significance of this data is under-appreciated, because Flood traditions have been under-reported and under-documented. I submit that these Flood traditions are even more pervasive and more compelling than previously thought! I believe their significance now needs to be reassessed. That is why I have sought to document these Flood traditions in a comprehensive and well-sourced manner. I have presented these in an open-handed manner to allow the reader to judge their significance for himself or herself. I trust the information speaks for itself.

I am nothing compared to the Ph. D. scientists cited in the previous section. I always thought that someone far more qualified, far more seasoned, and far better-suited for this subject ought to have written this book. And it ought to have been written many decades ago, I believe. Yet here we are, and the work was unfinished, so I stepped forward, albeit reluctantly. Much more remains to be found and written on the subject, but I hope my book (and my forthcoming second volume) is a step in the right direction, expanding our knowledge of the ubiquity of native Flood traditions.

Flood stories are not the only subject of this book. Many tribes also have ancient accounts which touch on Genesis accounts, including the creation of the world, the creation of man and woman, the Garden of Eden, and the Tower of Babel. These are documented as well, although doubtless there are many others that have escaped my notice. This is the first edition of this book. I hope that additional material can be found and included in future editions.

The Sources

The ultimate sources for the material contained in this volume are the tribe members and elders and chiefs from the First Nations peoples who have lived in North and South America from ancient times. Their histories and oral traditions have been recorded in a variety of settings, by a variety of individuals, at times ranging from the late 1400s to the present century. Those who recorded the information are historians, scientists, indigenous writers themselves, government officials, missionaries, ethnographers, and many others. As to the Flood traditions themselves, some are clearer than others. Some bear uncanny, specific resemblance to the Genesis account. Other Flood traditions are vague or fragmentary. Much has already been lost, due to the decimation of entire cultures, and due to the forgetfulness of time.

I do not claim to have located all these sources myself. I am thankful to the various historians and researchers whose work has made this volume possible, and who have provided very helpful leads in locating original sources. Many of these have been documented already. Others I found in the midst of thousands of hours of research, whether online or at countless libraries across multiple states, or in rare books obtained from foreign countries. But overall, the goal of this book was to assemble all of the relevant material so that it could be evaluated in a comprehensive manner.

I considered it very important to locate primary sources, which give the earliest and most direct access available to the information in question. Also, it was essential that the oral traditions of the Flood be aboriginal, rather than influenced by Christian or European ideas. I screened out and discarded those Flood traditions which had obvious signs of influence by settlers and missionaries. For instance, any oral traditions with biblical names such as Noah, Jesus, and the Holy Spirit, or the familiar Genesis phrase "forty days and forty nights" obviously bear the marks of Christian influence, and were thus discarded.

Overall, this process of searching netted over 300 significant Flood stories from North and South America, which the reader can consider and evaluate. Now if we love the truth, we must ask ourselves one important question: why? Why are there so many native, oral traditions that sound so similar to the Genesis Flood? Is such a finding possible in an atheistic universe? I emphatically say no. I contend that the only explanation that can truly account for all these flood traditions, which are so similar to the Genesis account, is that the Flood happened, just as Genesis says.

A GUIDE TO THIS VOLUME

The more than 300 Flood traditions and other Genesis-related traditions in this volume come from all over North and South America, and the neighboring islands, including the Caribbean and Greenland. They are organized by regions, beginning in Canada, and proceeding southward to the other end of this hemisphere.

I would also encourage the reader to check out the material in the appendices, which contains further information on several related topics. These include:

- **Appendix A:** Expanded Texts
- **Appendix B:** The Historicity of Genesis, Comparisons with the *Epic of Gilgamesh*, and North American Flood Traditions
- **Appendix C:** Earth Diver Stories and Other Variants
- **Appendix D:** Naturalistic Explanations of Flood Traditions
- **Appendix E:** Bibliography
- **Appendix F:** Recommended Reading
- **Appendix G:** Biblical Connections
- **Appendix H:** Index by Tribe, Nation, or Locale

While the focus of this volume is traditions of the Flood, scattered throughout this book are also numerous traditions of the Tower of Babel (and the resulting confusion of languages), Creation, the Garden of Eden, and the Fall, and even a few Native American prophecies of Jesus and of the coming message of salvation.

I hope you find the content of this book interesting. I pray that this book increases your faith in God and your confidence in the scriptures, including the book of Genesis. Genesis, like so many books of the Old Testament, prophesied of the coming Savior of the world, God in the flesh—Jesus, who would come to make atonement for sin and provide the way to a right relationship with God.

Finally, Jesus acknowledged the global Genesis Flood (Matthew 24:37-39). It is important that we believe in it too. Denial of the Bible's message about historical, earthly things (including the global Flood) leads to denial of the Bible's message about spiritual things. Let us heed the warning of Jesus, the ultimate author of all the Bible, who said the following:

> *"If I told you earthly things and you do not believe, how will you believe if I tell you heavenly things?"* (John 3:12).

EASTERN AND CENTRAL CANADA

The native peoples of Canada, like all nations on the earth, have passed down traditions of a great Flood. Let us begin with the Cree people, a great tribe that settled a vast section of Canada. Their tradition states that a good man named Wesaketchan built a large raft, which he boarded with his family and a pair of all kinds of birds and animals. The man sent out a duck and a muskrat, the latter of which returned carrying some soil in its mouth.

The Montagnais or Innu of eastern Canada say the survivor of the Flood was one of their deities, Messou, "the Great Hare." He sent a raven to try to find earth.

The Ojibwe, another tribe of Canada and the Great Lakes area, tell that their patriarch built a giant raft and rescued all sorts of animals and birds upon it. The Wyandotte or Huron attribute the Flood to a dispute between divine brothers, in which one shot an arrow into a giant bag of water in the sky containing all the world's waters, which drowned all the world except those led to safety by the benevolent deity. The Ottawa, around the year 1770, told fur trader Alexander Henry about their ancestor Nanibojou who originally lived "toward the going down of the sun." Being warned of the Flood in a dream, he built a raft to save his family and all types of animals, floating upon the waters for many moons before he created land and mankind anew.

Regional Tribes

1. Cree (Central Canada)
2. Montagnais (Quebec and Labrador Provinces)
3. Ojibwe (Ontario and Great Lakes Area)
4. Wyandotte (Ontario)
5. Ottawa (Ontario)

1

CREE

Central Canada

Cree Man, 1903

The Cree nation occupied a vast section of Canada south of the Hudson Bay. Their tradition about the Flood was recorded by an ethnologist named Émile Petitot in 1869. The tradition went as follows:

> A gigantic fish tried to destroy Wesaketchan, with whom he had quarreled. With his jumps and jolts he caused an inundation which covered the whole earth and even the highest mountains.
>
> But Wesaketchan built a large raft on which he boarded all his family, as well as a pair of all the birds and all the animals. It was thus that he preserved his life.[1]

Another relevant Cree text was reported by the Catholic Bishop Henri Faraud in 1864:

> As tradition, the Crees have a little confused idea of the creation of man, of his fall, and especially the flood; they say: "There was a time when men had become so large that they would no longer obey God and the Almighty destroyed them by raising the water. One man fashioned a large boat, called Micinapikivan (large canoe). Thus the flood arose, and all the men perished with the animals. After a certain period of time, the rescued man grew tired of floating on the water. Believing he saw a small island, he set free a raven, who did not return. To punish him for his disobedience, the raven, who was white, became black. A white dove was sent a while later; it returned with a piece of clay in its legs. The man concluded that the earth was quite dry, and he landed. That's about the tradition of the Cree and Ojibwa""[2]

Wesaketchan built a large raft on which he boarded all his family, as well as a pair of all the birds and all the animals.

2

MONTAGNAIS

Quebec and Labrador Provinces

The Montagnais, or Innu, have anciently inhabited eastern Canada, including much of what is now Quebec and Labrador. They were northern enemies of the Iroquois nations. The Montagnais held to a tradition of the Flood, which the Jesuit missionaries recorded in their annual report in 1634:

> As to the Messou [the Great Hare], they hold that he restored the world, which was destroyed in the flood; whence it appears that they have some tradition of that great universal deluge which happened in the time of Noë, but they have burdened this truth with a great many irrelevant fables. This Messou went to the chase, and his Lynxes, which he used instead of dogs, having gone into a great lake, were held there. The Messou, seeking them everywhere, was told by a bird that it had seen them in the midst of this lake. He went in, to get them out; but the lake overflowed, covering the earth and swallowing

Reindeer Hunting in Labrador

1. Émile Petitot, *Traditions Indiennes du Canada Nord-ouest* (Paris: Maissonneuve Fréres, 1886), p. 475–476.
2. Ibid., p. 387.

GRACE
to You

GRACE TO YOU PROGRAMS YOU'RE HELPING MAKE AVAILABLE IN MAY

RADIO

April 14–May 7
The Fulfilled Family
11-CD series
$47.00

May 10–25
The Grip of God
7-CD series
$31.00

May 26–June 4
Mishandled: Setting the Record Straight on Frequently Abused Bible Verses
5-CD series
$24.00

TELEVISION

Watch *Grace to You*, featuring John MacArthur, every Sunday on DIRECTV, channel 378, at 6:30 p.m. (Pacific), and anytime at gty.org.

For a complete listing of radio and television stations carrying *Grace to You*, or to listen or view online, visit **gty.org**.

800-55-GRACE

4 21 BK US

up the world. The Messou, very much astonished, sent a raven in search of a little piece of ground, with which to rebuild this element [the earth], but he could not find any; he made an Otter descend into the abyss of waters, but it could not bring back any; at last he sent a muskrat, which brought back a little morsel, and the Messou used this to rebuild this earth which we inhabit. . . . [Messou] married a muskrat, by whom he had children who have re-peopled this world.[3]

God, being angry with the giants, commanded a man to build a large canoe.

A second Flood tradition, from another subgroup of the Montagnais, was recorded by the aforementioned Henri Faraud in 1864:

> God, being angry with the giants, commanded a man to build a large canoe. The man did so, and when he had embarked in it, the water rose on all sides, and the canoe with it, till no land was anywhere to be seen. Weary of beholding nothing but a heaving mass of water, the man threw an otter into the flood, and the animal dived and brought up a little earth. The man took the earth or mud in his hand and breathed on it, and at once it began to grow. So he laid it on the surface of the water and prevented it from sinking. As it continued to grow into an island, he desired to know whether it was large enough to support him. Accordingly he placed a reindeer upon it, but the animal soon made the circuit of the island and returned to him, from which he concluded that the island was not yet large enough. So he continued to blow on it till the mountains, the lakes, and the river were formed. Then he disembarked.[4]

3 OJIBWE

Ontario and Great Lakes Area

"Before the general deluge," the Ojibwe elders told Peter Jones, "there lived two enormous creatures, each possessed of vast power." One was a great horned animal. The other was a giant toad, which possessed all the world's waters in his body, and which was in charge of watering the earth. "Between these two creatures, there arose a quarrel, which terminated in a fight." The horned animal rushed at the toad and pierced its side, "out of which the water gushed in floods, and soon overflowed the face of the earth."[5]

Sha-có-pay, The Six, Chief of the Plains Ojibwa

> At this time Nanahbozhoo [the Great Hare] was living on the earth, and observing the water rising higher and higher, he fled to the loftiest mountain for refuge. Perceiving that even this retreat would soon be inundated, he selected a large cedar tree which he purposed to ascend should the waters come up to him. Before they reached him he caught a number of animals and fowls, and put them into his bosom. At length the water covered the mountain. Nanahbozhoo then ascended the cedar tree, and as he went up, he plucked its branches and stuck them in the belt which girdled his waist.[6]

---

3. Paul le Jeune, "Relation of What Occurred in New France in the Year 1634," *The Jesuit Relations and Allied Documents*, ed. Reuben Gold Thwaites, vol. 6 (Cleveland: Burrow Brothers, 1898). p. 156.
4. Mgr. Faraud, "Missions de l'Amérique du Nord," *Annales de la Propagation de la Foi*, vol. 36 (Lyon: 1864), p. 388–389.
5. Rev. Peter Jones, *History of the Ojebway Indians* (London: A.W. Bennett, 1861), p. 33.
6. Ibid.

For a time, the tree grew upward at the same pace as the water. But later Nanahbozboo saw that the water would soon overtake him. He knew that he needed to construct a great raft, on which he could float along with the animals that were with him. Thus he built the raft, using the branches he had plucked. "On this raft he floated about for a long time, till all the mountains were covered, and all the beasts of the earth and fowls of the air, except those he had with him, perished."[7]

Boy Chief - Ojibbeway

Next, the tribal elders told Mr. Jones how Nanabozhoo sent the animals to dive for mud, which he then took and extended to form the new earth. He then traveled across the new world which he had made, and here and there he created various tribes of peoples. He placed them in their respective parts of the earth, and gave them different cultures, ways, and beliefs.[8]

In the 1860s, Émile Petitot recorded another Flood tradition from the Ojibwe peoples, which tells that a "deluge of snow" took place in the most ancient times. Instantly it turned into a great flood of water, after some mice released a reservoir of heat onto the earth. These waters "covered the earth to the tops of the highest firs, and it raised so greatly the level of the waters that they inundated our planet and rose above the Rocky Mountains."[9]

> A single man, an old man, who had foreseen this catastrophe, had vainly warned his countrymen. "We will seek refuge in the mountains," they said. They were drowned there. He himself had built a large canoe, and began to sail about, collecting on his passage all the animals which he met. But, as he could not live long in this frightful condition, he made the beaver, the otter, the muskrat and the Arctic duck dive by turns in search of the earth. The latter alone returned with a little mud in its claws.[10]

He knew that he needed to construct a great raft, on which he could float along with the animals that were with him.

Yet another Flood tradition, from the Tamigami branch of the Ojibwe, records the unleashing of a global Flood, and the construction of a great raft to save the animals. The man releases two birds (a crow and an owl) to fly to measure the earth. The crow abandons its mission and feasts on a dead animal, just as we find in Genesis.[11]

4 —WYANDOTTE—

Ontario

The elders of the Wyandotte, or Huron, told William Connelley the following: There was a quarrel between two divine brothers, Sesta and Skareh. In the night Skareh stole all the earth's waters and held them in a giant bag in the sky. The people cried out for lack of water. Sesta, being concerned for the people's survival, took as an arrow a giant trunk of a pine tree, and shot it into the sky, piercing the bag. Yet now he had another problem, for the water spilled upon the earth and covered everything, even the hills. "The Lower World was destroyed by the flood," they told. Then Sesta led his people to a heavenly forest above the earth, using the rainbow as a bridge. In that beautiful place they lived until the waters returned to their proper boundaries, leaving habitable dry land.[12]

Three Huron - Wyandotte Chiefs

7. Ibid.
8. Ibid., p. 34-35.
9. Émile Petitot, *Monograph of the Dene-Dindjie Indians*, trans. Douglas Brynner, p. 147. Retrieved from: https://archive.org/stream/cihm_15864.
10. Ibid.
11. Frank Speck, "Myths and folk-lore of the Timiskaming Algonquin and Timagami Ojibwa," *Geological Survey of Canada Memoir*, vol. 71, Anthropological Series (Ottawa: Government Printing Bureau, 1915), p. 36–38.
12. William Elsey Connelley, *Indian Myths* (New York: Rand McNally, 1928). Retrieved from: http://www.wyandotte-nation.org/culture/folk-lore-and-myths/indian-myths/.

5

OTTAWA

Ontario

The Ottawa (or Odawa) shared their traditions with an English fur trader named Alexander Henry (1739–1824). In their Flood tradition, they replace Noah with their deity Nanibojou, "the Great Hare."

Mid-18th Century Sketch of an Ottawa Family

> Traditions related of the Great Hare are as varied as his name. He was represented to me as the founder, and indeed creator, of the Indian nations of North America. He lived originally toward the going down of the sun, where being warned, in a dream, that the inhabitants would be drowned by a general flood, produced heavy rains, he built a raft, on which he afterward preserved his own family, and all the animal world without exception. According to his dream, the rains fell, and a flood ensued. His raft drifted for many moons, during which no land was discovered. His family began to despair of a termination to the calamity; and the animals, who had then the use of speech, murmured loudly against him. In the end, he produced a new earth, placed the animals upon it, and created man.[13]

According to his dream, the rains fell, and a flood ensued. His raft drifted for many moons, during which no land was discovered.

13. Alexander Henry, *Travels and Adventures in Canada and the Indian Territories between the years 1760 and 1766*, Part 1 (New York: J. Riley, 1809), p. 212–213.

Group of Crees

Kwakwaka'wakw
Harvesting Clams in Canoe

WESTERN CANADA

In western Canada, we find a multitude of tribes affirming this ancient Flood. Among these are the Kwakiutl, the Nootka, and the Haida. The Lillooet people in 1905 told anthropologist James Teit their sacred tradition. A man named Ntci'nemkin built a very large canoe, saving himself and his family, and several young children whose parents begged him to take them, thinking nothing of their own survival. The waters covered all the high mountains except one called Split, and the survivors later descended to repopulate the earth. We have a remarkable Flood memory told by Squamish chief Joe Capilano, recorded in this volume, and one from the Sarci, whose elders told in 1888 how one man and one woman escaped the Flood on a giant raft, together with all sorts of animals and birds which they had collected.

The Tsimshian, living in coastal British Colombia across from the Haida Gwaii Islands, around the year 1850, told one Mr. Duncan how a few people escaped the ancient Flood at the top of one of their high mountains. The Bella Coola remember not only the Flood, but also have a vague tradition of the confusion of languages. So do the Cowichan, of whom we have an early tradition of how their ancestors had dreams forewarning about the coming Flood. They built a giant raft and survived the Flood, having anchored it to a rock at the top of Cowichan Mountain by means of a cable of cedar rope. The Coastal Salish say that a man named Xals, and his wife and daughters escaped in a large canoe, and when the Flood ended, they went down into the Fraser River valley. The Carrier told that a boy survived the Flood on a

Regional Tribes

6. Lillooet (British Columbia)
7. Squamish (Southwestern British Columbia)
8. Saulteaux (Southern Manitoba)
9. Sarci (Alberta)
10. Western Cree (Alberta)
11. Beaver (Alberta)
12. Kwakiutl (Vancouver Island)
13. Nootka (Vancouver Island)
14. Thompson River Tribe (Pacific Northwest)
15. Kootenay (British Columbia)
16. Haida (British Columbia)
17. Tsimshian (British Columbia)
18. Bella Coola (British Columbia)
19. Shuswap (British Columbia)
20. Cowichan (Vancouver Island)
21. Coastal Salish Tradition (British Columbia)
22. Carrier (British Columbia)
23. Tahltan (British Columbia)

raft, and sent a wolf (instead of a bird) to see whether the newly appeared land was ready for habitation.

The Tahltan mention that a wise man was forewarned of the coming Flood, sent by God due to the wickedness of mankind. Their tradition also mentions a race of fallen beings (possibly giants) that existed in those days, and a confusion of languages that occurred after the Flood. The Tsetsaut said that children were placed in hollow trees, which were sealed watertight (we are not told how they breathed), and later repopulated the earth. And we have the Flood traditions of other tribes besides, including the Shuswap, Kootenay, and Beaver tribes.

The Western Cree say that the Great Spirit sent the Flood after mankind grew wicked. One man survived, and an otter, beaver, and muskrat with him. He sent the muskrat diving into the water, and it returned with a piece of earth. They also recognize the rainbow as "the mark of life," the sign that the Great Spirit will not again destroy the earth with a flood.

The Saulteaux tribe told a similar version to Lieutenant Hooper around the year 1850. Like Noah, their patriarch sent a raven to survey the size of the newly appeared earth.

6

LILLOOET

British Columbia

The Lillooet people lived along the Lillooet River, which is in British Columbia north of Vancouver. Around 1905, they told James Teit their tradition about a great flood and dispersion that took place in the ancient past:

St'at'imc (Lillooet) Nation, 1865

> All the Lillooet people lived together around Green Lake, and for some distance below it on Green River. At that time there came a great and continuous rain, which made all the lakes and rivers overflow their banks, and deluge the surrounding country. When the people saw the waters rise far above the ordinary high-water mark, they became afraid.
>
> A man called Ntci'nemkin had a very large canoe, in which he took refuge with his family. The other people ascended the mountains for safety; but the water soon covered them too. When they saw that they would probably all be drowned, they begged Ntci'nemkin to save their children. As for themselves, they did not care. The canoe was too small, however, to hold all the children; so Ntci'nemkin took one child from each family, a male from one, a female from the next, and so on.
>
> The rain continued falling and the waters rising, until all the land was submerged except the peak of the high mountain called Split. The canoe drifted about until the waters receded, and it grounded on Smimelc Mountain. Each stage of the water's sinking left marks on the sides of this mountain.
>
> When the ground was dry again, the people settled just opposite the present site of Pemberton. Ntci'nemkin with his wives and children settled there, and he made the young people marry one another. He sent out pairs to settle at all the good food-places through the country. . . . Thus was the country peopled by the offspring of the Green Lake people.[1]

The rain continued falling and the waters rising, until all the land was submerged except the peak of the high mountain called Split.

1. James Teit, "Traditions of the Lillooet Indians of British Columbia," *Journal of American Folk-lore*, vol. 25 (Lancaster, PA, and New York, NY: 1912), p. 342.

7

SQUAMISH

Southwestern British Columbia

Pauline Johnson interviewed a Squamish chief named Joe Capilano (1854–1910), one very rainy February day, when the subject of the Flood arose:

> One time, there was no land here at all; everywhere there was just water. . . .
>
> It was after a long, long time of this — this rain. The mountain-streams were swollen, the rivers choked, the sea began to rise — and yet it rained; for weeks and weeks it rained.
>
> It rained for weeks and weeks, while the mountain torrents roared thunderingly down, and the sea crept silently up. The level lands were first to float in sea-water, then to disappear. The slopes were next to slip into the sea. The world was slowly being flooded. Hurriedly the Indian tribes gathered in one spot, a place of safety far above the reach of the on-creeping sea. The spot was the circling shore of Lake Beautiful, up the North Arm. They held a Great Council and decided at once upon a plan of action. A giant canoe should be built, and some means contrived to anchor it in case the waters mounted to the heights. The men undertook the canoe, the women the anchorage. . . .

Chief Joe Capilano

> Then, with the bravest hearts that ever beat, noble hands lifted every child of the tribes into this vast canoe; not one single baby was overlooked. The canoe was stocked with food and fresh water, and, lastly, the ancient men and women of the race selected as guardians to these children the bravest, most stalwart, handsomest young man of the tribes and the mother of the youngest baby in the camp — she was but a girl of sixteen, her child but two weeks old; but she, too, was brave and very beautiful. These two were placed, she at the bow of the canoe to watch, he at the stern to guide, and all the little children crowded between.
>
> And still the sea crept up, and up, and up. At the crest of the bluffs about Lake Beautiful the doomed tribes crowded. Not a single person attempted to enter the canoe. There was no wailing, no crying out for safety. "Let the little children, the young mother, and the bravest and best of our young men live," was all the farewell those in the canoe heard as the waters reached the summit, and — the canoe floated. Last of all to be seen was the top of the tallest tree, then — all was a world of water.
>
> For days and days there was no land — just the rush of swirling, snarling sea; but the canoe rode safely at anchor, the cable those scores of dead, faithful women had made held true as the hearts that beat behind the toil and labour of it all.
>
> But one morning at sunrise, far to the south, a speck floated on the breast of the waters; at midday it was larger; at evening it was yet

It was after a long, long time of this — this rain. The mountain-streams were swollen, the rivers choked, the sea began to rise — and yet it rained; for weeks and weeks it rained.

larger. The moon arose, and in its magic light the man at the stern saw it was a patch of land. All night he watched it grow, and at daybreak looked with glad eyes upon the summit of Mount Baker. He cut the cable, grasped his paddle in his strong young hands, and steered for the south. When they landed, the waters were sunken half down the mountainside. The children were lifted out; the beautiful young mother, the stalwart young brave, turned to each other, clasped hands, looked into each other's eyes — and smiled.

A Sarcee Man and Woman

And down in the vast country that lies between Mount Baker and the Fraser River they made a new camp, built new lodges — where the little children grew and thrived, and lived and loved; and the earth was repeopled by them.[2]

8 SAULTEAUX

Southern Manitoba

The Saulteaux tribe lived south of the Crees, to the north of Minnesota and North Dakota. They also held a tradition of a universal deluge, which they told to a Lieutenant W.H. Hooper between 1849 and 1851. They told of a medicine-man named Wis who built a big canoe in which he put all classes of animals. A great deluge occurred and covered all land, hills, and trees. Finally, he sent animals diving into the water, each with a rope tied to its leg, in search of a piece of earth with which he could form land. First a diver bird, then an otter, then a beaver, and finally a rat. The rat returned to him, clutching a piece of earth in its paws. The man blew on it, and it magically grew to become a vast expanse of land. He thought it was large enough, so he sent out a wolf to explore, but the wolf returned quickly and said it was too small. Then he blew on the earth again, and it enlarged further. He sent out a crow and, when it did not return, he concluded it was now large enough for all to inhabit. So he and all the animals got out from the boat.[3]

Three Saulteaux Men, c1882

Earth-Diving Animals. The tradition above contains an example of the "earth diver" motif, where typically a man sends a few animals diving into the floodwaters in search of some mud. The reader may notice similarities between this motif and in Genesis, where Noah sends first a crow, followed by a dove, on a test flight to see whether there is any dry land. Indeed, the similarities run very deep. As we proceed, we will see plenty of evidence that these two themes are intimately connected. There is zero chance that these two elements coincide merely by chance. Further, I present in Appendix C evidence that the "earth diver" motif originated from the memory of Noah's dispatch of the birds, combined with a memory of the Creation event as told in Genesis.

They told of a medicine-man named Wis who built a big canoe in which he put all classes of animals. A great deluge occurred and covered all land, hills, and trees.

2. Emily Pauline Johnson, *Legends of Vancouver* (Vancouver: David Spencer, 1911), p. 53–58.
3. W.H. Hooper, *Ten Months Among the Tents of the Tuski* (London: John Murray, 1853), p. 285–292.

9 SARCI

Alberta

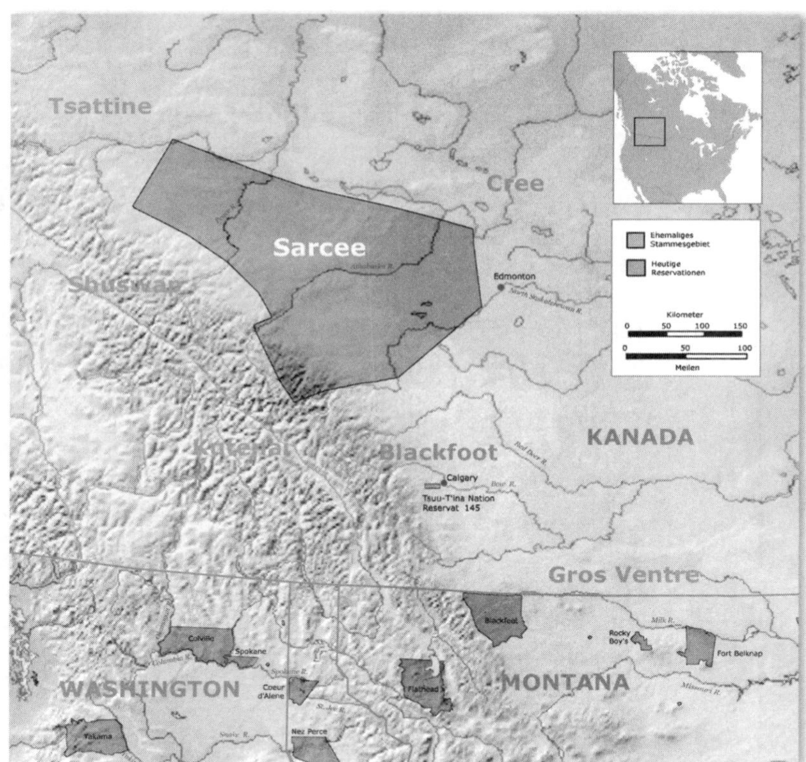

The Historical Tribal Territory of the Sarcee

In 1888, the Reverend E.F. Wilson interviewed a Sarci chief — a tall and powerful man named Bull's Head — together with other leading men. Wilson mentioned their belief concerning the Flood:

> They also have a tradition of the flood, which accords in its main features with that of the Ojibways, Crees, and other Canadian tribes. They say that when the world was flooded there were only one man and one woman left, and these two saved themselves on a raft, on which they also collected animals and birds of all sorts.[4]

After this, the man sent down several animals in search for a fragment of earth. Finally, a muskrat returned with a little mud. The man used it to remake the earth, and he created upon it rivers, mountains, trees, and everything else we see.

10 WESTERN CREE

Alberta

The fur trader and surveyor David Thompson (1770–1857) found an oral tradition of the Flood among the Western Crees in Alberta. This was told to him around the year 1800 by a group of older Cree men:

> After the Great Spirit made mankind, and all the animals, he told Weesarkejauk to take care of them and teach them how to live, and not to eat of bad roots; that would hurt and kill them; but he did not mind the Great Spirit; became careless and incited them to pleasure, mankind and the animals all did as they pleased, quarreled and shed much blood, with which the Great Spirit was displeased; he threatened Weesarkejauk that if he did not keep the ground clean he would take everything from him and make him miserable but he did not believe the Great Spirit and in a short time became more careless; and the quarrels of men and the animals made the ground red with blood, and so far from taking care of them he incited them to do and live badly; this made the Great Spirit very angry and he told Weesarkejauk that he would take everything from him, and wash the ground clean; but still he did not believe; until the rivers and lakes rose very high and overflowed the ground for it was always raining; and the Keeche Gahme (the Sea) came on the land, and every man and animal were drowned, except one Otter, one Beaver, and one Muskrat. Weesarkejauk tried to stop the sea, but it was too strong for him, and he sat on the water crying for his loss, the Otter, the Beaver and the Muskrat rested their heads on one of his thighs.

Cree Chief

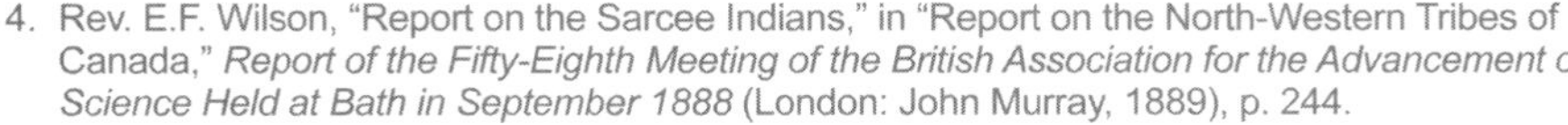

4. Rev. E.F. Wilson, "Report on the Sarcee Indians," in "Report on the North-Western Tribes of Canada," *Report of the Fifty-Eighth Meeting of the British Association for the Advancement of Science Held at Bath in September 1888* (London: John Murray, 1889), p. 244.

> . . . In this sad state, as he sat floating on the water he told the three animals that they must starve unless he could get a bit of the old ground from under the water of which he would make a fine island for them.
>
> He sends the Otter, the Beaver, and the Muskrat to dive for mud. The latter succeeds, and from this the man remakes dry land earth.[5]

A Dane-zaa Trapper Sells Pelts to the Hudson Bay Store, 1900

The Western Cree also associated the rainbow with the Flood. Thompson told that in late May 1806, an unusually heavy period of rain occurred for three weeks, causing them much anxiety. He told of their reaction when the rain ceased and the clouds parted, giving way to a rainbow. The parallel with the Genesis account of the rainbow is truly stunning.

> All was anxiety, they smoked and made speeches to the Great Spirit for the rain to cease, and at length became alarmed at the quantity of water on the ground; at length the rain ceased, I was standing at the door watching the breaking up of the clouds, when of a sudden the Indians gave a loud shout, and called out "Oh, there is the mark of life, we shall yet live." On looking to the eastward there was one of the widest and most splendid rainbows I ever beheld; and joy was now in every face. The name of the rainbow is Peeshim Cappeah (sun lines). I had now been twenty two years among them, and never before heard the name of the Mark of Life given to the rainbow (Peemah tisoo nan oo Chegun) nor have I ever heard it since; upon inquiring of the old men why they kept this name secret from me, they gave the usual reply: you white men always laugh and treat with contempt what we have heard and learned from our fathers, and why should we expose ourselves to be laughed at.[6]

11 BEAVER

Alberta

The Beaver, or Dane-zaa, lived in the northern parts of what is now British Columbia and Alberta, especially along the Peace River. In a letter dated December 1, 1808, a fur trader named George Keith wrote of a Flood tradition that an old woman of the tribe narrated to him:

> In former times, when people were very numerous upon the earth, it happened that the sun ceased to give heat or light. An unremitting fall of snow threatened to annihilate every living creature upon the earth; the tops of the loftiest trees were already almost buried in snow, and it was with great difficulty fire wood could be obtained.
>
> In order to discover the cause of this dreadful phenomenon, a party of Indians agreed to go upon discoveries, and after having marched many days without observing any difference in the climate, discovered a squirrel's nest.

They had not proceeded many days upon their return when they were threatened with a deluge arising from the impression that the heat of the sun made upon the snow.

5. J.B. Tyrrell (editor), *David Thompson's Narrative of his Explorations in Western America* (Toronto: Champlain Society, 1917), p. 85–86.
6. Ibid., p. 88–89.

> . . . They had not proceeded many days upon their return when they were threatened with a deluge arising from the impression that the heat of the sun made upon the snow. The waters increasing more and more, our adventurers redoubled their pace in order to get to the summit of a very high, rocky mountain. Unfortunately only two of them, a man and his wife, reached the top of the mountain, all the rest were drowned in the waters. Upon the summit of this mountain were gathered two of every living creature (male and female) that liveth upon the Earth, many of the drowned people transformed themselves into fowls of the air and had the sagacity to retire to this place.
>
> The waters continuing a long time, reduced those creatures to great extremities for want of food. It was at length proposed by the canard de France, the petit plongeux and the buzzard to dive into the waters in order to try to find ground. . . . After remaining some days inactive, they again dived, and the buzzard alone, after appearing upon the surface seemingly in a lifeless state, had his bill full of earth, which showed that the waters were decreasing.[7]

Kwakiutl Girl

12 KWAKIUTL — Vancouver Island

The Kwakiutl lived on Vancouver Island and neighboring parts of British Columbia. A chief of the tribe told a surveyor named George Dawson their Flood tradition in 1878:

> Very long ago there occurred a great flood, during which the sea rose so as to cover everything with the exception of three mountains. . . . Nearly all the people floated away in various directions on logs and trees. The people living where Kit-katla now is, for instance, drifted to Fort Rupert, while the Fort Ruperts drifted to Kit-katla. Some of the people had small canoes, and by anchoring them managed to come down near home when the water subsided. Of the Hailtzak there remained only three individuals: two men and a woman, with a dog. One of the men landed at Kâpa, a second at another village site, not far from Bella-Bella, and the woman and dog at Bella-Bella. From the marriage of the woman with the dog, the Bella-Bella Indians originated.[8]

Nootka on the Shore

13 NOOTKA — Vancouver Island

The Nootka lived on Vancouver Island and the Olympic Peninsula of Washington. An elderly, blind Nootka man told Edward Sapir this tradition concerning the Flood:

> Two brothers were the chiefs of the village. They had killed a whale and were preparing it for a village feast. This ritual preparation consisted of cutting off the dorsal fin, which

7. Louis Rodrigue Masson, "George Keith Letters to Mr. Roderic MacKenzie," *Les Borgeois de la Compagnie du Nord-Ouest*, vol. 2 (Quebec: Imprimerie Générale a Coté et Cie, 1890), p. 80–83.
8. George M. Dawson, "Notes and Observations on the Kwakiool People of the Northern Part of Vancouver Island," *Proceedings and Transactions of the Royal Society of Canada for the Year 1887* (Montreal: Dawson Brothers, 1888), p. 82–83.

was believed to contain the animal's soul, and singing to it for four days. Once this requirement was fulfilled, they believed the whale's soul departed its body, allowing for the feast to begin. However, as the ruling brothers were performing this ritual in their canoes, the whale's fin started singing back. The brothers joined in the singing, as did the people of the village. At the same time, a great flood ensued. The flood was not due to the whale, but to Thunderbird. The earth was not seen, for the flood was high and the mountains were under water, except that the big mountains stood dry above water.[9]

Nootka Woman Selling Baskets that She Made

Yet they were protected during the storm by the whale, to which they had sung. After many days of drifting, they came to the peaks of some mountains, and the brothers agreed to go to separate mountains. The older brother grew tired and fell asleep, and had a dream. And just as his dream foretold, he awoke to find that serpent which formed the belt of Thunderbird, coiled under him and singing. When he awoke, the snake glided away, but the man struck its tail and cut it off. The man took the tail and used it as an amulet. Thunderbird having been defeated, the flood began to go down slowly. The brothers landed when the earth was dry enough, having consumed most of the provisions which they had taken in their canoes.[10]

14 THOMPSON RIVER TRIBE

Pacific Northwest

The Thompson River tribe, dwelling in southern British Columbia and northern Washington, told James Teit the following tradition around 1899.

Members of a Nlaka'pamux (Thompson River Tribe) Community

> There was once a great flood which covered the whole country excepting the tops of some of the highest mountains. It was probably caused by the Qoa'qlqal (three magic-working brothers), who had great power over water. All the people were drowned except the Coyote, who turned himself into a piece of wood; and three men, who went into a canoe, and reached the Nzuke'ski Mountains, but who, with their canoe, were afterwards transformed into stone, and may be seen sitting there at the present day. When the waters subsided, the Coyote, in the shape of a piece of wood, was left high and dry. He then resumed his natural form, and looked around. He found that he was in the Thompson River country. He took trees for wives, and the Indians are said to be his descendants. Before the flood there were no lakes or streams in the mountains, and consequently no fish. When the waters receded, it left lakes in the hollows of the mountains, and streams began to run from them. That is the reason that we now find lakes in the mountains, and fish in them.[11]

9. Edward Sapir, "A Flood Legend of the Nootka Indians of Vancouver Island," *Journal of American Folk-lore*, vol. 32 (Lancaster and New York: American Folklore Society, 1919), p. 352–353.
10. Ibid., p. 355.
11. James Teit, *Traditions of the Thompson River Indians* (Boston and New York: Houghlin and Mifflin, 1898), p. 20.

Alexander Catcott (1725–1779) on the Certainty of the Flood

With regard to the certainty of the Flood, I may argue in the manner of Aristotle, 'What seems true to some wise men is somewhat probable; what seems so to most or to all wise men is very probable; what most men, both wise and unwise, assent unto, doth still more resemble truth. But what men generally consent in hath the highest probability, and approaches near to demonstrable truth.'

Surely then, what men universally agree in, what, I may say, all nations (otherwise differing in opinion, customs, language, religion, and even ignorant of one another's existence) have, throughout all known ages, assented unto, may well pass for an established axiom and a demonstrable truth. And such I have shown is the state of the case with regard to the knowledge of the deluge.

Again, the report of the Flood must have come from some quarter or other, and when or wherever it was first published, the relation of a fact so extraordinary, would naturally raise the curiosity of the first hearers, and excite them to inquire into the truth of it. Now if they discovered that the report was false or groundless, the history would have been immediately discredited, and the relater and his story no more heard of. But the tradition prevailing universally, it is certain that such an event did happen — and moreover that it was universal in its effects, else it could not have been universally believed.

Which (second) article is further evident from the afore-cited testimonies themselves. For in all those that are tolerably full and explicit, we find a method mentioned by which a few escaped out of the general destruction, from whom the world was afterwards peopled, which is a plain confession that according to their opinion the whole race of mankind (except the few allowed to be saved) was destroyed; and so the deluge universal.

But farther yet, a universal deluge is not an article of mere speculation, or a point, the certainty of which might be provide only by properly examining the asserter thereof, but is an Event, or Fact in Nature, and of such a peculiar kind that, did such ever happen, it could not but have left undeniable marks of its existence on every part of the earth; and so the relater of such an event might have been confuted or his adversaries convinced on the spot.

Especially was this confutation or confirmation easily to be established in the first ages of the world; or rather, this is a point which could not but be then settled. For as men began to multiply after the flood, they would of course separate and divide, and so repeople the earth. And as they thus separated, they could not fail of knowing whether the Flood was universal or not. For, if they could find no human inhabitants in the countries to which they came, nor any marks of their former works, as houses, palaces, temples, gardens, etcetera, and could see nothing but ruin and devastation in the things that did remain, they would certainly conclude that the deluge was universal. On the contrary, if, as they dispersed or endeavoured to disperse, they found the neighbouring countries still full of inhabitants, the lands cultivated, etcetera, they would as certainly conclude that the deluge had not been universal.

And from this infallible and unavailable means of knowing the truth, the relation of the flood would have been handed down to posterity. But posterity all over the world speak of it as universal, or allow that there has been a deluge, which comes to the same thing; for had it been partial, or extended only over a few countries, the remaining part of the world would have been utterly ignorant of such an event, or at least if they spoke of it, they would not have acknowledged, as they generally do, that it happened in their own country, and have supposed that a king, or an eminently righteous person of their own nation (including some others) was preserved from the destruction. All this abundantly proves that the deluge was universal.[12]

British Columbia

15 KOOTENAY

Alexander Chamberlain went to the Kootenay people of southeastern British Columbia in 1891. He heard the following story several times, which contains a memory of the Flood. As we proceed southward into Central and South America, we will find many similar versions in which the Flood commences after a woman is ravished by a serpent or a monster:

> Sukpeka, the wife of Intlak, is forbidden by her husband to go to a certain lake, to drink of its waters, or to bathe in it. One day her husband goes out after deer and repeats the warning before leaving. Sukpeka busied herself picking berries, and, what with climbing the mountain and being exposed to the hot sun, she feels very warm, and goes down to the lake. Suddenly the water rises, and a giant called Yawoenek comes forth, who seizes the woman and ravishes her. Intlak is very angry when he learns of this, and, going to the lake, shoots the monster, who swallows up all the water, so there is none for the Indians to drink. Intlak's wife pulls the arrow out of the giant's breast, whereupon the water rushes forth in torrents, and a flood is the result. Intlak and his wife take refuge on a mountain, and by-and-by the water sinks to its proper level.[13]

Very long ago there was a great flood by which all men and animals were destroyed, with the exception of a single raven.

Kootenay Girls

British Columbia

16 HAIDA

The Haida live on the Queen Charlotte Islands 70 miles off the coast of British Columbia. They told their origin story to George Dawson in 1878, which began like this:

> Very long ago there was a great flood by which all men and animals were destroyed, with the exception of a single raven. This creature was not, however, exactly an ordinary bird, but — as with all animals in the old Indians stories — possessed the attributes of a human being to a great extent. His coat of feathers, for instance, could be put on or taken off at will, like a garment. It is even related in one version of the story that he was born of a

The waters went down again; the canoes rested on the land, and the people settled themselves in the various spots whither they had been driven.

12. Alexander Catcott, *Treatise on the Deluge* (London: E. Allen, 1768), p. 123–126.
13. Dr. A.F. Chamberlain, "Report on the Kootenay Indians of South-eastern British Columbia," in *Eighth Report of the Committee on the North-Western Tribes of the Dominion of Canada*, in *Report of the Sixty-Second Meeting of the British Association for the Advancement of Science Held in Edinburgh, 1892* (London: John Murray, 1893), p. 575.

> woman who had no husband, and that she made bows and arrows for him.[14]

Haida House Exhibit

The tradition goes on:

> When the flood had gone down, Ne-kil-stlas [the raven] looked about, but could find neither companions nor a mate, and became very lonely. Finally he took a cockle [a type of bivalve mollusk] from the beach. In time, a woman came out of it and he married her. All the peoples of the world are descended from this pair.[15]

17 TSIMSHIAN

British Columbia

The Tsimshian tribe, dwelling on the coast opposite the Haida Gwaii Islands, told their Flood story to a local missionary some years prior to 1857:

> The Tsimsheans say that all people perished in the water but a few. Amongst that few there were no Tsimsheans; and now they are at a loss to tell how they have reappeared as a race. In preaching at Observatory Inlet he [Mr. Duncan] referred to the Flood, and this led the chief to tell him the following story. He said: "We have a tradition about the swelling of the water a long time ago. As you are going up the river you will see the high mountain to the top of which a few of our forefathers escaped when the waters rose, and thus were saved. But many more were saved in their canoes, and were drifted about and scattered in every direction. The waters went down again; the canoes rested on the land, and the people settled themselves in the various spots whither they had been driven."[16]

Totem Pole in Bella Coola

18 BELLA COOLA

British Columbia

The Bella Coola tradition of the Flood contains also an echo of the Tower of Babel event, where God confused the people's language:

> The following is said about the flood: After the sun was formed in the heavens, Masmasalaniz had connected the earth and the sun with a long rope, which kept both at a fixed distance from each other, and prevented the earth from sinking into the ocean. Once, however, he began to stretch and stretch the rope, and as a result the earth sank deeper and deeper, so that the surface of the waters covered all the land up to the peaks of the mountains. A terrible storm at the same time swept over the earth, and many people who had saved themselves into their boats were killed, while others were carried away. Masmasalaniz finally cut back the rope. The earth emerged from the floods and the

14. George M. Dawson, *Report on the Queen Charlotte Islands* (Montreal: Dawson Brothers, 1880), p. 149.
15. Ibid., p. 149–150.
16. Richard Charles Mayne, *Four Years in British Columbia and Vancouver Island* (London: John Murray, 1862), p. 273–274.

> people spread anew. But while the Stiksauas (Tinne tribes) had formerly lived on the ocean, they had now moved to the interior of the country. The Bilballa, who had previously lived there, now settled in the old home of the Stiksauas, and likewise the Vilzula and the Niskuali of Naztaz had changed their habitations, for the Vilzula had previously been in the south, the Niskuali in the north used. At the time, many different languages were formed, since all tribes had spoken only one language.[17]

Cowichan Girl, 1913

19 SHUSWAP

British Columbia

In 1900, several older men of the Shuswap tribe shared their origin story with James Teit. It preserves only a vague memory of the Flood:

> The Chinook (warm) wind was kept in a bag by the people of the south. The Fox and Hare stole the bag and liberated the wind, so that all people might be benefited. The people of the south, in revenge, tried to burn the world by a great fire, which spread over nearly all the earth. The latter was flooded — some say by the musk-rat or beaver — to drown the fire, and many people perished by either flood or fire.[18]

20 COWICHAN

Vancouver Island

The Cowichan are another tribe from Vancouver Island. They told their Flood history to Martha Harris sometime in the late 1800s, of which she later wrote:

> In the days after "Sowittan, or the Grumbler," the people were so numerous that they spread all over the land, till the hunting became scarce. The Cowichan, Saanich, Kuper Island and Nanaimo people increased so rapidly that they began to quarrel over their boundaries. They had also increased their store of knowledge, and were becoming skilled in the art of shaping paddles, weaving baskets, dressing skins, and making dresses from cedar bark, which they wove into stout material for the purpose. . . .

At last they decided to build a huge raft of many canoes tied together, the like of which was never seen before.

> They also had wise men, who had power to foretell the future, and these men were greatly troubled on account of certain dreams, which foretold destruction of the people, if they were true. One man said, "I have dreamed a strange thing," and the others were eager to hear what he had to say. "I dreamed that such rain fell that we all were drowned."
>
> "I," said another, "dreamed that the river rose and flooded the place, and we were all destroyed."
>
> "So did I," chimed in another. "And I too." They could not understand what these dreams could mean; so they called a council to decide what they had better do. At last they decided to build a huge raft of many canoes tied together, the like of which was never seen before. So they set to work, amidst the jeering of the people who would not believe in these dreams. After many months they finished the raft and tied it with long cedar-bark ropes and made a huge rope of cedar bark that could reach the top of Cowichan Mountain, where they passed it through the middle of a huge stone, to serve as the anchor. The stone is still there, as a witness of the truth. They were a long time at work. At length all was ready. The

17. Franz Boas, "Mitteilungen über die Vilzula Indianer," *Original Mittheilungen aus der Ethnologischen Abtheilung der Königlichen Museen zu Berlin* (Berlin: W. Spemann, 1885), p. 179.
18. James Teit, "The Shuswap," *The Jesup North Pacific Expedition*, editor Franz Boas, vol. 2, part 3 (New York: G.E. Stechert, 1909), p. 598.

Cowichan Village, 1912

raft floated in Cowichan Bay, a wonderment to all about. Not long afterwards the rain commenced. The drops were as large as hailstones, and so heavy that they killed the little babies. The river rose and all the valleys were covered. People took refuge in the mountain, but that was soon under water. When the rain began, the wise people, and the friends who believed, took their families and placed them on the raft and took food and waited. By and by the raft rose with the water, and was the only thing seen for many days. How terrified they all were, and could not divine why this terrible calamity had been sent for.

They prayed to the Great Spirit for help, but none came. As the rain fell, they were kept busy bailing out the rain with their cedar-bark bailers. At length the rain stopped, and they felt the waters going down, and their raft rested on the top of Cowichan Mountain, being held by the anchor and cedar rope. Then they saw land, but what desolation met their eyes! How their hearts were wrung with anguish! It was indescribable, but they took courage and landed, and went to where their old homes had been. They began to rebuild the village and take up their old life again. After this they increased rapidly, and soon filled their lands with people. Then they quarreled among themselves so bitterly that they agreed to separate, and in this way was the world peopled.[19]

At length the rain stopped, and they felt the waters going down, and their raft rested on the top of Cowichan Mountain, being held by the anchor and cedar rope.

"The history and legends of the Indians of the Pacific Northwest is especially interesting from the fact that they have not been so long or so closely in touch with the white races as the other aboriginal inhabitants of North America."

—Martha Harris, author of *History and Folklore of the Cowichan Indians*)[20]

19. Martha Harris, *History and Folklore of the Cowichan Indians* (Victoria, BC: Colonist Publishing, 1901), p. 10–12.
20. Ibid., p. 4.

21 COASTAL SALISH TRADITION

British Columbia

Salish Wooden Carvings at the Field Museum in Chicago.

An elderly member of the Coastal Salish told the following Flood tradition to James Teit around the year 1916:

> At one time there was a flood that covered the earth, and most of the people were drowned. When the waters rose, the people fled to the mountains; but some were overtaken and drowned on the way, and others were drowned on the tops of the lower mountains. All the land was flooded except the tops of a few very high mountains. Xals and his wife and daughters escaped in a large canoe. They were chiefs. After paddling about for many days and nights, they became very tired. They drifted against the top of Qotselis Mountain, and there they made a hole through a stone, and moored their canoe by passing a heavy cedar-bark cable through the hole. Here they stayed and gauged the increase and decrease of the water with stakes as marks. After flowing and receding several times, the water at last receded, and they cast off their canoe. The flood now subsided rapidly, and they found themselves in the Lower Fraser Valley. Some say they had drifted there from the south. Now all the water was gone, excepting some that remained in the form of lakes and ponds, filling up the hollows and depressions.
>
> After this Xals travelled over the world, and taught the survivors of the flood how to act and how to work. He was very wise, and taught the people how to pray, and do every kind of work. He travelled among all the neighboring coast tribes.[21]

22 CARRIER

British Columbia

Adrien Gabriel Morice

The Carrier (also known as Dakelh) are a tribe of central British Columbia. In 1895, a woman of the tribe narrated a lengthy tradition to Reverend Adrien-Gabriel Morice, which concluded with a story of the great Flood.

A core of truth consistent with the Genesis narrative can be clearly seen, even with the mythical elements which are added in this version:

> The child then put his brother-wolf on his raft and set out in company with a muskrat and a young beaver. The water was soon noticed to rise up at a prodigious rate. It rose and rose until it covered the highest mountains. Rising still higher, it almost touched the sky, when the child, striking at it with his dagger, the flood began gradually to subside.
>
> He waited a long time, and then sent down in search of land both the muskrat and the young beaver. Very long after, they both came up to the surface, dead. The young beaver had his paw clutched, but empty, while the muskrat's contained a little mud. This the child took out and kneaded with his hands so as to extend it into an island. After additional handling, it became a large island on which he and his brother-wolf landed.
>
> He then sent his brother-wolf to see how the land was. On taking leave of his brother, the wolf said: "If I come back silent, you shall know thereby that the land is not yet inhabitable. If I howl from a very long distance, it shall be a sign that the land is well." Then he added: "Know you also that you shall die before me."

The water was soon noticed to rise up at a prodigious rate. It rose and rose until it covered the highest mountains. Rising still higher, it almost touched the sky, when the child, striking at it with his dagger, the flood began gradually to subside.

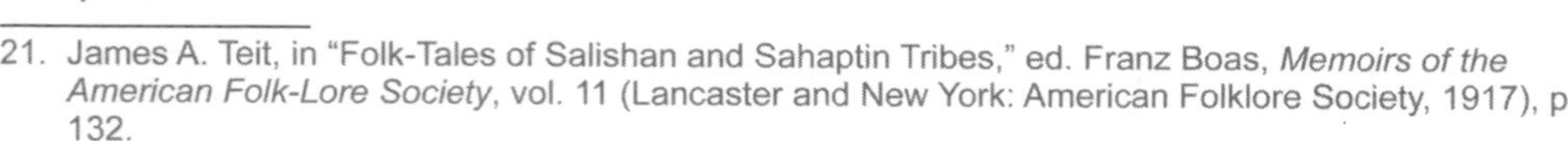
21. James A. Teit, in "Folk-Tales of Salishan and Sahaptin Tribes," ed. Franz Boas, *Memoirs of the American Folk-Lore Society*, vol. 11 (Lancaster and New York: American Folklore Society, 1917), p. 132.

So he said, and went. Long thereafter he came back in silence, as the land was not yet inhabitable. But the second time that he had set out to explore the island, he was heard howling from a very great distance. Therefore Estas settled definitely. As for the wolf, he is still in existence, while Estas is no more.[22]

23 TAHLTAN

British Columbia

The Tahltan tribe lived along the Telegraph Creek and surrounding foothills in northern British Colombia. Around the year 1900, they told James Teit many of their traditions, including this remarkable account of the Flood and of the confusion of languages (Tower of Babel):

Tahltan Men on Boat to Go Hunting

Very long ago, when the world was very young, all the people were together in one country. They talked one language, and were of one race. Many of them were highly gifted with knowledge and magic, while others knew very little. In some respects the people were very wise; and in other respects they were very helpless, simple, and ignorant. In appearance they were similar to the people of today, and most of them were well-meaning and good. Besides these people, there were many others in the same country who were not altogether human, but more like animals with human characteristics. They were nearly all highly gifted with certain kinds of knowledge, and possessed of magical powers of many kinds, often of a high order. Besides these humans and semi-human beings, there were many kinds of animals, some of them of immense size, and different from any on the earth at the present day. Most of the semi-human beings were very wicked, and some of them were cannibals. There were also giants in those days.

A wise man of the people said, "Something is going to happen, maybe a great flood will come;" but the people would not believe him. Now the animals became very tame and came into people's houses. They seemed to have a foreboding of something. Then the people said to one another, "Something is going to happen. See how tame the animals are!" Many people laughed. They said, "Let the flood come! We shall save ourselves on rafts." Others said, "We shall climb the trees. We shall climb the mountains." Yet others said, "We shall subdue the flood with our magic. We shall escape by our magical powers." At last a heavy rain set in, and it rained for many days and nights. The creeks and rivers overflowed their banks, and the ocean rose and flooded the land. At the same time the earth tipped, and the water ran to that place where the people dwelt. Now there was a great flood, and the waters rose so rapidly that people were surrounded in many places and could not escape. Some climbed trees and rocks and hills and mountains; but the water overtook them, and they were drowned. For ten days it rose continually and rapidly. The rain and flood were accompanied by storms, high winds, and darkness. The sun, moon, and Dipper stars were lost. The whole earth was covered by water excepting the highest peaks. Only two peaks in the Tahltan country were not covered by the deluge, Takitstsitla on the west side

22. Reverend Adrien-Gabriel Morice, "Three Carrier Myths," *Transactions of the Canadian Institute*, vol. 5 (Toronto: Canadian Institute, 1895), p. 10.

of Chesley River, and Tsetoxtle on the south side of the Stikine River. Some people tried to save themselves on rafts, large and small. In the darkness the wind and sea drove them hither and thither. They all became separated and lost. They did not know where they were. Some saw mountain-peaks exposed above the water, and tried to reach them. Some succeeded, and others did not. Some rafts were driven off a very long way; others went to pieces, and the people on them died or were washed off. Rats and mice got aboard some of the large rafts, and gnawed the wires binding the logs together; so that they came apart, and the people were drowned.

Tahltan Tribe Members

Some people reached the two mountains in the Tahltan country, and went ashore. Some others went ashore on the high peaks which were not submerged in other countries. However, only a few were saved, and they were at widely-separated points. They became the ancestors of all the people in the world at the present day. Very few of the wicked semi-animal people survived, and only a few giants. Some animals escaped by taking refuge on the high unsubmerged peaks in various countries, but most of them were drowned. Some kinds of animals became extinct. The surviving animals spread afterwards from the high peaks into neighboring parts of the country, and multiplied. They are the animals now known to us.

After ten days the flood subsided; the rain, storms, and darkness lessened; and in another ten days the waters had receded completely. The people who survived the Flood increased in number at the several points where they had located, and gradually spread over the country. In time some of them migrated here and there into other districts in search of better living-conditions; others did likewise when they became too many in one place.

After a long time, some people came into contact with others at certain points, and thus they learned that there were people in the world besides themselves. When they met, they found that they spoke different languages and had difficulty in understanding one another. This came about by their being separated and living isolated for a long period of time. That all the people were one originally, is evidenced by their many customs, beliefs, and traditions which are common to all (the narrator instanced several beliefs regarding bear and salmon held in common by all the neighboring tribes). These customs survived the Flood. … Some people say that the Flood came to destroy all the bad people that were on the earth long ago.[23]

Tahltan Girls

23. James Teit, "Tahltan Tales," *Journal of American Folk-lore*, vol. 32, no. 124 (1919), p. 232–234.

Inupiat Family from Noatak, Alaska, 1929

THE ARCTIC REGION

In the far northern regions of this continent, we find the Dene people group, who inhabit much of Alaska and the northwestern parts Canada. According to their tradition, an old man named Tchapewi built a large raft to escape the Flood, taking with him many animals. The Flood covered the entire earth for a long time, including the highest mountains of the Rockies. The Yupiks of Alaska tell of a great flood, which only a few people survived in their fur boats, and then landed on the highest mountains. The Kaigani, an Alaskan tribe, told that a good man had been saved from the waters of the deluge in a great canoe, which landed on a high mountain. He later sent a crow to see if the waters had gone down.

The Netsilik Inuit told the explorer Knud Rasmussen about the great Flood which drowned all but two people. The Inuit of Baffin Island, in the Arctic region north of Hudson Bay, told the early explorers of a great Flood which submerged even the high mountains. As evidence of this Flood, they pointed to the bones of whales, seals, and fish which have been found on top of the local mountains. Even in Greenland, the natives in the 1730s told the early Moravian missionaries about the ancient Flood which had been sent because God was displeased with mankind, destroying all but one man. They also related that the first man was created from the earth, and the first woman was created from his body, specifically, from his thumb.

Tribes of the Arctic Region

24. Hareskin (Northwest Territories)
25. Dene Tribes (Northern Canada)
26. Gwich'in (Northwest Canada and Alaska)
27. Tlingit (Pacific Northwest)
28. Kaska (Yukon Territory)
29. Yupik / Eskimo (Alaska)
30. Inuit of Baffin Island (Nunavut)
31. Greenland
32. Tchiglit Inuit
33. Tsetsaut (British Columbia and Alaska)
34. Netsilik Eskimo (Nunavut Territory)
35. Other Alaska Traditions

The Hareskin (also known as Sahtú), in what they told Dr. Tache in 1852, made mention of a race of fallen beings (possibly giants) that lived before the Flood. From this Flood four persons escaped, along with several animals and birds, by means of a floating island. In 1870, the Gwich'in or Kutchin people told the missionary Émile Petitot their tradition about their ancestor, an old man called the Mariner, who survived the global Flood inside of a large hollow straw, sealed watertight. They pointed to the mountain where they said he landed, in the Rocky Mountains of extreme northwest Canada, a place which they called "the place of the old man." In addition, we could relate the Flood histories the Kaska of Yukon Territory, the Tchiglit Inuit of the Arctic coast, and the Tlingit of southeastern Alaska, the latter of whom also had a vague Tower of Babel reference within their Flood tradition.

24

HARESKIN

Northwest Territories

The Hareskin (also known as Sahtú) told an account of the Flood to the Catholic missionary, Dr. Tache, in 1852. He wrote:

Crossing an Open Lead North of Annootok on a Seal Hunt

> These savages had retained some of the leading notions of the history of the human race, besides a vague tradition of the creation, and of the fall of man through the woman, and this tradition is connected with the narrative transmitted by Moses, and agrees with him in stating, 'There were giants on the earth; the waters overflowed and covered the surface of the earth; men were afterwards dispersed into all regions; fire fell from heaven and consumed the whole world.
>
> In the history of their deluge, they substitute for the ark a floating island, on which, four persons with a number of animals and birds found safety, and escaped from the general destruction. A tradition like this, found in the nineteenth century among a Pagan people, would be enough, one might imagine, to astonish the ignorant incredulity of the philosophers of the eighteenth. [1]

The Star People (a Lakota tradition)

Genesis 6:1–4 refers to a race of *nephilim* (Hebrew: "fallen ones") in the ancient world that resulted from the union of fallen angels with women.

This is not without parallel in Native American tradition. A Lakota chief named Pipe Carrier told: "They fell from the heavens in the ancient times.

They took our women. They were not washte [good] and there are some who continue to visit Turtle Island [North America] today."

1. Rev. Dr. Tache, "Hudson's Bay Missions," *Annals of the Propagation of the Faith*, vol. 13 (London: 1852), p. 254.

Joseph RiverWind, a Taino chief and author, then shared the tradition of his tribe regarding these fallen ones.

"Pipe Carrier confirmed what I have heard from many other tribal elders. My father told me that there was a great battle in the Sky World where good spirits and bad spirits were fighting one another. The bad spirits were thrown from the heavens down to the earth below where they made themselves out to be gods.

These star people took our women by force and the resulting children became the race of giants that we read about in historical accounts from cultures around the world, including the Bible. Interestingly enough, the repeating similarity is these beings came from the sky, took the human women, and produced a race of giants."[2]

Émile Petitot recorded another Flood story from the Hareskin:

> After that, the wise man said to his sister, "There, at the foot of heaven, I will build a large raft."
>
> "And what do you want to do with this chest?" She replied. "If there is an inundation, as I foresee, we will take refuge there," he said. He told his plan to the men that were still left on the earth. They laughed at him. "Oh! Oh! Oh! If there is an inundation, we will take refuge on the trees," they replied. "It's good, it's good," he said. "If there is an inundation, I will sail on my box."
>
> So he braided big ropes; he made a great number of them, he worked much, he assembled large pieces of wood, and he built a large raft.
>
> All of a sudden there was such an inundation that we never saw anything like it. It was as if water were pouring from all sides. The men eagerly saved themselves on the trees, but the water ascended, ascended, reached them, and drowned them. All the men died.
>
> As for the wise man, who possessed a good and large raft in which all the pieces were joined and bound with ropes, he floated on the waters and did not perish. While floating, he thought of the future and collected two by two all the herbivorous animals, all the birds and even all the carnivores he encountered on the way. "Place yourself on my raft," said he, "for soon there will be no more land." In fact, the earth disappeared for a very long time and no one felt to go search for it. Nobody, as it is said." [3]

So he braided big ropes; he made a great number of them, he worked much, he assembled large pieces of wood, and he built a large raft.

Sahtú People in a Canoe

The account went on to tell that the animals dove into the water, and eventually the Muskrat returned, nearly dead, with a little soil in his paws. From this the wise man remade the world, they left the raft, and the world was repopulated.

2. Joseph RiverWind, *That's What the Old Ones Say* (Middletown, DE: Firekeepers, 2015), p. 162.
3. Petitot, *Traditions Indiennes*, p. 145–149.

25

DENE TRIBES

Northern Canada

A Dene Chief in Full Dress

The Dene are a group of tribes of the Athabaskan language group, located in northwestern and north-central Canada. Petitot heard a tradition of the Flood from them in 1868:

> After Tchapewi (the old man) had driven his two children out of his presence, he retreated into a strait that united two immense waters (seas) to the north. There he lived alone, angry and sulky, because his children had broken his orders.
>
> Suddenly the roar of the abyss was heard, as if it were going up and down the earth. A torrential rain fell from the sky during the sleep of the old man, and the water of the seas climbed and climbed, and soon covered this little earth.
>
> Then Tchapewi, or Etewekwi, standing on the strait, with one leg on both sides of the river, draws with his broad hands the animals and men dragged by the waters, and places them on the mainland. But as the water was still rising, he made a large raft, on which he placed a couple of each kind of animal, and he drifted away on his raft. Then the water covered the whole earth. The rain fell for a long time, and the water surpassed the highest summits of the Rocky Mountains.[4]

Then Tchapewi sent animals diving into the water in search of a little mud. The muskrat finally succeeded, and he used this to create dry earth again.

Other traditions told by the Dene include one in which the man who survived the Flood sent out a raven, followed by a dove. Émile Petitot recorded this around the year 1860:

> Other Denes say that the old man first let loose the crow — which, finding a supply of food in the corpses floating on the water, did not return — then the dove, which returned twice after having made the circuit of the earth. Having been sent a third time, it returned in the evening, tired out, and holding in its foot a green branch of fir.[5]

But as the water was still rising, he made a large raft, on which he placed a couple of each kind of animal, and he drifted away on his raft.

The Chipewyan (not to be confused with the Chippewa or Ojibwe) are a Dene tribe of northwestern Canada. In 1789, they told the explorer Alexander MacKenzie an interesting tradition of their migration during ancient times, which seems to describe the crossing of the Bering Strait from northeast Asia into Alaska. Similar statements have been found from other tribes as well.[6]

> They have also a tradition amongst them, that they originally came from another country, inhabited by very wicked people, and had traversed a great lake, which was narrow, shallow, and full of islands, where they had suffered great misery, it being always winter, with ice and deep snow.[7]

MacKenzie also mentioned their tradition not only of the Flood, but of the great longevity of the people of that time:[8]

---

4. Petitot, *Traditions Indiennes*, p. 317–318.
5. Émile Petitot, *Monograph of the Dene-Dindjie Indians*, trans. Douglas Brynner, p. 147. Retrieved from: https://archive.org/stream/cihm_15864.
6. See, for example: Charles Beatty, *The Journal of a Two Months Tour* (London: William Davenhill, 1768), p. 91, and Antoine-Simon Le Page du Pratz, *The History of Louisiana* (London: T. Becket, 1774), p. 289.
7. Alexander MacKenzie, *Voyages from Montreal*, vol. 1 (Toronto: George Morang, 1902), p. 173.
8. See page 182 for more sources, cited by Josephus, which confirm the long lifespans of the ancients.

> They believe, also, that in ancient times their ancestors lived till their feet were worn out with walking, and their throats with eating. They describe a deluge, when the waters spread over the whole earth, except the highest mountains, on the tops of which they preserved themselves.[9]

Dene Wampum (Beads)

Yet another Flood tradition from a Dene group of people, recorded by Reverend Jetté, goes as follows in summarized form: A young man traveled across the sea to make a marriage proposal to a young woman, but she rejected his offer. Later he saw her sinking in mud, but he refused to save her. As he departed, a woman of the village gave him her little daughter to take in his canoe. The mother of the young woman who died, burning with anger, sent four tame bears to the water to make giant waves. "A great inundation occurred, which drowned everyone except the young man and the little girl in his canoe, and the mother of the little girl and her husband. In the great, stormy flood, the young man threw a harpoon and it struck a wave. That wave became Mount Denali, on which his canoe came to rest. Land formed again." The girl grew up and became the young man's wife. These repopulated the earth. But the other man and woman repopulated the earth on the other side of the sea.[10]

This last tradition, despite its great uniqueness, has parallels with a version told over 2,000 miles away by the Potawatomi (page 106) and other tribes.

26

GWICH'IN

Northwest Canada and Alaska

In December 1870, a member of the Gwich'in (or Kutchin) tribe told Émile Petitot a legend of the Flood. This legend tells of a man called the Mariner who built a great canoe. One day, the rocking of his boat created waves, which spread and created a great flood over the whole earth. Even his canoe was overthrown, and in the passing debris he found a giant hollow straw, into which he is able to climb, sealing it behind him. He floated in this straw until the flood receded, finally coming to rest on a high mountain:

> The mariner floated in a gigantic straw until the waters had evaporated and the earth had dried up. He then dismounted on a high mountain where his straw had rested.
>
> The mariner remained long in this highland. He did not leave until several days had elapsed. This place is called the place of the Old Man, because it was there that Etpoetchokpen remained. It is this peaked rock that you saw to the right of Fort MacPherson, in the Rocky Mountains.[11]

The mariner floated in a gigantic straw until the waters had evaporated and the earth had dried up. He then dismounted on a high mountain where his straw had rested.

The story goes on to tell how the Mariner, with the help of a magical raven, created women out of a dead pike and a dead loach, and thus the world was repopulated.

9. MacKenzie, Voyages from Montreal, vol. 1, p. 173–174.
10. Rev. J. Jetté, "On Ten'a Folk-Lore," *Journal of the Royal Anthropological Institute*, vol. 38 (London: 1908), p. 312–314.
11. Petitot, *Traditions Indiennes*, p. 34–38.

Dance of the Kucha-Kutchi

Why Should We Be Surprised? "As the American continent had been possessing for ages a variety of populations in different states of civilized and savage life, unknown to the rest of mankind, and maintaining no relations with them before Columbus revealed the new world to the old one; it is a natural inquiry of our curiosity if any traditions of the Deluge existed there. To our surprise we find them in every part. Yet I would correct this expression, because the awful event being an actual truth, it would be surprising if no intimation of it could have been traced there. It is therefore quite natural, and it indicates to us the reality of the catastrophe, that both in South and North America, traditions prevail about it, sometimes whimsical indeed in the circumstances, but decided as to the fact."[12]

—Sharon Turner, English historian

---

27 TLINGIT

Pacific Northwest

Alaska was still a Russian colony in 1850, when the Tlingit told Henrik Holmberg their tradition of the Flood. This also seems to contain a vague memory of the Tower of Babel:

> The myths of the Tlingits also speak of a universal flood or deluge, in which the people rescued themselves in a large floating ark. When the water was drained, it fell on a rock under the surface, and, in consequence of its great weight, broke into two parts when the water had assumed its former position. And hence the difference of languages. The Tlingits remained on the one half, and on the other half all the other peoples of the earth.[13]

In a second version that they told Holmberg, an evil raven was responsible for the destruction of the world through a flood that covered all of the mountains and surged upward toward the skies. But a good raven survived the flood by hooking his beak to the ceiling of heaven.[14]

Tlingit Couple

12. Sharon Turner, *The Sacred History of the World, as Displayed in the Creation and Subsequent Events to the Deluge*, vol. 2 (London: Longman, 1834), p. 327–328.
13. H.J. Holmberg, "Ethnographische Skizzen über die Völker des Russischen Amerika," *Acta Societatis Scientiarum Fennicae*, vol. 4 (Helsingfors, 1856), p. 345–346.
14. Ibid., p. 332–336.

The Tlingits told a similar version to John Swanton, in which the raven destroyed all mankind through a global flood, but later recreated them out of leaves. For this reason, we are told, many humans die during the fall just as leaves do.[15]

We see here that while many particulars of the Flood event were forgotten or lost in translation at Babel, others such as Noah's raven were not entirely forgotten.

28 KASKA

Yukon Territory

The Kaska, a Dene tribe living in the Yukon Territory and northeastern British Columbia, told this tradition to James Teit between 1912 and 1915:

> Once there came a great flood which covered the earth. Most of the people made rafts, and some escaped in canoes. Great darkness came on, and high winds which drove the vessels hither and thither. The people became separated. Some were driven far away. When the flood subsided, people landed wherever they found the nearest land. When the earth became dry, they lived in the places where they had landed. People were now widely scattered over the world. They did not know where other people lived, and probably thought themselves the only survivors. Long afterwards, when in their wanderings they met people from other place, they spoke different languages, and could not understand one another. This is why there are now many different centers of population, many tribes, and many languages. Before the flood, there was but one centre; for all the people lived together in one country, and spoke one language.[16]

Once there came a great flood which covered the earth. Most of the people made rafts, and some escaped in canoes.

YUPIK/ESKIMO

Alaska

Around the year 1882, the Yupiks or Eskimos living south of Norton Sound in Alaska told this Flood tradition to the explorer Johan Jacobsen:

> Eisig [Jacobsen's Eskimo associate] told me that in this area, such earthquakes occur frequently during the winter, while in summer one does not hear of it. He also added that among the Eskimos who lived here, the legend goes that an earthquake had passed over the country with a strong flood, and that only a few people were then able to do so with their fur boats on the peaks of the highest Mountains. Thus we find the saga of the Flood also spread among the Eskimos of Alaska as with so many people of the earth.[17]

Yupik Woman with Child on Back

They also shared a tradition of the Flood with Edward Nelson between 1877 and 1881:

> The Norton Sound Eskimo have a legend that in the first days the earth was flooded except a very high mountain in the middle. The water came up from the sea and

15. John R. Swanton, *Tlingit Myths and Texts* (Washington: GPO, 1909), p. 16–18.
16. James Teit, "Kaska Tales," *Journal of American Folk-lore*, vol. 30 (Lancaster and New York: American Folklore Society, 1917), p. 442–443.
17. Adrian Woldt, Captain Jacobsen's Reise an der Nordwestküste, 1881–1883 (Leipzig: 1884), p. 252.

covered all the land except the top of this mountain; only a few animals were saved, which escaped by going up the mountain side. A few people escaped by going into an umiak (furskin boat) and subsisting on the fish they caught until the water subsided. Finally, as the waters lowered, the people who were saved went to live upon the mountains, eventually descending to the coast; the animals also came down and replenished the earth with their kind. During the flood the waves and currents cut the surface of the land into hollows and ridges, and then, as the water receded, it ran back into the sea, leaving the mountains and valleys as they are today. Legends very similar to this are widely spread among other Eskimo on the coast of the Bering Sea.[18]

During the flood the waves and currents cut the surface of the land into hollows and ridges, and then, as the water receded, it ran back into the sea, leaving the mountains and valleys as they are today.

Oral Traditions of Alaskan Tribes

One writer described the wealth of Alaskan traditions related to Genesis as follows:

"The recent intercourse of our Presbyterian Missionaries, with the Mongolian and Ugrian tribes of Alaska, has laid open a wonderful inheritance of tradition. Some of these tribes have not only tradition of the Noachic Deluge, but also of the original Chaos, the first dividing of the waters, and the creation of heavenly bodies, plants, animals and men in nearly the Mosaic order of succession. And these traditions have evidently no touch of "white men's teaching." The grotesque form attests the originality and antiquity of the myth."[19]

— Julia McNair Wright

---

30 INUIT OF BAFFIN ISLAND

Nunavut

Baffin Island is an extremely cold place, located north of Hudson Bay in northeast Canada. The local Inuit told Franz Boas their oral history of the Flood around 1883:

> A long time ago the ocean suddenly began to rise, until it covered the whole land. The water even rose to the top of the mountains and the ice drifted over them. When the flood had subsided the ice stranded and ever since forms an ice cap on the top of the mountains. Many shellfish, fish, seal, and whales were left high and dry and their shells and bones may be seen to this day. A great number of Inuit died during this period, but many others, who had taken to their kayaks when the water commenced to rise, were saved.[20]

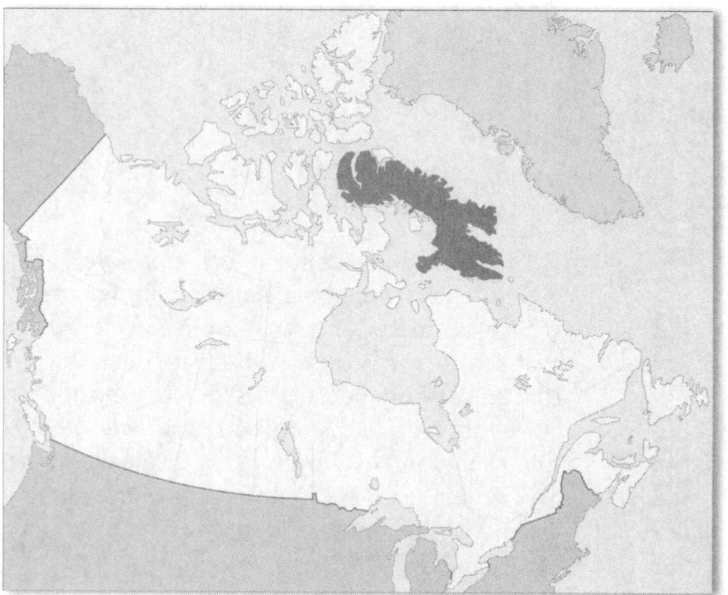

Map Locating Baffin Island, Canada

The explorer Charles Hall — who later died on the ill-fated Polaris Expedition to the North Pole — heard an account of the Flood from the Inuit at Baffin Island as well:

18. Edward William Nelson, *The Eskimo About Bering Strait* (Washington: GPO, 1900), p. 452.
19. Julia McNair Wright, *Bricks from Babel: A Brief View of the Myths, Traditions and Religious Belief of Races* (New York: John B. Alden, 1885), p. 128.
20. Franz Boas, "The Central Eskimo," *Sixth Annual Report of the Bureau of American Ethnology* (Washington: GPO, 1888), p. 637–638.

They have a tradition of a deluge, which they attribute to an unusually high tide. One one occasion, when I was speaking with Tookoolito concerning her people, she said, "Inuits all think this earth [was] once covered with water." I asked her why they thought so. She answered, "Did you never see little stones, like clams and such things as live in the sea, away up on the mountains?"[21]

Greenlandic Inuit in 1903

GREENLAND

31 Greenland

The Moravian missionaries arrived at the island of Greenland in 1733. The natives told them a Flood tradition, which David Cranz (1723–1777) mentioned in his *History of Greenland*:

> Almost all heathen nations know something of Noah's Flood, and the first missionaries found also some pretty plain traditions among the Greenlanders; namely, that the world once overset, and all mankind, except one, were drowned; but some were turned into fiery spirits. The only man that escaped alive, afterwards smote the ground with his stick, and out sprung a woman, and these two re-peopled the world. As a proof that the deluge once overflowed the whole earth, they say that many shells, and relics of fishes, have been found far within the land where men could never have lived, yea that bones of whales have been found upon a high mountain.[22]

As a proof that the deluge once overflowed the whole earth, they say that many shells, and relics of fishes, have been found far within the land where men could never have lived, yea that bones of whales have been found upon a high mountain.

The Greenlanders also told a tradition of the Flood to a Danish expedition around 1883:

> The first earth which came into existence had neither seas nor mountains, but was quite smooth. When the One above was displeased with the people upon it, he destroyed the world. It burst open, and the people fell down into the rifts and became "ignerssuit" [spirits], and the water poured over everything. When the earth reappeared, it was entirely covered by a glacier. Little by little this decreased, and two human beings fell down from heaven, by whom the earth was peopled. One can see every year that the glacier is shrinking. In many places signs may yet be seen of the time when the sea rose over the mountains.[23]

David Cranz also recorded a creation story, which has some parallels to Genesis:

> They call the first man Kallak, and say he sprung out of the earth, and soon afterward his wife sprung from his thumb, and from this pair all mankind proceeded. There are many that ascribe the origin of all things to this man. The woman is said to have brought death into the world, by saying: "Let these die to make room for their posterity."[24]

Greenlandic Inuit Man

21. Charles Francis Hall, *Life with the Esquimaux*, vol. 2 (London: Sampson Low, Son, and Marston, 1864), p. 318.
22. David Cranz, *History of Greenland*, vol. 1 (London, 1767), p. 204–205.
23. Gustav Holm, "Den Østgrønlandske Expedition udført I Aarene 1883–85," *Meddelelser om Grønland*, vol. 10 (Copenhagen: 1888), p. 144.
24. Cranz, *History of Greenland*, vol. 1, p. 204.

An Inuit Family

32 TCHIGLIT INUIT

Tchiglit Inuit

The Tchiglit, who live along the Arctic Sea coast of Alaska and part of Canada, told a tradition of the Flood to Émile Petitot in July 1870:

> The water overflowed the terrestrial disk. It was terrified, because the wind blew and made disappear the houses of men.
>
> The Eskimos tied together several boats to form a large raft. The water was still rising and the waves surpassed the Rocky Mountains. A great wind blew them to the ground, and the wind did not stop. No doubt that men could first be dried in the sun; but they soon disappeared and the universe with them because they died a horrible heat, as well as by the waves of the sea that was still rising.
>
> The unfortunate lamented, and trees that had been uprooted floated with the waves. Those that had boats tied them together, shivering with cold, while they were floating on the water, packed together, alas! under a large tent.
>
> So a juggler named An-odjium or Son of Owl, threw his bow into the sea, crying: "Wind, that is enough. Calm down!" Then he threw her earrings. This was enough to stop the flood.[25]

The Eskimos tied together several boats to form a large raft. The water was still rising and the waves surpassed the Rocky Mountains.

Interestingly, we will find parallels to this version in Indonesia and other places.

25. Petitot, *Traditions Indiennes*, p. 6–7.

33 TSETSAUT

British Columbia and Alaska

In the winter of 1894–1895, Franz Boas visited the Portland Inlet on the southern border of Alaska and British Columbia, where he met the few remaining members of the Tsetsaut. They told him this legend of the Flood:

Franz Boas

> Once upon a time a man, his wife, and his mother-in-law went up the mountains to hunt marmots. When they had reached the higher parts of a hill, they saw the waters rising. They climbed higher and higher, but the waters rose steadily. All the people fled up the mountains. Finally, when the water was about to reach them, they resolved to enclose their children in hollow trees, hoping that there they might be safe until the waters would retreat. They hollowed out two trees, in one of which they placed the children of the eagle clan, while in the other one they placed the children of the wolf clan. They gave them an ample supply of food, and then closed up the trees with wooden covers, which they caulked with pitch. The water continued to rise, and all the people were drowned. The children who were enclosed in the trees heard the waves breaking in the branches and felt the swaying of the trees. Finally, the trees were entirely covered by water. After a few days the water began to retreat. Again the trees were swaying. The children heard the waves breaking, first in the highest branches, then farther down, and finally everything was quiet. They went to sleep, and when they awoke one of the boys opened the hole. They saw that the water had disappeared, but the branches were still dripping. The ground was wet and soggy, and everything was covered with seaweeds. Then the children came forth from the trees, but the ground was so wet that they were unable to start a fire, so that many died of cold. Finally the ground dried up. They made a fire, which they fed with their supplies of mountain-goat tallow. They married, and became the ancestors of the Tsetsaut.[26]

Finally, when the water was about to reach them, they resolved to enclose their children in hollow trees, hoping that there they might be safe until the waters would retreat.

34 NETSILIK ESKIMO

Nunavut Territory

The Netsilingmiut (or Netsilik), who live on the Arctic coast of Canada, told the following Flood tradition to a Danish explorer named Knud Rasmussen in 1923:

> Woman was made by man. It is an old, old story, difficult to understand. They say that the world collapsed, the earth was destroyed, that great showers of rain flooded the land. All the animals died, and there were only two men left. They lived together. They married, as there was nobody else, and at last one of them became with child.[27]

Asen Balikci visited the Netsilik between 1959 and 1965. They told him the same flood story, but also containing a reference to a race of giants:

> There were still no women on earth. They came into being only after a dreadful deluge. Incessant rain flooded the

Alaskan Eskimo Woman

26. Franz Boas, "Traditions of the Tsetsaut," *Journal of American Folk-lore*, vol. 9 (Boston and New York: Houghton, Mifflin and Co., 1896), p. 262.
27. Knud Rasmussen, *The Netsilik Eskimos: Social Life and Spiritual Culture* (Copenhagen; 1931), p. 209. Also in Report of the Fifth Thule Expedition, vol. 8.

Inuit Constructing an Igloo With Blocks of Snow

> land and great destruction followed. All the animals and men died, with the exception of two shamans. . . .
>
> It was during these times also that giants fought and people ridiculed Narssuk, the monstrous baby who later gained control of the weather, so important to the Netsilik.[28]

A Billy Graham Prophecy? "You, as Indians, are a sleeping giant. The original American, you are now awakening. Just around the corner, you may become a spiritual superpower in this country that could change not only America, but the world."

—Evangelist Billy Graham, at a conference with First Nations Christian missionaries in Albuquerque, 1975.

35 Other Alaska Traditions

Charles M. Skinner (1852–1907) collected oral traditions from tribes scattered across North America. The native peoples of Alaska told him two Flood traditions:

> The manitou of Edgecumbe, Ahgishanakon, saved herself from the universal deluge by catching at this peak, and standing on it held up and saved the world from drowning, too, while her brother, Chethl, struggled so hard to rise out of the water that wings appeared on his shoulders and he became the osprey.[29]

The second text is from the Kaigani, a tribe who inhabited Prince of Wales Island in southeastern Alaska.

> Alaskan Kaiganees say that the big canoe in which a good man was saved in the time of a great flood rested on a mountain just back of Howkan, and one old fellow claimed, a dozen or two of years ago, that he had a piece of its bark anchor-rope. The crow that flew out the ark still nests in the crater of Mount Edgecumbe, near Sitka, and catches whales.[30]

28. Asen Balikci, *The Netsilik Eskimo* (Garden City, NY: Natural History Press, 1970), p. 210.
29. Charles Montgomery Skinner, *Myths and Legends Beyond Our Borders* (Philadelphia and London: J.B. Lippincott, 1899), p. 199.
30. Ibid., p. 27.

Nez Perce
Horse Warrior

PACIFIC NORTHWEST

We come to the Pacific Northwest where, during the 1870s, Myron Eells found that very many tribes had a tradition of the Deluge. He recorded the traditions of the Twana or Coastal Salish, the Klallam, Lummi, Puyallop, Spokane, Nez Perce, Cayuse, and other tribes. "When the earliest missionaries came," he said, "they found that those Indians had their tradition of a flood, and that one man and wife were saved on a raft. Each of those three tribes also, together with the Flathead tribes, has their separate Ararat in connection with this event." The sending of the crow figures in some of these traditions.

Tribes of the Region

36. Tolowa (Northwestern California)
37. Ashochimi (Northern California)
38. Maidu (Northern California)
39. Northern Miwok (Central and Northern California)
40. Miwok of Bodega Bay (Central California)
41. Miwok of Clear Lake (Northern California)
42. Chehali and Cowlitz (Washington State)
43. Coastal Salish (Washington State)
44. Klallam (Washington State)
45. Lummi and Puyallop (Washington State)
46. Cascade Mountains Tradition (Washington State)
47. Spokane, Nez Perce, and Cayuse (Eastern Washington)
48. Yakama (Washington State)
49. Nez Perce (Eastern Washington and Idaho)
50. Mount Jefferson Tradition (Oregon)
51. Skokomish (Washington State)
52. Three Sisters Peaks (Oregon)
53. Skagit (Washington State)
54. Yurok (Northwest California)
55. Wiyot (Northern California)
56. Mattole (Northern California)
57. Karok (Northern California)
58. Sinkyone (Northwest California)
59. Shasta (Northern California and Southern Oregon)
60. Quileute (Washington State)
61. Ohlone (Northern California)
62. Nisqually (Washington State)
63. Kalapuya (Oregon)
64. Klallam (Puget Sound)
65. Cahto (Northern California)
66. Pomo (Northern California)
67. Alsea and Molala (Oregon)
68. Chilula (Northern California)
69. Takelma (Oregon)
70. Modoc (Northern California)
71. Coos (Western Oregon)
72. Makah (Washington State)
73. Kathlamet (Washington State)
74. Wintun (Northern California)
75. Chemetunne (Oregon)
76. Chimariko (Northern California)
77. Achomawi (Northern California)

The Yakama spoke of a great Flood that came, "one time in the early suns, back near the beginning." Mankind provoked the Creator with their evil ways, but a good man prophesied about the Flood, and made a boat out of the largest cedar tree, in which the good people were saved. We find other Flood accounts from the Coos of coastal Oregon, the Makah, Skokomish, and other tribes. An old woman of the Swinomish Reservation narrated a well-preserved Tower of Babel tradition to Ella Clark, and a Flood tradition associated with the Three Sisters Peaks in Oregon. The Skagit of Washington State have also preserved a strong memory of the Flood and the confusion of languages, which they say occurred during the Flood itself.

A Tolowa Man Wearing Dancing Head-dress

36 TOLOWA

Northwestern California

The Tolowa, or Smith River tribe, lived along the Pacific coast of northwestern California and southwestern Oregon. The historian Stephen Powers heard a Flood tradition from the oldest living woman of the tribe. This appeared in his 1877 work, Tribes of California:

> At one time there came a great rain. It lasted a long time and the water kept rising till all the valleys were submerged, and the Indians (who were very populous at that time) retired to the high land. As the water rose, covering their retreat, they were swept away and drowned. There was one pair however who were more successful. They reached the highest peak in the country and were saved. They subsisted on fish — cooking them by placing them under their arms. They had no fire and could not get any, as everything was water-soaked to such an extent that no fire could be produced. At length the water began to subside and continued to do so till it returned to its former level, and from that forlorn hope are all the Indians of the present day descended as also all the game, insects, etc. As the Indians died, their spirits took the forms of deer, elk, bear, insects, snakes, etc., as the fancy of the departed prompted. By those means the earth became again peopled by the same kind as formerly existed.[1]

As the water rose, covering their retreat, they were swept away and drowned. There was one pair however who were more successful. They reached the highest peak in the country and were saved.

37 ASHOCHIMI

Northern California

The Ashochimi, or Wappo, inhabited the Napa Valley of Northern California. They told Stephen Powers their tradition of the Flood between 1871 and 1876:

> They have a legend of the Deluge which runs as follows: Long ago there was a mighty flood which prevailed over all the land and drowned all living creatures save the coyote alone. He set himself to restore the population of the world in the following manner: He collected together a great quantity of owls', hawks', eagles', and buzzards' tail-feathers, and with these in a bundle he journeyed over the face of the earth and carefully sought out all the sites of the Indians' villages. Wherever a wigwam had stood before the flood, there he planted a feather in the ground and scraped up muck around the same. In due time the feathers sprouted, took root, grew up, branched and flourished greatly, finally turning into men and women; and thus was the world repeopled.[2]

A Wappo Woman

1. Stephen Powers, *Tribes of California* (Washington: GPO, 1877), p. 70.
2. Ibid., p. 200.

38 MAIDU

Northern California

The Maidu of the Sacramento Valley told Stephen Powers the following tradition between 1871 and 1876:

> Of old the Indians abode tranquilly in the Sacramento Valley, and were happy. All on a sudden there was a mighty and swift rushing of waters, so that the whole valley became like the Big Water, which no man can measure. The Indians fled for their lives, but a great many were overtaken by the waters, and they slept beneath the waves. Also, the frogs and the salmon pursued swiftly after them, and they ate many Indians. Thus all the Indians were drowned but two, who escaped into the foothills. But the Great Man gave these two fertility and blessed them, so that the world was soon repeopled.[3]

Northern California Tribal Areas at Time of European Contact

39 NORTHERN MIWOK

Central and Northern California

Sometime prior to 1910, the Northern Miwok people of California told their legend of the Flood to Clinton Merriam. "When water covered the world only the top of the highest mountain rose above it. The people had climbed up on this mountain, but could find no food and were starving." The people ventured down in search of food, but the ground was soft and muddy, and they sank and died. Later, ravens went out, and when the ground dried up, they turned into people.[4]

40 MIWOK OF BODEGA BAY

Central California

The Olamentko Miwok of Bodega Bay told Merriam another legend of the great Deluge. In this version, the Flood was caused by Coyote-man because of a quarrel between him and Falcon-man. "He made the rain come and cover the world with water. The water grew deeper and deeper and covered all the trees and all the hills and all the mountains until nothing was left but water." Falcon-man flew around searching for a place to rest, but found none and nearly died. Finally Coyote-man let down the water and recreated people.[5]

Miwok on Merced River

41 MIWOK OF CLEAR LAKE

Northern California

The Tuleyome tribe of the Miwok people, living near Clear Lake, told Merriam another Flood tradition. This bears similarities to the previous version, attributing the Flood to the vengeance of Coyote-man. He warned, "It is

3. Ibid., p. 290.
4. Clinton Hart Merriam, *The Dawn of the World* (Cleveland: Arthur H. Clark Company, 1910), p. 100–101.
5. Ibid., p. 156–157.

going to rain for ten days and ten nights." And it did rain, and the rain covered the whole country till all the land and all the hills and all the mountains were under water — everything except the top of Oo-de'-pow-we (Mount Konokti, on the west side of Clear Lake) which was so high that its top stuck out a little. . . . On the tenth day the rain stopped, and after that the water began to go down and each day the mountain stood up higher. Wek'wek stayed on the mountain about a week, by which time the water had gone down, and the land was bare again.[6]

42 CHEHALI AND COWLITZ

Washington State

The Chehalis of western Washington State told Thelma Adamson their Flood legend in 1926. This attributed the Flood to a personified bird (Thrush), which was forbidden to wash his face lest something should happen. However, one day he was coerced to wash his face by his wife's parents, and a great flood broke out. "It began to rain and rained all day. 'Move back from the river. I washed my face as you asked,' Thrush said to his father-in-law. The river continued to rise. It rained for many days and nights. The water rose and covered everything. There was no place for the people to stand but in the water and no place for them to go. Many drifted away and were never found." Muskrat dove into the water, and found some dirt. He used this to make a mountain, where the people could land and be safe. "After the water fell and the earth dried off, the ground was found to be covered with dried (fossil) whales. The earth was just like new, and the people could begin all over again."[7]

Adamson also found a few variants of this legend, as well as a similar story among the neighboring Cowlitz.[8] She also heard a different Flood story from another Chehali tribe member in 1927: "The flood began and all the people were drowned. They tried to go to the highest hills but could not save themselves; they tried to swim but drowned. Pheasant flew up to the highest hill and sat on the tallest tree there. Even there he thought that he would soon die for the water began to rise over his tail. At last the water fell and only Pheasant was saved. When the water fell it left a mark on Pheasant's tail."[9]

43 COASTAL SALISH

Washington State

The Coastal Salish, or Twana, are not a single tribe but rather a group of tribes which are linguistically related. They have inhabited western Washington State for many centuries. Myron Eells, a missionary and scholar of the Pacific Northwest, heard a Flood tradition from them between 1874 and 1877:

> Many of the Indians on this coast have a tradition of a Deluge. The Twanas on Puget's Sound speak of it, and that only good Indians were saved, though there were quite a number of them. It occurred because of a great rain, and all the country was overflowed. The Indians went in their canoes to the highest mountains near them, which is in the Olympic range; and as the waters rose above the top of it, they tied their canoes to the tops of the trees on it, so that they should not float away. Their ropes were made of the limbs of the cedar trees, just as they sometimes make them at the present time. The waters continued to rise, however, above the tops of the trees, until the whole length of their ropes was reached, and they supposed

Coast Salish "Quilcene Boy"

6. Ibid., p. 138–146.
7. Thelma Adamson, Folk-tales of the Coast Salish (New York: American Folklore Society, 1934), p. 1–2.
8. Ibid., p. 178.
9. Ibid., p. 3.

that they would be obliged to cut their ropes and drift away to some unknown place, when the waters began to recede. Some canoes, however, broke from their fastenings, and drifted away to the west, where they say their descendants now live, a tribe who speak a language similar to that of the Twanas. This they also say accounts for the present small number of the tribe. In their language, this mountain is called by a name which means "Fastener," from the fact that they fastened their canoes to it at that time. They also speak of a pigeon which went out to view the dead.[10]

In their language, this mountain is called by a name which means "Fastener," from the fact that they fastened their canoes to it at that time. They also speak of a pigeon which went out to view the dead.

44

KLALLAM

Washington State

Myron Eells also mentioned a Flood tradition which the Klallam tribe told him between 1874 and 1877.

> The Clallams, whose country adjoins that of the Twanas, also have a tradition of a flood, but some of them believe that it is not very long ago, perhaps not more than three or four generations since. One old man says that his grandfather saw the man who was saved from the flood, and that he was a Clallam. Their Ararat, too, is a different mountain from that of the Twanas.[11]

Klallam People Near a Canoe

45

LUMMI & PUYALLOP

Washington State

Of the Lummi and Puyallop tribes of Washington State, Eells wrote:

> The Lummi Indians, who live very near the northern line of Washington Territory, also speak of a flood, but I have not learned any particulars in regard to it. The Puyallop Indians, near Tacoma, say that the flood overflowed all the country except one high mound near Steilacoom, and this mound is called by the Indians "The Old Land," because it was not overflowed.[12]

46

CASCADE MOUNTAINS TRADITION

Washington State

Myron Eells heard another Flood story from a tribe living in the Cascade Mountains. He did not specify which tribe it was, but the most likely candidates are the Wenatchi, Yakama, and Sahaptin tribes:

> "Do you see that high mountain over there?" said an old Indian to a mountaineer, as they were riding across the Cascade Mountains, about seventeen years ago. "I do," was the reply. "Do you see that grove to the right?" the Indian then said. "Yes," said the white man. "Well," said the Indian, "a long time ago there was a flood, and all the country was overflowed. There was an old man and his family on a boat or raft, and he floated about, and the wind blew him to that mountain, where he touched bottom. He stayed there some time, and then sent a crow to hunt for land, but it came back without finding any. After some time he sent the crow again, and this time it brought a leaf from that grove, and the old man was glad, for he knew that the water was going away."[13]

There was an old man and his family on a boat or raft, and he floated about, and the wind blew him to that mountain, where he touched bottom. He stayed there some time, and then sent a crow to hunt for land, but it came back without finding any. After some time he sent the crow again, and this time it brought a leaf from that grove, and the old man was glad, for he knew that the water was going away.

A Lummi Woman

10. Rev. Myron Eells, "Traditions of the Deluge Among the Tribes of the North-West," *The American Antiquarian and Oriental Journal*, vol. 1 (1878), p. 70.
11. Ibid.
12. Ibid.
13. Ibid., p. 71.

47 SPOKANE, NEZ PERCE, & CAYUSE

Eastern Washington

Eells mentioned the existence of Flood traditions held by the Spokane, Nez Perce, and Cayuse tribes of interior Washington:

> When the earliest missionaries came among the Spokanes, Nez Perces, and Cayuses, who with the Yakimas live in the eastern part of the Territory, they found that those Indians had their tradition of a flood, and that one man and wife were saved on a raft. Each of those three tribes also, together with the Flathead tribes, has their separate Ararat in connection with this event.[14]

Nez Perce Baby in Cradleboard

The Gospel Comes to the Plateau Tribes. During a smallpox outbreak in the 1780s, a Spokane shaman named Circling Raven went to the top of Mount Spokane to fast and pray for healing for his people for four days. According to their oral traditions, he then received a vision in which he saw white men wearing strange clothes, carrying leaves bound together. He was told that his people should prepare themselves for the coming of these "white skinned ones" and to pay attention to the teaching that came from the leaves bound together.

A similar prophecy was given to an eastern Salish chief named Shining Shirt.

In 1824–1825, George Simpson, a representative from the Hudson Bay Company, was accosted by a dozen chiefs requesting teachers to come and teach their people from the book they had caught glimpses of at company posts. Simpson knew nothing of the prophecies that had fueled these requests! This led to a powerful work of God among the Plateau tribes, with many people coming to faith in the Lord Jesus for forgiveness of their sins. Chief Spokane Garry was one of the leading men used by God in this period.[15]

"I have heard from the Land Above, the land of the spirits, that a big water is coming — a big water that will cover all the land. Make a boat for the good people. Let the bad people be killed by the water."

48 YAKAMA

Washington State

The Yakima (or Yakama) lived around the Yakima River in Washington State. They shared an ancient tradition with Lucullus McWhorter, which he recorded in an unpublished manuscript called "Yakima Tradition of the Flood":

> There was a flood in the Yakima country, one time in the early suns, back near the beginning. Before the big water came, there had been wars and blood between the tribes. Even the medicine men had killed people. But there were some good people who remembered what they had been told by the old people who were gone.
>
> One of the good men told the others, "I have heard from the Land Above, the land of the spirits, that a big water is coming — a big water that will cover all the land. Make a boat for the good people. Let the bad people be killed by the water."

Yakama Woman

14. Ibid.
15. Richard Twiss, One Church Many Tribes (Minneapolis: Baker Publishing, 2000), p. 140–141.

The good people held a council and decided to make the boat from the cedar tree, the biggest and best cedar they could find. They chipped it with stone and with antlers of elk and burned it hollow with fire.

When the cedar canoe was finished, it went over the water like a good canoe. Soon the flood came. It filled the valleys. It covered the hills and the mountains. The bad people were drowned by the big water. The good ones were saved in the boat.

We do not know how long the flood stayed. At last the canoe came down where it was built. It is still there. You can see it on the Toppenish ridge, on the side toward the rising sun. The earth will again be destroyed by a big water if the people do wrong a second time — if they fight in wars, if they steal and murder and do other wrongs.[16]

Yakama Warrior

The Accuracy of the Genesis Flood Record.

By now you may be noticing the trend, that these North American tribal traditions say it was atop some mountain near them, where the "great canoe" landed. Indeed, that is a global trend. As Arthur Custance wrote: "This is a quite exceptional circumstance. All other traditions report that the ark landed locally. In Greece on Mount Parnassus; in India the ark landed in the Himalayas; in America one story has it landing on Keddie Peak in the Sacramento Valley. And so it goes; everywhere the same — always a local mountain. This circumstance surely suggests that here in the Bible we have the genuine account. And it also underscores the great respect which the Hebrew people had for the Word of God and the requirement that they never tamper with it. It would surely, otherwise, have been most natural for them to land the ark on their most famous mountain, Mount Zion.[17]

The Book of Genesis, unlike these global traditions, places the landing of the ark at a far-away mountain in Armenia. This is near 800 miles away from Jerusalem as the crow flies, but much farther on foot!

I have seen hundreds of Flood records from all over the world, and the Genesis account clearly stands apart from the rest, as the most historical, original, and well-preserved account. The Genesis account is sober, detailed, and reads exactly like a log book written by an eyewitness.

For more discussion of the historical accuracy of the Book of Genesis, see Appendix B (The Historicity of Genesis, Comparisons with the Epic of Gilgamesh, and North American Flood Traditions).

16. Lucullus V. McWhorter, "Yakima Tradition of the Flood," McWhorter Manuscript Collection, Washington State University Library. Box 43, Folder 420, No. 16. As quoted by Ella Clark, *Indian Legends of the Pacific Northwest* (Berkeley: University of California Press, 1953), p. 45.
17. Arthur C. Custance, "Flood Traditions of the World," Symposium on Creation IV (Grand Rapids, MI: Baker, 1972), p. 17.

49 — NEZ PERCE

Eastern Washington and Idaho

Nez Perce Warrior Yellow Wolf

The Nez Perce were a powerful tribe living on the western slopes of the Rocky Mountains in central Idaho and eastern Washington. A missionary named Kate McBeth spent 27 years among the Nez Perce from about 1881 to 1907. She recorded a brief reference to the Flood in one of their legends:

> Now that mountain, Yamastas, is where the Nez Perces took refuge at the time of the great flood, when all other places but that one had been submerged. The stone is there yet in which they pounded their food. The people say it looks just like one of their old mortars.[18]

In 1910, a tribe member named Otis Halfmoon told Ella Clark their beliefs about the Flood:

> The great flood, some people say, took place long before the human race was created, back in the days of the animal people. It rained for a long, long time. The valleys were filled with water, and the animals lived on the tops of the hills. Some of the animals were saved, but the big animals perished. That is why people have found the bones of big animals along the Salmon River and big hip bones near Lewiston. Watermarks and driftwood carried by the flood have been found on Steptoe Butte in southeastern Washington.[19]

Also, a Nez Perce woman named Lucy Armstrong Isaac told Ella Clark this about the Flood:

> Steptoe Butte stood above the waters at the time of the great flood, and many Indians were saved there from drowning. Below the top, there used to be a water line, the mark of where the water had once been.[20]

50 — MOUNT JEFFERSON TRADITION

Oregon

The following tradition comes from an unspecified tribe of Oregon — the Kalapuya and Molala tribes are strong candidates. A Portland resident who had spent a great length of time with the tribes of Oregon recorded this sometime prior to 1930:

> A great flood covered the land. Then the waters flowed away, and the land became dry again. A second time a flood covered the land, and a second time the waters sent away. Afraid that another and greater flood might come, the people cut the biggest cedar they could find and made the biggest canoe any of them had ever seen.
>
> When they saw the flood coming the third time, they chose the bravest and finest of their young men and the fairest and choicest of their maidens. They put the young people in the canoe, with enough food for them for many days. Then a flood bigger and deeper than any before swallowed all the land and the people.

They put the young people in the canoe, with enough food for them for many days. Then a flood bigger and deeper than any before swallowed all the land and the people.

18. Kate C. McBeth, *The Nez Perces Since Lewis and Clark* (New York and Chicago: Fleming H. Revell Co., 1908), p. 260.
19. Ella E. Clark, *Indian Legends of the Northern Rockies* (Norman, OK: University of Oklahoma Press, 1966), p. 39.
20. Ibid., p. 40.

Mount Jefferson, Oregon's Second Highest Peak

> For many days and many nights rain fell, and the canoe floated over the water. Once the dark clouds opened up and the young man and young woman saw blue sky, but the clouds closed again. A second time the dark clouds opened, and they saw blue sky. But again the dark clouds closed. When the clouds opened a third time, the people saw dry land. The man paddled the canoe toward it.
>
> This time the clouds stayed open. The rain stopped. The flood waters went down, and the canoe rested on the top of the peak now called Mount Jefferson. When the valleys were dry again, the two people left the canoe and made their new home at the foot of the mountain. All the Indians are their grandchildren and their grandchildren's children.[21]

The flood waters went down, and the canoe rested on the top of the peak now called Mount Jefferson. When the valleys were dry again, the two people left the canoe and made their new home at the foot of the mountain.

51 SKOKOMISH

Washington State

The Skokomish people have inhabited the Pacific coast of Washington for centuries. They told the following account to Ella Clark, probably around 1950:

> Once a big flood came to this world. . . . My people made ropes by twisting cedar limbs. They tied the ropes to their canoes and fastened the canoes to a mountain near the canal. When the world got flooded, the Skokomish people went higher and higher into the Olympic Mountains. The Olympics got flooded. Some of the ropes broke and the canoes drifted away. They kept on going and kept on going —down, down, down. They kept their canoes tied together until they reached the country of the Flathead Indians. They became known as the Flatheads. A long time afterwards, when there was war around where Seattle is now, the Skokomish people were trapped on the bay. They heard strange people talking in the Skokomish language. When my people spoke to them, they said, "We are the people who drifted away from here." That is why the Skokomish and the Flatheads speak the same language.[22]

Skokomish Fishing Camp

21. Ella Elizabeth Clark, *Indian Legends of the Pacific Northwest*, p. 14–15.
22. Ibid., p. 44.

52 THREE SISTERS PEAKS

Oregon

Three Sisters, Looking North

The Three Sisters Peaks, part of the Cascade Mountains in Oregon, are the subject of a legend that seems to refer to both the Flood and the Tower of Babel. Ella Clark collected this at the Swinomish Reservation in 1952:

> Three sisters built a very high house, a long time ago. They made it tall because they wanted to go up to the sky to see the Creator. They kept building it higher and higher and higher. By the time the house was finished, they could not speak the same language. They could not understand each other. That is why there are so many different languages today. During the great flood, the three women drifted away. After the flood, the Changer came to make the world over. He transformed the sisters into a mountain with three peaks. It is the Sisters Peak up there by Mount Baker.[23]

53 SKAGIT

Washington State

The Skagit people inhabited the river by the same name in Washington State and southwest British Columbia. An older man of the tribe shared the Skagit creation story with Ella Clark around 1952:

> After the world had been created for a while, everyone learned the four names of the earth. Everyone and everything spoke the Skagit language. When the people began to talk to the trees, then the change came. The change was a flood. Water covered everything but two high mountains — Kobah and Takobah. Those two mountains — Mount Baker and Mount Rainier — did not go under.
>
> When the people saw the flood coming, they made a great big canoe. They loaded it with two of everything living on earth, with the male and female of every animal and plant. When the flood was over, the canoe landed on the prairie in the Skagit country. Five people were in the canoe. After the flood, when the land was dry again, they made their way back here. A child was born to the man and his wife who had been in the canoe. He became Doquebuth, the new creator. He created after the flood, after the world changed.[24]

When the people saw the flood coming, they made a great big canoe. They loaded it with two of everything living on earth, with the male and female of every animal and plant.

Illustration of a Skagit Camp

23. Ibid., p. 43.
24. Ella E. Clark, *Indian Legends of the Pacific Northwest* (Berkeley: University of California Press, 1953), p. 139.

54

YUROK

Northwest California

The anthropologist Alfred Kroeber recorded a Flood tradition of the Yurok tribe of northern California. His source was a Yurok man named Tskerkr, who narrated this between 1902 and 1907. Blind and in his seventies when Kroeber met him, Tskerkr had been born before the arrival of white man.

Yurok Man in a Boat

> There used to be a settlement at Siwitsu just north of Orekw. Then it happened that there almost came to be no people left in the world on account of what happened at this settlement. For an old man and his brother went into the sweathouse to sleep. But a man was outside, and when they slept, he went in and tied their hair together. Then he went out and shouted, "They have come! Somebody will be killed! They are going to fight!"
>
> Then the ocean began to turn rough from the anger of the old men. A breaker came over the settlement of Siwitsu, washed the whole of it away, and drowned everyone. Then all the people of Orekw ran off to the top of the hill, wearing their woodpecker headbands: they were afraid.
>
> Then he at Orekw who knew the formula for the sacred sweat house there ran to Oketo, for now the water was already all around Orekw. He looked into the sweathouse at Oketo. There was the one who know that formula. He spoke to him, but that one did not answer. Four times he spoke to him. Then he said, "Were they drowned?" "Yes, I saw them drowned," said he of Orekw, "but I am afraid the water will cover the whole land."
>
> And now the breakers were already dashing against one side of that sweathouse at Oketo. Then that one began to speak his formula in that sweat house. He had to do it hastily; therefore he used old boards to make the fire. Then the ocean went down.[25]

Two men and two women were saved in a boat; all others drowned. Sky-Owner gave them a song. When they sang, the water receded. This song is used to prevent the ocean from again covering the land.

Another tribe member told Kroeber this regarding the Flood:

> Once the ocean covered the earth. That is why there are redwood logs on the high ridges. The flood was caused by the surf. Two men and two women were saved in a boat; all others drowned. Sky-Owner gave them a song. When they sang, the water receded. This song is used to prevent the ocean from again covering the land.[26]

Illustration of a Yurok Burial

25. Alfred L. Kroeber, *Yurok Myths* (Berkeley: University of California Press, 1976), p. 186–187.
26. Ibid., p. 430.

55 WIYOT

Northern California

The Wiyot (sometimes called Wishosk) living near Humboldt Bay told their Flood story to the photographer and ethnologist Edward Curtis between 1916 and 1917:

> Old-man-above was alone. There was nothing but water. He thought there should be people and some land for them to live on. So he made the land, but it was barren. He thought it did not look right, because it had no trees and no grass. So he made vegetation on the earth. Then he made people. These people were not good; they quarreled and talked ill, so he sent a tidal wave and drowned all except two, Shatash (condor) and his sister. These two, knowing that a flood was coming, had made a large storage basket, and in it they floated about on the water. When the water subsided, the man went to look for food, and to observe the country. When he came back he said, "My sister, are you home?" "Yes," she answered. But she would not say, "Yes, my brother." Seeing that she would not so address him, he became suspicious that she might not regard him as her brother. One day he returned from his travels and said to her, "Are you here, my wife?" Then she laughed. She liked it. So this man married his sister, and they were the ancestors of all who afterward peopled the earth.[27]

These two, knowing that a flood was coming, had made a large storage basket, and in it they floated about on the water.

Self-Portrait of Edward S. Curtis

56 MATTOLE

Northern California

The Mattole come from a part of northwestern California which is now Humboldt County. They shared a tradition of the Flood with Stephen Powers during the 1870s, which he briefly mentioned:

> They have also a tradition of the flood, and as usual this occurrence took place in their immediate vicinity. Taylor's Peak is the mountain on which the surviving Indians took refuge.[28]

57 KAROK

Northern California

In 1901 and 1902, a seventy-five-year-old man Karok man told the following to Alfred Kroeber. This man — known simply as Dick Richards' father-in-law — had never been given an English name, nor spoke any English (it was considered uncouth to ask for one's tribal name if it was not volunteered).

> In the middle of the world in this land here, there grew two people. They knew that the water would spread out here and cover the world, and that all the people would die. They took a shipnuk storage basket, and getting pitch, they rubbed it over the basket, covering all its stitches until it would not leak, and on top they had a cover. But one of them came too late and did not get into it and was left behind. The other jumped into the basket, and his dog jumped with him. When he heard the water about him, he drew the cover

They took a shipnuk storage basket, and getting pitch, they rubbed it over the basket, covering all its stitches until it would not leak, and on top they had a cover.

27. Edward S. Curtis, *The North American Indian*, vol. 13 (Norwood, MA: Plimpton Press, 1924), p. 190–191.
28. Stephen Powers, *Tribes of California*, p. 111.

over the top. With a deer-bone awl he prepared to make a small hole, holding pitch ready in his hand to stop the hole if water entered; he wanted to see if the water had stopped rising. Finally no water came in at the hole. Then he made the hole larger, and larger. He could see nothing but endless sand hills. He uncovered the basket and looked around. The water had gone. All people were dead. Not a single person was left; only the man and his dog were saved.[29]

They knew that the water would spread out here and cover the world, and that all the people would die.

58 SINKYONE

Northwest California

The Eel River Athapaskans were a group of tribes that included the Sinkyone, Wailaki, Lassik, and Nongatl peoples. Between 1902 and 1918, a Sinkyone woman told Dr. P.E. Goddard their belief about the Flood:

> The ocean came up and covered the land. Two eel-baskets [people], a brother and a sister, went on Bear Butte, a mountain southwest of Phillipsville. There they were saved. Everyone else was drowned. People are afraid to climb this mountain.[30]

59 SHASTA

Northern California and Southern Oregon

An Aged Shasta

The Shasta people lived to the north of the Wintun, extending from California into southern Oregon. The memory of the Flood lived on in their understanding of the weather, as they told Stephen Powers:

> When it rains, some Indian, sick in heaven, is weeping. Long, long ago, there was a good young Indian on earth. When he died the Indians wept so that a flood came upon the earth, and drowned all people except one couple.[31]

A second version, told to Roland Dixon around 1910, has similarities to that of other North American tribes, such as the Menominee tribe of Wisconsin:

> Coyote was traveling about. There was an evil being in the water. Coyote carried his arrows. Now, the evil being rose up out of the water, and said, "There is no wood." Then the water rose up toward Coyote, it covered him up, Coyote was covered by the water. Then the water went down, dried off, and Coyote shot the evil being.
>
> Now, Coyote ran away, and the water followed after him. He ran up on Mount Shasta, ran up to the top of the mountain. The water was very deep. Coyote made a fire, for there only was any ground left above the water. Grizzly-Bear swam thither, Deer swam thither, Black-Bear swam thither, Elk swam thither, and Gray-Squirrel, and Jack-Rabbit, and Ground-Squirrel, and Badger, and Porcupine, and Coon, and Wild-Cat, and Fisher, and Wolf, and Mountain-Lion. . . . Then there was no more water. It was swampy all about. People scattered everywhere.[32]

29. Alfred L. Kroeber and Edward W. Winslow, Karok Myths (Berkeley and Los Angeles: University of California Press, 1980), p. 55–56.
30. Alfred Louis Kroeber, "Sinkyone Tales." *Journal of American Folk-lore*, vol. 32 (Lancaster and New York: American Folklore Society, 1919), p. 347.
31. Stephen Powers, *Tribes of California* (Washington: GPO, 1877), p. 251.
32. Roland B. Dixon, "Shasta Myths," *Journal of American Folk-lore*, vol. 23, no. 87 (Boston and New York: Houghton Mifflin, 1911), p. 8, 36. A similar version was collected by the late Hap Gilliland in The Great Flood (Billings, MT: Council for Indian Education, 2008), p. 14–15.

Josephus on the Flood (ca. A.D. 90)

> Now all the writers of barbarian histories make mention of this flood and of this ark; among whom is Berosus the Chaldean; for when he is describing the circumstances of the flood, he goes on thus: "It is said there is still some part of this ship in Armenia, at the mountain of the Cordyaeans; and that some people carry off pieces of the bitumen, which they take away, and use chiefly as amulets for the averting of mischiefs. Hieronymous the Egyptian, also, who wrote the Phoenician Antiquities, and Mnaseas, and a great many more, make mention of the same. Nay, Nicolaus of Damascus, in his ninety-sixth book, hath a particular relation about them, where he speaks thus: "There is a great mountain in Armenia, over Minyas, called Baris, upon which it is reported that many who fled at the time of the Deluge were saved; and that one who was carried in an ark came on shore upon the top of it; and that the remains of the timber were a great while preserved. This might be the man about whom Moses, the legislator of the Jews wrote.[33]

Josephus

60 Washington State

QUILEUTE

Between 1905 and 1909, a Quileute tribe member told this tradition pertaining to the Flood to a government agent named Alfred Reagan:

> Thunderbird was very angry one time. He caused the ocean to rise. When the water began to cover things, the Quileute got into their boats. The waters rose for four days. They rose until the very tops of the mountains were covered with water. The Quileute in their boats sailed wherever the wind and the currents carried them. They had no way to direct themselves. There was no sun. There was no land. For four days the water receded. But now the people were much scattered. When they reached land, some of the people were at Hoh; so they lived there from that time on. Others landed at Chemakum and stayed there. Only a few succeeded in finding their way back to Quileute.[34]

When the water began to cover things, the Quileute got into their boats. The waters rose for four days. They rose until the very tops of the mountains were covered with water.

Quileute Girl

61 Northern California

OHLONE

The Ohlone (or Costanoan) populated what is now the San Francisco Bay Area. Their creation story records a memory of a great flood that destroyed the earth. As two old women of the tribe told Alfred Kroeber:

> The eagle, hummingbird, and Coyote were standing on the top of Pico Blanco. When the water rose to their feet, the eagle, carrying the hummingbird and Coyote, flew to the Sierra de Gabilan. There they stood until the water went down. Then the eagle sent Coyote down the mountain to see if the world were dry. Coyote came back and said: "The whole world is dry." The eagle said to him: "Go and look in the river. See what there is there." Coyote came back and said: "There is a beautiful

33. Josephus, *Antiquities of the Jews, in The Works of Josephus*, trans. William Whiston (Peabody, MA: Hendrickson, 1987), 1.3.6.
34. Albert B. Reagan and L.V.W. Walters, "Tales from the Hoh and Quileute," *Journal of American Folklore*, vol. 46, no. 182 (Lancaster and New York: American Folklore Society, 1933), p. 322.

girl." The eagle said: "She will be your wife in order that people may be raised again."[35]

The children of this union went out and founded five rancherias with five different languages.

62 Washington State

NISQUALLY

Myron Eells also shared a tradition from the Nisqually people. The reader will be able to see striking similarity to the Kwakiutl (page 29) and Karok (page 62) traditions:

> A great many years ago — so many that man cannot enumerate them — the tribes became so numerous that they ate up all the game and fish, and then they turned cannibals; after a time they became worse than wild animals, so much so that the Great Spirit sent a great rain which flooded the whole country, and all living things were drowned, excepting one squaw [woman] and a dog, who both happened to be on the headwaters of the Nisqually River, and they, seeing the waters rising rapidly, fled to Mount Tacoma and remained upon its summit until the waters subsided. From the squaw and the dog sprang the present Nisqually Indians.[36]

...the tribes became so numerous that they ate up all the game and fish, and then they turned cannibals; after a time they became worse than wild animals, so much so that the Great Spirit sent a great rain which flooded the whole country, and all living things were drowned, excepting one squaw [woman] and a dog...

63 Oregon

KALAPUYA

In 1877, Albert Gatschet recorded oral traditions from the Kalapuya tribe of the Willamette Valley in Oregon. Gatschet named one of these traditions "The Four Generations of Mankind." It gives the Kalapuya cosmology and refers to the Flood, which they say occurred in the "Third Age" of the world:

Kalapuya Woman

> The third age of persons became many. Now then two women stole one infant, and they kept it all the time. . . . Then one flint boy found her, and he brought her to her mother. Then the two women who had stolen the girl from her mother became angry, they stood and danced, they made rain with their rain spirit-power, and then it rained twenty days. The earth was flooded, the mountains sank, and then the third age of people died. Only one boy and one girl were left on the flooded earth (except also the two women who had caused the flood), flint was the male. The man put the girl under his armpit, he hid her. Then the water receded.[37]
>
> After this, the man killed the two women who had caused the flood, and cursed them so that they became rain clouds. All mankind who died in the flood became beavers, fish, and other marine animals. These animals used to be the people in the pre-flood world.[38]

...they stood and danced, they made rain with their rain spirit-power, and then it rained twenty days. The earth was flooded, the mountains sank, and then the third age of people died.

35. Alfred L. Kroeber, "Indian Myths of South Central California," *University of California Publications American Archaeology and Ethnology*, vol. 4, no. 4 (Berkeley: University Press, 1907), p. 191, 199.
36. Myron Eells, "The Religion of the Indians of Puget Sound," *American Antiquarian*, vol 12 (Chicago: 1890), p. 74.
37. Albert S. Gatschet, Leo J. Frachtenberg, and Melville Jacobs, "Kalapuya Texts," *University of Washington Publications in Anthropology*, vol. 11 (Seattle: University of Washington, 1945), p. 173–175.
38. Ibid., p. 175.

64 KLALLAM

Puget Sound

Evening on Puget Sound

The Klallam people are from the Olympic Peninsula in northwestern Washington. An older woman of narrated this Flood tradition to Erna Gunther around 1925:

> There was a man who told his people to make some canoes and to make them large and strong so they could endure storms. There was a flood coming. The people said the mountains were high and they could just go up to the mountains when the flood came. He warned them again. Soon it began to rain and rained for many days. And the rivers became salt. The people said they would go up to the mountains. When the flood came they took their children by the hand and packed
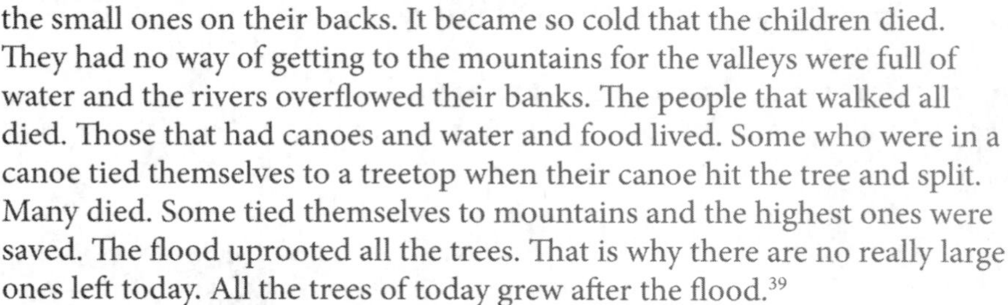
> the small ones on their backs. It became so cold that the children died. They had no way of getting to the mountains for the valleys were full of water and the rivers overflowed their banks. The people that walked all died. Those that had canoes and water and food lived. Some who were in a canoe tied themselves to a treetop when their canoe hit the tree and split. Many died. Some tied themselves to mountains and the highest ones were saved. The flood uprooted all the trees. That is why there are no really large ones left today. All the trees of today grew after the flood.[39]

The flood uprooted all the trees. That is why there are no really large ones left today.

65 CAHTO

Northern California

The Cahto people inhabited what is now Mendocino County, in California's northern coastal area. Around 1923, A Cahto man shared his tribe's knowledge of the Deluge with Edward Curtis:

Cahto Woman

> There were people living on the earth. For a long time it had not rained, and the wise men said there would be some catastrophe, but others saw no cause for alarm. Then it began to rain, and it rained day and night for an entire moon; and every day it grew warmer, until the people had to leap into the streams. Some died from the heat. By the end of the month it was raining large stones instead of drops of water, and these killed nearly all the people. A great wall of water came from the southwest and covered the world. A few who had saved their lives from the falling stones by hiding in caves now took refuge from the water on the top of Solchokut (Bald Mountain), the peak of which remained above the waters. At Bee Rock, Hawk saved himself and his sister. He put her on the end of a long pole and lifted her up to the hole, and then she drew him up to her. The people on Bald Mountain had nothing but leaves to eat, and at last they became deer. Hawk and his sister never came out of the cave.[40]

39. Erna Gunther, "Klallam Folk Tales," *University of Washington Publications in Anthropology*, vol. 1 (Seattle: University of Washington Press, 1927) p. 119.
40. Edward S. Curtis, *The North American Indian*, vol. 14, p. 165.

A second version was told to Edward Gifford. The world that existed prior to the Flood, as the Cahto told him, was very different than our present world:

A Pomo Dancer

> But the creations of the two gods were not to endure, for flood waters came. Every day it rained, every night it rained. All the people slept. The sky fell. The land was not. For a very great distance there was no land. The waters of the oceans came together. Animals of all kinds drowned. The waters completely joined everywhere. There was no land or mountains or rocks, but only water. Trees and grass were not. There were no fish, or land animals, or bids. Human beings and animals alike had been washed away.[41]

POMO

66 Northern California

The Pomo told Samuel Barrett their tradition in 1904, is similar to that of the Miwok tribe.

> Coyote dreamed that water was going to cover up the world but no one believed him. At that time there were no mountains or hills. Coyote told the people, "There is going to be water all over the world. It will come tonight and tomorrow. Tomorrow the water will be over the world." Still the people did not believe him. Next morning, however, it was raining and presently the water began to rise. The people got on whatever little elevation there were on the land and climbed trees because there were no mountains up which they might go to escape. Coyote took a tree and broke it so that he had a large log. He, with a number of people, climbed on this log and floated around. The log did not move or try to roll over and the people were able to sit upon it easily. Coyote said to those with him, "Don't be afraid. The water will go down by and by.[42]

Coyote dreamed that water was going to cover up the world but no one believed him.

Coyote later hired Mole to create mountains, which made the waters go down. Then he created more people out of willow and elder wood sticks, and dispersed them in groups to inhabit different parts fo the world.[43]

Yet there is another Flood account from the Pomo tribe, which is noteworthy because it resembles versions that we find in East and Southeast Asia. Specifically, it contains the "fire fetching" theme, which tells of the recovery or rediscovery of fire in the damp and muddy post-Flood world. This theme is also found in texts from certain parts of South America. I believe this element is derived from the memory of what Noah did when he went out from the ark: he built an altar, lit a fire, and offered burnt offerings to the Lord on the altar (Genesis 8:20–22). The confusion of languages at Babel undoubtedly gave rise to differences in how that event, and other details of the Flood, would later be retold.

> During the Deluge everyone except Gopher was killed. He saved himself by climbing to the top of Mt. Kanaktai. As the water rose he climbed higher and higher, and just as the water was about to wash him off the top of the mountain it began to recede and finally left Gopher high and dry on the top of the mountain.

41. Edward Winslow Gifford and Gwendoline Harris Block, *Californian Indian Nights* (Glendale, CA: Arthur H. Clark, 1930), p. 79–81.
42. Samuel Alfred Barrett, "Pomo Myths," *Bulletin of the Public Museum of the City of Milwaukee*, Vol 15 (Milwaukee: Order of the Board of Trustees, 1933), p. 129–130.
43. Ibid., p. 130–131.

Gopher was, of course, without fire and he had no neighbors from whom to borrow fire as was the custom in the olden times, so he began to dig down from the top of the mountain. He dug on and on down into the mountain until he finally found fire inside of it. In this way he got fire again for the world.[44]

67 ALSEA AND MOLALA

Oregon

Leo Frachtenberg reached the Alsea tribe in 1910, and collected their origin story from the few remaining tribe members. Their tradition told of an old man who had the gift of dreams, and who warned the people of an impending flood. The parallels with Noah are striking.

William Smith, an Alsea Indian

> Not very long were the people living (on their allotted rivers), when the weather was getting rough all over. A terrible rain the earth brought forth, when winter set in all over the world. Then one person there was who knew what to do whenever it rained very hard. At that time usually that one person would dance because of it. . . . One man (there was) who was habitually dreaming a great deal. He was a very important personage because he knew very well how to dream. Thus he acted. All the people acted thus everywhere. One man there was who always acted thus. He knew very well what such a thing meant when the elements acted thus. Indeed, he knew everything as soon as it began to thunder hard all over. And for that reason all the people were simply afraid.
>
> "It will not be long before it will commence to rain. The water will come ashore from the ocean. Thus I was told constantly. For that reason you shall take good care of yourselves, when it will commence to rain hard all over, for at that time the water will come ashore from inside the ocean." Thereupon every year was counted, and that man continually spoke to all the people: "Do you take good care of yourselves! It will not be long before the water will begin to overflow from the ocean. At that time the earth will be washed clean."
>
> In fear all had their minds upon themselves when that person was heard (to say) this. . . . So whenever he was singing all the people would gather around him listening carefully whenever he would announce that not long (afterward) the water would overflow.
>
> . . . Finally one year went by, and then surely not long afterward the water of the ocean was going to come ashore. And then, verily, thus it happened all over. The water of the ocean came ashore everywhere. No matter how high some mountains there were, nevertheless the water would cover them all up when it finally began to come ashore. . . .[45]

The water of the ocean came ashore everywhere. No matter how high some mountains there were, nevertheless the water would cover them all up when it finally began to come ashore…

44. Ibid., p. 135.
45. Leo Frachtenberg, "Alsea Texts and Myths," Bureau of American Ethnology Bulletin, vol. 67 (Washington: GPO, 1920), p. 113–115.

Frachtenberg also made a passing reference to a Flood tradition from the Molala tribe of Oregon.

> In like manner the Molala believe that the Flood was caused by the Water People in order to avenge on Panther the death of their daughter.[46]

Yellow Hammer of the Modoc People

68 CHILULA

Northern California

The Chilula people lived in the redwood forests of northern California. In 1912, a very aged Chilula woman living at Redwood Creek shared their tribal memory of the Flood with Pliny Goddard:

> Water came. The water flowed over every part of the world. Then only so much of the hill was not covered by the water. All kinds of animals swam to it. Then the water which came dried up again. The people lived happily again after the ground was dry. Just the Kixunnai lived on this butte. Here is the end. He-who-came-down-for-this-earth thought the people had talked very badly. Because of that the flood came. Thus they will live well. After that he made it good.[47]

69 TAKELMA

Oregon

The Takelma people inhabited the Rogue Valley in southwestern Oregon. From Edward Sapir's interviews at the Siletz Reservation in 1906 we have a fragment of their flood account:

> Long ago there were people, all beings were people. Birds, ducks, deer; bluejays were all people; all sorts of beings. Buzzards, those were all people, crows were all people. Now then beavers were not ear-holed, while ducks were nose-holed. For that reason did they become beavers.
>
> Then a flood did come and cover all, all this world became a mass of water. And then, 'tis said, they were submerged, all beings were submerged. Then Beaver got to be at the bottom of the water, up to this day he is there. Then all the birds flew up, and for that reason they all fly today. Since Beaver was not nose-holed, since he was not ear-holed, for that reason did Beaver, for his part, get to be in the water, indeed. Thus it is.[48]

70 MODOC

Northern California

The Modoc were a powerful tribe of northeastern California and southern Oregon. They lived along the Lost River, and the volcanic regions around Lakes Klammath and Tula. Jeremiah Curtin wrote that Lake Klammath is "as beautiful as are the famed lakes of Italy and Switzerland," nearly entirely surrounded by mountains, some of which remain snow-capped nearly all year long.[49]

Big Eagle, a Modoc Chief

46. Frachtenberg, "Alsea Texts and Myths," p. 114.
47. Pliny Earle Goddard, "Chilula Texts," *University of California Publications in American Archaeology and Ethnology*, vol. 10, no. 7 (Berkeley: University of California Press, 1914), p. 373–374.
48. Edward Sapir, "Takelma Texts," *Anthropological Publications of the University of Pennsylvania Museum*, vol. 2, no. 1 (Philadelphia: University Museum, 1909), p. 167.
49. Jeremiah Curtin, *Myths of the Modocs* (Boston: Little, Brown & Co., 1912), p. v.

A.B. Meacham (1826–1882), the Oregon Superintendent of Indian Affairs, knew the Modoc well, and was wounded by them in a failed peace attempt in 1873. He recorded their Flood tradition in his 1876 work, *Wi-ne-ma (The Woman Chief)*:

Wi-ne-ma (The Woman Chief)

> The Modoc tradition recites the history of the Deluge, that it was sent to destroy the human family, except, one pair; that before the Deluge the people were very much larger than the present race. They are represented in this tradition to have been twelve to fifteen feet in height, and of proportionate weight, hence were very destructive. God had warned them against killing each other, threatening to destroy them, but this warning was disregarded. Selecting the smallest man and the smallest woman of all the people, he bade them go to the top of a very high mountain, taking with them a pair of crows, a pair of hawks, a pair of white rabbits and one pair of white deer; and they obeyed the command.
>
> The waters rose up round the mountain, covering all the land about it, and destroying every living thing, save the small man and woman, and the birds and animals which they had taken to the mountain-top. When the waters began to reach them, the man and woman were frightened and began to make a canoe. God came and talked to them, and said if they would trust in Him He would not permit them to be drowned. He caused a wall of spirits to form round the mountaintop, which held back the waters, although it rose high above them. Such is the tradition regarding the Deluge.[50]

The waters rose up round the mountain, covering all the land about it, and destroying every living thing, save the small man and woman, and the birds and animals which they had taken to the mountain-top.

Other Texts (See Appendix A on page 241)

71 **Coos (Western Oregon)**

72 **Makah (Washington State)**

73 **Kathlamet (Washington State)**

74 **Wintun (Northern California)**

75 **Chemetunne (Oregon)**

76 **Chimariko (Northern California)**

77 **Achomawi (Northern California)**

50. Alfred Benjamin Meacham, *Wi-ne-ma (the Woman Chief) and Her People* (Hartford: American, 1876), p. 114–115.

Two Havasupai Women

SOUTHWEST UNITED STATES

The tribes that inhabit the Grand Canyon in Arizona, which are the Havasupai and Hualapai, attribute the carving out of the Canyon to the global Flood, adding that one girl survived inside a hollow, floating log. The Tohono O'odham of Arizona told that their ancestor was forewarned of the Flood, and constructed a boat, by which he survived the Flood, and landed on a high mountain. He sent a coyote to inspect the drying of the land. The Pima said it was a floating ball of resin by which their old prophet survived. The Zuñi said they escaped on a high mesa outside their pueblo. The Hopi said they floated in hollow reeds. The Washoe tribe, near Lake Tahoe, say there were giants before the Flood.

The Cochiti, a pueblo people of New Mexico, narrated a remarkable Flood tradition which differs from the Genesis account only in minor details. Instead of an olive leaf, the pigeon returned carrying a flower. The Owens Valley Paiute claimed that pre-Flood artifacts were found on high mountains. The Navajo say that the Flood came because of man's sinning and quarreling. The Apache say the Flood covered the earth for twelve days, and the floating vessel landed on a hill. The pigeon and crow are involved in the account, to which they also add a turkey. We have found Flood traditions from many other tribes of the Desert Southwest as well.

Tribes of the Region

78. Havasupai (Grand Canyon)
79. Hualapai (Arizona and Nevada)
80. Papagos (Arizona)
81. Pima (Arizona)
82. Zuñi (New Mexico)
83. Juaneño (Southern California)
84. Luiseño (California)
85. Mutsun (California)
86. Salinan (California)
87. Chumash (Southern California)
88. Tewa (New Mexico)
89. Northern Paiute (Nevada and Oregon)
90. Zia (New Mexico)
91. Apache (Eastern Arizona to Western Texas)
92. Western Shoshone (Utah and Nevada)
93. Maricopa (Arizona)
94. Mojave (Arizona, Nevada, and California)
95. Cochiti Pueblo (New Mexico)
96. Kitanemuk (Southern California)
97. Wukchumni (California)
98. Hopi (Northeast Arizona)
99. Washoe (Lake Tahoe)
100. Navajo (Desert Southwest)
101. Owens Valley Paiute (Nevada and California)
102. Acoma Pueblo (New Mexico)
103. Tubatulabal (Southern California)

78

HAVASUPAI

Grand Canyon

The Havasupai people inhabit the Grand Canyon and surrounding area of Arizona. They recite an oral tradition which tells that the Grand Canyon was carved out by the ancient Flood. What is most striking about this legend is that fact that the Havasupai, located as they were in the middle of the desert, would have likely had little concept of such large quantities of water. Therefore, it seems highly unlikely that they would have invented this story all on their own:

> The two gods of the universe . . . are Tochopa and Hokomata. Tochopa he heap good. Hokomata . . . heap bad — all same white man's devil. Him Hokomata make big row with Tochopa, and he say he drown the world. . . . Tochopa was full of sadness at the news. He had one daughter whom he devotedly loved, and from her he had hoped would descend the whole human race for whom the world had been made. If Hokomata persisted in his wicked determination she must be saved at all hazard. So, working day and night, he speedily prepared the trunk of a pinion tree by hollowing it out from one end. In this hollow tree he placed food and other necessaries, and also made a lookout window. Then he brought his daughter, and telling her she must go into this tree and there be sealed up, he took a sad farewell of her, closed up the end of the tree, and then sat down to await the destruction of the world. It was not long before the floods began to descend. Not rain, but cataracts, rivers, deluges came, making more noise than a thousand Hack-a-tai-as (Colorado River) and covering all the earth with water. The pinion log floated, and in safety lay Pu-keh-eh while the waters surged higher and higher and covered the tops of Hue-han-a-patch-a (the San Franciscos), Hue-ga-wool-a (Williams Mountain), and all the other mountains of the world.
>
> But the waters of heaven could not always be pouring down, and soon after they ceased, the flood upon the earth found a way to rush into the sea. And as it dashed down it cut through the rocks of the plateaus and made the deep Chic-a-mi-mi (canyon) of the Colorado River (Hack-a-tai-a). Soon all the water was gone.

...he speedily prepared the trunk of a pinion tree by hollowing it out from one end. In this hollow tree he placed food and other necessaries, and also made a lookout window.

Havasupai Women With Kathaks on Back

> Then Pu-keh-eh found her log no longer floating, and she peeped out of the window Tochopa had placed in her boat, and, though it was misty and almost dark, she could see in the dim distance the great mountains of the San Francisco range. And nearby was the canyon of the Little Colorado, and to the north was Hack-a-tai-a and to the west was the canyon of the Havasu.[1]

They say the Flood lasted so long that this girl had grown to be a woman. Then, one day, feeling the longings for maternity, she wandered through the Canyon and found a glorious waterfall, which fathered her children. For this reason Havasupai girls are called "daughters of the water." The children of this union repopulated the earth.[2]

Havasupai Man

79

HUALAPAI

Arizona and Nevada

The Hualapai, or literally, "People of the Ponderosa Pine," occupy the western end of the Grand Canyon and the southeastern tip of Nevada. At Spirit Mountain (Wikahme) they possess ancient pictographs which recount both the great Flood and the tribe's ancient history. Spirit Mountain is held as a sacred place by several tribes of the Yuman language group, which share a common history with the Hualapai. Lucille Watahomigie, a tribal elder and the authority on the tribe's traditions, gave the interpretation of these pictographs:

Rains fell on the earth for 45 days. The rising waters wiped out all peoples with the lone exception of an old man atop Spirit Mountain.

> Rains fell on the earth for 45 days. The rising waters wiped out all peoples with the lone exception of an old man atop Spirit Mountain. The Creator eventually sent a bird to the man with instructions to dig with a ram's horn into the foot of the mountain to enable the waters to drain. The man obeyed and soon the bird returned a second time with grass in its beak to inform the man that the waters had receded.[3]

Another pictograph depicts eight people being carried across the waters of the Flood, departing from Wikahme mountain, and coming to a place where they are told to scatter and dwell all over the land.[4] Although our materialistic friends may be inclined to doubt it, Mrs. Watahomigie insisted that this oral tradition has been passed down from generation to generation, and is not the product of Christian influence.

Hualapai Hunter

1. George Wharton James, *The Indians of the Painted Desert Region* (Boston: Little, Brown, and Co.: 1903), p. 209–211.
2. Ibid., p. 211.
3. Jeremy D. Lyon and Bill Hoesch, "Flood Tales from the Canyon" (January 1, 2015). Retrieved from https://answersingenesis.org/the-flood/flood-legends/flood-tales-canyon/. Also told in expanded form in Leanne Hinton and Lucille J. Watahomigie, "Spirit Mountain: An Anthology of Yuman Story and Song," *Sun Tracks*, vol. 10 (Tuczon, AZ: Sun Tracks and University of Arizona Press, 1984), p. 15–42.
4. Hilton and Watahomigie, "Spirit Mountain," p. 41.

80 PAPAGOS

Arizona

The Tohono O'odham, or Papagos, told this Flood tradition to a U.S. Indian Agent in 1865:

> The coyote informed Montezuma that the flood was coming to destroy all living things upon the earth. Believing in the truthfulness and sagacity of the coyote, Montezuma built a boat, in which he survived the deluge; his boat, on the subsidence of the waters, rested on the topmost summit of Santa Rosa. The coyote gnawed down a large cane growing upon the river bank, entered the cane, and sealed up the end with some resinous gum. In this receptacle he floated during the prevalence of the waters, when his ark also found a resting place on dry land.
>
> . . . Montezuma immediately sent the coyote toward the south, to ascertain if he could find the sea; the animal returned after a short absence and reported that he found it; he sent him to the west, and he soon returned and told him that the sea was there. He sent him to the east also; after a much longer absence he returned and reported that he was again successful. The coyote was then sent to the north; in this journey he was gone so long a time that Montezuma despaired of ever seeing him again. At last he came back, wearied and worn with sore travel, and reported that he could find no sea to the north.
>
> By these means Montezuma was enabled to ascertain the boundaries of the dry land remaining after the flood. . . . Following the Indian legend, Montezuma, aided by the Great Spirit, again repeopled the earth.[5]

Papagos Man

Montezuma built a boat, in which he survived the deluge; his boat, on the subsidence of the waters, rested on the topmost summit of Santa Rosa.

81 PIMA

Arizona

The Pima tribe once inhabited the area where Phoenix is now located. The historian H.H. Bancroft interviewed five of their chiefs in October 1873 who shared with him the following tradition:

Pima Women

> The Creator took clay in his hands and mixing it with the sweat of his own body, kneaded the whole into a lump. Then he blew upon the lump till it was filled with life and began to move; and it became man and woman. This Creator had a son called Szeukha, who, when the world was beginning to be tolerably peopled, lived in the Gila valley, where lived also at the same time a great prophet, whose name has been forgotten. Upon a certain night when the prophet slept, he was wakened by a noise at the door of his house, and when he looked, a great Eagle stood before him. And the Eagle spake: Arise, though thou healest the sick, thou shouldest know what is to come, for behold a deluge is at hand. But the prophet laughed the bird to scorn and gathered his robes about him and slept. Afterwards the Eagle came again and warned him of the waters near at hand; but he gave no ear to the bird at all. . . . A third time, the Eagle came to warn the prophet, and to say that all the valley of the Gilla should be laid waste with water; but the prophet gave no heed. Then, in the twinkling of an eye, and even as the flapping of the Eagle's wings died away into the night, there came a peal of thunder

The Creator took clay in his hands, and mixing it with the sweat of his own body, kneaded the whole into a lump. Then he blew upon the lump till it was filled with life and began to move; and it became man and woman.

5. M.O. Davidson, in "Arizona Superintendency," *Annual Report of the Office of Indian Affairs for the Year 1865* (Washington: GPO, 1865), p. 131.

> and an awful crash; and a green mound of water reared itself over the plain. It seemed to stand upright for a second, then, cut incessantly by the lightning, goaded on like a great beast, it flung itself upon the prophet's hut. When the morning broke there was nothing to be seen alive but one man — if indeed he were a man: Szeukha, the son of the Creator, had saved himself by floating on a ball of gum or resin. On the waters falling a little, he landed near the mouth of the Salt River, upon a mountain where there is a cave that can still be seen, together with the tools and utensil Szeukha used while he lived there.[6]

Kaviu, a Pima Elder

Szeukha, angry with the Great Eagle, climbed to his nest and killed him. Finding a multitude of dead bodies in his nest, Szeukha raised them to life again in order to repeople the earth.[7]

Members of the Pima tribe told another Flood story to Frank Russell in 1901 or 1902:

> Earth Doctor then called his people together and told them there would be a great flood. After describing the calamity that would befall them, he sang: ". . . Weep, my unfortunate relatives! You will learn all. The waters will overwhelm the mountains." He thrust his staff into the ground, and with it bored a hole quite through the other side of the earth. Some of the people went into the hole, while others appealed to Elder Brother. Their appeals were not heeded, but Coyote asked his assistance, and he was told to find a big log and sit upon it. This would carry him safely on the surface of the water along with the driftwood. Elder Brother got into his olla and closed the opening by which he entered. . . . As he was borne along by the flood he sang: "Running water, running water, herein resounding, as on the clouds I am carried to the sky. . . ."[8]

Earth Doctor then called his people together and told them there would be a great flood. ... "The waters will overwhelm the mountains."

82

ZUÑI

New Mexico

The Zuñi inhabited a pueblo village by the same name in northwestern New Mexico. They held the belief that a prominent mesa, which they called Dowa Yalanne, was the site where their ancestors found shelter from the primeval Deluge. They shared this tradition with Tilly Stephenson around 1883:

> Tradition tells that they were driven by a great flood from the site they now occupy, which is in the valley below the mesa, and that they resorted to the mesa for protection from the rising waters. The waters rose to the very summit of the mesa, and to appease the aggressive element a human sacrifice was necessary. A youth and a maiden, son and daughter of two priests, were thrown into this ocean. Two great pinnacles, which have been carved from the main mesa by weathering influences, are looked upon by the Zuñi as the actual youth and maiden converted into stone, and are appealed to as "father" and "mother."[9]

Zuni Girl Headcarrying a Jar

6. Hubert Howe Bancroft, *The Native Races of the Pacific States of North America*, vol. 3, (New York: D. Appleton and Co., 1875), p. 78–79. A related version can be found in Charles M. Skinner, *Myths and Legends of Our Own Land*, vol. 2 (Philadelphia and London: J.J. Lippincott, 1896), p. 215–218.
7. Ibid., p. 218.
8. Frank Russell, "The Pima Indians," *Twenty-Sixth Annual Report of the Bureau of American Ethnology* (Washington: GPO, 1908), p. 210.
9. Mrs. Tilly E. Stevenson, "The Religious Life of the Zuñi Child," *Fifth Annual Report of the Bureau of American Ethnology* (Washington: GPO, 1887), p. 539.

It is interesting that several tribes around the world say that a sacrifice was made in order to stop the Flood. Perhaps this is a distorted memory of what Noah did after he left the Ark: he offered a burnt offering to God (Genesis 8:20-21).

Image of a Zuni Pueblo

83 JUAÑENO

Southern California

The Acagchemem, or Juaneño, of California's southern coast shared their Flood tradition with Geronimo Boscana sometime between 1812 and 1826. Boscana wrote:

> These Indians were not entirely destitute of a knowledge of the universal deluge, but how, or from whence, they received the same, I could never understand. Some of their songs refer to it; and they have a tradition that, at a time very remote, the sea began to swell and roll in upon the plains, and fill the valleys, until it had covered the mountains; and thus nearly all the human race and animals were destroyed, excepting a few, who had resorted to a very high mountain which the waters did not reach. But the songs give a more distinct relation of the same, and they state that the descendants of Captain Ouiot asked of Chinigchinich vengeance upon their chief — that he appeared unto them, and said to those endowed with the power, "Ye are the ones to achieve vengeance — ye who cause it to rain! Do this and so inundate the earth, that every living being will be destroyed." The rains commenced, the sea was troubled, and swelled in upon the earth, covering the plains, and rising until it had overspread the highest land, excepting a high mountain, where, the few had gone with the one who had caused it to rain, and thus every other animal was destroyed upon the face of the earth. These songs were supplications to Chinigchinich to drown their enemies. If their opponents heard them, they sang others in opposition, which in substance ran thus: "We are not afraid, because Chinigchinich does not wish to, neither will he destroy the world by another inundation." Without doubt this account has reference to the universal deluge, and the promise God made, that there should not be another.[10]

These Indians were not entirely destitute of a knowledge of the universal deluge ... Some of their songs refer to it; and they have a tradition that, at a time very remote, the sea began to swell and roll in upon the plains, and fill the valleys, until it had covered the mountains; and thus nearly all the human race and animals were destroyed, excepting a few.

84 LUISEÑO

California

The Luiseño, another tribe of coastal southern California, shared their account of the Flood with Constance DuBois in 1906:

> There is a wonderful little knoll, near Bonsai, the Spanish name of it Mora, the Indian name Katuta; and when there was a flood that killed all the people, some stayed on this hill and were not drowned. All the high mountains were covered, but this little hill remained above the water. One can see heaps of sea shells and seaweed upon it, and ashes where those people cooked their food, and stones set together, left as they used them for cooking; and the shells were those of shell-fish they caught to eat. They stayed there till the water went down.[11]

10. Friar Geronimo Boscana, Chinigchinich, trans. Alfred Robinson (New York: Wiley and Putnam, 1846), p. 44–45.
11. Constance Goddard DuBois, *The Religion of the Luiseño Indians of Southern California* (Berkeley: University of California Publications, 1908), p. 157.

They also have a song called the "Song of the Flood," which mentions Katuta, or Mora, "the little hill that was the only dry land when the water covered the high mountains."[12]

Luiseño Men at Pala

85 MUTSUN

California

The Mutsun, a tribe of the Costanoan language group, lived to the east of Monterey Bay in California. We have only a fragmentary reference to their Flood tradition. However, it includes an interesting note about of their migration after the Flood. This comes from their responses to a list of questions, which the Mexican government sent to the recently established missions in 1811:

> They say that the first Indians to settle this country came from the north after a great flood; that some went back and did not return; and that here sprung the single common language which is spoken in the seven missions about here, although somewhat changed.
>
> They did not have chiefs. The bravest and strongest were those who went out to their wars. Every man acted as he wished.[13]

86 SALINAN

California

Alexander Taylor visited the Salinan people in Monterey County around 1856. He mentioned that the tribe had a tradition of the great Deluge:

> The Indians of San Antonio believed in a Superior Being; they believed he made the sun, moon, stars, earth, men and other visible things. . . . They had a superstition or tradition of a deluge of water which covered the land in the old times, and had their priests, who were the sorcerers.[14]

They shared more information with H.W. Henshaw in 1884:

> After the deluge the animals wished to get some earth. First the diving ducks dived into the water but failed to bring up any earth. Then the Eagle put a heavy weight on the back of the Kingfisher and he dived into the water for the earth and succeeded in reaching the bottom.
>
> But the sea was so deep that when he came to the surface, he was dead. Between his claws the Eagle found some earth, and after reviving the Kingfisher he took the dirt and made the world. Then he revived all the other animals who had been drowned in the deluge, the Coyote next after the Kingfisher. When the Coyote found himself alive again, he shouted for joy and ran around reviving the rest of the animals that he found dead, and then sending them to the Eagle.[15]

Family of Pedro Encinales, a Miguelino Salinan

12. Ibid., p. 116.
13. Alfred L. Kroeber, "A Mission Record of the California Indians: From a Manuscript in the Bancroft Library," *University of California Publications in American Archaeology and Ethnology,* vol. 8, no. 1 (Berkeley: University Press, 1908), p. 24.
14. Alexander Smith Taylor, "The Indianology of California," *The California Farmer,* April 27, 1860.
15. John Alden Mason, *The Ethnology of the Salinan Indians* (Berkeley: University of California Publications, 1912), p. 190.

Genesis Parallels in the Salinan Creation Story

The above tradition went on to tell that "from some of the earth brought up by the Kingfisher, Eagle made man, and then made woman from one of man's ribs."[16] In another account, which told of the creation of men and women, it was said that Eagle "saw that the world was incomplete and decided to make some human beings. So he took some clay and modeled the figure of a man and laid him on the ground." Then he said, "It is impossible that he should be left alone; he must have a mate." So he pulled out a feather and laid it beside the sleeping man. Then he left them and went off a short distance, for he knew that a woman was being formed from the feather. Then, when the woman was complete, Eagle woke the man, who opened his eyes and saw the woman, to his great surprise.[17]

87

CHUMASH

Southern California

J.P. Harrington visited the Chumash people of southern California between 1912 and 1922 and recorded many of their oral traditions. The majority of his work remains in unpublished manuscripts filling the space of some 400 boxes at the Smithsonian Institution. In these manuscripts, Anita Goos found a creation story referring to the Flood:

Chumash Musicians

> The five men and the woman sent out a crow (or raven) to see if there was a piece of dry land after the flood. They wanted a piece large enough to hold all the people if they were sent out. The crow acted badly by staying out long and eating some people. The five men and the woman then sent out the wild dove. The dove stayed out a long time because it got its feet stuck in the mud. That is why the marks on its feet are as they are. When the dove finally came back it was so late that it missed the blessing that had been given to all the other animals. That is why the dove now cries, "u, u, u, u" all the time.
>
> The five men and one woman sent out all the animals. They told each animal what he was going to be and sent him away to live. Only the dog did not want to leave, but to stay and be with the new people. That is why he stays around all the time and barks to warn us against other animals. Some say that the bear of the present time was the dog of the five brothers and the sister. They called him "hunakis." All the animals of today were the people of ancient times.[18]

The five men and the woman sent out a crow (or raven) to see if there was a piece of dry land after the flood. ... The crow acted badly by staying out long and eating some people. The five men and the woman then sent out the wild dove. The dove stayed out a long time because it got its feet stuck in the mud.

In another manuscript, we find a Flood tradition told by an older Chumash woman, who was well-informed on the tribe's traditions.

> Maqutikok, the Spotted Woodpecker, was the only one saved in the flood. He was Sun's nephew. Maria doesn't know why the flood came or how it started, but it kept raining and the water kept rising higher and higher until even the mountains were covered. All the people drowned except Maqutikok who

16. Ibid.
17. Ibid, p. 191–192.
18. Anita Goos, *The Legends*, p. 64. Retrieved from: https://archive.org/details/ChumashFolkloreStories.

found refuge on top of a tree that was the tallest in the world. The water kept rising until it touched his feet, and the bird cried out, "Help me, Uncle, I am drowning, pity me!" Sun's two daughters heard him and told their father that his kinsman was calling for help. "He is stiff from cold and hunger," they said. Sun held his firebrand down low and the water began to subside. Maqutikok was warmed by the heat. Then Sun tossed him two acorns. They fell in the water near the tree and Maqutikok picked them up and swallowed them. Then Sun threw two more acorns down and the bird ate them and was content. That is why he likes acorns so much — they are still his food. And after the water was gone only Maqutikok remained. Maria has seen rocks in the mountains that are the exact shape of human arms and hands: they are the remains of the people who died in the flood. Those first people, the molmoloqiku, were very tall. They used to wade across the channel without needing boats, taking chia and acorns and other things to the islanders in carrying nets. The very old men told Maria that people had found bones on Santa Rosa Island and at Mikiw which were human, but which were yards long.[19]

Tewa Man

88

TEWA

New Mexico

The Tewa have a tradition about a flood that happened long ago. A young boy was found in the wild, abandoned, living with the animals. A hunter took him back to the village and adopted him. This boy had a prophetic gift, and could foretell when it would rain or snow. Later, he forewarned the people of a coming flood unlike any other, and that they must take shelter at a high hill. Those who believed him took refuge on the mountain Mawolo, together with the animals. The turkeys were closest to the water, and their tails got wet, which is why their tails are white to this day.[20]

> Then the rain stopped, and the water went down, down, down. The wind came and blew hard over the earth, and the earth dried up. And they went to see if it was good. There were lots of mud, and the wind was blowing and blowing. One of them went down to see if it was no longer muddy. Then they all went down. And when they went home they found no people, they had all died. Then they believed in whatever he said, the little boy who was now a man.[21]

Those first people, the molmoloqiku, were very tall. They used to wade across the channel without needing boats ... The very old men told Maria that people had found bones on Santa Rosa Island and at Mikiw which were human, but which were yards long.

89

NORTHERN PAIUTE

Nevada and Oregon

In 1930, the Northern Paiute shared several of their traditions with the archaeologist Isabel Kelly. An elderly man of the tribe named Billy Steve told her the tribe's creation story, which contains an account of the Flood. It also contains a "preservation of fire" story, which has noticeable parallels with the biblical account of Noah building an altar, lighting a fire, and offering burnt offerings. Interestingly, we will see other "preservation of fire" stories in which a raven or other bird returns to the survivors of the Flood, carrying a burning stick in its beak. The memory of the Noahic Flood is very evident, even if the details are distorted.

Tewa Girl

19. Thomas C. Blackburn, *December's Child: A Book of Chumash Oral Narratives* (Berkeley and Los Angeles: University of California Press, 1975), p. 94–95.
20. Elsie Clews Parsons, "Tewa Tales," *Memoirs of the American Folk-lore Society*, vol. 19 (New York: American Folk-lore Society, 1926), p. 106–108.
21. Ibid., p. 108.

A long time ago there used to be the first Indian here. I don't know just what he was. Then something came and covered these mountains with water to kill those Indians. The Sagehen [sage grouse] was the only kind of bird saved from the water. He saved fire on a tall mountain. He covered it with his breast; he had it under his breast; he lay on it. Then that Sagehen, he made a fire stick of sagebrush. It was about three inches long and had a hole in one end. He tied on a handle of willow. He made a fire hearth about a foot long. He put sagebrush bark outside and underneath for tinder. He put a little sand in the hole. Then pretty soon it began to smoke; the smoke fell on the bark; he picked it up and blew; and then he had fire. He had to cover the fire all the time so it wouldn't go out.[22]

Zia Dancer

Did you know that Native Americans have the highest military participation rate of any ethnic group, and have fought in every war this country has ever been in? The call to be a warrior runs deep for Native Americans. Even though they were wronged by the U.S. government in so many ways, the duty to protect the land of their ancestors motivates so many of them to serve valiantly in the military.[23]

90 ZIA

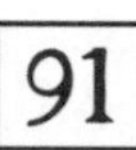

New Mexico

The Zia (or Sia) people of New Mexico had a creation story which, like their Hopi and Navajo neighbors, told of their escape from a flooded underworld by means of a giant reed. This was told to Matilda Stephenson in the 1880s:

> For eight years after the fight (years referring to periods of time), the people were very happy, but the ninth year was very bad, the whole earth being filled with water. The water did not fall in rain, but came in as rivers between the mesas, and continued flowing from all sides until the people and all animals fled to the mesa. The waters continued to rise until nearly level with the mesa top, and Sus'sistinnako (the spider god) cried, "Where shall my people go? . . . Alas, I see the waters are everywhere." And all of his theurgists sang four days and nights before their altars and made many offerings, but still the waters continued to rise as before.[24]

Finally, the people climbed up a huge reed, cut a hole into the next world, and thus escaped the rising floodwaters.

91 APACHE

Eastern Arizona to Western Texas

We have a few Flood traditions from the Apache peoples. The first comes from the creation story that appeared in Volume 1 (1907) of Edward Curtis' twenty-volume work, *The North American Indian.*

> The earth was smooth, flat, and barren, so Kuterestan (God or "Sky Man") made a few animals, birds, trees, and a hill. Then he sent Agocho, the pigeon, to see how the world looked. Four days later Agocho returned and said all was beautiful, but that in four days more the water on the opposite side would rise and flood the land. Kuterestan

Alchise, an Apache Man

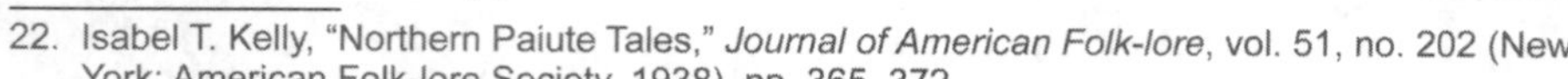

22. Isabel T. Kelly, "Northern Paiute Tales," *Journal of American Folk-lore*, vol. 51, no. 202 (New York: American Folk-lore Society, 1938), pp. 365, 372..
23. Kevin Gover, "American Indians Serve in the U.S. Military in Greater Numbers Than Any Ethnic Group and Have Since the Revolution," December 6, 2015. Retrieved from https://www.huffingtonpost.com/national-museum-of-the-american-indian/american-indians-serve-in-the-us-military_b_7417854.html.
24. Matilda Coxe Stevenson, "The Sia," *Eleventh Annual Report of the Bureau of American Ethnology* (Washington: GPO, 1894), p. 34–35.

at once created a pinion tree. This Stenatliha skillfully tended until it grew to be of gigantic size at the end of four days. Then with four great limbs as a framework she made a very large water bottle, ("tus") covering it with gum from the pinion. When the water appeared as predicted Kuterastan went up on a cloud, taking his twenty-eight helpers with him, while Stenatliha summoned all the others and put them into the tus, into which she climbed last, closing the mouth at the top.

Apache Bride

The flood completely submerged the earth for twelve days. Then the waters subsided, leaving the tus on the summit of the hill Kuterastan had made. The rush of the waters had changed the once smooth, level plain into series of mountains, hills, rivers, and valleys, so that Stenatliha hardly knew where they were when she opened the tus and came out. Tazhi, the Turkey, and Gage, the Crow, were the first to make a tour of the land. At the base of the hill they descended into a small muddy alkaline creek, in which the Turkey got the tips of his tail-feathers whitened, and they have been white ever since. On return they reported that all looked beautiful as far as they had travelled. Stenatliha then sent Agocho to make a complete circuit and let her know how things appeared on all sides. He came back much elated, for he had seen trees, grass, mountains, and beautiful lakes and rivers in every direction.[25]

The flood completely submerged the earth for twelve days. Then the waters subsided, leaving the tus (floating vessel) on the summit of the hill Kuterastan had made.

The Apache told a Flood tradition to George Catlin sometime between 1852 and 1857:

Like the Crows, their tradition is, that "their tribe is the father of all the existing races — that seven persons only were saved from the Deluge by ascending a high mountain, and that these seven multiplied and filled again the valleys with populations; and that those who built their villages were very foolish, for there came a great rain, which filled the valleys with water, and they were again swept off."[26]

Among the Chiricahua branch of the Apache, in New Mexico, Morris Opler heard this version between 1931 and 1935:

The old world was destroyed by water, by a flood. There was only one mountain at the time of this flood that was not entirely covered by the water. And that mountain is called today "White-Ringed Mountain." No human beings lived through this flood, but there was a rooster that floated on top of the water and got on top of that mountain. The water almost got to the top of that mountain, almost covered it. Now you can see the mountain with the white ring at the highest point the water reached. I think that mountain is in Old Mexico.[27]

Apache Hattie Tom

25. Edward Sheriff Curtis, *The North American Indian*, vol. 1 (Cambridge, MA: University Press, 1907), p. 27–28.
26. George Catlin, *Last Rambles Amongst the Indians of the Rocky Mountains and the Andes* (London: Sampson Low, Son, and Marston, 1868), p. 186.
27. Morris Edward Opler, "Myths and Tales of the Chiricahua Apache Indians," *Memoirs of the American Folk-lore Society*, vol. 42 (New York: 1942), p. 1.

92 WESTERN SHOSHONE

Utah and Nevada

A Western Shoshone told a brief account of the Flood to Julian Steward in 1935:

> At one time the world was filled with water. Only the Inyo mountains were left above it. All the people went to the summit of these mountains. (Probably New York Butte.) The water ran off toward the south.[28]

Pakit, a Young Maricopa Woman

93 MARICOPA

Arizona

The Maricopa tribe of southwestern Arizona told Louis Meeker their creation story in 1904. They told him that we are currently living in the fourth age of the world, and the three previous ages were destroyed by three floods.

> Now all the things that were made then were of the first generation. The first flood came because the Brother made so much trouble and claimed to have more power than Earth Doctor, who at length drove him off the earth. . . . The waters rose, washing away all except the mountains and the representative races and animals that took refuge there. . . .
>
> The Brother met Coyote and called him brother, but Coyote would not reply. So a flood was sent to destroy Coyote and the earth and all its inhabitants. Small numbers were saved by clinging to trunks of trees that floated on the water. Coyote insisted the Brother should address him as Elder Brother. This was conceded. Coyote made a ball of mud from the root of the tree on which he floated. He stuck in a bunch of grass from the bill of the duck the Brother had made. This he cast upon the water to be the nucleus of a new world, and the Flood subsided.

At one time the world was filled with water. Only the Inyo mountains were left above it.

> Then Earth Doctor proceeded to construct the third generation.... Men increased rapidly. They had no diseases. There were no wars. The few deaths were from snake bites or accidents. The earth was crowded. There was not food for all. . . . A council was held in the skies. . . . They agreed to have the great flood, so that there would not be too many people.
>
> ...The flood that followed continued for four years. . . . The vessel containing the seed of future generations floated upon the water, and, as the waters subsided, touched ground at the highest point; Che-o-tmaka, as the Pima call him, the Maricopa Kokmat, crossed over the sky to get the vessel. But Coyote was just ahead of him, and took refuge in the joint of a great reed that floated upon the water. There were three other joints of reed floating by it, and Coyote having sealed up his reed with resin from the mesquite and chaparral bushes, Kokmat could not tell in which he was concealed. . . . From the ashes of the woman and the ashes of all the woods and from all the seeds that were powdered sprang up the present generation.[29]

Yellow Feather, Maricopa

28. Julian Haynes Steward, "Some Western Shoshoni Myths," *Bureau of American Ethnology Bulletin 136*, No. 31 (Washington: GPO, 1943), p. 284.
29. Stewart Culin, "Games of the North American Indians," *Twenty-fourth Annual Report of the Bureau of American Ethnology* (Washington: GPO, 1907), p. 203–204.

94 MOJAVE

Arizona, Nevada, and California

Alfred Kroeber visited the Mojave people along the Colorado River in 1900 and 1902. He made a passing reference to their flood story, saying their traditions speak of a woman named Mastamho who "made the Colorado river, produced light, shaped the land, saved the people from flood, separated the tribes, taught agriculture, and instituted the clans."[30]

Long ago the people knew that there would be a great flood. Up in the north among the high mountains they built a great boat. When it was nearly time for the water to rise, they began to load it with much corn and they took all the different animals into the boat and a white pigeon.

95 COCHITI PUEBLO

New Mexico

An older woman of the Cochito Pueblo in New Mexico narrated a stunning tradition related to the Flood to Ruth Benedict in 1924:

> Long ago the people knew that there would be a great flood. Up in the north among the high mountains they built a great boat. When it was nearly time for the water to rise, they began to load it with much corn and they took all the different animals into the boat and a white pigeon. When everything was ready the sons of the builder of the boat and their sons came into the ship. When they were all in, they put pitch all over the cracks of the boat. The flood came. The boat floated on the water. The people that were left on the earth fled to the highest mountain to try to escape from the waters. The ones who could not get to the high mountains were all drowned and floated about on the waters of the flood. The ones who climbed the mountains were overtaken by the water and turned into rocks. Some were embracing each other, and some held one another on their laps, and there they are still just as the water overtook them. Every living thing on the earth was drowned, but the boat still floated.
>
> When the waters went down, the boat grounded on a high place in the mountains to the north. Then they knew the waters were subsiding. The chief said to the rest, "We will send the white pigeon to see if the earth is uncovered again." The white pigeon was let out. At last he returned and told the chief, "I have seen the earth and the water has gone down. But it is a terrible thing to see. The people are all drowned and their bodies piled upon the ground." In the boat there was also a crow as white as the pigeon. They sent out the crow to look over the earth. She went out and saw the earth as the pigeon had. But she flew down to the dead bodies and began to pick out their eyes. When she came back to the boat, they knew she had done mischief. They said to her, "What is it that you have done when you were out flying over the earth? You were white and now your feathers are all black." Again they let the pigeon out to see if the earth was firm again. She went out and as she was flying she saw a flower in blossom. She picked the flower for a sign that the earth was getting firm again, and she took it back to the boat. She said to the owner of the boat, "The plants are all growing again, and I settled on the ground and did not sink into the mud. This flower is a sign of the growing of the plants." So the people on the boat were saved from the first-ending-of-the-world-by-flood.[31]

Mosa, Mohave Girl

When the waters went down, the boat grounded on a high place in the mountains to the north. Then they knew the waters were subsiding. The chief said to the rest, "We will send the white pigeon to see if the earth is uncovered again." The white pigeon was let out.

30. Alfred L. Kroeber, "Preliminary Sketch of the Mohave Indians," *American Anthropologist*, vol. 4 (new series), no. 2 (New York: G.P. Putnam's Sons, 1902), p. 283.
31. Ruth Benedict, "Tales of the Cochiti Indians," *Bureau of American Ethnology Bulletin*, vol. 98 (Washington: Smithsonian, 1931), p. 2–3.

96 KITANEMUK

Southern California

The Kitanemuk live around the Tehachapi Mountains on the western end of the Mojave Desert in south-central California. Our knowledge of their Flood tradition comes from John Harrington, who met with members of the tribe in 1917 and 1918:

Cochiti Pueblo between c. 1871-c. 1907

> This world was circular and floated on a surrounding ocean supported by two gigantic serpents whose movements caused earthquakes. Later there was a great deluge that covered all but the tops of the highest mountains. All First People were drowned or turned to animals with the exception of the six siblings, who were safe in their home at Aiykitsa Tivat, a beautiful place in the south where flowers bloomed continually and it was never hot.[32]

The tradition adds that their deity "sent them off in different directions, telling each man to marry a certain woman, and where to live and what languages to speak. Thus, different tribes of people were created."[33]

Later there was a great deluge that covered all but the tops of the highest mountains. All First People were drowned or turned to animals with the exception of the six siblings…

Other Texts (See Appendix A on page 241)

97 **Wukchumni (California)**

98 **Hopi (Northeast Arizona)**

99 **Washoe (Lake Tahoe)**

100 **Navajo (Desert Southwest)**

101 **Owens Valley Paiute (Nevada and California)**

102 **Acoma Pueblo (New Mexico)**

103 **Tubatulabal (Southern California)**

32. Thomas C. Blackburn and Lowell John Bean, "Kitanemuk," *Handbook of North American Indians*, vol. 8, ed. Robert F. Heizer (Washington: Smithsonian, 1978), p. 568.
33. Ibid.

Chief Bearman and Chief Mad Bull of the Cheyenne Tribe

GREAT PLAINS AND NORTHERN ROCKIES

A most remarkable ceremony was held by the Mandan of North Dakota every year to remember Nu-mohk-munk-a-nah, "the only man," who landed his big canoe on a mountain far to the west. Their elaborate ceremony is described further in this volume, derived from the descriptions by Catlin and Curtis. The Mandans also highly esteemed the turtle dove, which they say returned to their Noah carrying a willow bough in its mouth as a sign of the retreating waters. The Blackfoot tribe have their Flood tradition, which also tells of the confusion of languages that God caused shortly after the Flood. The Lakota acknowledge the Flood which the Creator sent because people did not know how to behave. The Crow and Assiniboine tribes have preserved a memory of the Flood as well.

The Pawnee of Nebraska told G.B. Grinnell in 1870 of the Flood which the creator Ti'rawa sent to destroy a wicked race of giants, whose bones they claimed to have found in canyons and underground. A bluebird and a crow were sent to see if the earth was dry. The bluebird fulfilled its mission, and has since been commemorated by its symbol on their ceremonial prayer pipes.

Continuing westward to the Rocky Mountains, the Arapaho of Colorado and Wyoming have a Flood tradition which mentions the sending of a pigeon to search for land, and the changing of languages after the Flood. The Utes told the early settlers how the ark had landed at the top of one of the mountains to the west of what is now Palmer Lake in Colorado. Another branch of the Utes say Pikes Peak was where the boat landed. The Eastern Shoshone told that after the Flood, God sent a crow and a chickadee in search of earth, and the latter fulfilled the mission. The Bannock tribe of Idaho told of a Flood that covered even the mountains, and that their divine ancestor sent a muskrat diving in search of earth after the Flood.

Tribes of the Region

104. Mandan (North Dakota)
105. Pawnee (Nebraska and Kansas)
106. Blackfoot (Montana and Alberta)
107. Assiniboine (Northern Great Plains)
108. Lakota (Nebraska through Montana)
109. Crow (Montana and Wyoming)
110. Arapaho (Colorado and Wyoming)
111. Ute (Utah and Colorado)
112. Ute Pikes Peak Tradition (Colorado)
113. Northern Shoshone (Idaho)
114. Eastern Shoshone (Wyoming)
115. Wichita (Kansas to North Texas)
116. Gros Ventres (Montana)
117. Cheyenne (Wyoming and South Dakota)
118. Flathead (Montana)
119. Arikara (North Dakota)
120. Tonkawa (Texas)
121. Yellowstone Valley Tradition (Wyoming)
122. Bannock (Idaho)
123. Hidatsa (North Dakota)

The Cheyenne held a Sun Dance ceremony, in which a representation of the rainbow must be erected; otherwise a flood will come. They remember a flood which covered all but the highest hills, and which killed all the animals. This flood also separated the people into different groups, and resulted in different languages. The Gros Ventres of Montana also have a well-preserved Flood tradition mentioning also the scattering of people groups after the Flood. They replace the ark with a chief pipe which, once unrolled, contained all types of animals. And there are other Flood traditions from the Rocky Mountains besides these. The Arikara say that God hid some righteous persons in an underground cave during the Flood. The Hidatsa tribe guarded certain ancient pots, which they filled with water to commemorate the Flood, remembering also the large bird which returned from its dive with earth to remake dry land.

Shakoka (Mint), a Mandan Girl

104 MANDAN — North Dakota

George Catlin, an American traveler and painter of the early 1800s, recorded one of the most remarkable Flood traditions in North America from the Mandan tribe of North Dakota. The Mandans, as it turned out, commemorated this event annually, and Catlin was privileged enough to witness the event:

..."the twig that the bird brought home was a willow bough, and had full-grown leaves on it," and the bird to which they allude, is the mourning or turtle-dove, which they took great pains to point out to me...

> In the centre of the Mandan village is an open, circular area of 150 feet diameter, kept always clear, as a public ground for the display of all their public feasts, parades, etc. . . . In the middle of this ground, which is trodden like a hard pavement, is a curb (somewhat like a large hogs head standing on its end) made of planks (and bound with hoops), some eight or nine feet high, which they religiously preserve and protect from year to year, free from mark or scratch, and which they call the "big canoe" — it is undoubtedly a symbolic representation of a part of their traditional history of the Flood; which it is very evident, from this and numerous other features of this grand ceremony . . . this exciting and appalling scene, then, which is familiarly (and no doubt correctly) called the "Mandan religious ceremony" commences, not on a particular day of the year (for these people keep no record of days or weeks), but at a particular season which is designated by the full expansion of the willow leaves under the bank of the river, for according to their tradition, "the twig that the bird brought home was a willow bough, and had full-grown leaves on it," and the bird to which they allude, is the mourning or turtle-dove, which they took great pains to point out to me, as it is often to be seen feeding on the sides of their earth-covered lodges, and which, being, as they call it, a medicine-bird, is not to be destroyed or harmed by anyone, and even their dogs are instructed not to do it harm.[1]

Crow's Heart, a Mandan

The ceremony began with the appearance of a mystery man known as Nu-mohk-munk-a-nah (the first or only man). The villagers, according to Catlin, would spot him on the horizon, and all eyes would be fastened on him as he slowly walked towards the village. He was painted with white clay, dressed in wolf skins and raven feathers, and carried a ceremonial pipe.

...the "big canoe" — it is undoubtedly a symbolic representation of a part of their traditional history of the Flood...

> After passing the chiefs and braves as described, he approached the medicine or mystery lodge, which he had the means of opening, and which had been religiously closed during the year except for the

1. George Catlin, *The North American Indians*, vol. 1 (Edinburgh: Jon Grant, 1926), p. 178-179.

> performance of these religious rites. Having opened and entered it, he called in four men whom he appointed to clean it out, and put it in readiness for the ceremonies. . . . During the whole of this day, and while these preparations were making in the medicine lodge, Nu-mohk-munk-a-nah (the first or only man) travelled through the village, stopping in front of every man's lodge, and crying until the owner of the lodge came out, and asked who he was, and what was the matter? to which he replied by relating the sad catastrophe which had happened on the earth's surface by the overflowing of the waters, saying that he was the only person saved from the universal calamity; that he landed his big canoe on a high mountain in the west, where he now resides, that he had come to open the medicine lodge, which must needs receive a present of some edged-tool from the owner of every wigwam, that it may be sacrificed to the water, for he says, "if this is not done, there will be another flood, and no one will be saved, as it was with such tools that the big canoe was made."[2]

Packs-Wolf as Numak-Mahana

Catlin continued:

> Their tradition says, that at a very ancient period such a man did actually come from the West — that his body was of the white color, as this man's body is represented. . . . He said, "he was at one time the only man — he told them of the destruction of every thing on the earth's surface by water — that he stopped in his big canoe on a high mountain in the West, here he landed and was saved. . . . The annual religious ceremony invariably lasts four days, and the other following circumstances attending these strange forms, and seeming to have some allusion to the four cardinal points, or the "four tortoises," seem to me to be worthy of further notice. Four men are selected by Nu-mohk-muck-a-nah (as I have said), to cleanse out and prepare the medicine-lodge for the occasion — one he calls from the north part of the village — one from the east — one from the south, and one from the west. The four sacks of water, in form of large tortoises, resting on the floor of the lodge . . . and also the four buffalo, and the four human skulls resting on the floor of the same lodge — the four couples of dancers in the "bull dance," as before described; . . . The bull-dance in front of the medicine-lodge, repeated on the four days, is danced four times on the first day, eight times on the second, twelve times on the third, and sixteen times on the fourth . . . which added together make forty, the exact number of days that it rained upon the earth, according to the Mosaic account, to produce the Deluge.[3]

He said, "he was at one time the only man — he told them of the destruction of every thing on the earth's surface by water — that he stopped in his big canoe on a high mountain in the West, here he landed and was saved…

Catlin tells of various objects he saw within the mystery lodge — their "holy of holies" — which he could only see from outside. Among these were four sacks of water which, to Catlin, had "the appearance of very great antiquity, and by inquiring of my very ingenious friend and patron, the medicine man, after the ceremonies were over, he very gravely told me, that those four tortoises contained the waters from the four quarters of the world — that these waters had been contained therein ever since the settling down of the waters!"[4]

2. Catlin, *North American Indians*, p. 180.
3. Ibid., p. 201, 205.
4. Ibid., p. 184.

At the end of the ceremony, this mystery man or high priest of the Mandans bade the people goodbye, saying "that he was going back to the mountains in the west, from whence he should assuredly return in just a year from that time, to open the lodge again."[5]

A Pair of Mandan Men

105 PAWNEE

Nebraska and Kansas

George Grinnell spent over 20 years with the Pawnee beginning in 1870. Their history contained a memory of the Flood, which they said God used to destroy an antediluvian race of giants:

> Now, these giants did not believe in any of these things (the creator Tira'wa and life after death). They did not pray to Tira'wa, and they thought that they were very strong, and that nothing could overcome them. They grew worse and worse. At last Tira'wa got angry, and he made the water rise up level with the land, and all the ground became soft, and these great people sank down into the mud and were drowned. The great bones found on the prairie are the bones of these people, and we have been in deep canyons, and have seen big bones underground, which convinces us that these people did sink into the soft ground.
>
> After the destruction of the race of giants, Tira'wa created a new race of men, small, like those of today. He made first a man and a woman. They lived on the earth and were good. To them was given the corn. From this man and this woman the Pawnees sprung.[6]

...after the people were drowned, Tirawa sent a little messenger, a bird, to visit the earth, to see if the ground was all hard.

They told a related version to George Dorsey between 1899 and 1902, which mentions the bursting of water from within the earth as a contributing cause of the Flood, as well as the dispatch of birds after the Flood. They said it was the bluebird which returned to its master:

> Now after the people were drowned, Tirawa sent a little messenger, a bird, to visit the earth, to see if the ground was all hard. Then Tirawa sent another bird, the crow, to visit the earth, saying: "Now you will find creeks, people, and animals upon the earth, but don't touch them; I will take care of you while you go down there." But when this bird came down to the earth it saw the dead people, and ate of the people. Tirawa was displeased, and when the bird tried to fly back to Heaven, Tirawa said: "Stop, you shall stay there forever! You have disobeyed my order; you shall hereafter live upon dead carcasses," so the crow was ordered to stay upon the earth.

Tribal Territory of Pawnee, Ponca, Omaha, Oto, Kansa Peoples

5. Ibid., p. 181.
6. George Bird Grinnell, *Pawnee Hero Stories and Folk-Talks* (New York: Charles Scribner's Sons, 1893), p. 355–366. See also: George A. Dorsey, The Pawnee, vol. 1 (Washington: Carnegie, 1906), p. 134–135, 296.

> Now Tirawa had sent another bird, and this bird went down. Tirawa said to the bird when it came back: "You shall be chief of all the birds; you did not do as the other bird did." The little bird was told that he had done right, he would be known as the messenger bird between Tirawa and the people; that when the people were put upon the earth, it would always be present with them; that it would be tied close to the mouth-piece of the holy pipe-stem; so, to this day we have this little bird [the bluebird] upon the pipe-stem of the pipe that belonged to the bundle ceremonies.[7]

Pawnee Sharitarish (Wicked Chief)

106 **Montana and Alberta**

BLACKFOOT

The Blackfeet living in northwest Montana told this account to George Grinnell around the year 1900:

> In the beginning, all the land was covered with water, and Old Man and all the animals were floating around on a large raft. One day Old Man told the beaver to dive and try to bring up a little mud. The beaver went down, and was gone a long time, but could not reach the bottom. Then the loon tried, and the otter, but the water was too deep for them. At last the muskrat dived, and he was gone so long that they thought he had drowned, but he finally came up, almost dead, and when they pulled him on to the raft, they found, in one of his paws, a little mud. With this, Old Man formed the world, and afterwards he made the people.[8]

In the beginning, all the land was covered with water, and Old Man and all the animals were floating around on a large raft.

A separate account, told to Robert Lowie in the first decade of the 1900s, added: "During the flood, Old Man was sitting on the highest mountain with all the beasts. The flood was caused by the above people, because the baby of the woman who married a star was heedlessly torn in pieces by an Indian child."[9]

The Northern Blackfeet also had a tradition of the confusion of languages, which they said occurred shortly after the Flood:

> After the flood, Old Man mixed water with different colors. He whistled, and all the people came together. He gave one man a cup of one kind of water, saying, "You will be chief of these people here." The Blackfoot, Piegan, and Blood all received black water. Then he said to the people, "Talk," and they all talked differently; but those who drank black water spoke the same. This happened on the highest mountain in the Montana Reservation.[10]

A Blackfoot Warrior on Horseback

7. George A. Dorsey, *Traditions of the Skidi Pawnee* (Boston: Houghton, Mifflin & Co., 1904), p. 23–24.
8. George Bird Grinnell, *Blackfoot Lodge Tales* (New York: Charles Scribner's Sons, 1908), p. 272.
9. Clark Wissler and D.C. Duvall, "Mythology of the Blackfoot Indians," *Anthropological Papers of the American Museum of Natural History*, vol. 2 (New York: Order of Trustees, 1909), p. 19.
10. Ibid.

Blackfoot Creation Story with Genesis Parallels

In 1972, Percy Bullchild, a 67-year-old man of the Blackfoot tribe, recorded his tribe's oral traditions and history, writing them down for future generations. According to the Blackfoot account of creation, the eternal God, or "Creator Sun," first made life in the form of snakes, who rebelled against him and were punished for their disobedience. Creator Sun then made a wife for himself out of mud, which came to life when he blew into the nostrils of the wooden figure. One day she was looking for food when she was tempted by a "snakeman" who deceived her and caused her to disobey the Creator, her husband. But being merciful and wise, he forgave her.

He also went on to create the human race, which was to be in his own shape and image. So he molded a form of himself and blew into its nostrils, and "mudman" came to life. Then he created a companion for man, because he did not want him to be lonely. Using a strange power, Creator Sun put the mudman into a deep sleep, so he was unaware of what was happening. Then Creator Sun took out mudman's smallest rib, and from this rib he made an image after the mudman and himself. The woman would be to bear fruit, and to bear offspring.[11]

107

ASSINIBOINE

Northern Great Plains

The Assiniboine lived in the northern Great Plains, their territory stretching from North Dakota to Saskatchewan. They had a flood story, which they told to Robert Lowie at Fort Belknap in August 1907:

> All the earth was flooded with water. Inktonmi sent animals to dive for dirt at the bottom of the sea. No animal was able to get any. At last he sent the Muskrat. It came up dead, but with dirt in its claws. Inktonmi saw the dirt, took it, and made the earth out of it.[12]

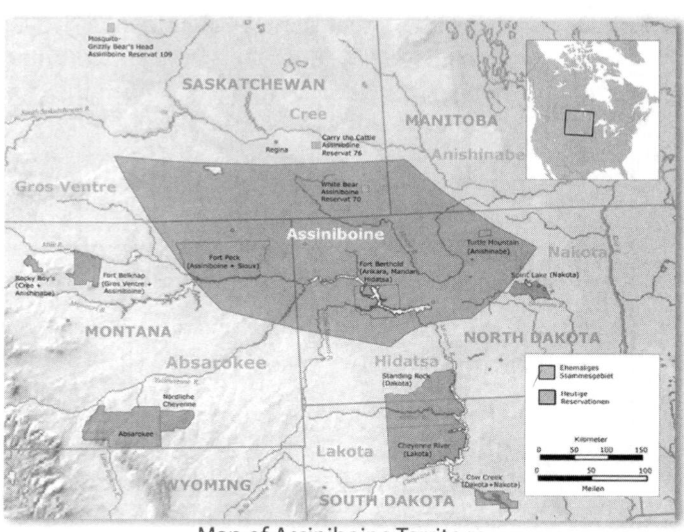

Map of Assiniboine Territory

Three Mounted Piegan Chiefs

11. Percy Bullchild, *The Sun Came Down: The History of the World as my Blackfeet Elders Told It* (New York: Harper & Row, 1985), p. 5–8, 38–43.
12. Robert H. Lowie, *The Assiniboine* (New York: Order of the Trustees, 1909), p. 101.

108 LAKOTA

Nebraska through Montana

In 1974, at Rosebud Indian Reservation in South Dakota, a Lakota man named Leonard Crow Dog shared his tribe's flood tradition with Richard Erdoes:

There was a world before this world, but the people in it did not know how to behave themselves or how to act human. The creating power was not pleased with that earlier world. He said to himself: "I will make a new world."

> There was a world before this world, but the people in it did not know how to behave themselves or how to act human. The creating power was not pleased with that earlier world. He said to himself: "I will make a new world." He had the pipe bag and the chief pipe, which he put on the pipe rack that he had made in the sacred manner. He took four dry buffalo chips, placed three of them under the three sticks, and saved the fourth one to light the pipe. The Creating Power said to himself: "I will sing three songs, which will bring a heavy rain. Then I'll sing a fourth song and stamp four times on the earth, and the earth will crack wide open. Water will come out of the cracks and cover all the land." When he sang the first song, it started to rain. When he sang the second, it poured. When he sang the third, the rain-swollen rivers overflowed their beds. But when he sang the fourth song and stamped on the earth, it split open in many places like a shattered gourd, and water flowed from the cracks until it covered everything. The Creating Power floated on the sacred pipe and on his huge pipe bag. He let himself be carried by waves and wind this way and that, drifting for a long time. At last the rain stopped, and by then all the people and animals had drowned. Only Kangi, the crow, survived, though crow asked him to make a place for it to light. The Creating Power thought: "It's time to unwrap the pipe and open the pipe bag." The wrapping and the pipe bag contained all manner of animals and birds., from which he selected four animals known for their ability to stay under water for a long time.[13]

Sitting Bull and Buffalo Bill

> He sent a loon to dive for mud, but it failed to reach the bottom. "All the time, the crow was flying around and begging for a place to light." A turtle was sent, and it returned with a little mud, which God used to create land.[14]

> From the earth the Creating Power formed the shapes of men and women. He used red earth and white earth, black earth and yellow earth, and made as many as he thought would do for a start. He stamped on the earth and the shapes came alive, each taking the color of the earth out of which it was made. The Creating Power gave all of them understanding and speech and told them what tribes they belonged to. The Creating Power said to them: "The first world I made was bad; the creatures on it were bad. So I burned it up. The second world I made was bad too, so I drowned it. This is the third world I have made. Look: I have created a rainbow for you as a sign that there will be no more Great Flood. Whenever you see a rainbow, you will know that it has stopped raining.[15]

Look: I have created a rainbow for you as a sign that there will be no more Great Flood. Whenever you see a rainbow, you will know that it has stopped raining.

We have another Lakota tradition, which they told to "Buffalo Bill" Cody in the 1860s.

> It was taught by the wise men of this tribe that the earth was originally peopled by giants, who were fully three times the size of modern men.

13. Richard Erdoes and Alfonzo Ortiz, *American Indian Myths and Legends* (New York: Pantheon Books, 1984), p. 496–497.
14. Ibid., p. 497–498.
15. Ibid., p. 498.

They were so swift and powerful that they could run alongside a buffalo, take the animal under one arm, and tear off a leg and eat it as they ran. So vainglorious were they because of their own size and strength that they denied the existence of a Creator. When it lightened they proclaimed their superiority to the lightning; when it thundered they laughed. This displeased the Great Spirit, and to rebuke their arrogance he sent a great rain upon the earth. The valleys filled with water and the giants retreated to the hills. The water crept up the hills and the giants sought safety on the highest mountains. Still the rain continued, the waters rose, and the giants, having no other refuge, were drowned. The Great Spirit profited by his former mistake. When the waters subsided he made a new race of men, but he made them smaller and less strong. This tradition has been handed down from Sioux father to Sioux son since earliest ages. It shows, at least, as the legends of all the races do, that the story of the Deluge is history common to all the world.[16]

It was taught by the wise men of this tribe that the earth was originally peopled by giants, who were fully three times the size of modern men … So vainglorious were they because of their own size and strength that they denied the existence of a Creator.

No doubt, there is some exaggeration in the above text. But the core content is clearly consistent with Genesis.

Lakota Prophecy of Jesus

Chief Joseph RiverWind is a man of the Taino tribe who has traveled extensively among the other First Nations peoples. He recorded the following Lakota prophecy of Jesus. This ancient tradition has existed from the time when the Sioux people lived on the east coast (their original territory before they were pushed westward to the plains, although a remnant of them still live in North Carolina). In abbreviated form, the story went as follows:

> A terrible sickness had come over the land, and the Lakota were dying, and none of the remedies were working. So the Chief of the tribe went up on the mountain to fast and pray to the Great Spirit on behalf of the people. This went on for four days. On the fourth day of his fervent praying, the Creator sent an angel who hovered in the sky above him. The angel drew a window in the sky and said to the old Chief, "Look through this window, and you will see the answer to your prayers."
>
> The Chief looked through the large opening in the sky, and he saw a man who was pierced and hanging on a tree. The angel said, "He is dying so that your people may live."
>
> As the angel began to depart, the old Chief said, "Wait! What is his name so that we can remember him and his sacrifice for our people? There is no greater honor among our people than to give your life for another." The angel said, "His Name is Bright Morning Star. Remember His Name." [see Revelation 22:16]
>
> The old Chief fell to his knees, weeping and thanking the Creator, for he knew his people would be healed.[17]

16. Helen Cody Wetmore, *Last of the Great Scouts: The Life Story of Col. William F. Cody ("Buffalo Bill") as Told by His Sister Helen Cody Wetmore* (Chicago: Duluth Press, 1899), p. 165–166.
17. Chief Joseph RiverWind, *That's What the Old Ones Say* (Middletown, DE: FireKeepers, 2015), p. 84–88.

Lakota Sioux Man Radically Saved

Richard Twiss, a Lakota Sioux man, shared in his own words how Jesus saved him from his lost and empty way of life, to know and serve the living God:

> I was drawn to the Eastern religions: Buddhism, Taoism, Hinduism. Still searching for meaning in my life, I practiced yoga, prayed mantric prayers and sought enlightenment through the use of hallucinogenic drugs. I spent many nights praying and sleeping under the stars. But the combination of drugs, Eastern religions, my Catholic upbringing and Native American spirituality only led to further confusion. When I wasn't searching for God, I partied with friends and tried relationships with a number of women. I felt empty inside. I knew there had to be more to life than what I was experiencing.
>
> While hitchhiking to the other side of Maui one afternoon, I was picked up by a couple of guys who talked to me about God, about Jesus Christ and His plan for my life. I thought they were narrow-minded, self-righteous Jesus freaks and Bible thumpers, and after giving them a piece of my mind, I got out of the car. . . . The last thing I wanted was to be a Christian. But then a few weeks later, while alone on a beach in Maui, I remembered what these two Christian men had said to me about Jesus.
>
> There is a place on the coast of Maui called the Seven Sacred Pools, where a small river cascades down a valley in a series of waterfalls. In a nearby meadow, psilocybin mushroom plants — a very strong hallucinogenic — grew in great numbers. Often, many spiritual seekers could be found there picking and eating the plants and tripping out. One day, I had eaten numerous magic mushrooms (as they are referred to in street jargon) and at 2:30 in the morning, I found myself completely engulfed in paranoia and the fear of dying or losing my mind. I tried my Eastern meditations and prayers for relief, but to no avail. I could imagine going crazy and running down the beach with men in white uniforms chasing me. It was a horrible moment mentally and emotionally.
>
> At last, fearing the worst, I literally yelled at the top of my lungs, "Jesus, if You're real and You can do what those people said You could do, then I want You to come into my heart and life and to forgive me for the wrong I've done!" At that moment an incredible thing happened. The effect of the drugs left, the fear disappeared, and the most incredible sensation of peace flooded my being from the top of my head to the bottom of my feet. I felt clean, forgiven and filled with joy.
>
> It was there on that beach that the Creator revealed Himself to me in the person of Jesus Christ, and I became a follow of the Jesus Way.[18]

Twiss went on to found Wiconi International, a ministry which serves and shares Jesus with the First Nations peoples.

18. Richard Twiss, *One Church Many Tribes* (Bloomington, MN: Chosen Books, 2000), p. 32–33.

109 CROW

Montana and Wyoming

Hó-ra-tó-a, a Crow Warrior

The Crow or Absahrokee tribe did not always live in the Northern Rockies of Montana and Wyoming. Their ancestors lived in the Ohio area. With the arrival of the Europeans on the eastern shore, pressure from warring tribes drove them further west.

According to George Catlin, who visited them in 1832, "They say that their people were a great nation before the Flood, and that a few who reached the summits of the mountains were saved when all the tribes of the valleys were destroyed by the waters."[19]

110 ARAPAHO

Colorado and Wyoming

The Reverend John Roberts was a missionary to the Shoshone and Arapaho peoples at the Wind River Reservation, where he arrived in 1883. He was respected and trusted by the Arapaho to such a degree that he was one of the few white men ever to see the Arapaho's most sacred vessel, the Flat Pipe. Regarding their version of the Flood, he wrote:

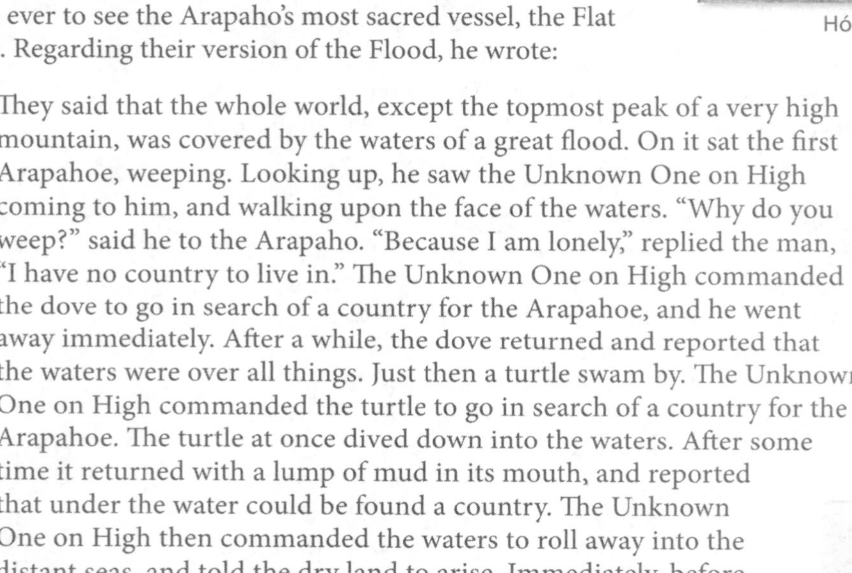

> They said that the whole world, except the topmost peak of a very high mountain, was covered by the waters of a great flood. On it sat the first Arapahoe, weeping. Looking up, he saw the Unknown One on High coming to him, and walking upon the face of the waters. "Why do you weep?" said he to the Arapaho. "Because I am lonely," replied the man, "I have no country to live in." The Unknown One on High commanded the dove to go in search of a country for the Arapahoe, and he went away immediately. After a while, the dove returned and reported that the waters were over all things. Just then a turtle swam by. The Unknown One on High commanded the turtle to go in search of a country for the Arapahoe. The turtle at once dived down into the waters. After some time it returned with a lump of mud in its mouth, and reported that under the water could be found a country. The Unknown One on High then commanded the waters to roll away into the distant seas, and told the dry land to arise. Immediately, before the Arapahoe's view, a beautiful country appeared, with wooded mountains and green valleys and shining rivers.[20]

… the whole world, except the topmost peak of a very high mountain, was covered by the waters of a great flood … The Unknown One on High commanded the dove to go in search of a country for the Arapahoe, and he went away immediately.

That the "earth diver" motif, so widespread among North American tribes, originated from the memory of Noah sending the raven and the dove to search for a sign of land, can be discerned from the oral tradition narrated above. **See Appendix B** for more on earth diver stories and their relation to the Genesis Flood and Creation accounts.

Arapaho Youth

19. George Catlin, *Last Rambles Amongst the Indians of the Rocky Mountains and the Andes*, p. 152.
20. Sarah E. Olden, *Shoshone Folk Tales, as Discovered from the Rev. John Roberts, a Hidden Hero, On the Wind River Indian Reservation in Wyoming* (Milwaukee: Morehouse Publishing Co., 1923), p. 41.

The Prayer Pipe

> The ceremonial prayer pipe was widely used among the tribes of North America. It was symbolic of one's prayer life, and the smoke that arose represented one's prayers ascending to God. Four herbs were most commonly used: tobacco, sage, sweet grass, and cedar. A popular misconception is that marijuana or other mind-altering drugs were used in First Nations' prayers, but that is not the case. Otherwise, it would not be known if any revelation received through prayer came from the Great Spirit or from one's own disoriented mind. Use of the prayer pipe carried great honor and responsibility, and one needed to be trained by the elders to use it properly.

Edward Curtis visited the Arapaho at the Wind River Reservation in 1910. He described their most sacred pipe, the Flat Pipe, in this way:

> The object of highest veneration is the Flat Pipe, which is held in a family of the Northern band. It consists of a wooden stem about two feet long, inserted, without angle, into a straight, cylindrical bowl of black steatite inlaid with a whitish stone. Carefully concealed in a mass of skin wrappings, the pipe is kept in the back part of the custodian's ceremonially painted lodge, on a stand consisting of four sticks driven into the ground. The lodge of the keeper occupied a position just inside the camp-circle and opposite the entrance of the camp. Like the priest of the Lakota Calf Pipe, he proceeded in advance of the moving column, but unlike the former he himself, and not a virgin, carried the precious bundle. Only occasionally was the sacred pipe revealed to a favored few who could afford the expense attendant upon the ceremony. On such occasions those who were present smoked the pipe, praying for health, prosperity, and any special boon desired, and the keeper related the story of the pipe. This was not a simple myth of the creation; it began with that episode, explaining thus the manner in which the pipe came into the possession of the people, and continued with a mythical history of the first people. From several descriptions by Arapaho who have heard it, the lore of the pipe-keeper seems to be a mass of myths, folk-tales, traditions, rules governing the social relations and ceremonial procedure, precepts and injunctions to the moral life. It constitutes in fact the unwritten bible of the Arapaho. It can be recited only when the pipe is exposed and only by the pipe-keeper, and four nights must be consumed in the telling. When the pipe-keeper, Weasel Bear, died in 1908, he had no male heir of mature age, and the sacred bundle was given, without instruction in the mythology, to his daughter, a young woman. There is no one now living able to repeat the myth in full if he would.[21]

Another Flood story was narrated to George Dorsey by an old Southern Arapaho man known as Blindy, around 1902 or 1903. Notice also the similarity with the Tower of Babel account in Genesis:

21. Edward Curtis, *North American Indian*, vol. 6, p. 140–141.

The water began to rise. They (Blue-bird, his brother Magpie, and Nihaca) went to the top of a high mountain. Nihaca lay down on the very summit, which had been reserved for the children. When they told him to move away he feigned to be sick in his back. Then the waters came up. When the water almost touched them, Rock stretched out his foot with the turtle moccasin on it and the water receded. Four times the water came up and he caused it to go back by means of the turtle moccasin. After the third time he told the people: "Go down and gather mushrooms which are light. My power is good only four times." So Crow, Magpie, and Blue-bird went and gathered small mushrooms, and putting cobwebs around them, made a boat or raft. When the water rose they all entered it. But he with the turtle moccasins remained on the mountain peak, and Nihaca, knowing that he would not drown, remained with him. The water remained high a very long time. The mushrooms began to become soft, and the people called for help. The one with the turtle moccasins knew that he had made the boat and that it was not in his power to make it over. Therefore, he sent the white-nosed duck down to see whether the earth was far down, but the duck came up exhausted. Then he took off his moccasin and it changed into a turtle and it dived and finally came up with mud in each of its four arm pits. Then he took the mud and sent the turtle down to bring up a short rib. When it brought this, he sent it up to bring a bulrush. It brought this also. Then he sprinkled the earth which the turtle had brought him about the place where he was, and with the rib he pointed in the four directions. As he pointed, the land spread out in those directions to the ends of the earth. Then he pointed above and made the vault of the sky. Now the earth was bare. Then the one with the turtle moccasins made corn from the bulrush. After this Nihaca lived in the sky and was called our father. Now there was doubt whether the people should all speak one language or whether they should speak many, for they still spoke alike. Then a council was held and it was decided that most of them should change their languages from the original (Arapaho). And Nihaca gave the Arapaho the middle of the earth to live in, and all the others were to live around them.[22]

Old Blindy Arapahoe

UTE

111 Utah and Colorado

Frank Hall (1836–1917) — a general, pioneer, and miner — was a very influential leader in the early years of the territory and state of Colorado. He arrived in Colorado in 1860. Among other things, he authored the four-volume work, *History of the State of Colorado*, in which he preserved a Flood tradition from the Tabeguach band of the Ute Indians:

> The Tabeguaches, like all other races of people, have a tradition of the Deluge, and, while not in accord with the Scriptural account, is nevertheless quite unique. They believe that the ark or boat which contained all the people and all the animals to be saved from the universal inundation landed, not on Mount Ararat, but on top of a spur of mountains just back of Palmer Lake, 52 miles south of Denver, and that when the waters subsided and the dry land appeared, they departed from the boat and went down upon the plain. There they pitched their tepees, and the animals went with them.[23]

They believe that the ark or boat which contained all the people and all the animals to be saved from the universal inundation landed, not on Mount Ararat, but on top of a spur of mountains just back of Palmer Lake, 52 miles south of Denver.

22. James A. Dorsey and Alfred L. Kroeber, *Traditions of the Arapaho* (Chicago: Field Columbian Museum, 1903), p. 15–16.
23. Frank Hall, *History of the State of Colorado*, vol. 4 (Chicago: Blakely Printing Co., 1895), p. 93.

112 UTE PIKES PEAK TRADITION

Colorado

A poet from Colorado Springs named Ernest Whitney (1858–1893) heard a Flood tradition of the Ute tribe who historically lived in the mountains above Colorado Springs:

Ute Chief Sevara and Family

> At the beginning of all things the Lesser Spirits possessed the earth, and dwelt near the banks of the Great River. They had created a race of men to be their servants, but these men were far inferior to the present inhabitants of the earth, and made endless trouble for their creators. Therefore the Lesser Spirits resolved to destroy mankind and the earth itself; so they caused the Great River to rise until it burst its banks and overwhelmed everything. They themselves took each a large portion of the best of the earth, that they might create a new world, and a quantity of maize which had been their particular food, and returned to heaven. Arriving at the gate of heaven, which is at the end of the plains, where the sky and the mountains meet, they were told that they could not bring such burdens of earth into heaven. Accordingly they dropped them all then and there. These falling masses made a great heap on the top of the world which rose far above the waters, and this was the origin of Pike's Peak, which is thus shown to be directly under the gate of heaven. Formerly it was twice as high as it is now, but lost its summit as we shall see later on. The rock masses upon it and all about it, show plainly that they have been dropped from the sky. The extent and variety of mineral wealth in the region prove that the earth's choicest materials are deposited here. . . .
>
> Now among the inhabitants of the earth left to destruction, was one man who by secretly feeding upon the food of the Spirits, the sacred maize, had become much stronger and superior in every way to his fellow beings. Such was his strength that he succeeded in sustaining himself and his wife above the waters for a very long time. Suddenly a maize stalk rose before him and blossomed into fruit. Breaking a joint from it, he soon fashioned this into a rude boat in which he took refuge with his wife. . . . Not knowing what direction to take on the pathless waters, he paddled toward the only other object visible upon the face of the deep. On approaching, this proved to be another maize stalk. Upon it were a pair of field mice which shared with him their supply of grain. Launching forth again he paddled toward another object visible in the distance, which proved to be another maize plant. . . . Thus unconsciously following the course of the Lesser Spirits, he passed in turn the maize plants of the prairie dog, the squirrel, the rabbit, and all the animals, and then came to the maize plants of the birds, until passing from one to another he came to the mountain. Having landed his boat upon it, the man died of exhaustion, and the woman died soon after, in the pains of maternity, giving birth to a boy and girl.[24]

Therefore the Lesser Spirits resolved to destroy mankind and the earth itself; so they caused the Great River to rise until it burst its banks and overwhelmed everything.

Pikes Peak in Colorado

24. Ernest Whitney, *Legends of the Pikes Peak Region* (Denver: Chain & Hardy Co., 1892), p. 25–29.

113 NORTHERN SHOSHONE

Idaho

The Northern Shoshone living in Idaho told Robert Lowie their memory of the Flood, when he met them in the spring of 1906:

> Coyote saw some wild geese flying and begged them for some feathers. They flew down and gave him some. Then he was able to join them. When they got to the summit of a high mountain, they saw that the water below was moving a little. They had a council there, debating whether they should wash the whole world. They decided to do so, and raised the water until it filled all the low parts of the earth. Everyone except Coyote and his companions was drowned. Someone shut off the water; no one knows who. When everything was drying up again, the survivors took sticks and placed them on the slopes of the mountains. That is why we have trees on the mountains now. They made little creeks and lakes. Then they also created the fish and all the other animals for the Indians.[25]

Shoshoni Chief Washakie

114 EASTERN SHOSHONE

Wyoming

Around 1908, the Eastern Shoshone living at the Wind River Reservation in Wyoming told H.H. St. Clair a fragmentary account of the Flood. As in many "earth diver" versions, the memory of Noah sending the two birds is very evident:

> Our Father sent the Crow, who was sitting on a high mountain, to bring earth. "Get earth! I will once more create the drowned people." Then the Crow flew away, and after a while came back to the creator. "You must have been eating the drowned people. You stink. Go back! — Now, you, little Chickadee, bring dirt! Then I'll create all the people again." When the Chickadee returned with dirt, our Father made the earth and sky. We now walk on the ground he made. He said, "Now, my children, pray to me; then I will listen to you, and take pity on you."
>
> The whole earth was covered with water. Only on a high mountain was there a dry spot.[26]

115 WICHITA

Kansas to North Texas

The Wichita lived on the plains from northern Texas to Kansas for countless centuries. George Dorsey described them as generally shorter and stockier, and somewhat darker in skin tone than their neighbors, the Cheyenne, Arapaho, Comanche, Apache, and Kiowa.[27] Dorsey met with a Wichita chief named Towakoni Jim in 1903. This chief shared several oral traditions with Dorsey, including a Flood tradition:

> The prophet was told by a voice from above that he had a work that was soon to begin, for everything was going wrong; that he was to begin a work; that things were getting worse. The prophet was told to get a tall cane, and place in between the joints all kinds of seeds, grass, corn, etc., using joint after joint of the cane. Then he was told to select in pairs those animals he thought best should be saved. He was to save all the good ones and leave out

The prophet was told to get a tall cane, and place in between the joints all kinds of seeds, grass, corn, etc., … Then he was told to select in pairs those animals he thought best should be saved.

25. Robert Harry Lowie, "The Northern Shoshone," *Anthropological Papers of the American Museum of Natural History*, vol. 2, part 2 (New York, 1909), p. 247.
26. Harry Hull St. Clair, ed. Robert H. Lowie, "Shoshone and Comanche Tales," *Journal of American Folk-lore*, vol. 22 (Boston and New York: Houghton Mifflin, 1909), p. 273.
27. George Amos Dorsey, *The Mythology of the Wichita* (Washington: Carnegie, 1904), p. 2.

all the bad ones. The voice said it would attend to the bad ones. He also told to prophet to tell him when he had everything ready; he should set up the pole in the ground, crawl into it himself and then let him know that everything was ready. He was then told to go to the north where he would see someone standing; that he should tell him that he had everything ready, and beg him to go ahead with his work and to the rest. After the prophet had put everything in the cane he went to the man in the north and told him that everything he wished to save was in the cane, and he asked him to go ahead with the work and finish it. The man at the north replied that he would soon send someone back to the village of the prophet; that when the time should come there would be a sign indicating that dire things were going to happen; that the fowls and animals would be seen coming from the north and going to the south. On a certain day the fowls of the air appeared in the north, like a cloud, and they flew toward the south. The prophet crawled into the cane. The people wondered what was the reason for this. Finally the animals came, and the people began to find out what was about to happen. They began to cry and to run for the mountains and for other places, but it did them no good. After the birds and the animals had passed there came a flood, and the water was all over, and it got deeper and deeper. The bad people were drowned and everything else that was not in the cane. … When the man and the woman were placed on the high point and the water had gone down, they noticed foam where the high points of land had been, as far as they could see. While they were up on the mountains the prophet thought he had better go down to the bottom and see how the land was, whether it had got dry or was still soft. When he got down to the foot of the mountain he noticed that the ground was getting harder, because the wind blew hard. A long time after this the prophet was told that the ground had dried up and they must go down from the mountain. . . .[28]

They began to cry and to run for the mountains and for other places, but it did them no good. After the birds and the animals had passed there came a flood, and the water was all over, and it got deeper and deeper. The bad people were drowned and everything else that was not in the cane

Wichita and Skidi Dancers

116 **Montana**

GROS VENTRES

In 1901, a young man of the Gros Ventres ("big bellies"), or A'ani, told Kroeber this Flood tradition:

The people before the present world were wild. They did not know how to do anything. Nixat did not like the way they lived and did. He thought, "I will make a new world." He had the chief pipe. He went out doors and hung the pipe on three sticks. He picked up four buffalo chips. One he put under each of the sticks on which the pipe hung, and one he took for his own seat. He said, "I will sing three times and shout three times. After I have done these things, I will kick the earth, and water will come out of the cracks. There will be a heavy rain. There will be water over all the earth." Then he began to sing. After he sang three times, he shouted three times. Then he kicked the ground and it cracked. The water came out, and it rained for days, and over all the earth was water. By means of the buffalo chips he and the pipe floated. Then it stopped raining. There was water everywhere. He floated wherever the wind took him. For days he drifted thus. Above him the Crow flew about. All the other birds and animals were drowned. The

The people before the present world were wild. … Nixat did not like the way they lived and did. He thought, "I will make a new world. … I will kick the earth, and water will come out of the cracks. There will be a heavy rain."

28. Ibid., p. 292–293.

> Crow became tired. It flew about crying, “My father, I am becoming tired. I want to rest.” Three times it said this. After it had said so three times, Nixat said, “Alight on the pipe and rest.” . . . Nixat became tired sitting in one position. He cried. He did not know what to do. After he had cried a long time, he began to unwrap the chief pipe. The pipe contained all animals. He selected those with a long breath to dive through the water. First he selected the Large Loon. . . . Nixat sang, and then commanded it to dive and try to bring mud. . . . Then the Small Loon dived. . . . Then he took the Turtle. He sang and it became alive and he sent it and it dived. . . . On the inside of its feet he found a little earth. … Then he said to the Crow, “Come down and rest. I have made a little piece of land for myself and for you.” . . . He decided to make persons and animals. He took earth, and made it into the shape of a man. He made also the shape of a woman. Then he made more figures of earth, until he had many men and women. When he thought he had enough persons, he made animals of all kinds in pairs. When he had finished making these shapes, he named the tribes of people and the kinds of animals. . . . Then he showed them the rainbow, and said to them, “This rainbow is the sign that the earth will not be covered with water again. Whenever you have rain, you will see the rainbow; and when you see it, it will mean that the rain has gone by. There will be another world after this one.” He told the people to separate in pairs and to select habitations in the world for themselves. That is why human beings are scattered.[29]

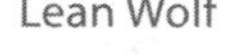
Lean Wolf

Then he showed them the rainbow, and said to them, “This rainbow is the sign that the earth will not be covered with water again.”

117 Wyoming and South Dakota

CHEYENNE

The Cheyenne people held an annual Sun Dance ceremony, which they believed reanimates the earth and its vegetation and animal life. George Dorsey got to witness this ceremony in 1901 and 1903. On the fifth day, part of this ceremony featured certain “rainbow sticks” — sticks painted with multiple colors. The chief priest formed an arch of these sticks, which he drove into the ground. They were said to be symbolic of a rainbow, or of rain, and if the rainbow sticks were not set up, they believed a flood will come.[30] This was very reminiscent of Genesis 9:11–17.

The Cheyenne also had a notion that three floods occurred in the early times of creation. To one of these floods they attributed the creation of different languages and the dispersion of people groups by language:

> There were many different groups with different languages, for the people were never united after the second flood.[31]

> While they were traveling southward there came a great rain and flood all over the country. The rivers rose and overflowed, and still the rain kept falling. At last the high hills alone could be discerned. . . . Nearly all the animals were either drowned or starved to death.[32]

Cheyenne Chief White Buffalo

29. Alfred L. Kroeber, “Gros Ventre Myths and Tales,” *Anthropological Papers of the American Museum of Natural History*, vol. 1 (New York: Order of the Trustees, 1907), p. 59–61.
30. George A. Dorsey, *The Cheyenne, Field Columbian Museum Publication 99*, vol. 9, no. 1 (Chicago: Field Columbian Museum, 1905), p. 144–145.
31. Ibid., p. 36.
32. Ibid., p. 38.

118 FLATHEAD

Montana

The Flathead or Salish people lived on the eastern slopes of the Rockies in modern-day Montana. They shared their memory of the Flood with Lucullus McWhorter in 1923:

> The great water first came to the valley where Flathead Lake has remained until this day. The flood grew bigger and bigger, spreading over all the lower lands. Most of the people were drowned in the valleys, but others fled to the highest mountain. As they climbed, the water followed them. At last all the land was covered except for the solitary peak where a few Indians had gone for refuge.
>
> Then the chief said, "I will try to stop the water. I will ask for my guardian spirit to help me."
>
> He shot an arrow toward the ground at the edge of the water, but the arrow floated away and the flood was not stopped. He sent a second arrow. It also floated away and the waters continued to creep upward. He sent a third arrow. It stayed in the ground at the very edge of the waters. The water reached the third feather on the shaft of the arrow but went no farther.
>
> Gradually the water went down, the tops of the mountains appeared, then the hills, then the valleys. The floodwater that remained formed Flathead Lake.
>
> And so a few people were saved. Their wise men prophesied that through them the tribe would grow again, but that after several generations they would all perish from the earth.[33]

Flathead Child

George Catlin on the Ubiquity of Flood Traditions

The early 18th century explorer and painter George Catlin visited some 50 tribes of the United States and southern Canada. Regarding the Flood tradition of the Mandan tribe, he wrote:

> That these people should have a tradition of the Flood is by no means surprising; as I have learned from every tribe I have visited, that they all have some high mountain in their vicinity, where they insist upon it the big canoe landed.[34]

119 ARIKARA

North Dakota

We again find an account of the Flood in another origin story, from the Arikara people of present-day North Dakota. They told this to Edward Curtis during the first decade of the 1900s:

> The earth was inhabited by a race which Neshanu, Chief, had brought into being. But some of these people mocked the powers above, and their creator resolved to destroy them. First he transformed into grains of corn those who had not derided the mysteries, and placed them in

33. Lucullus V. McWhorter, "The Rattlesnake as Guardian of Good Water Springs," April 1923, *McWhorter Manuscript Collection*, Washington State University Library. Box 44, Folder 430, No. 24. As quoted in Ella Clark, *Indian Legends from the Northern Rockies* (Norman, OK: University of Oklahoma Press, 1966), p. 90.
34. Catlin, *North American Indians*, vol. 1, p. 200.

safety with the animal people in a cavern far underground. Then upon the earth descended a heavy, constant rain, and the rising flood drowned all whom Neshanu had not chosen to save.[35]

Since their Flood history replaces a floating ark with a cavern, they also replace the sending of animals in search of land, with the sending of animals to dig out a hole out from the cavern.

Tonkawa Man

TONKAWA

120 Texas

The Tonkawa were a small tribe from southern Texas. According to the ethnographer James Mooney, they were one of the few cannibalistic tribes of North America. We have but a fragment of their Flood tradition, which was told to Mooney in 1898.

> In the spring of 1898 I met some Tonkawas in Washington, who were there at Congress, and a few months later I met with them again in Omaha. The chief Sentali, also called Grant Richards, was a strong man of about 45 years and his companion John Williams was the oldest living Tonkawa. Both men had witnessed the butchery in 1862 [the Dakota War]. . . . The chief told me all sorts of things about the customs of his tribe. . . . Sentali still knew the names of the ancient Tonkawa tribes in Texas and told me the story of the ancestors who were swept away by a flood, and who must have lived somewhere beyond the great water.[36]

Sentali…told me the story of the ancestors who were swept away by a flood, and who must have lived somewhere beyond the great water.

Other Texts (See Appendix A on page 241)

121 Yellowstone Valley Tradition (Wyoming)

122 Bannock (Idaho)

123 Hidatsa (North Dakota)

35. Curtis, *The North American Indian,* vol. 5, p. 80–81. See also: George A. Dorsey, *Traditions of the Arikara* (Washington: Carnegie, 1904), p. 12–13.
36. James Mooney "Die Tonkawas, der letzte Kannibalenstamm in den Vereinigten Staaten," *Globus*, vol. 82 (Brunswick, Germany: Friedrich Vieweg, 1902), p. 79.

Aerial View of Lake Huron

MIDWEST UNITED STATES

In 1766, a certain First Nations tribe of Ohio told Charles Beatty their tradition of the Flood and the Great Canoe. They also have a well-preserved tradition of the Tower of Babel and the resulting confusion of languages. The Sauk and Fox tribes of Wisconsin and Michigan told how a race of giants conspired to kill the patriarch Wesahkah and his people by sending a flood. This Wesahkah, which is their Noah, prayed to the Great Spirit and obtained help. He built a great raft and survived with his family and all kinds of creatures, and the giants were killed by their own flood.

We have also the Flood traditions of the Menominee, Potawatomi, Winnebago, and others. The Shawnee tribe of Ohio and Kentucky told the Methodist minister J. Spencer their Creation and Flood tradition, of which he remarked that it "agrees in all essential points with the Mosaic record."

Tribes of the Region

124. Shawnee (Ohio River Valley)
125. Pipestone Quarry Tradition (Minnesota)
126. Iowa (Iowa)
127. Omaha (Ohio and Indiana)
128. Potawatomi (Michigan through Illinois)
129. Dakota (Dakotas and Minnesota)
130. Menominee (Wisconsin)
131. Sauk and Fox (Michigan, Wisconsin and Ontario)
132. Ohio Tradition
133. Winnebago (Wisconsin)
134. Osage (Missouri)
135. Missouri Tradition

The Iowa tribe told Reverend Hamilton their history about the Flood which lasted twenty or thirty days and destroyed all mankind. The deity Ictinike drifted along in his canoe, and he sent the muskrat diving, which resurfaced with a piece of earth in his paws. He also sent a bird, which returned with a twig and few leaves. Finally, the Great Spirit made a new man and woman from the red clay of the earth. The Osage tribe of Missouri spoke of a mighty elk which battled the waters in order to cause the earth to drain.

In Minnesota, we find the most sacred site of the First Nations people, the Pipestone Quarry, where tribes from across the country used to obtain the red stone from which they fashion their prayer pipes. At a hill here, they say the Indians made their final stand before succumbing to the rising waters of the Flood. As Catlin was told, "The pipe stone, which is the flesh of their ancestors, is smoked by them as the symbol of peace."

124 SHAWNEE

Ohio River Valley

Charles Bluejacket

Charles Bluejacket was a Shawnee man born in 1816, and the son of the famous war chief Jim Bluejacket. He was very knowledgeable about the tribe's traditions, which he shared with the Methodist missionary J. Spencer between 1858 and 1860.

Their Flood tradition identifies the survivor as an old woman known as *Kukumthena* ("Grandmother"). She was the one to whom the Shawnee, and several tribes of the Algonquian language group, attributed the origin of their race. As Spencer wrote:

> The Shawnee tradition of the creation and the antediluvian period, as told to me, agrees in all essential points with the Mosaic record. The first real divergence is in connection with the Flood. The tradition gives an account of the white man's canoe, and of the saving of a white family, just about as the Bible also has it; but, in addition, it states that an old Indian woman was also saved. After the Flood she lived in a valley, with a hill intervening between her and her white brother and his family, over which she could see the smoke rise from the white man's wigwam. When the sense of her loneliness and destitution came over her, she began to weep very bitterly. There then appeared a heavenly messenger, and asked her why she was so sorrowful. She told him that the Great Spirit had left her white brother his family but she was just a poor old woman alone, and that there was to be an end of her people. Then said the visitor, "Remember how the first man was made," and then he left her. From this she knew that a new creation was meant: so she made small images of children from the earth, as directed, as the Great Spirit had made the first man. When, however, she saw that they had no life, she again wept. Again the messenger appeared, and inquired the cause of her grief. She said she had made children from clay, but that they were only dirt. Then said the visitor, "Remember how the Great Spirit did when the first man was made." At once she understood, and breathed into their nostrils, and they all became alive. This was the beginning of the red men. The Shawnees to this day venerate the memory of the one they call their Grandmother as the origin of their race.[1]

"The Shawnee tradition of the creation and the antediluvian period, as told to me, agrees in all essential points with the Mosaic record."

125 PIPESTONE QUARRY TRADITION

Minnesota

The Pipestone Quarry, located on the Coteau des Prairies region of southwest Minnesota, was a sacred site to many tribes from all across a vast section of North America. For hundreds of years, they traveled great distances to mine out small quantities of the beautiful red stone. It is from this that they made their ceremonial pipes.

William Clark of the Lewis and Clark Expedition found that all the tribes he encountered along the Missouri River made their pipes of the stone from here. The explorer George Catlin also found evidence that all the tribes quarried their pipestone from here.[2] It was considered a neutral site to all Natives, who believed the Great Spirit designated it as a place of peace and unity for all the First Nations people. Tribes that warred against one another away from this place smoked together in peace while here. Catlin was told, "This red pipe was given to the red men by the Great Spirit — it is a part of our flesh, and therefore is great medicine."[3]

Ten-squat-a-way the Shawnee Prophet

1. J. Spencer, "Shawnee Folk-lore," *Journal of American Folk-lore*, vol. 22 (Lancaster, PA and New York, NY: 1909), p. 319.
2. Catlin, *North American Indians*, vol. 2, p. 191.
3. Ibid.

Regarding this Pipestone Quarry, it is even referred to in some Flood traditions from North American tribes.[4] The following was told to Catlin by a distinguished man from the Cree tribe:

Pipestone National Monument Quarry Bluff

> That in the time of a great flood, which took place many centuries ago, and destroyed all the nations of the earth, all the tribes of the red men assembled on the Coteau du Prairie, to get out of the way of the waters. After they had all gathered here from all parts, the water continued to rise, until at length it covered them all in a mass, and their flesh was converted into red pipe stone. Therefore it has always been considered neutral ground — it belonged to all tribes alike, and all were allowed to get it and smoke it together.
>
> While they were all drowning in a mass, a young woman, K-wap-tah-w (a virgin), caught hold of the foot of a very large bird that was flying over, and was carried to the top of a high cliff, not far off, that was above the water. Here she had twins, and their father was the war-eagle, and her children have since peopled the earth.
>
> The pipe stone, which is the flesh of their ancestors, is smoked by them as the symbol of peace, and the eagle's quill decorates the head of the brave.[5]

That in the time of a great flood, which took place many centuries ago, and destroyed all the nations of the earth, all the tribes of the red men assembled on the Coteau du Prairie, to get out of the way of the waters. After they had all gathered here from all parts, the water continued to rise, until at length it covered them all in a mass.

As Christians, we find our place of peace — our "Pipestone Quarry," if you will — in the person of Jesus Christ Himself, who died in our place as an atoning sacrifice for our sins, and for the whole world. This of course took place at a hill in Jerusalem, in the sight of Jews, Romans, Greeks, and visitors from Asia, Africa, and Europe. But his life did not end there at that hill or in the tomb. Three days later, Jesus rose from the dead, just as the Scriptures prophesied centuries earlier. Many eyewitnesses testified to his resurrection, and did not deny it when threatened with death. Anyone who believes in Him is forgiven of their sins, gets a restored relationship with God, and receives the Holy Spirit. Our prayer pipe is Jesus. He reigns in heaven, but He comes to live in us as well.

---

4. See also a Lakota legend on page 91 of this book
5. Catlin, *North American Indians*, vol. 2, p. 191–192.

126 Iowa

IOWA

The White Cloud, Head Chief of the Iowas

From late 1837 to 1853, William Hamilton served at a Presbyterian mission located at the Iowa tribe's reservation in Kansas. They told him their tradition of the Flood, which was eventually published in 1853:

> Of the Flood, hear the Indians: "Our fathers tell us, that a long time ago, it rained a long time; perhaps twenty or thirty days; and all animals and all Indians were drowned. The Great Spirit then made another man and woman out of red clay, and we came from them. Don't know what became of the whites in the flood: they may have been saved in boats or canoes. The Great Spirit told our fathers all this, or told the first man he made.[6]

In an article in 1892, the ethnologist James Dorsey shared more information on what the Iowa tribe believed:

> The Iowa story, of which only a small part was recorded by the late Rev. William Hamilton, places Ictinike in a canoe with a few animals as his servants. The muskrat brings up a little mud between his paws from the submerged earth, and a bird returns to the canoe with a branch on which are a few leaves. Ictinike removes the leaves, mixes them and the twigs with the mud, and scatters the compound over the waters, causing the new earth to appear.[7]

Of the Flood, hear the Indians: "Our fathers tell us, that a long time ago, it rained a long time; perhaps twenty or thirty days; and all animals and all Indians were drowned.

127 Ohio and Indiana

OMAHA

Before migrating to Nebraska, the Omaha tribe lived farther east in present-day Ohio and Indiana. We have a passing reference to their Flood tradition, which James Dorsey heard from them during the 1870s:

> Ictinike . . . met a Turtle, whom he persuaded to flee to the bluffs on account of a great flood which the gods were to send, a flood so violent that even turtles would be in danger of death.[8]

128 Michigan through Illinois

POTAWATOMI

The Potawatomi tribe settled in parts of Michigan, Wisconsin, and Illinois. At Two Rivers, Wisconsin, in 1804, a frontier trader named Thomas Anderson met a Potawatomi chief who recounted the tribe's origin story containing a memory of the Flood. We read this from Anderson's diary:

> I put up at the lodge of an old Indian chief, named Nanaboujou, who gave the following account of the origin of his tribe, in answer to my inquiry on the subject: "I take my name," said he, "from my original ancestors, who were the first living man and woman. They found themselves in a big canoe; all the animals were also in the same canoe, floating on thick water. After a while the ancestors insisted that there must be something much more substantial beneath the water. To test it, they wanted the

Little Snake, an Omaha Interpreter

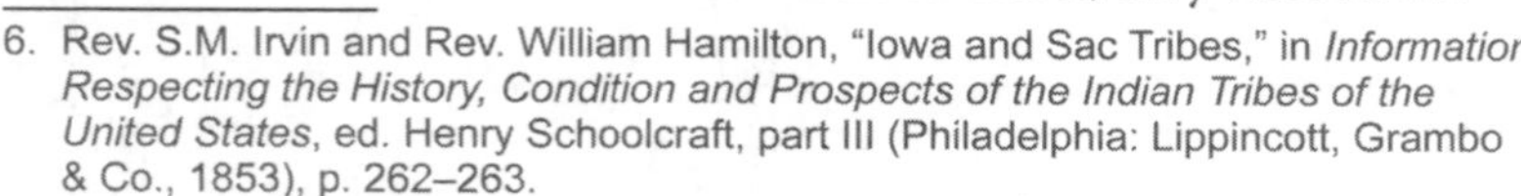

6. Rev. S.M. Irvin and Rev. William Hamilton, "Iowa and Sac Tribes," in *Information Respecting the History, Condition and Prospects of the Indian Tribes of the United States*, ed. Henry Schoolcraft, part III (Philadelphia: Lippincott, Grambo & Co., 1853), p. 262–263.
7. James Owen Dorsey, "Nanibozhu in Siouan Mythology," *Journal of American Folk-lore*, vol. 5, no. 19 (Boston and New York: Houghton, Mifflin and Co., 1892), p. 300.
8. Ibid., p. 301.

deer, or some other animal, to dive down and ascertain. None would venture on so perilous and uncertain an undertaking. At length a beaver volunteered to make the effort, and jumped overboard, plunging beneath the waters. After a long time he rose to the surface, almost dead, without being able to relate anything satisfactory. But the ancestors still persisted that there must be a hard substance upon which the waters rested. Finally they persuaded the muskrat to go on a trip of discovery. He, too, was gone a long time on his sub-watery exploration; but at length he emerged from the flood of waters quite exhausted. The woman ancestor took him up in her arms, and on nursing and drying him to bring him to, found a little clay adhering to one of his forepaws. This she carefully scraped off, worked it between her thumb and finger, and placed it on the water to see if it would float. It immediately began to increase in size, and in three days it was more than three fathoms broad.[9]

They found themselves in a big canoe; all the animals were also in the same canoe, floating on thick water.

More context comes from Simon Pokagon (1830–1899), a Potawatomi writer in the 1898 issue of *The Forum* journal. According to Pokagon, the deity Nenawbozhoo ("the great hare") shot an arrow at the sea monster, or water go Neven Manito, because the latter had seized and drowned his dog. The arrow struck the great sea monster, piercing his heart. He cried "Revenge!" and sent other sea monsters to cause a great flood in an attempt to kill Nenawbozhoo:

Me-Te-A, A Pottawatomie Chief

The prophet fled in consternation before the outraged creatures that hurled after him mountains of water, which swept down the forests like grass before the whirlwind. He continued to flee before the raging flood, but could find no dry land. In sore despair he then called upon the God of Heaven to save him, when there appeared before him a great canoe in which were pairs of all kinds of land beasts and birds, being rowed by the most beautiful maiden, who let down a rope and drew him up into the boat. The flood raged on; but, though the mountains of water were continually being hurled after the prophet, he was safe.

When he had floated on the water many days, he ordered Aw-mik (the beaver) to dive down and, if he could reach the bottom, to bring up some earth. Down the latter plunged, but in a few minutes came floating to the surface lifeless. The prophet pulled him into the boat, blew into his mouth, and he became alive again. He then said to Waw-jashk (the musk-rat), "You are the best diver among all the animal creation. Go down to the bottom and bring me up some earth, out of which I will create a new world; for we cannot much longer live on the face of the deep." Down plunged the musk-rat; but, like the beaver, he, too, soon came to the surface lifeless, and was drawn into the boat, whereupon the prophet blew into his mouth, and he became alive again. In his paw, however, was found a small quantity of earth, which the prophet rolled into a small ball, and tied to the neck of Ka-ke-gi (the raven), saying, "Go thou, and fly to and fro the surface of the deep, that dry land may appear." The raven did so; the waters rolled away; the world resumed its former shape; and, in course of time, the maiden and prophet were united and repeopled the world.[10]

… there appeared before him a great canoe in which were pairs of all kinds of land beasts and birds, … The flood raged on; but, though the mountains of water were continually being hurled after the prophet, he was safe.

9. "Narrative of Capt. Thomas G. Anderson, 1800–28," ed. Lyman Copeland Draper, *Collections of the State Historical Society of Wisconsin*, vol. 9 (Madison: State Historical Society, 1909), p. 155–156. For a related version recorded in 1923, see: Alanson Skinner, "The Mascoutens or Prairie Potawatomi Indians, Part III, Mythology and Folklore," *Milwaukee Public Museum Bulletin*, vol. 6, part 3 (Milwaukee: Order of the Trustees, 1927), p. 332.
10. Simon Pokagon, "Indian Superstitions and Legends," *The Forum*, vol. 25 (New York: Forum Publishing Company, 1897), p. 621–622.

129 Dakotas and Minnesota

DAKOTA

James W. Lynd (1830–1862) was a Minnesota State Senator, and the first person killed in the Dakota Uprising of 1862. Prior to his death, he spent a great deal of time among the Dakotas, learning their language, customs, and legends.

In his unpublished manuscript, Lynd wrote of the Flood tradition he had heard from them in the 1850s:

> The tradition that occurs among the Iroquois, that the sea once invaded the land and swept off all but a few living creatures, is found also among the Sioux; and the presence of the bones of the mastodon and of the remains of immense Pachydermata in the interior, has been more than once accounted for to us by adducing this tradition. In cases of this kind, however, the Dakotas do not pretend to reason upon doubtful points, but have the matter either with skepticism as to inferences, or apathetic indifference.[11]

130 Wisconsin

MENOMINEE

The Menominee Flood tradition is very similar to that of the Potawatomi, and can be found in the Appendix on page 255.

131 Michigan, Wisconsin and Ontario

SAUK AND FOX

We possess, in general, fewer native legends from Wisconsin and Michigan than from other parts of the continental United States. However, the missionary Cutting Marsh recorded an outstanding tradition of the Flood from the Sauk (or Sac) and Fox, a closely related pair of tribes from this region. Marsh wrote the following in a letter dated March 25, 1835:

> [The] Ai-yam-woy [were] men of terrible size, or giants. . . . The Ai-yam-woy were a race of supernatural beings, descendants of the gods of the sea and inhabited the ancient world. . . .
>
> At length the Ai-yam-woy became very numerous and over-ran both elements at their pleasure, so that the children of We-sah-kah were in danger of being totally destroyed by those terrible demi-gods. We-sah-kah seeing this, sent his brother to the gods of the sea to remonstrate against the depredations committed by their children amongst the race of the chief god of the earth. But instead of listening they slew Nah-pat-tay [his brother].
>
> We-sah-kah prepared himself with the great spear, and went with the speed of an eagle to fight the Ai-yam-woy, the murderers of his brother.

11. James W. Lynd, "History, Religion, Legends, Language, and General Condition of the Dakota Nation," *James W. Lynd Papers*, Minnesota Historical Society Library, St. Paul, MN. Chapter 3: Early History, p. 72–73. Approx. date 1859.

He met and slew them; this occasioned a war with the gods which lasted for a long time. The gods of the sea having the great deep at their disposal resolved upon destroying We-sah-kah and his race even at the loss of their own lives. A great council was therefore called for the purpose, and all the chiefs were assembled and agreed upon the destruction of the world by flood. We-sah- kah hearing of this fasted again for ten days. At the end of the tenth day his voice reached the Great Spirit; his prayer was heard and answered and mankind, the beasts and birds, etcetera, were preserved. Then the waters began to overflow the plains and We-sah-kah fled before them with his family, etcetera, until he reached a high mountain. But the water soon overtook them and he built a great raft upon which he put all kinds of creatures and then let it loose, so it floated upon the surface of the great waters. After a long time We-sah-kah began to be sorry and fasted ten days. At the end of the tenth day he dreamed he saw the dry land. Awaking out of sleep he sent down the tortoise, but he returned without any clay; he then sent down the musk- rat, and he brought up clay between his claws, out of which We-sah-kah formed the dry land. Then mankind and all the creatures which had been preserved were spread abroad upon the face of it. They now lived in peace and happiness because there were no Ai-yam-woy or any spirits of destruction to trouble them having all been exterminated by the flood.[12]

…all the chiefs were assembled and agreed upon the destruction of the world by flood. We-sah- kah hearing of this fasted again for ten days. At the end of the tenth day his voice reached the Great Spirit; his prayer was heard and answered and mankind, the beasts and birds, etcetera, were preserved. … he built a great raft upon which he put all kinds of creatures and then let it loose, so it floated upon the surface of the great waters.

132 Ohio Tradition

OHIO TRADITION

Charles Beatty (c. 1715–1772) was a Presbyterian preacher who served in the frontier west of the Alleghany Mountains, ministering to both colonists and Indians. In Ohio during the fall of 1766, he met with an old Indian man who had converted to Christianity. This man at an early age learned from his uncle the ancient traditions of his people. Among these were a tradition of a great flood, and of the confusion of languages that occurred during the construction of a very high edifice:

> The same person likewise told me, that once the water overflowed all the land, and drowned all the people then living, except a few, who made a great Canoe, (which is a kind of boat, made of a large tree, hollowed out, and commonly used by them) and were saved in it.
>
> Another tradition he heard, was, that a long time ago, the people went to build a high place to reach up a great way; and that, while they were building it, they lost their language, and could not understand one another; that, while one, perhaps, called for a stick, another brought him a stone, etcetera. And that, from that time, they (the Indians) began to speak different languages.[13]

Kee-shes-wa, A Fox Chief

12. Cutting Marsh, "Expedition to the Sacs and Foxes," *Collections of the State Historical Society of Wisconsin*, vol. 15 (Madison: Democrat Printing Co., 1900), p. 130–132.
13. Charles Beatty, *Journal of a Two Months Tour: With A View Of Promoting Religion Among The Frontier Inhabitants of Pennsylvania, and of Introducing Christianity Among the Indians to The Westward of the Alegh-Geny Mountains* (London: William Davenhill, 1768), p. 90.

The Alleghany Mountains

The Fighting Prowess of the First Nations People

The frontier preacher Charles Beatty, who lived through the French and Indian War, described the fighting skill of the First Nations tribes:

> No people in the world, perhaps, have a higher sense of liberty than the Indians, and, consequently, are more jealous of it, many of them preferring death to either captivity or slavery. They have a great disposition for war, and are far from being destitute of courage, however they may be looked upon by some to be dastardly, because their manner of fighting in the woods, and maxims of war are so different from ours, and indeed most other nations; yet, whoever truly considers their situation and circumstances, must own their art of war is best calculated for them. Britain now, as well as America, knows, by experience, that they are far from being contemptible enemies, when one hundred of them have courage enough to attack, and, perhaps, are a match for a thousand British troops in the wilderness, unacquainted with their manner of fighting.[14]

14. Ibid., p. 88–89.

133 **Wisconsin**

WINNEBAGO

Little is known about the Winnebago tribe's tradition of the Deluge, except that it existed. There is a passing reference to it in the 1854 report from a U.S. Indian Agent who interviewed chiefs of the tribe:

> Taw-nee-nuk-kaw [one of the oldest chiefs of the tribe] said that his father had told him the story of the Deluge, which had been handed down by their forefathers; but said he did not believe it was true, because he could not believe the Great Spirit would destroy the people and animals on the earth, after taking the trouble to create them. The tradition of the Deluge is believed by a majority of the tribe. Naw-hu-hu-kaw, one of the chiefs, in speaking of the Deluge, gave it as his opinion that it was produced, in part, by a heavy rain, but principally by a strong wind blowing the waters out of the great lakes, and overflowing the land.[15]

Hoo-Wan-Ne-Ka,
A Winnebago Chief.

Other Texts (See Appendix A on page 241)

134 **Osage (Missouri)**

135 **Missouri Tradition**

15. Jonathan E. Fletcher, "Origin and History of the Winnebagoes," in, *Schoolcraft, Information Respecting the History, Condition and Prospects of the Indian Tribes of the United States*, Part IV (Philadelphia: Lippincott, Grambo & Co., 1854), p. 231.

Adirondack Mountains by John Henry Dolph

NORTHEAST UNITED STATES

Now we come to the northeastern United States. We have, in general, less information on these tribes, due to the warfare that took place and the early destruction of their way of life. Nevertheless, a tribe of the White Mountains area of New Hampshire told John Josselyn, in 1663, how a man and his wife in ancient times foresaw the coming Flood. According to these natives, the pair fled to the White Mountains for refuge, taking only a rabbit. Later he set loose the rabbit, and when it no longer returned to him, he knew the Flood had receded. The Passamaquoddy and Penobscot tribes of Maine and New Brunswick have traditions in which their chief deity sent a flood to destroy a rebellious race of giants. The Lenape or Delaware tribe of New Jersey and eastern Pennsylvania told David Zeisberger and the early Moravians how the earth had been submerged under the water. A small number, including two or three women, survived on the back of a giant turtle. These sent a loon, which flew far away and returned with some earth in its bill.

Tribes of the Region

136. Lenape (Pennsylvania, New Jersey, Delaware, and New York)
137. New York Tradition
138. Seneca (New York)
139. Oneida (New York)
140. White Mountains Tradition (New Hampshire)
141. Penobscot and Passamaquoddy (Maine and New Brunswick)

An old man of an Iroquois tribe, around the year 1856, related a tradition about the Flood which destroyed all life — including the great, reptile-like animals which used to inhabit the world — except for the people who foresaw the Flood. These, being warned by the Great Spirit, fled with their chosen animals to the highest peak of the Adirondack Mountains, which was the only place not submerged.

These Indians remembered not only the fact of the Flood, but also the date! The old man told how his people had commemorated the 4,000-year anniversary of their salvation from the Flood, not many generations ago, giving thanks to the Great Spirit on the slopes of that great Adirondack mountain. This matches the biblical chronology very well — 4,000 years from the biblical Flood date of approximately 2,348 B.C. places us at approximately A.D. 1,653. Each of the Iroquois tribes have their tradition of the Flood, some of which have changed significantly over time.

LENAPE

136 Pennsylvania, New Jersey, Delaware, and New York

The Lenape (also known as Delaware) were a powerful tribe which occupied Delaware, New Jersey, eastern Pennsylvania, and parts of New York and Long Island.

The Moravian missionary David Zeisberger labored among the Delaware beginning in 1749. The Flood story they told him is characteristic of the Algonquian-language tribes. The memory of Noah sending the birds to look for land is still apparent. See Appendix C for more analysis of this parallel theme.

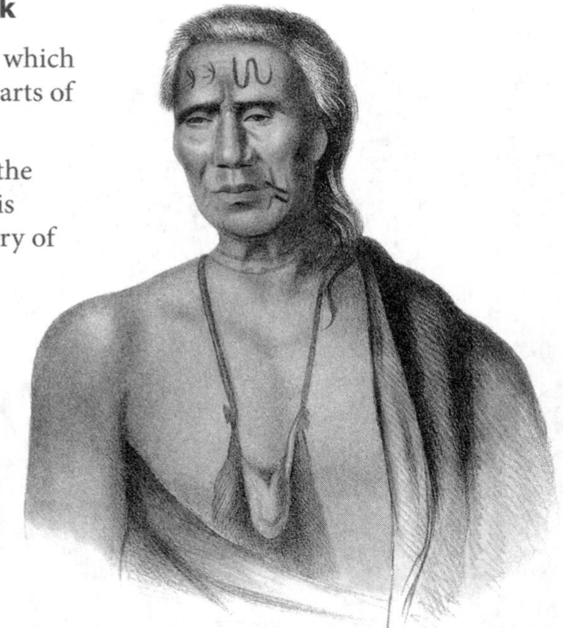
Lapowinsa, Chief of the Lenape

> The earth, he was told, having been submerged, several human beings, among them two or three women, saved themselves on the back of a turtle, who had reached so great an age that his shell bore moss. These requested a loon (bird), who happened to cross their path, to look for land. He complied, diving to the depths of the waters; but found none. At last he flew far away, and returned with a small quantity of earth in his bill. Guided by him, the turtle swam to the place, where a little spot of dry land was seen, on which the survivors settled and repeopled the world. Hence the illustrious position of the Turtle clan among the Indians.[1]

NEW YORK TRADITION

137 New York Tradition

The following is one of the more remarkable Flood traditions from North America. But first, it is fitting to describe the unique story that led to its discovery.

In 1856, a farmer named James Hennessy from Clinton County, Pennsylvania, discovered antlers of moose or caribou while removing tree stumps in a field on the edge of Tamarack Swamp, which is now part of Sproul State Park.

The folklorist Henry Shoemaker learned of this find. He observed that while the earliest settlers had never seen these animals in Pennsylvania, fossilized antlers had been found in many places, including caves at Riegelsville and Stroudsburg. This indicated that moose or caribou must have inhabited Pennsylvania in ancient times. But the antlers found in 1856 were not fossilized, and appeared to be more recent.

Shoemaker then mentioned this finding to an old Indian man from Nichols Run, who was in McElhattan selling medicinal herbs. Shoemaker recorded the man's response. Note the stunning similarities to the Genesis account:

The Reflection of Tamarack Trees on the Swamp

1. Edmund de Schweinitz, *The Life and Times of David Zeisberger* (Philadelphia: J.B. Lippincott and Co., 1870), p. 218–219.

> He smiled and said [he] recalled a story of how moose and caribou were imported into the Tamarack Swamp by a powerful Indian Chieftain, named Kowatgochee, or Wild Cat. He was the ruler of the redmen in the upper valley of the Otzinachson, being known far and wide for his historical knowledge, fine character and powers as an orator.
>
> He was often asked to be the guest of honor at Indian ceremonials and anniversaries in distant parts of the country, and not infrequently accepted and he delivered interesting addresses on the history and destiny of his race. Of king rank, he was not compelled to secure a wife upon reaching his majority, but postponed this happy event, from year to year, saying he was too busy preserving the glorious traditions of his forefathers to think of such a thing.
>
> There was a tradition among many of the tribes of New York State that the "big water" or Atlantic Ocean once overflowed its banks causing a tremendous flood. The Indian people had received advance tidings on the subject from Gitchie Manito, the Great Spirit, which enabled them to save themselves and their chosen animals and birds by ascending to the summit of Tahawus, now Mt. Marcy, the highest peak in the Adirondack Mountains, the only point not submerged. All their human enemies, races of gigantic white and yellow men who were constantly at war with them and the huge, serpentine sea and land animals, bat-winged and griffin-clawed, which preyed on them, were drowned.[2]

There was a tradition among many of the tribes of New York State that the "big water" or Atlantic Ocean once overflowed its banks causing a tremendous flood.

Mount Marcy in New York

Notice the seeming reference to dinosaurs in the previous text. What the tribal man told Shoemaker next is also very significant:

> On what would be to modern reckoners, the four thousandth anniversary of their deliverance from the great overflow, the Indians from far and wide gathered on the slopes of the big mountain to hold appropriate exercises of thanksgiving and observance, Kawatgochee was selected to deliver the historic oration.[3]

Who were the tribes that gathered on the slopes of Mount Marcy to commemorate the 4,000-year anniversary of the Flood? No doubt the Mohawk, since this mountain was in their territory. Their Iroquoian allies would have been there also: the Oneida, Seneca, Cayuga, Onandaga, and Tuscarora. Other neighboring tribes might have been there, including the Iroquoian-language Huron and Laurentians, and possibly the Abenaki, Mohicans, Delaware, Erie, and others.

This great gathering probably occurred around the year 1653, according to the biblical chronology (4,000 years after the Flood, which is dated at approximately 2,348 B.C.).

On what would be to modern reckoners, the four thousandth anniversary of their deliverance from the great overflow, the Indians from far and wide gathered on the slopes of the big mountain to hold appropriate exercises of thanksgiving and observance…

2. Henry Wharton Shoemaker, "History of Tamarack Swamp: Another Page from Indian Antiquity," *Reading Times*, January 6, 1912.
3. Ibid.

138 SENECA

New York

In the autumn of 1896, J.N.B. Hewitt met with four elderly men of the Seneca tribe and recorded several of their legends. Among these was an interesting Flood story, which began like this:

> There is a story that in ancient times there occurred a great calamity, which was caused by a rain that lasted three months. The result of this long rain was that the waters rose high and soon flooded the whole extent of the dry land. Only one man was saved. He climbed a tree to save himself from the waters.
>
> The waters rose high in every place except on one tract of land on which stood a village of about six families, from which all the game had disappeared; so the people of these families had nothing to eat.[4]

...the waters rose high and soon flooded the whole extent of the dry land. Only one man was saved. He climbed a tree to save himself from the waters.

As the families were beginning to starve — reduced to eating tree bark — a mysterious woman approached from over the waters. "No one knew whence she came, for they were surrounded by water, and there was no land in site."[5]

The mysterious woman, who was described as "beyond measure attractive in person, in manner, and in her words and actions," said that she was sent by her mother to save the people from starvation, and to marry the man whom she approached. He then married her, and she began to work miracles of food provision for the families. We read later that "The waters of the great flood had then gone down, and the earth had become new. She gave him food for his people; also, for seeding . . . It is from these seeds that were propagated all the food plants which the human race had in ancient times."[6]

Seneca Chief

139 ONEIDA

New York

James Dean (1748–1823) spent much of his adolescent years with the Oneida and became fluent in their language. He became a missionary to the tribe, and later was an American agent to the Oneida during the Revolutionary War, in which he helped to keep the Oneida neutral.

In the creation story that they told him, there is an account of the Flood. Sky Woman's daughter died while giving birth to twin boys, who represented good and evil, and struggled against each other. The younger and benevolent one was named Tanlong Hyauwangoon, and the older, malevolent one was named Thanwiskalaw. The benevolent young man lost his arrow, and swam to the bottom of the sea, where he found an old man living in a cottage. This man turned out to be his father. His father told him he must kill his evil, older brother in order that the world could be re-peopled. Tanlong Hyauwangoon followed the old man's guidance and, finding the weakness of his older brother, finally succeeded in killing him. However, this roused the fury of the Grandmother (formerly the Sky Woman), who sent forth a flood. "For many days successively she caused the rain to descend in torrents from the clouds until the whole surface of the earth and even the highest mountains were covered. The inhabitants fled to their canoes and escaped impending destruction." She then sent a deluge of snow, but they took to their snowshoes and escaped. Finally, she decided to inflict the human race with all the evils that we now see. But the benevolent god Taulong Hyauwaugoon shows kindness to the world, and provides all the good things that we enjoy.[7]

For many days successively she caused the rain to descend in torrents from the clouds until the whole surface of the earth and even the highest mountains were covered. The inhabitants fled to their canoes and escaped impending destruction.

4. John Napoleon Brinton Hewitt and Jeremiah Curtin, "Seneca Fiction, Legends, and Myths," *32nd Annual Report of the Bureau of American Ethnology* (Washington: GPO, 1918), p. 636.
5. Ibid.
6. Ibid., p. 637–641.
7. Wonderly, *Oneida Iroquois Folklore, Myth, and History* (Syracuse: Syracuse University Press, 2004), p. 65–68.

140 WHITE MOUNTAINS TRADITION

New Hampshire

John Josselyn was an early English traveler who journeyed twice to New England. The first time, in 1638, was only eight years after Boston had been settled. It was only a village at that time. By his second voyage in 1663 it had become a thriving seaport.

Josselyn traveled around the New England area and wrote about its natural environment, its indigenous peoples and its animals. In his 1674 work, *An Account of Two Voyages to New England*, he recorded a native Flood tradition in connection with the White Mountains. He does not say which tribe is the source of this tradition, but based on their territory it was likely the Abenaki or the Pennacook:

> Their Theologie is not much, but questionless they acknowledge a God and a Devil, and some small light they have of the Souls immortality: for ask them whither they go when they dye, they will tell you pointing with their finger to Heaven beyond the White Mountains, and so hint at Noah's Floud [Flood], as may be conceived by a story they have received from Father to Son, time out of mind, that a great while agon their Countrey was drowned, and all the People and other Creatures in it, only one Powaw [man] and his Webb [wife] foreseeing the Floud, fled to the White Mountains carrying a hare along with them and so escaped; after a while the Powaw sent the Hare away, who not returning emboldned thereby they descended, and lived many years after, and had many Children, from whom the Countrie was filled again with Indians. Some of them tell another story of the Beaver, saying that he was their Father.[8] [archaic spelling preserved]

...only one Powaw [man] and his Webb [wife] foreseeing the Floud [Flood}, fled to the White Mountains carrying a hare along with them and so escaped...

The White Mountains of New Hampshire

8. John Josselyn, *An Account of Two Voyages to New England Made During the Years 1638, 1663* (Boston: William Veazie, 1865), p. 105.

The Indian Mother

The following testimony comes from the ecclesiastical records of the Puritans in New England in the 17th century:

> Pammehanuit, an Indian of prime quality, on Martha's Vineyard [island], and his wife, having buried their five first children successively, every one of them within ten days of their birth, notwithstanding all their use of Powaws [Indian priests] and medicines, to preserve them. They had a sixth child, a son, born about the year 1638, which was a few years before the English first settled on that Vineyard. The mother was greatly perplexed with fear that she should lose this child, like the former: and utterly despairing of any help form such means as had been formerly tried with so little success, as soon as she was able (which among the Indians is quickly and within less than ten days) with a sorrowful heart, she took up her child, and went out into the field, that she might there weep out her sorrows. While she was here musing on the insufficiency of all human help, she felt it powerfully suggested unto her mind, that there is one Almighty God who is to be prayed unto: that this God hath created all the things that we see, and that the God who had given being to herself, and all other people, and given her child unto her, was easily able to continue the life of her child.
>
> Hereupon this poor blind pagan resolved, that she would seek unto this God for that mercy, and she did accordingly. The issue was, that her child lived; and her faith (such as it was) in Him, who thus answered her prayer, was wonderfully strengthened. The consideration whereof caused her to dedicate this child unto the service of that God, who had preserved his life, and educate him as far as might be, to become the servant of God.
>
> Not long after this, the English came to settle on Martha's Vineyard; and the Indians, who had been present at some of the English devotions, reported, that they assembled frequently together, and that the man who spoke among them often looked upwards. This woman, from this report, presently concluded, that their assemblies were for prayers, and that their prayers were unto that very God, whom she had addressed for the life of her child. She was confirmed in this, when the Gospel was not long after preached by Mr. Mayhew to the Indians there, which Gospel she readily, and cheerfully, and heartily embraced. And in the confession that she made publicly at her admission into the church, she gave a relation of the preparation for the knowledge of Christ, wherewith God in this wonderful way had favoured her.
>
> But that which adds to this wonder, is, that this very child has proved an eminent preacher of Christ unto the other Indians. He is living at this time (1696) a very religious Christian, and a laborious minister, and one, who not only is pastor to an Indian church on Martha's Vineyard, consisting of some scores of regenerate souls, but also has taken pains to carry the Gospel unto other Indians on the main land with a notable effect thereof. His name is Japhet.[9]
>
> The author went on to describe some of the deeds of Japhet, and wonderful answers to prayer that were seen among him and the Christian Indians. He adds: "Our Christian Indians are distinguished by the name of Praying Indians: and when they have become Christian, they have been favoured by Heaven, with notable successes of their praying."[10]

9. Cotton Mather, *The Ecclesiastical History of New England* (London: Thomas Parkhurst, 1702), Book 6, p. 63.
10. Ibid., p. 63–65.

141 Maine and New Brunswick

The Penobscot and Passamaquoddy tribes of Maine and New Brunswick had Flood legends associated with their god, Glooskap. The first version comes from Charles Godfrey Leland, who interviewed an old woman of the Passamaquoddy tribe sometime prior to 1884. This story told how the creator, Glooskap, planned to send a great flood on some irreverent Indians:

When the great Flood was coming Glooskap told them about it. They said they did not care.

> Long ago the Rattlesnakes were very saucy Indians. They were very saucy. They had too much face. They could not be put down by much, and they got up for very little.
>
> When the great Flood was coming Glooskap told them about it. They said they did not care. He told them the water would come over their heads. They said that would be very wet. He told them to be good and quiet, and pray. Then those Indians hurrahed. He said, "A great Flood is coming." Then they gave three cheers for the great Flood. He said, "The Flood will come and drown you all." Then these Indians hurrahed again, and got their rattles, made of turtle-shells, in the old fashion, fastened together, filled with pebbles, and rattled them and had a grand dance. . . . Yes, they had a great dance. The rain began to fall, but they danced. The thunder roared, and they shook their rattles and yelled at it. Then Glooskap was angry. He did not drown them in the Flood, however, but he changed them into rattlesnakes. Nowadays, when they see a man coming, they lift up their heads and move them about. That's the way snakes dance. And they shake their rattles in their tails just as Indians shake their rattles when they dance.[11]

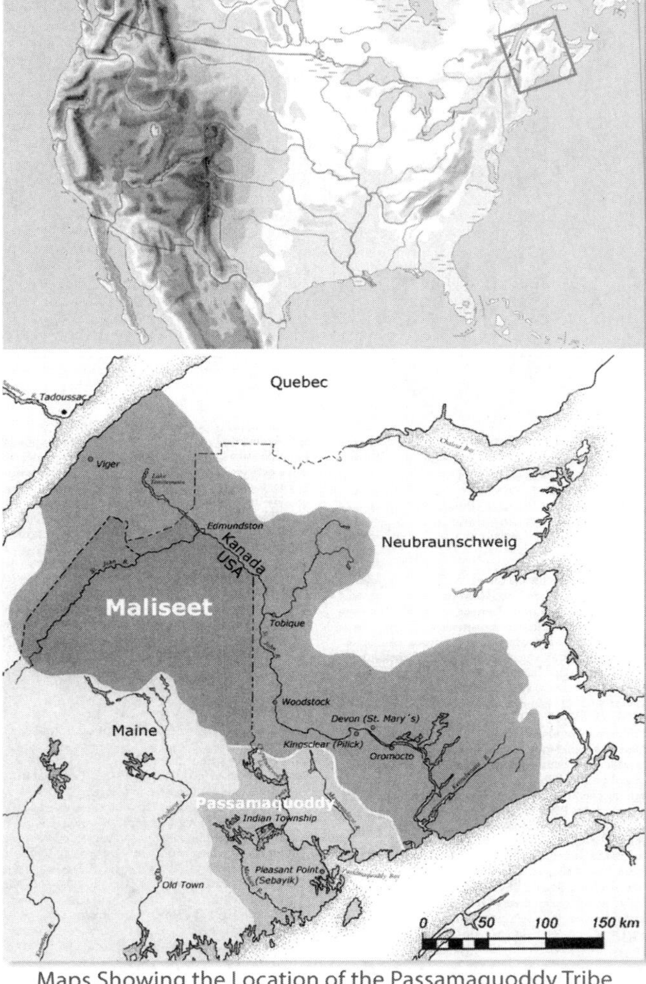

Maps Showing the Location of the Passamaquoddy Tribe

The neighboring Penobscot tribe told Leland another tradition, which referred to both the Flood and an ancient race of giants.

> There was a father who had three sons and a daughter: they were m'teoulin, or mighty magicians; they were giants; they ate men, women, and children; they did everything that was wicked and horrible; and the world grew tired of them and of all their abominations. . . . And they (the giant magicians) tried to smoke with him (Glooskap), and the wigwam was closed; they hoped to smother him with smoke, but he sat and puffed away as if he had been on a mountain-top, till they could bear it no longer. And one said, "This is idle; let us go and play at ball." The place where they were to play was on the sandy plain of Samgadihawk, or Savo, on the bend of the river. And the game begun, but Glooskap found that the ball with which they played was a hideous skull; it was alive and snapped at his heels, and had he been as other men and it had bitten him, it would have taken his foot off. Then Glooskap laughed, and said, "So this is the game you play. Good, but let us all play with our own balls." So he

. . . they were giants; they ate men, women, and children; they did everything that was wicked and horrible; and the world grew tired of them and of all their abominations . . .

11. Charles Godfrey Leland, *The Algonquin Legends of New England* (London: Sampson Low, Marston, Searle & Riverton, 1884), p. 110–111.

stepped up to a tree on the edge of the river-bed and broke off the end of a bough, and it turned into a skull ten times more terrible than the other. And the magicians ran before it as it chased them as a lynx chases rabbits; they were entirely beaten. Then Glooskap stamped on the sand, and the waters rose and came rushing fearfully from the mountains adown the river-bed; the whole land rang with their roar. Now Glooskap sang a magic song, which changes all beings, and the three brothers and their father became the chinahmess, a fish which is as long and as large as a man, and they went headlong down on the flood, to the deep sea, to dwell there forever.[12]

Then Glooskap stamped on the sand, and the waters rose and came rushing fearfully from the mountains adown the river-bed; the whole land rang with their roar.

12. Ibid., p. 122–126.

Choctaws at the Mississipi River

SOUTHEAST UNITED STATES

Moving toward the Southeast, we find the Cherokee, who told Henry Schoolcraft in 1846 that "the water once prevailed over the land, until every person was drowned but a single family." The man had been forewarned that "he must make a boat, and put in it all he wished to save." The Chitimacha of Louisiana say the floating vessel was a giant earthen pot. They call the pigeon "ground-watcher" because it saw the ground come out when the Flood subsided. They replace Noah's raven with a woodpecker. The Natchez, Tunica, Atakapa, Yuchi, and other tribes of the Southeast have their Flood histories. The Catawba, a tribe of modern-day North Carolina, say that the dove was sent and came back, first with a leaf, and later with corn.

"Seven or eight people had survived the Flood in a great canoe," said the Powhatan to the early colonists in the 1600s. The Chickasaw hold that two of all kinds of animals were saved on a giant raft, along with one family. The Choctaw of Mississippi and Alabama have very well-preserved traditions of the Flood and the Tower of Babel, differing mainly in that they say Babel occurred before the Flood. The Caddo of Texas, and many other tribes of the region, used to meet on a special day every year, upon the hill where they believed their ancestors found refuge from the Flood. Here they would offer sacrifices to God for not destroying all of mankind. The Coushatta, Alabama, and Tuskegee all have their own versions of how the Flood happened, as well as the Apalachee of Florida, who say that two people were saved on a high mountain, together with many animals. An elder of the Creek tribe told that two doves were sent, and returned with a blade of grass as a sign that the Flood was subsiding.

Regional Tribes

142. Cherokee (Kentucky through Georgia)
143. Natchez (Louisiana)
144. Chitimacha (Louisiana)
145. Tunica (Louisiana and Mississippi)
146. Atakapa (Louisiana)
147. Catawba (North Carolina)
148. Powhatan Tribes (Virginia)
149. Chickasaw (Tennessee, Alabama, and Mississippi)
150. Choctaw (Mississippi and Alabama)
151. Caddo (Texas to Arkansas)
152. Alabama (Alabama)
153. Coushatta (Tennessee, Georgia, and Alabama)
154. Tuskegee (Alabama)
155. Creek (Tennessee, Georgia, and Alabama)
156. Apalachee (Florida)
157. Santee (South Carolina)

142 CHEROKEE

Kentucky through Georgia

The Cherokee occupied the southern Appalachians from North Carolina and Kentucky to Georgia and Alabama. In 1846, a Cherokee chief named Stand Watie recited his tribe's ancient tradition to Henry Schoolcraft, which he described thus:

Stand Watie

> It is affirmed by Cherokee tradition, said my informant, that the water once prevailed over the land, until every person was drowned but a single family. The coming of this calamity was revealed by a dog to his master. This dog was very pertinacious in visiting the banks of a river, for several days, where he stood gazing at the water, and howling piteously. Being sharply spoken to, by his master, and ordered home, he revealed to him the coming evil. He concluded his prediction by saying, that the escape of his master and family from drowning, depended upon their throwing him into the water; that to escape drowning himself, he must make a boat, and put in it all he wished to save; that it would then rain hard, a long time, and a great overflowing of the land would take place. The dog then told his master to look for a sign of the truth of what he had said, to the back of his neck. On turning round, and doing so, the dog's neck was raw and bare, the bone and flesh appearing. By obeying this prediction, one man and his family were saved, and from these rescued persons, the earth, they believe, was again peopled.[1]

It is affirmed by Cherokee tradition, … that the water once prevailed over the land, until every person was drowned but a single family.

Cherokee Prophecy of Jesus

Lynn Lossiah, a Cherokee author and artist, told a story which is called the "oldest Cherokee story ever told." It tells about when a great star appeared in the eastern sky, the Cherokee gathered near modern day Tallulah Falls (in northern Georgia) and how angels brought the message to the Cherokee that the greatest Holy Man the world had ever seen was born. According to the Cherokee, these angels brought stories from across the great waters about miracles this great Holy Man performed.

> "But one day the sky grew dark, the earth shook, and the spirit beings came across the great waters crying because this great Holy Man had been killed in a cruel and unusual way. Their tears hit the stones and the stones turned into crosses that can still be found to this day."

When Chief RiverWind shared this story with a Lakota man named PipeCarrier, he nodded and said, "We know the Holy Man that story was about. There are many stories like that I have heard among other plains tribes."[2]

1. Henry Schoolcraft, *Notes on the Iroquois* (Albany, NY: Erastus H. Pease & Co., 1847), p. 358–359.
2. RiverWind, *That's What the Old Ones Say*, p. 125–126.

143 NATCHEZ

Louisiana

In his *History of Louisiana*, the historian Du Pratz (1695–1775) wrote of the Flood memory that the Natchez people told him:

> At the beginning of Spring in 1725 my friend, the Chief of the Temple Guardians, came to see me with an urgency and anxiousness that were not ordinary for him. But I pretended not to perceive this, so as to have the time to know from him if his nation believed as the others did on the subject of the Deluge. I asked him if they had any knowledge of the deluge. He replied that the ancient word taught all the red men that almost all men were destroyed by waters, except a very small number who had saved themselves on a very high mountain; that he knew nothing more regarding this subject except that these few people had repeopled the earth.[3]

Natchez Hut Reproduction

From a manuscript written in the early 1800s by a Natchez men, we learn that their Flood tradition is very similar to that of the Cherokees: Namely, the coming Flood was announced to the ancients by a little dog, which "bade him who could fly to the mountains for safety and escape death, so they fled. Only a few of them reached the mountains, however, most being overtaken and overwhelmed by the waving torrent of water." Among the few survivors was an "old man of sorrow," who mourned for all who perished, and instructed the other survivors how they should live to avoid the paths of destruction. "The earth was overwhelmed by the billows of water and no one survived that did not attain the summit of the mountains. From these was the earth repeopled.[4]

When the great deluge came the people baked a great earthen pot, in which two persons saved themselves, being borne up upon the surface of the waters.

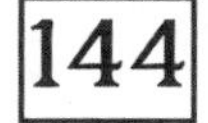

144 CHITIMACHA

Louisiana

Around 1910, a member of the Chitimacha tribe recounted this tradition to John Swanton:

> When the great deluge came the people baked a great earthen pot, in which two persons saved themselves, being borne up upon the surface of the waters. With them went two rattlesnakes. So the rattlesnake was thought to be the friend of man, and it is maintained that in ancient times each house was protected by one of these serpents, which entered whenever its owner went away and retired when he came back. While the flood prevailed the redheaded woodpecker hooked his claws into the sky and hung there. The water rose so high that his tail was partly submerged and sediment deposited upon it by the disturbed waters marked it off sharply from the rest of the body as it is today. After the sea had subsided considerably this bird was sent to find land, but after a long search he came back empty-handed. Then the dove was sent and returned with a single grain of sand. This was placed upon the surface of the sea and made to stretch out in order to form the dry land. Therefore the dove is called Ne-he'tcmon, "Ground-watcher," because it saw the ground come out when the great flood subsided.[5]

Chitimacha Mother and Daughter

3. Antoine-Simon Le Page Du Pratz, *L'Histoire de la Louisiane*, vol. 3 (Paris: 1758), p. 27.
4. John R. Swanton, "Early History of the Creek Indians and their Neighbors," *Bureau of American Ethnology Bulletin*, No. 73 (Washington: GPO, 1922), p. 316.
5. John R. Swanton, "Indian Tribes of the Lower Mississippi Valley," *Bureau of American Ethnology Bulletin*, No. 43 (Washington: GPO, 1911), p. 357–358.

145 TUNICA

Louisiana and Mississippi

The Tunica people lived in the Mississippi valley area of northern Louisiana and adjacent Mississippi. John Swanton described what this tribe said touching on the Flood:

> The flood legend of the Tunica has been almost forgotten, but it must have been similar to that of the Chitimacha, because the episode of the red-headed woodpecker is recognized as having formed a part.[6]

Migration to America

The historian Du Pratz met an old man of the Yazoo tribe (a sub-group of the Tunica), who shared a tradition of how they reached their current location in the Mississippi Valley. He told Du Pratz that the direction from which they came is "between the north and the sun-setting," and then it proceeds west, and then it is cut by the Great Water from north to south.[7]

146 ATAKAPA

Louisiana

The Atakapa tribe inhabited southwestern Louisiana. The name "Atakapa" is a Choctaw word which means "man-eaters."[8] Their belief regarding the Flood was made known in a letter written by a French military officer, dated April 23, 1802:

> The Atacapas pretend that they are come out of the sea, that a prophet or man inspired by God laid down the rules of conduct to their first ancestors, which consists in not doing any evil. They believe in an author of all things: that those who do well go above, and that those who do evil descend under the earth into the shades. They speak of a deluge which swallowed up men, animals, and the land, and it was only those who resided along a high land or mountain (that of San Antonio, if we may judge) who escaped this calamity.[9]

They speak of a deluge which swallowed up men, animals, and the land, and it was only those who resided along a high land or mountain who escaped this calamity.

Creek Creation Story

According to the creation story of the Creek or Muskogee people, in the beginning the world was covered with water except for a hill called Nunne Chaha, which had emerged from the waves. The god Esaugetuh Emisee, whose name meant "Master of Breath," created the first men out of clay on the hill. Then he directed the water off of the earth, for the newly created human race to inhabit.[10]

6. John R. Swanton, "Mythology of the Indians of Louisiana and the Texas Coast," *Journal of American Folklore*, vol. 20, no. 79 (Huffton Mifflin, 1907), p. 287.
7. Du Pratz, *The History of Louisiana*, p. 285–289.
8. Swanton, "Indian Tribes of the Lower Mississippi Valley," p. 360.
9. Ibid., p. 355–356, 363.
10. Lewis Spence, *The Myths of the North American Indians* (London: George G. Harrap, 1916), p. 108.

147 CATAWBA

North Carolina

At the Catawba tribe's reservation in Rock Hill, South Carolina, an 85-year-old woman related this tradition of the Flood to Frank Speck in 1922:

> A long time ago it rained so much that the river rose and the big earth was completely under the water and the people were washed away. A few climbed up trees on an island and remained there a long time. The dove left and went far away. The first time the dove came back it brought a leaf back and the next time brought back corn. It brought back corn in its mouth. Now the people knew that there was dry land to go to. This is true it is said.[11]

Blue Ridge Mountains in North Carolina

148 POWHATAN TRIBES

Virginia

In 1959, Stanley Pargellis brought to light an unpublished manuscript from the 1600s, with information on the Powhatan tribes. This early manuscript, stored in the Ayer Collection of the Newberry Library in Chicago, was written in the 1680s by an English clergyman. Although the manuscript is anonymous, Pargellis' analysis points to a Reverend John Clayton (1656–1725) as the likely author.

A long time ago it rained so much that the river rose and the big earth was completely under the water and the people were washed away.

Among other things, this 17th century manuscript recorded a tradition of the Deluge held among the native peoples of Virginia:

> They have a tradition of the floud [flood], that all the world was once drowned, except a few that were saved, to wit, about seven or eight in a great canoro [canoe].[12]

And in another place we read:

> They have but 7 great men in a nation, and no more besides the king, because (according to their tradition) there were but seven saved in the great deluge.[13]

A second document also bears witness to a memory of the Flood from the tribes of Virginia. William Byrd II, who is considered the founder of the city of Richmond, wrote the following in a letter to a John Woodward on August 14, 1697:

> According to your desire I have here sent you the Indian account of the manner how shells and other marine bodies came to be reposited in the bowels of the earth, and at great distance from their original habitation. And indeed, if your quarrelsome adversaries did but know it, they might with equal probability assert that you pillaged some part of your Book from the Indians as well as from the Ancients.

Powhatan Indian Village Home

11. Frank G. Speck, "Catawba Texts," *Columbia University Contributions to Anthropology*, vol. 24 (New York: Columbia University Press, 1934), p. 23.
12. Stanley Pargellis, "An Account of the Indians of Virginia," *William and Mary Quarterly*, vol. 16, no. 2 (Williamsburg, VA: Omohundro Institute of American History and Culture, 1959), p. 236.
13. Ibid., p. 235. Parentheses are original.

Their notions concerning that matter are not very disagreeable, as appears by the following instance. An Indian priest came one day to an Englishman's house, that happened at that time to be sinking of a well, and amongst other things he threw up several shells which seemed to be the Spolia [spoils] of some fish, and asked the Indian how it came about that they should straggle so far from their proper element, and be lodged so deep in the Earth? "I admire," says the Indian, "that you should be an English man and not know that. I'll tell you presently how it came to pass." And so taking a pail, and having put into it a little dirt, he filled it up with water.

…there happened a terrible Deluge that drowned all the world except an old man and his wife.

"Now you must know a multitude of years ago," says he, "there happened a terrible Deluge that drowned all the world except an old man and his wife." And then with a stick stirring the dirt and water together, thus says he "by the means of some violent convulsion was the earth and the water jumbled together, and when that ceased the earth presently subsided and all shells and other heavy bodies sunk down along with it, and each took its place according to its gravity. And these shells which you dug up, have lain where you found them out of harm's way, ever since."

They say that the world was once destroyed by water; that the water covered all the earth; that some made rafts to save themselves…

This remarkable story I had from a minister who was told it by the man himself that was digging the well, so that there's a great deal of reason to believe 'tis true. And so much I can say upon my own knowledge that many of them have a tradition of a Deluge.[14]

149 CHICKASAW

Tennessee, Alabama, and Mississippi

In the Chickasaw tribe's oral history, recorded by Henry Schoolcraft sometime in the 1820s or 30s, there is a reference to the Flood:

> They say that the world was once destroyed by water; that the water covered all the earth; that some made rafts to save themselves; but something like large white beavers would cut the strings off the raft and drown them. They say that one family was saved, and two of all kinds of animals.[15]

A Choctaw Woman

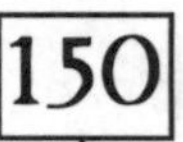

150 CHOCTAW

Mississippi and Alabama

The Choctaw nation lived in what is now Mississippi and Alabama. The explorer and painter George Catlin (1796–1872) heard their Flood tradition during his visit to Fort Gibson:

> Our people have always had a tradition of the Deluge, which happened in this way: There was total darkness for a great time over the whole of the earth; the

14. William Byrd II, *Letter from William Byrd, Lincoln's Inn, London, to Dr. John Woodward, 1697 August 14.* Manuscript X.C.50, Folger Shakespeare Library, Washington, DC. Retrieved from: https://emmo.folger.edu/view/Xc50/regularized.
15. Henry R. Schoolcraft, *Historical and Statistical Information Respecting the History, Conditions and Prospects of the Indians Tribes of the United States*, Part 1 (Philadelphia: Lippencott, Grambo & Co., 1851), p. 310.

> Choctaw doctors or mystery-men looked out for daylight for a long time, until at last they despaired of ever seeing it, and the whole nation were very unhappy. At last a light was discovered in the North, and there was great rejoicing, until it was found to be great mountains of water rolling on, which destroyed them all, except a few families who had expected it and built a great raft, on which they were saved.[16]

Choktaw Stickball Player

Horatio Cushman recorded the same story, but in greater detail, in his *History of the Choctaw, Chickasaw and Natchez Indians*. It is worth noting that the story told of a raven approaching the man while he was floating and seeking dry land. He tried to persuade the bird to help him find land, but it refused. Next, a dove flew toward him and did him the kindness of leading the way toward land. "After many days the waters passed away; and in the course of time Puchi Yushabah [the dove] became a beautiful woman, whom the prophet soon after married, and by them the world was again repeopled."[17]

> ...great mountains of water rolling on, which destroyed them all, except a few families who had expected it and built a great raft, on which they were saved.

The Choctaw also had a tradition remarkably similar to the Tower of Babel, though they thought this event happened before the Flood and not after.

> They continued to wonder and talk among themselves and at last determined to endeavor to reach the sky. So they brought many rocks and began building a mound that was to have touched the heavens. That night, however, the wind blew strong from above and the rocks fell from the mound. The second morning they again began work on the mound, but as the men slept that night the rocks were again scattered by the winds. Once more, on the third morning, the builders set to their task. But once more, as the men lay near the mound that night, wrapped in slumber, the winds came with so great force that the rocks were hurled on them. The men were not killed, but when daylight came and they made their way from beneath the rocks and began to speak to one another, all were astounded as well as alarmed — they spoke various languages and could not understand one another. Some continued thenceforth to speak the original tongue, the language of the Choctaw, and from these sprung the Choctaw tribe. The others, who could not understand this language, began to fight among themselves. Finally they separated. The Choctaw remained the original people; the others scattered, some going north, some east, and others west, and formed various tribes. This explains why there are so many tribes throughout the country at the present time.[18]

Peter Pitchlynn, the Choctaw Principal Chief

16. George Catlin, *The North American Indians*, vol. 2, p. 145.
17. Horatio Bardwell Cushman, *History of the Choctaw, Chickasaw and Natchez Indians* (Greenville, TX: Headlight Printing, 1899), p. 283–284.
18. David I. Bushnell Jr., "The Choctaw of Bayou Lacomb, St. Tammany Parish, Louisiana," *Bureau of American Ethnology Bulletin*, No. 48 (Washington: GPO, 1909), p. 30.

Map of the 1806 Red River Expedition

151 CADDO

Texas to Arkansas

The Caddo tribe inhabited an area stretching across parts of Texas, Oklahoma, Arkansas, and Louisiana. Thomas Freeman and Peter Custis, of the 1806 Red River Expedition, met the Caddo and recorded a Flood tradition from them:

> From the similarity of one of their traditions to the Mosaical account of the deluge it deserves notice. They say that long since, a civil war broke out amongst them, which so displeased Enicco, the Supreme Being, that he caused a great flood, which destroyed all but one family; consisting of four persons, the father, mother, and children. This family was saved by flying to a knoll at the upper end of the prairie, which was the only spot uncovered by the water. In this knoll was a cave, where the male and female of all the kinds of animals were preserved. After the flood had continued one moon, they set a bird, called by them O-Wah, at liberty, which returned in a short time with a straw.
>
> The family then set out on a raft in search of the place, from whence this straw was brought, and pursuing a west course for two leagues, they came to land. All the Mexican and Louisiana Indians are supposed to be the offspring of this family.[19]

In this knoll was a cave, where the male and female of all the kinds of animals were preserved. After the flood had continued one moon, they set a bird, called by them O-Wah, at liberty, which returned in a short time with a straw.

Notice what is said next. Here, like among the Iroquois tribes and others, we have an annual commemoration of the Flood by many tribes assembled together:

> It is said that some other of the nations have a similar tradition; and that many of the tribes used to meet, on a certain day in every year at the knoll upon which this family was supposed to have been preserved; and there offer sacrifices to the Supreme Being, for not destroying the whole race.[20]

A Caddo Woman

19. Thomas Freeman and Peter Custis, *An Account of the Red River, in Louisiana, Drawn Up From the Returns of Messrs. Freeman and Custis to the War Office of the United States, Who Explored the Same, In the Year 1806* (Washington: 1806), p. 28–29.
20. Ibid., p. 29.

John Sibley, a U.S. Indian Agent in Louisiana, recorded a similar account in 1801:

> By the side of this lake the Caddoques have lived from time immemorial. About one mile from the lake is the hill on which, they say, the Great Spirit placed one Caddo family, who were saved when, by a general deluge, all the world were drowned; from which family all the Indians have originated. To this little, natural eminence, all the Indian tribes, as well as the Caddoques, for a great distance, pay a devout and sacred homage.[21]

Sho-e-tat (Little Boy)
Louisiana Caddo leader

And in another place Sibley wrote:

> They have a traditionary tale, which not only the Caddoes, but half a dozen other smaller nations believe in, who claim the honor of being descendants of the same family: they say, when all the world was drowning by a flood, that inundated the whole country, the Great Spirit placed on an eminence, near this lake, one family of Caddoques, who alone were saved; from that family all the Indians originated.[22]

Another Flood tradition attributed to the Caddo can be found in the Appendix on page 256.

152 Alabama

ALABAMA

Between 1908 and 1914, John Swanton interviewed members of the Alabama tribe and recorded many of their traditions, including this one pertaining to the Flood:

> When this world was almost lost in the waters a frog predicted it. One man seized the frog and threw it into the fire, but another said, "Don't do that." He took it, cared for it, and healed it, and it said to him, "The land will almost disappear in the waters. Make a raft and put a thick layer of grass underneath so that the beavers cannot cut holes through the wood." So he cut long dry sticks of wood and tied them together and put a quantity of grass underneath.
>
> When other people saw this they said, "Why did you make it?" He answered, "A flood is going to cover the whole country." "Nothing like that can happen," they said. Some persons stayed about laughing at him. After some time he finished his raft and the flood came. When it arrived fish came with it and some of the people killed them and said, "We are having a good time." The man and his family got upon the raft along with the frog.

He answered, "A flood is going to cover the whole country." "Nothing like that can happen," they said. Some persons stayed about laughing at him. After some time he finished his raft and the flood came.

Alabama River

21. Eds. Walter Lowrie and Matthew St. Clair Clarke, *American State Papers, Class II: Indian Affairs*, vol. 1, (Washington: Gales and Seaton, 1832), p. 729. For another Caddo version, see George A. Dorsey, Traditions of the Caddo (Washington: Carnegie, 1905), p. 18–19.
22. John Sibley, "Lewis and Clarke's Expedition, Communicated to Congress, February 10, 1806," *American State Papers. Class 2, Indian Affairs* (Washington: Gates and Seaton, 1832), p. 721.

> When the water rose the raft went up also, and some of the people said, "We want to get on," but no one got on. When it rose higher all of the other people were drowned. Then those on the raft floated up with it. The flying things flew up to the sky and took hold of it, with their tails half in the water. The ends of their tails got wet. The red-headed woodpecker was flat against the sky and said, "My tail is half in the water."[23]

A second version can be found on page 257 in the Appendix.

Selocta, a Muskogee Chief

COUSHATTA

153 Tennessee, Georgia, and Alabama

The Coushatta tribe had a Flood story which was very similar to that of the Alabama tribe, except they replace the frog with a lizard. The lizard predicted the flood, saying, "I am not going to die before the flood comes." The story then continued on in similar fashion to the Alabama version.[24]

When the water rose the raft went up also, and some of the people said, "We want to get on," but no one got on. When it rose higher all of the other people were drowned.

TUSKEGEE

154 Alabama

It is not clear whether the Tuskegee — the native inhabitants of a village called Taskigi in Alabama — were Muskogee, Cherokee, or a separate tribe. The anthropologist Frank Speck recorded a tradition from them in 1904 or 1905 which, like many earth diver stories, retains a mixed memory of the Creation and Flood events:

> The time was, in the beginning, when the earth was overflowed with water. There was no earth, no beast of the earth, no human being. They held council, to know which would be best, to have some land or to have all water. When the council had met, some said, "Let us have land, so that we can get food," because they would starve to death. But others said, "Let us have all water," because they wanted it that way.

> So they appointed Eagle as chief. He was told to decide one way or another. Then he decided. He decided for land. So they looked around for someone whom they could send out to get land. The first one to propose himself was Dove, who thought that he could do it. Accordingly they sent him. He was given four days in which to perform his task. Now, when Dove came back on the fourth day, he said that he could find no land. They concluded to try another plan. Then they obtained the services of Crawfish. He went down through the water into the ground beneath, and he too was gone four days. On the fourth morning he arose and appeared on the surface of the waters. In his claws they saw that he held some dirt. He had at last secured the land. They took the earth from his claws and made a ball of it. When this was completed they handed it over to the chief, Eagle, who took it and went out from their presence with it. When

The time was, in the beginning, when the earth was overflowed with water. There was no earth, no beast of the earth, no human being.

23. John R. Swanton, "Myths and Tales of the Southeastern Indians," *Bureau of American Ethnology Bulletin*, Vol. 88 (Washington: GPO, 1919), p. 121.
24. Ibid.

he came back to the council, he told them that there was land, an island. So all the beasts went in the direction pointed out, and found that there was land there as Eagle had said. But what they found was very small. They lived there until the water receded from this earth. Then the land all joined into one.[25]

They [the Creeks] believe that before the Creation there existed a great body of water.

155 Tennessee, Georgia, and Alabama

CREEK

The Creeks or Muskogee were a loose confederation of peoples spread across Tennessee, Alabama, and Georgia, united for strength against outside threats. We have a fragment of a Flood history from them. This version, like that of the Tuskegee, seems to blur the lines between the Noahic memory of the Flood and Creation. It was recorded sometime prior to 1857 from a man named Sekopechi, one of the oldest Creek men:

> They [the Creeks] believe that before the Creation there existed a great body of water. Two pigeons were sent forth in search of land, and found excrements of the earthworm; but on going forth the second time, they procured a blade of grass, after which, the waters subsided, and the land appeared.[26]

Creek Chief Red Eagle

156 Florida

APALACHEE

The Apalachee tribe spoke a Muskogean language and occupied the panhandle region of Florida and southwestern Georgia. The French missionary Charles de Rochefort (1605–1683) wrote an early history of the Caribbean region, in which we find this concerning the Apalachees:

> The Indians of Apalachee count themselves the ancestors of those who populate the lands of New Spain, and the most ancient people of the world. They say that the sun, after not rising for an entire day, overturned the Lake Tami, in the province of Bemarin. The waters covered the earth, with the result that only two people were saved from the inundation, along with various animals. These climbed Mount Olaimy (located one league from Melilot, the court of the Apalachee chiefs), at the peak of which was located the Temple of the Sun. Later the survivors came down from the mountain and repopulated the earth.[27]

The waters covered the earth, with the result that only two people were saved from the inundation, along with various animals … Later the survivors came down from the mountain and repopulated the earth.

25. Frank Speck, "The Creek Indians of Taskigi Town," *Memoirs of the American Anthropological Association*, vol. 2 (Lancaster, PA: New Era Printing Co., 1907), p. 145–146.
26. Henry Rowe Schoolcraft, *Information Respecting the History Conditions and Prospects of the Indian Tribes of the United States*, Part I (Philadelphia: Lippincott, Grambo & Co., 1853), p. 266.
27. Charles de Rochefort, *Historia des Antilles*, Book 1, Chapter 8. Quoted in: Gregorio Garcia, *Origen de los Indios de el Nuevo Mundo, e Indias Occidentales* (Madrid: Francisco Martinez Abad, 1729), p. 330.

157 SANTEE

South Carolina

Not all of the Siouan-language tribes settled in the Great Plains and Midwest. The Santee lived further east, in South Carolina near Lake Marion, where today there is a town called Santee. An elderly Santee woman told this Flood tradition to a Lakota man named Lame Deer, probably sometime in the 1950s:

Lame Deer

> This story was told to me by a Santee grandmother. A long time ago, a really long time when the world was still freshly made, Unktehi the water monster fought the people and caused a great flood. Perhaps the Great Spirit, Wakan Tanka, was angry with us for some reason. Maybe he let Unktehi win out because he wanted to make a better kind of human being.
>
> Well, the waters got higher and higher. Finally everything was flooded except the hill next to the place where the sacred red pipestone quarry lies today. The people climbed up there to save themselves, but it was no use. The water swept over that hill. Waves tumbled the rocks and pinnacles, smashing them down on the people. Everyone was killed, and all the blood jelled, making one big pool. The blood turned to pipestone and created the pipestone quarry, the grave of those ancient ones. That's why the pipe, made of that red rock, is so sacred to us. Its red bowl is the flesh and blood of our ancestors, its stem is the backbone of those people long dead, the smoke rising from it is their breath. I tell you, that pipe, that chanunpa, comes alive when used in a ceremony; you can feel power flowing from it. Unktehi, the big water monster, was also turned to stone. Maybe Tunkashila, the Grandfather Spirit, punished her for making the flood. Her bones are in the Badlands now. Her back forms a long, high ridge, and you can see her vertebrae sticking out in a great row of red and yellow rocks. I have seen them. It scared me when I was on that ridge, for I felt Unktehi. She was moving beneath me, wanting to topple me. Well, when all the people were killed so many generations ago, one girl survived, a beautiful girl. It happened this way: When the water swept over the hill where they tried to seek refuge, a big spotted eagle, Wanblee Galeshka, swept down and let her grab hold of his feet. With her hanging on, he flew to the top of a tall tree which stood on the highest stone pinnacle in the Black Hills. That was the eagle's home. It became the only spot not covered with water. If the people had gotten up there, they would have survived, but it was a needle-like rock as smooth and steep as the skyscrapers you got now in the big cities. My grandfather told me that maybe the rock was not in the Black Hills; maybe it was Devils Tower, as white men call it—that place in Wyoming. Both places are sacred.[28]

The people climbed up there to save themselves, but it was no use. The water swept over that hill.

28. Erdoes and Ortiz, *American Indian Myths and Legends*, p. 93–94.

Toltec Sculptures at Tula, Mexico

MEXICO

The knowledge of the Flood pervades Central and South America, just as it does in North America. The great civilizations of Mexico all knew about the Flood. The Toltecs had a tradition and historical paintings, which told of an ancient flood, from which only a few escaped inside a "toplipetlacali," an enclosed vessel. They had a Tower of Babel account also and spoke of the dispersion of all peoples to different parts of the world — 104 years after this dispersion, they arrived in Mexico where they settled. The Aztecs too have ancient paintings which depict the Flood, showing one couple safely floating inside a hollow tree as the world was destroyed by water. Old paintings representing the Flood are found also among the Mixtecs, Tlascaltecs, Zapotecs, and Michoancáns. The latter tribe told that a priest and his wife took refuge in an enclosed wooden vessel with many animals and seeds. As the Flood was waning, he sent two birds to search for a sign of land. One bird went about eating from floating corpses, but the other bird returned with a branch in its beak. The Mayans had a tradition of the Flood, as did the Tarahumara, Core, Tlapanec, and many other tribes of Mexico.

Tribes of the Region

158. Toltec (Hidalgo State)
159. Cholula (Puebla)
160. Aztecs (Central Mexico)
161. Mayans (Yucatan Peninsula)
162. Purepecha (Michoacán State)
163. Zapotec (Oaxaca)
164. Tarahumara (Chihuahua State)
165. Huichol (Sierra Madre Occidental Mountains)
166. Cora (Nayarit State)
167. Tlapanec (Guerrero)
168. Mixtecs (Oaxaca, Puebla, and Guerrero)
169. Totonac (Veracruz and Puebla)
170. Tepehua (Durango)
171. Tlaxcalan (Tlaxcala)
172. Chiapaneco (Chiapas)
173. Paipai (Baja California)
174. Huastec (Northeastern Mexico)
175. Trique (Oaxaca)
176. Copala Trique (Oaxaca)
177. Tzeltal (Chiapas)
178. Chol (Chiapas)
179. Chontal (Oaxaca)
180. Hauve (Oaxaca)
181. Tzotzil (Chiapas)
182. Opata (Sonora)
183. Tlahuica (Mexico State)
184. Lacandon (Chiapas)
185. Guarijio (Chihuahua and Sonora)
186. Yaqui (Northwest Mexico)
187. Kiliwa (Baja California)

158 TOLTEC

Hidalgo State

The Toltecs, predecessors of the Aztecs, were a people of central Mexico who are known for their impressive structures and civilization. These were centered at their capital city of Tula, less than 50 miles north of modern-day Mexico City.

Our main source for the Toltecs' tradition of the Flood is Fernando de Alva Ixtlilxochitl (1568 or 1580 to 1648), a mestizo historian and a direct descendant of previous rulers of the city-states of Texcoco and Tenochtitlan. He was highly informed on the oral traditions of his people through his relationships with the tribal elders and authorities, and he knew how to interpret the ancient hieroglyphs. The historian Clavigero said that he "was so cautious in writing, he made his accounts conform exactly with the historical paintings, which he inherited from his illustrious ancestors."[1]

In his *Relación Histórica de la Nación Tulteca* (produced between 1600 and 1608), Ixtlilxochitl wrote thus concerning the Toltecs' history, and their account of the Flood and the Tower of Babel:

> They say that the world was brought up in the year of Ce Tecpatl, and this period until the flood they call Atonatiuh, meaning the age of the water sun, because the world was destroyed by the flood. We find in the stories of the Toltecs that this first age and world, as they call it, lasted 1716 years; that the men were destroyed with great showers and lightning from the sky and the entire world, and the highest mountains were submerged beneath the water for "caxtolmoletltli," that is, fifteen cubits deep. And to this they also add other fables, and of how the few who escaped from this destruction within a "toptlipetlacali," which almost means an enclosed ark, multiplied again.[2]

> And afterwards the men multiplied and made a very high zacuali, and it was this, which means the highest tower, at which they sought to find shelter when the Second World would be destroyed. In time, the languages were changed and, not understanding each other, the people went to different parts of the world. And the Toltecs, who were seven companions with their women who understood the language, came to these parts, having first passed through great lands and seas, living in the caves and enduring great difficulties before coming to this land, that they found good and fertile for their habitation; And they say that they lived 104 years in different parts of the world before arriving in Huehue Tlapalan, which was in (the age of) Ce Tecpatl, that which was 520 years after the flood had passed, which are five ages; And 1715 years after the flood they were destroyed by a great hurricane which wiped out the trees, rocks, houses and people and great buildings, although many men and women escaped, mainly those who escaped in caves and parts where the great hurricane could not reach. . . . They called this the second age or world, or as they call it, Ecalchitonatiuh, which means, the age of the sun of air. . . . They also have it in their history, that one day the sun stood still in its place for a day without moving.[3]

We find in the stories of the Toltecs that this first age and world, as they call it, lasted 1716 years; that the men were destroyed with great showers and lightning from the sky and the entire world, and the highest mountains were submerged beneath the water for "caxtolmoletltli," that is, fifteen cubits deep.

And afterwards the men multiplied and made a very high zacuali, and it was this, which means the highest tower, at which they sought to find shelter when the Second World would be destroyed. In time, the languages were changed and, not understanding each other, the people went to different parts of the world.

1. Francesco Saverio Clavigero, *The History of Mexico*, trans. Charles Cullen (London: J. Johnson, 1807), p. xviii.
2. Fernando de Alva Ixtlilxochitl, P*rimera Relación de la Historia de los Tultecas, in Antiquities of Mexico*, ed. Lord Kingsborough, vol. ix (London: Henry G. Bohn, 1848), p. 321.
3. Ibid., p. 321–322.

Ixtlilxochitl also wrote about the Flood in another passage, mentioning also an antediluvian race of giants:

Toltec Temple Ruins in Tula, Mexico

> The Toltecs were second settlers of this land after the destruction of the giants, especially in this corner which today is called New Spain. These Toltecs had knowledge of the creation of the world, and how it was destroyed by the deluge, and many other things which they had in painting and history. These also touched on the end of the world, and how it is to be destroyed by fire. "Toltec" means crafty and wise man, because the people of this nation were great craftsmen, as is seen today in many parts of New Spain in the ruins of their structures, especially in this town of San Juan, Teotihuacan, Tula and Cholula, and many other towns and cities. These Toltecs came from toward the West with seven elders or captains: the first Zaca, the second Chalcatzin, the third Ecatzin, the fourth Cohuazon, the fifth Tzihuacohuatl, the sixth Tlapalmetzotzin, and the seventh Metzoltzin. They brought with them many people—men as well as women. They were banished from their country and nation, and thus they brought corn, cotton, and the other seeds and legumes which exist in this land. And they were great workers of gold and precious stones and many other arts, as shown in their histories and paintings.[4]

These Toltecs had knowledge of the creation of the world, and how it was destroyed by the deluge, and many other things which they had in painting and history.

159 CHOLULA

Puebla

Cholula is an ancient city in Mexico, well-known for its pyramid by the same name. It is located a little over 50 miles east of Tenochtitlan, which is modern-day Mexico City. This pyramid's origins perhaps predate even the ancient Toltecs. The historian Alexander de Humboldt (1769–1859) described this pyramid as "the greatest, most ancient, and most celebrated of the whole of the pyramidal monuments of Anahuac [Mexico]."[5]

Cholula Pyramid

Of interest to our study, Humboldt recorded the following tradition held by the locals:

> Another very remarkable tradition still exists among the Indians of Cholula, according to which the great pyramid was not originally

4. Ixtlilxochitl, *Relación Sucinta En Forma de Memorial de las Historias de Nueva España, Relación 1, in Antiquities of Mexico*, vol. ix, p. 450.
5. Alexander de Humboldt, *Researches Concerning the Institutions & Monuments of the Ancient Inhabitants of America*, trans. Helen Maria Williams, vol. 1 (London: Longman, 1814), p. 87.

> destined to serve for the worship of Quetzalcoatl [the "green-feathered serpent"].[6]

Rather, as Humboldt writes, this pyramid was originally intended as a memorial of the high mountain, in which the ancient survivors were saved from the Flood:

> After my return to Europe, on examining at Rome the Mexican manuscript in the Vatican library, I found, that this same tradition was already recorded in a manuscript of Pedro de Los Rios, a Dominican monk, who, in 1566, copied on the very spot all the hieroglyphical paintings he could procure. "Before the great inundation, which took place four thousand eight hundred years after the creation of the World, the country of Anahuac was inhabited by giants (tzocuillixeque). All those who did not perish [in the great inundation] were transformed into fishes, save seven, who fled into caverns. When the waters subsided, one of these giants, Xelhua, surnamed the architect, went to Chololan, where, as a memorial of the mountain Tlaloc, which had served as an asylum to himself and his six brethren, he built an artificial hill in form of a pyramid. He ordered bricks to be made in the province of Tlamanalco, at the foot of the Sierra of Cocotl, and to convey them to Cholula he placed a file of men, who passed them from hand to hand. The gods beheld with wrath this edifice, the top of which was to reach the clouds. Irritated at the daring attempt of Xelhua, they hurled fire on the pyramid. Numbers of the workmen perished, the work was discontinued, and the monument was afterwards dedicated to Quetzalcoatl, the god of the air."[7]

When the waters subsided, one of these giants, Xelhua, surnamed the architect … built an artificial hill in form of a pyramid. … The gods beheld with wrath this edifice, the top of which was to reach the clouds. Irritated at the daring attempt of Xelhua, they hurled fire on the pyramid …

Humboldt notes the similarity with the Genesis account of the Flood and Tower of Babel. Then he adds further evidence:

> Rios, to prove the high antiquity of this fable of Xelhua, observes, that it was contained in a hymn, which the Cholulans sang at their festivals, dancing round the teocalli [pyramid], and that this hymn began with the words "Tulanian hululaez," which are words belonging to no dialect at present known in Mexico.[8]

160 AZTECS

Central Mexico

The Aztec, or Mexica, flood story was recorded in a text called the *Leyenda de los Soles*, or *Legend of the Suns*. The legend, found in a manuscript bearing the date May 22, 1558, represents the second part, following the *Anales de Cuauhtitlan*, of an 83-page codex known as the *Codex Chimalpopoca*. The document is written in the Nahuatl language of the Aztecs by an anonymous author who identifies himself as a fellow Aztec. This text was evidently written at the request of the Spanish to explain the Aztecs' creation story and beliefs, their history, and their traditions.

I am indebted to John Bierhorst for his translation of the *Legend of the Suns* from the Nahuatl into English, which he published in 1992. Bierhorst tells that the *Legend* is rooted in earlier material, which the document's author no doubt understood and used:

6. Ibid., p. 95.
7. Ibid., p. 95–96.
8. Ibid., p. 97.

> It is more than likely that the author of the Annals of Cuauhtitlan had access to pictographic sources in addition to oral accounts. . . . But in Legend of the Suns, the second of the two Nahuatl texts preserved in the Codex Chimalpopoca, the reliance on pictures is much more obvious. Here the author speaks to us as though we were looking over his shoulder, while he points to the painted pictures. "This sun was 4 Jaguar," he writes; "these people . . . were blown away"; "here's when . . ."; "this is when. . . ." In places the text reads like a sequence of captions, as though the unseen pictures could carry the burden of the tale. Yet the narrative relaxes into an easier style wherever the story implied by the paintings happens to be already on the author's lips. The overall effect is of a knowledgeable traditionalist making his way through a single, well-integrated work of mytho-history. Despite moments of awkwardness, Legend of the Suns is one of the finest — one of the purest sources of Aztec myth that has come down to the present time. Moreover, it is the only creation epic to have survived in the Nahuatl language.[9]

Titlacahuan gave a command to the one called Tata, and to his wife, who was called Nene. He said to them, "Put aside your cares. Hollow out a big cypress … get inside." And so they got inside. Then he sealed them in …

The portion touching on the Flood occurs near the beginning of the *Legend*. According to this text, we are now in the fifth age or "Sun." The great Flood occurred in the fourth sun:

They died by drowning. … All the mountains disappeared. And the water lay for fifty-two years. … The log has stopped moving. Then it opens.

> The sun is named 4 Water. And for fifty-two years there was water. These people lived in the fourth one, in the time of the sun 4 Water. And it was 676 years that they lived. And they died by drowning. They turned into fish. The skies came falling down. They were destroyed in only one day. And what they ate was 4 Flower.[10] That was their food. And their year was that of Ce-calli. And on the first day they were destroyed. All the mountains disappeared. And the water lay for fifty-two years. And when they were to be destroyed, then Titlacahuan gave a command to the one called Tata, and to his wife, who was called Nene. He said to them, "Put aside your cares. Hollow out a big cypress, and when it is Tozoztli [April] and the skies come falling down, get inside." And so they got inside. Then he sealed them in and said, "You must eat only one of these corn kernels. And your wife must eat only one." Well, when they had eaten it all up, they went aground.
>
> It can be heard that the water is drying. The log has stopped moving. Then it opens. They see a fish. Then they drill fire and cook fish for themselves. Then the gods Citlalinicue and Citlalatonac looked down and said, "Gods, who is doing the burning? Who is smoking the skies?" Then Titlacahuan, Tezcatlipoca, came down and scolded them. He said, "What are you doing, Tata? What are you people doing?" Then he cut off their heads and stuck them on their rumps, and that way they were turned into dogs.[11]

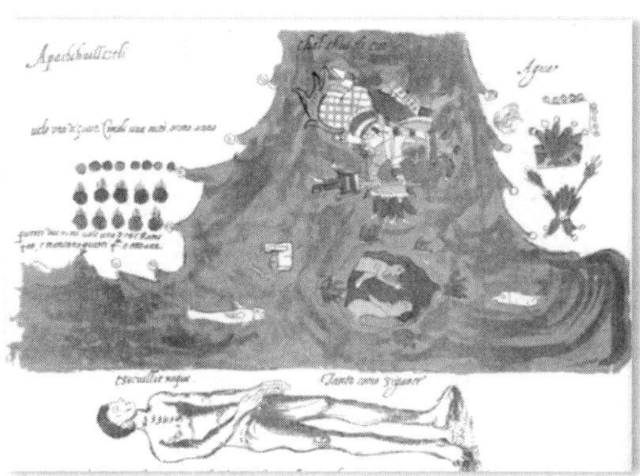

Aztec Painting from Codex Vaticanus 3738 Showing a Deluge and a Couple Saved Inside a Tree Trunk

9. John Bierhorst, *History and Mythology of the Aztecs: The Codex Chimalpopoca* (Tucson: University of Arizona Press, 1992), p. 7.
10. Ibid., p. 142. Bierhorst points out that these cryptic references such as "4 Flower" refer to calendric names. "Although the foods in our text remain unidentified, it may be conjectured that these early staples are wild seeds or primitive grains. . . ."
11. *Codex Chimalpopoca*, in Bierhort, *History and Mythology of the Aztecs*, p. 143–144.

The Aztec flood tradition is further confirmed by Codex Vaticanus 3738. This Codex consists of Aztec manuscript paintings, copied using transparency paper during the mid-1500s by a Dominican priest, Pedro de los Rios. Among these is a painting (right) which depicts water being poured over the earth, people drowning and turning into fish, and one couple safely housed inside a tree trunk.

Regarding this painting, the historian Alexander de Humboldt explained:

> A great inundation, which began the year "ce calli," the day "4 water" (nahui alt), destroyed mankind. . . . Men were transformed into fish, except one man and one woman, who saved themselves in the trunk of an ahahuete, or cupressus disticha [a type of cypress]. The drawing represents the goddess of water, called Matlalcueje, or Chalchiuhcueje, and considered as the companion of Tlaloc, descending towards the earth. Coxcox, the Noah of the Mexicans, and his wife Xochiquetzal, are seated in a trunk of a tree covered with leaves, and floating amidst the waters.[12]

The Flood is also depicted in the Aztec Stone of the Sun (right), an exquisite 15th-century rock sculpture which was found in the Aztec capital of Tenochtitlan (Mexico City). This monolith contains the cosmological beliefs of the Aztecs. Experts are in agreement that the four previous eras or "Suns" are depicted near the center of the disk, in four boxes. Going counter-clockwise from the top right, these are the Sun of Jaguar, Sun of Wind, Sun of Rain, and Sun of Water. The Sun of Water, or fourth age, ends with a destruction by water.

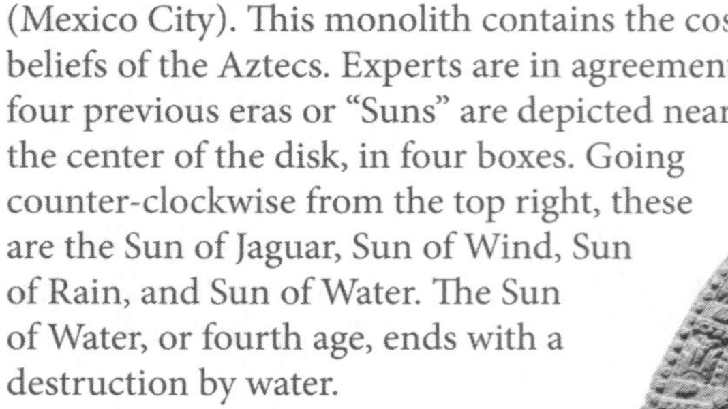

A great inundation, . . . destroyed mankind. . . . Men were transformed into fish, except one man and one woman, who saved themselves in the trunk . . .

12. Alexander de Humboldt, *Researches Concerning the Institutions & Monuments of the Ancient Inhabitants of America*, trans. Helen Maria Williams, vol. 2 (London: Longman, 1814), p. 23.

Various Mexican Paintings Attesting to the Deluge

The early scientist of the Americas, Alexander de Humboldt (1769–1859, right), summarized Mexican histories of the Flood:

> Of the different nations that inhabit Mexico, paintings representing the deluge of Coxcox are found among the Aztecks, the Miztecks, the Zapotecks, the Tlascaltecks, and the Mechoacanese. The Noah, Xisuthrus, or Menou of these nations, is called Coxcox, Teo-Cipactli, or Tezpi. He saved himself conjointly with his wife, Xochiquetzel, in a bark, or, according to other traditions, on a raft of "ahuahuete" (Cupressus disticha). The painting represents Coxcox in the midst of the water, lying in a bark. The mountain, the summit of which, crowned by a tree, rises above the waters, is the Peak of Colhuacan, the Ararat of the Mexicans. The horn, which is represented on the left, is the phonetic hieroglyphic of Colhuacan. At the foot of the mountain appear the heads of Coxcox and his wife. . . .
>
> The men born after the deluge were dumb: a dove, from the top of a tree, distributes among them tongues, represented under the form of small commas. We must not confound this dove with the bird which brings Coxcox tidings that the waters were dried up. The people of mechoacan preserved a tradition, according to which Coxcox, whom they called Tezpi, embarked in a spacious "acalli" with his wife, his children, several animals, and grain, the preservation of which was of importance to mankind. When the great spirit, Tezcatlipoca, ordered the waters to withdraw, Tezpi sent out from his bark a vulture, the "zopilote" (vultur aura). This bird, which feeds on dead flesh, did not return on account of the great number of carcasses, with which the earth, recently dried up, was strewed. Tezpi sent out other birds, one of which, the hummingbird alone, returned, holding in its beak a branch covered with leaves. Tezpi, seeing that fresh verdure began to cloth the soil, quitted his bark near the mountain of Colhuacan.[13]

MAYANS

161 **Yucatan Peninsula**

Diego de Landa was a Franciscan missionary who arrived at Yucatan in 1549 and became a bishop over the province in 1561. His unchecked zeal to wipe out idolatrous practices led him to commit atrocities and harsh persecutions against the natives. For this he faced trial in Spain in 1566 but was ultimately exonerated.

Though he ordered the destruction of thousands of Mayan books, Diego de Landa obtained valuable information on the ways and religion of the Mayan peoples of the Yucatan Peninsula, having mastered the language, and through his extensive involvement with the native peoples of Yucatan. In his landmark work, *Relacion de las Cosas de Yucatan* (1566), he also mentions a native Flood tradition:

> Among the multitude of gods worshipped by these people were four whom they called by the name Bacab. These were, they say, four

They also say that these Bacabs [or gods] escaped when the world was destroyed by the deluge.

13. Ibid., p. 64–65.

brothers placed by God when he created the world, at its four corners to sustain the heavens lest they fall. They also say that these Bacabs escaped when the world was destroyed by the deluge. To each of these they give other names, and they mark the four points of the world where God placed them holding up the sky.[14]

Pages from the Book of Chilam Balam of Ixil

There came a sudden rush of water … Then the sky fell, it fell down upon the earth, … brought about the destruction of the world

This is confirmed by the *Chilam Balam*, which is a collection of fragments from the historical writings of the Mayans. These manuscripts were collected and copied by Dr. Karl H. Berendt in the visits throughout Yucatan and Guatemala between 1855 and 1862 and later translated.

> Then they were buried in the sands in the sea. There came a sudden rush of water when the theft of the insignia of Oxlahuntiku occurred. Then the sky fell, it fell down upon the earth, when the four gods, the four Bacabs, were set up, who brought about the destruction of the world.[15]

The American anthropologist Alfred Tozzer conducted field work among the Mayan peoples of Yucatan and Chiapas states in Mexico between 1902 and 1905. He was told a legend of the Flood by the native peoples in eastern Yucatan:

> According to the information obtained from the Mayas in the vicinity of Valladolid, this world is now in the fourth period of its existence. In the first epoch there lived the Saiwamwinkoob, the Adjusters. These composed the primitive race of Yucatan. They were dwarfs and were the ones who built the ruins. This work was all done in darkness before there was any sun. As soon as the sun appeared, these people turned to stone. Their images are

Observatory El Caracol at Chichen Itza

14. Diego de Landa, *Relation des Choses de Yucatan, ed. Arthus Bertrand* (Paris: London, Trubner and Co., 1864), p. 206.
15. *The Book of Chilam Balam of Chumayel, trans. Ralph Roy L. Roys* (Washington: Carnegie, 1933), p. 99–100. See also *Los Libros de Chilam Balam de Chumayel*, trans. Domingo Dzul Poot and Juan Ramon Bastarrachea Manzano (Caracas: Fundacion Editorial, 2008), p. 50.

found today in many of the ruins. It was at this period that there was a road suspended in the sky, stretching from Tuloom and Coba to Chichen Itza and Uxmal. This pathway was called kusansum or sabke (white road). It was in the nature of a large rope (sum) supposed to be living (kusan) and in the middle flowed blood. It was by this rope that the food was sent to the ancient rulers who lived in the structures now in ruins. For some reason this rope was cut, the blood flowed out, and the rope vanished forever. This first epoch was separated from the second by a flood called Haiyoqokab (water over the earth).

Kabah, Maya Archaeological Site, Yucatan, Mexico

In the second period of the history of the earth there lived the "Tsolob," the Offenders. Again a flood destroyed the greater part of the world, after which the Masehualli, or Mayas of the present time, came into power. Still again there was a flood which gave way to the fourth period. In this last epoch, there is a mixture of all the previous peoples inhabiting Yucatan.[16]

162 PUREPECHA

Michoacán State

The Purepecha or Tarascan people lived in what is now the state of Michoacán, west of Mexico City. Information on their religion comes from the Spanish historian Antonio de Herrera's four-volume work, *Décadas*. Herrera published his magnum opus between 1601 and 1615, in which he chronicled a vast amount of manuscript material from the Spanish archives. Regarding the Flood tradition of the Tarascan people, he wrote:

> [The Michoacans believed] that there was a flood, and one Indian named Tezpi, who was a priest, entered, along with his wife, into a wood vessel like an ark. They took different animals and seeds, and thus they escaped the flood. As the water subsided, he sent a bird, which they call aura, and it did not return but went about eating from corpses. And he sent other birds, and these too remained outside. And he sent a small bird, highly esteemed for its colorful plumage, and this bird returned with a branch. [17]

HISTORIA GENE
RAL DE LOS HECHO
DE LOS CASTELLANOS
EN LAS ISLAS I TIERRA FI
RME DEL MAR OCEANO ES
RITA POR ANTONIO DE
HERRERA CORONISTA
MAYOR DE SV Md DE LAS
INDIAS Y SV CORONISTA
DE CASTILLA.
En quatro Decadas desde el Año de
1492 hasta el de 1531.
Decada primera
Al Rey Nro Señor.
EN MADRID EN LA
EMPLENTA REAL
1601.

Title Page of *Décadas*

16. Alfred M. Tozzer, *A Comparative Study of the Mayas and the Lacandones* (New York: MacMillan, 1907), p. 153–154.
17. Antonio de Herrera y Torsedillas, *Historia General de los Hechos de los Castellanos, Década Tercera*, Book 3 (Madrid: Royal Office of Nicolas Rodriguez, 1726), p. 94.

163 **Oaxaca**

ZAPOTEC

Monte Alban, the Capital of the Zapotec Empire, in the Oaxaca Valley

The Zapotecs have inhabited the Oaxaca Valley of southern Mexico since approximately 500 B.C., where they built a powerful empire. When the Spanish came in the 1500s, they told the colonizers their tradition of the Flood. For locating this source we refer to the Mexican historian Francisco del Paso y Troncoso (1842–1916), who tirelessly sifted through the Spanish archives and published many manuscripts from the 16th century. The manuscript cited below, dated May 15, 1580 was written by Nicolas Espindola, the mayor of the district of Chichicapa. From his interviews with older members of the village of Ocelotepeque, he recorded this Flood legend:

> There was once a great deluge. A number of persons were able to escape in a boat. They found themselves on top of a hill when the waters subsided. A great Zapotec chieftain of Ocelotepeque, Petela (Dog), was descended from the survivors of the deluge. And these people chose Petela as a child of one of those who there escaped, being the bravest and strongest. So he governed them for ten or twelve years until he died.[18]

There was once a great deluge. A number of persons were able to escape in a boat. They found themselves on top of a hill when the waters subsided.

The natives from the village of Coatlan, in the same district, also told a similar account to the first Spanish colonists. Herrara presents this account in Volume 3 of *Décadas* (1601):

> In the town of Coatlan, they had a chief, named Petela, which means dog, whom they say came from those who escaped the general Deluge.[19]

Julio de la Fuente (1905–1970) found another Flood tradition from the Zapotec people of the village of Yalalag:

> When the earth was dark and cold, the only inhabitants were the giants. God was angry with them because of their idolatry. A number of giants, feeling that the deluge was coming, carved great slabs of rock to make houses for themselves under the earth. Some escaped destruction in this way and are still to be found hidden in certain caverns under the ground. Other giants hid themselves in the forests and became monkeys.[20]

…the only inhabitants were the giants. God was angry with them because of their idolatry. A number of giants, feeling that the deluge was coming, carved great slabs of rock to make houses for themselves under the earth. Some escaped destruction in this way…

---

18. Nicolas Espindola, *Relacion del Pueblo de Ocelotepeque, in Papeles de Nueva Espana*, ed. Francisco del Paso y Troncoso, vol. IV (Madrid: Successors of Ribadeneyra, 1905), vol. IV, p. 139.
19. Antonio de Herrera, *Historia General de los Hechos de los Castellanos, Década Tercera*, Book 3, p. 101.
20. Julio de la Fuente, *Yalalag: Una Villa Zapoteca Serrana* (Mexico City: Museo Nacional de Antropologia, 1949), p. 237.

164 TARAHUMARA

Chihuahua State

The Tarahumara, or Raramuri are a tribe from northwestern Mexico who have long been admired for their long-distance running prowess. They are known to run for up to 200 miles at a time, and they have other games in which a wooden ball is kicked in a relay race over extremely long distances. There is no outrunning a Tarahumara.

The explorer Carl Lumholtz met the Tarahumara in 1890 and recorded their memory of the Flood:

> When the world became full of water, a little girl and a little boy climbed up on a mountain, called Lavachi (gourd), which is south of Panalachic, and when the waters subsided they came down again. They brought three grains of corn and three beans with them. The rocks were soft after the flood, and the footprints of the little boy and the little girl may still be seen. They planted the corn and went to sleep and had a dream that night; then they harvested and all the Tarahumares are descended from them.[21]

> The Tarahumares were fighting among themselves, and Tata Dios sent much rain, and all the people perished. After the flood he sent three men and three women to people the earth. They planted corn at once, bringing three kinds, the same varieties still found here — soft corn, hard corn, and yellow corn.[22]

Two Tarahumara Men

When the world became full of water, a little girl and a little boy climbed up on a mountain, … when the waters subsided they came down again. … The rocks were soft after the flood, and the footprints of the little boy and the little girl may still be seen.

165 HUICHOL

Sierra Madre Occidental Mountains

The Huichol live in the Sierra Madre Occidental mountains, including parts of Nayarit, Zacatecas, Durango, and Jalisco states. This isolated tribe was able to avoid being subdued by the Spanish conquerors until 1722. Even after that, Lumholtz indicates, they resisted the influence of the Franciscan missionaries.[23]

The Huichol told Lumholtz their tradition of a Flood during his visit in the 1890s. This tradition has parallels to many that we will see in southeast Asia, where a man working in a field finds his work undone, and then is warned by a stranger to prepare for the coming flood.

Sierra Madre Occidental Mountains

> A Huichol was felling trees to clear a field for planting. Every morning he found that the trees he had cut down on the previous day had grown up again. He worried over this and grew tired of working. On

21. Carl Lumholtz, *Unknown Mexico*, vol. 1 (New York: Charles Scribner's Sons, 1902), p. 298–299.
22. Ibid.
23. "The ancient beliefs, customs, and ceremonies still have a firm hold on the minds of the people, and the Huichols jealously guard their country against the encroachments of the whites. The impress the victors made was superficial, and today the natives are practically in the same state of barbarism as that which they enjoyed the day when Cortes first set foot on American soil." Lumholtz, *Unknown Mexico*, vol. 1, p. 23.

the fifth day he came to try once more, determined to find the cause of the disturbance. Soon there rose from the ground in the middle of the clearing an old woman with a staff in her hand. She was Great grandmother Nakawe, the goddess of earth, who causes vegetation to spring forth from the neither world. But the man did not know her. With her staff she pointed toward the south, north, west, and east, above and below; and all the trees with the young man had cut down immediately stood up again. Then he understood how it happened that his clearing was always covered with trees.

Annoyed, he exclaimed: "Is it you who are undoing my work all the time?" "Yes," she said, "because I want to talk to you." Then she told him that he was working in vain. "A great flood is coming," she said. "It is not more than five days off. There will come a wind, very bitter, and as sharp as chile, which will make you cough. Make a box from the salate (fig) tree, as long as your body, and fill it with a good cover. Take with you five grains of corn of each colour, and five beans of each colour; also take the fire and five squash stems to feed it, and take with you a black female dog."

Hidden Beach in the Marietas Islands

The man did as the woman told him. On the fifth day he had the box ready and placed in it the things she had told him to take. Then he entered, with the black female dog; and the old woman put the cover on, and caulked every crack with glue, asking the man to indicate wherever there was an opening. Then she seated herself on the top of the box with a macao perched on her shoulder. The box rode on the waters for one year toward the south, for another year toward the north, during the third year toward the west, and in the fourth year toward the east. In the fifth year it rose upward, and all the world was filled with water. The next year the flood began to subside, and the box settled on a mountain near Santa Catarina, where it may still be seen. The man took off the cover and saw that all the world was still covered with water. But the macaos and the parrots made valleys with their beaks, and as the waters began to run off the birds separated them into five seas. Then the land began to dry, and trees and grass sprang forth.[24]

On the fifth day he had the box ready and placed in it the things she had told him to take. Then he entered, with the black female dog; and the old woman put the cover on…

The story continues to tell that the dog turned into a woman, and they married and repopulated the world. The fact that this theme of 'work undone by a stranger who warns of the coming flood' recurs in southeast Asia and certain American tribes is an observation worthy of further study.

166 CORA

Nayarit State

The Cora Indians are an isolated people group from the mountainous terrain of the state of Nayarit in western Mexico. Konrad Preuss recorded this fragmentary Flood account from an elderly Cora man, who passed away in 1905:

God told the zopilote (vulture) to see if the earth was sufficiently dry to get out of the canoe. But he did not return because he ate the dead. Then God sought him and struck him, turning his white color into black, and letting only the tips of the wings be white, so as to know what color he had formerly possessed. Now he commanded the pigeon to see if the world was

Now he commanded the pigeon to see if the world was already good. Then the pigeon went and saw that the world was good.

24. Ibid., p. 191–193.

already good. Then the pigeon went and saw that the world was good. She reported that it was good, but that the rivers were very large. Then God asked all the animals to drink water until the rivers were empty, and all came to the mourning dove. She did not come. That's why she always goes to drink water at nightfall because she is ashamed to show herself, and by day she always cries.[25]

Sierra Madre del Sur Mountains

167 TLAPANEC

Guerrero

The Tlapanec people have inhabited the Sierra Madre del Sur mountains in the state of Guerrero in southern Mexico. They have a Flood legend which is similar to that of the Huichol people, in which a man is told to stop working and to prepare a floating vessel:

> A buzzard came to talk with a man that was working in the mountains and said to him: "Don't work anymore for now the world is going to come to an end."
>
> The buzzard then said to a tree: "Arise," and to a rock: "Arise." The tree arose but the rock did not. Then the buzzard said to the man: "Make yourself a box and tell nobody, not even your family, for they will cry and therefore it is better that you tell them nothing."
>
> When the man finished making the box the buzzard put the man inside and shut up the box with a dog and a chicken also inside. Soon the man saw through a crack in the box that it was raining and he also heard the animals that live in the water were bothering his box, desiring, as it seemed, to eat the man. He also saw that the world was full of water. Later he saw that the land was very swampy, so much so that it was not possible to walk. Then he drew his head into the box again. Later he left his box when he saw that the shrubs were growing and he went to work the ground.
>
> The chicken changed herself into a buzzard and flew over the land. Wherever the buzzard flew there sprang up behind him [sic] mountains and valleys.[26]

When the man finished making the box the buzzard put the man inside and shut up the box with a dog and a chicken also inside.

Like the Huichol version, they said that the dog turned into a woman and became the man's wife.

25. Konrad Theodor Preuss, *Die Nayarit-Expedition*, vol. I (Leipzig: B.G. Teubner, 1912), p. 201.
26. H.V. Lemley, "Three Tlapaneco Stories from Tlacoapa, Guerrero," *Tlalocan*, Vol. 3, No. 1 (Mexico: Universidad Nacional de Mexico, 1949), p. 76–78.

168 MIXTECS

Oaxaca, Puebla, and Guerrero

The Sierra Mixteca

The Mixtecs are a nation of south-central Mexico, who lived to the south of the Aztecs and west of the Zapotecs, Gregorio Garcia recorded their knowledge of the Flood in his 1607 work, *Origen de los Indios*, derived from the ancient writings and books of the Mixtecs:

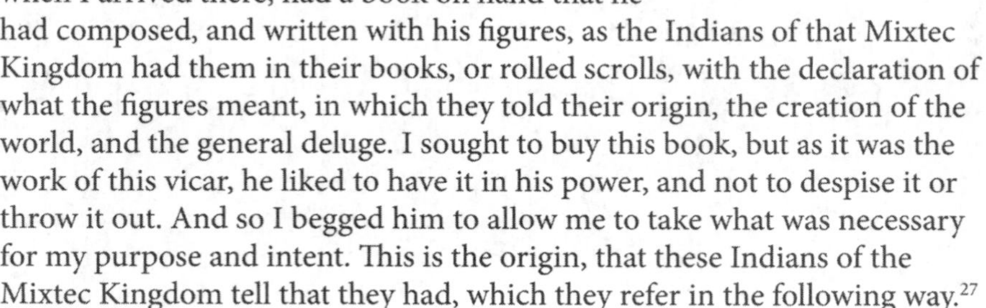

> One and a half leagues from the city of Guaxaca, bordering with the Mixteca, in an Indian town called Cuilapa, we have a famous convent of my [Dominican] Order, whose vicar, who was there when I arrived there, had a book on hand that he had composed, and written with his figures, as the Indians of that Mixtec Kingdom had them in their books, or rolled scrolls, with the declaration of what the figures meant, in which they told their origin, the creation of the world, and the general deluge. I sought to buy this book, but as it was the work of this vicar, he liked to have it in his power, and not to despise it or throw it out. And so I begged him to allow me to take what was necessary for my purpose and intent. This is the origin, that these Indians of the Mixtec Kingdom tell that they had, which they refer in the following way.[27]

> …the Indians of that Mixtec Kingdom had them in their books, or rolled scrolls, … in which they told their origin, the creation of the world, and the general deluge.

The Mixtecs' creation story began with the appearing of two gods — Puma Snake and Jaguar Snake — who become the father and mother of other gods, and take human form. Yet they were drowned in a great Flood which followed. After this, say the Indians, was a general flood, where many gods drowned. After the flood had passed, the creation of heaven began, and the earth began by the god, who in their language is called the Creator of all things. The human race was restored, and in that way the Mixtec Kingdom was populated.[28]

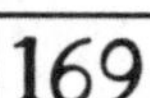

169 TOTONAC

Veracruz and Puebla

Totonacs Performing the "Voladores" Ritual

The Totonac tribe live along the Gulf Coast of Mexico to the east of Mexico City. Their Flood history was evidently very similar to that of the Huichol and Tlapanecs, based on the version Fernando Horcasitas recorded in 1953:

> When the deluge was over, no one was saved except a man and a female dog. Every day, when the man came home from work, he found that someone had prepared beans and tortillas for him. One day he hid himself and discovered that the dog took off her skin in a temazcal and then prepared food for him. He followed her and caught her. The dog said, "God wants it this way. Now we will be married and have children." They repopulated the world.[29]

27. Gregorio Garcia, *Origen de los Indios del Nuevo Mundo e Indias Occidentales* (Madrid: 1729), p. 327.
28. Ibid., p. 328–329.
29. Fernando Horcasitas, "An Analysis of the Deluge Myth in Mesoamerica," in *The Flood Myth*, ed. Alan Dundes (Berkeley: University of California Press, 1988), p. 206.

170 Durango

TEPEHUA

The Tepehua people live some 450 miles northwest of Mexico City in the state of Durango. The version Robert Gessain collected in 1953 went like this:

> After clearing his fields a man was surprised to find that the vegetation grew again overnight. He spied and found that a monkey was responsible for this harm. The monkey told him that God did not want him to work anymore, since a great flood was coming. Following the instructions of the monkey the man built a coffinlike craft and got into it. When the deluge began, the monkey sat on top of the coffin. When the waters subsided the man climbed out, picked up some fish he found on the ground, and built a small fire to cook them. But out of the sky appeared the Almighty, who, irritated with the man for having built the fire, turned him into a monkey.[30]

A Tepehua Family

171 Tlaxcala

TLAXCALAN

The Tlaxcalans or Tlaxcaltecs, lived east of the Aztecs and allied with the Spanish, led by Hernan Cortes, in their war against the Aztecs. Our primary source on the Tlaxcalans is Diego Camargo's work, *Historia de Tlaxcala*, which he wrote around 1580. Camargo was a mixed-race Spanish-Tlaxcala man who served as an interpreter to the Spanish. He noted that the Tlaxcalans, like many other tribes of Mexico, believed that two great cataclysms had occurred in the earth's past:

One of these destructions was by deluges and stormy waters, ... in those remote times there were giants, the bones of which have been found...

> One of these destructions was by deluges and stormy waters, and that the earth had been turned upside down. They also say that in those remote times there were giants, the bones of which have been found by the ravines as we have treated previously.[31]

The second cataclysm, according to the Tlaxcalans, may be the Tower of Babel event recorded in Scripture, for it describes the dispersal of peoples and a loss of the power of communication:

> Likewise, as a result, they say there was another end of the world, which was by winds and hurricanes which were so great that what was in them was ravaged, even the plants and trees of the very high mountains. And the winds battered the men of that time, and they were carried away by the wind until they disappeared from sight, and then they fell they were crushed to pieces. And some of these people who escaped were entangled in the mountains and hidden ridges, and were converted to monkeys and lost the use of reason and speech.[32]

Próspero Cahuantzi, a Colonel of Tlaxcalan Descent

30. Horcasitas, "An Analysis of the Deluge Myth in Mesoamerica," p. 198.
31. Diego Muñoz Camargo, *Historia de Tlaxcala*, ed. Alfredo Chavero (Mexico: 1892), p. 153–154.
32. Ibid.

172 Chiapas

CHIAPANECO

Francesco Clavijero

The Chiapanecos since ancient times have inhabited the southeastern part of Mexico in what is now the state of Chiapas. The Jesuit historian Francesco Clavijero (1731–1787) recorded an ancient tradition of the Chiapanecos in his *Historia Antigua de Mexico*. This tradition narrates their history and includes a reference to the Flood:

> The Chiapanecas, if we are to believe their traditions, were the first settlers of the New World. They said that Votan, grandson of that revered old man who made the big boat to save himself and his family from the flood, and one of those who undertook the work of the great building that was made to ascend to heaven, was by an express mandate of the Lord to populate that land. They also said that the first settlers had come from the north; and when they arrived at Xoconochco, they separated, some of them going to live in the country of Nicaragua, and the others remaining in that of Chiapan. This nation, as their historians say, was not governed by a king, but by two military chiefs, appointed by the priests. Thus they remained until the last Mexican kings submitted them to that crown. They make the same use of paintings as Mexicans, and had the same way of computing time; but they used different figures than those to represent the years, the months and the days.[33]

...Votan, grandson of that revered old man who made the big boat to save himself and his family from the flood, and one of those who undertook the work of the great building that was made to ascend to heaven...

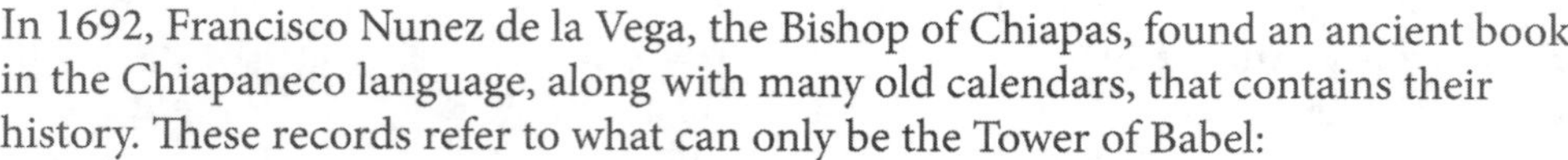

In 1692, Francisco Nunez de la Vega, the Bishop of Chiapas, found an ancient book in the Chiapaneco language, along with many old calendars, that contains their history. These records refer to what can only be the Tower of Babel:

> Votan is the third patriarch who is placed in the calendar, and in the historical book written in the Indian language, he named all the places and towns where he was. And even in the town of Teopisca there has been a generation called the Votanes. It also says he is the keeper of the musical instrument called Tepanaguaste, that he saw the great edifice [the Tower of Babel], which his grandfather built from the ground toward heaven, and that he is the first man whom God sent to divide and distribute this land of the Indies, and that in the land where he saw the great edifice is where God gave to each people their own language.[34]

There is also an ancient genealogy which lists 20 generations of their leaders. Votan is the third one named in this list, preceeded by Ygh and Mox.

> . . . in their calendars, corresponding to the twenty generations of leaders, they appear in the following order: Mox (also known as Ninus), Ygh, Votan, Ghanan, Abagh, Tox, Moxic, Lambat, Molo (in other places Mulu), Elab, Batz, Evob, Been, Hix, Tziquin, Chabin, Chic, Chinax, Cahogh, and Aghual.[35]

Could one of these names be positively identified with someone named in Genesis 10? We can only speculate. Perhaps their patriarch Votan is a grandson of Nimrod, who built the Tower at Babel. Alternatively, Votan may be Joktan (Genesis 10:25), the great-great grandson of Shem, Noah's firstborn son.

33. Francisco Javier Clavigero, *La Antigua Historia de Mexico y de su Conquista*, trans. Joaquin de Mora, vol. 1 (Xalapa, MX: Agustin Ruiz, 1868), p. 83.
34. Francisco Nunez de la Vega, *Constituciones Diocesanas del Obispado de Chiappa* (Rome: 1702), p. 9.
35. Ibid., p. 10.

173 PAIPAI

Baja California

The Paipai people of Baja California have a tradition very similar to the Tower of Babel. Mauricio Mixco collected this during his time among the Paipai between 1974 and 1975, from two men who were "experts" in the tribe's traditions.

> When they were in the house of God, the people would fill the house. So they were inside, and later they departed. When they were inside, all people understood each other. As they went out the door, their languages changed completely. They went out and migrated. So they came here to the northwest side. They came to a star there. They came closer, they saw. No one can cross the sea. There he stood (a shaman) singing. He stood, and when he had sung the sea was reduced. It looked like a stream. Then they all jumped, and crossed, and came here.[36]

When they were inside, all people understood each other. As they went out the door, their languages changed completely. They went out and migrated.

174 HUASTEC

Northeastern Mexico

In 1978, Neville Stiles recorded the Flood tradition of the Huastec people of northeastern Mexico. Note the similarity to the Genesis account, in which a raven is sent out first, which eats from the floating corpses, followed by a dove:

> Our god wanted to help his creatures. Then he decided to fertilize the earth by a universal flood. By that, that rabbit that rests on the moon came here to earth to explain to them how the flood would be. It began to rain day and night. It was flooding everywhere. Only one family was saved: a father, a mother, a son, and two daughters. When the flood was over, the one who was saved sent his son to the land to see if it was yet possible to settle. The one young man came to the land. And when he came, he saw many animals that had drowned and died. And he began to eat those who were decaying. That young man fed on rotten flesh. However, his father who was waiting for him, seeing that his son was not returning, sent his daughter. And he commanded that son to return. And when she came to the land, that girl turned into a bird which is called chiltota, because she started to scream, because she was surprised to see her brother eating rotten meat.
>
> Then the father who watched from above, commanded his youngest daughter. When she came to land and saw what her brother was doing, she invited him to return with his father. But her brother would not. Then that great father turned his little daughter into a hummingbird. And his son who did not want to see him, he transformed into a buzzard. This buzzard begat us Huastec.[37]

It was flooding everywhere. Only one family was saved: a father, a mother, a son, and two daughters. When the flood was over, the one who was saved sent his son to the land to see if it was yet possible to settle.

36. Mauricio J. Mixco, "Textos Para La Etnohistoria En La Frontera Dominicana De Baja California," *Tlalocan*, Vol. 7 (Mexico: Universidad Nacional Autonoma de Mexico, 1977), p. 213.
37. Neville Stiles, "El Diluvio y Otros Relatos Nahuas de la Huasteca Hidalguense," *Tlalocan*, vol. 10 (Mexico: Universidad Nacional Autonoma de Mexico, 1985), p. 18–21.

175 **Oaxaca**

TRIQUE

Prior to 1890, little was known about the Trique people, an isolated tribe from mountainous western Oaxaca, a state in southern Mexico. Cayetano Esteva visited them at that time and recorded what he learned in a little booklet titled *Teogonia Trique*, which also includes their Flood tradition:

> The world became full of people who turned evil. Men had forgotten the divine words, and Nexkiriac wanted to punish them. He called to his sons and told them to wipe the earth clean of those evil men. But first he spoke to a good man who still was left on the earth, and told him to make a great box in which to preserve the seed of the plants, and many animals, because he would send his sons to wipe the world clean, and whatever else that would be lacking the gods would restore. The good man enclosed himself in his box. Cuhui (the son) came and warmed the earth. Cunma caused it to rain very much. Nimah (death) destroyed all who had still remained alive, and Nanec (the air), for his part, came and dried the earth.
>
> So the man went out from his box, and Nexkiriac appeared before him. He said to the man: "Do not go forth yet on the earth. It is necessary to purify it. Dig a trench sevenfold my arm (pointing from the ground and raising his arm) and bury yourself with your box. The man obeyed and after having burned the surface of the earth Nexkiriac took the man from his box, with the animals and plants, and said: "The world is as pure as the first day. Inhabit it and populate it.
>
> The man saw that the waters were going toward the seas, and believed that the earth would be dry soon. So he rushed to sow and to cultivate the plants, so that he and the animals could live, multiply, and make progress. This man who survived and was saved from the water and fire, say the Triques, is the father of them and of all the inhabitants that exist on our planet.[38]

The world became full of people who turned evil. Men had forgotten the divine words, and Nexkiriac wanted to punish them. … But first he spoke to a good man who still was left on the earth, and told him to make a great box in which to preserve the seed of the plants, and many animals …

So the man went out from his box,… The man saw that the waters were going toward the seas, and believed that the earth would be dry soon.

Petrified Waterfall in Oaxaca, Mexico

38. Arturo Monzon, "Teogonia Trique," *Tlalocan*, Vol. 2, No. 1 (Mexico: Universidad Nacional Autonoma de Mexico, 1945), p. 8–9.

176 COPALA TRIQUE

Oaxaca

Copala is a dialect of Trique, spoken by those in Santiago Juxtlahuaca, a locality in western Oaxaca. In October 1972, a native and monolingual speaker of Copala Trique shared his people's tradition of the Flood, which was translated from the audio tape recording as follows:

Craftswoman Making Banana Leaf Bun in Tavehua, Oaxaca

> In the beginning the flood came to the world. The flood came to the world, but there wasn't any mountain that was able to grow more than the flood. Only the mountain that Saint John is on [San Juan Copala] grew more than the flood back then. The flood came to the world, but that mountain grew more than the flood. The mountain was growing, and the water was growing. The water was growing, and the mountain was growing. The water couldn't reach the top of the mountain. That mountain was able to grow taller than the water. The water stopped growing, and the mountain stopped growing. That mountain was able to conquer the water.
>
> And so it was that only a few people remained on the top of that mountain. The water stopped growing. The mountain stopped growing. And then the water turned back again and dried up.[39]

Next, they tell that God was not pleased with the people who survived, and he turned them into monkeys. Then he remade man.

177 TZELTAL

Chiapas

The Tzeltal people are from the central highlands of the state of Chiapas in southeastern Mexico. According to a tradition recited in 1947, their account of the Flood went like this:

> One day, through a misunderstanding, a wife killed and cooked her child. She and her husband ate it and enjoyed it very much. Soon everyone was killing and cooking children. God became very angry and sent down the deluge. One intelligent man was saved in a canoe. After the waters subsided he lit a fire. God smelled the smoke. He sent down the buzzard, the turkey buzzard, and a churn-owl to see what was happening upon the earth, but they all remained behind to eat dead bodies. God condemned them to eat only dead bodies thereafter. Then God sent down the hawk, which fulfilled his mission. The man was turned into a monkey.[40]

God became very angry and sent down the deluge. One intelligent man was saved in a canoe.

39. Barbara K. Hollenbach, "A Copala Trique Deluge Story," *Latin American Indian Literatures*, vol. 6, no. 2 (1982), p. 123–124.
40. Marianna Slocum, unpublished texts obtained at Oxchuc, Chiapas, around 1947. From Barlow Archive, Mexico City College. Presented in Horcasitas, "An Analysis of the Deluge Myth in Mesoamerica," p. 198.

178 CHOL

Chiapas

The Chols are from the highlands of northern Chiapas. Their Flood story, which John Beekman recorded around 1949, is similar to that of the Copala Triques:

> When the deluge came, a few people climbed to the top of the highest trees and were saved. But Ahau became angry with them and, reversing their faces and their hind parts, turned them into monkeys.[41]

When the deluge came, a few people climbed to the top of the highest trees and were saved.

179 CHONTAL

Oaxaca

The anthropologist Pedro Carrasco described the Chontal people as among the least known tribes of Mexico. He visited the Chontal for the first time in 1949, and in 1951 he was able to record several oral traditions from an authority of the tribe. This informant had possessed written records of the tribe's rituals, along with oral traditions that explain these rituals. Carrasco published these traditions, which included a Flood tradition:

Hierve el Agua in the Central Valleys of Oaxaca, Mexico

> At the time of the great flood the mountain of San Lorenzo Jilotepequillo saved the people. Everything was covered by water except the top of that mountain; the water reached to 10 meters below the top. You can still see the line the water reached; that mountain has a sort of a neck.
>
> God had his own people with Him, and after the flood He sent a man to the earth to see what he could find. Many fish had died and the man saw many animals about to die, but God had not blessed them yet; there was as yet no permission to eat. The man however did not waste any time. He made a fire and started to roast fish to eat right away.
>
> God waited for a while and when He realized his man was not coming back He sent a second one. But when this one met the first man, he invited him to eat, and seeing him eat, he took something to eat and there he stayed.
>
> God saw that His second man was not coming, so He sent a third one. But again He realized that this man was not coming back either because he also stayed behind in order to eat. God then sent a new man and ordered him to punish the others.[42]

At the time of the great flood … Everything was covered by water except the top of that mountain; the water reached to 10 meters below the top.

As punishment, the first man was turned into a dog, and the second and third men were turned into buzzards.

41. John Beekman, unpublished text from the Chol at Yajalon, Chiapas around 1949. Presented in Horcasitas, "An Analysis of the Deluge Myth in Mesoamerica," p. 198.
42. Pedro Carrasco, "Pagan Beliefs and Rituals Among the Chontal Indians of Oaxaca, Mexico," *Anthropological Records*, Vol. 20, No. 3 (Berkeley and Los Angeles: University of California Press, 1960), p. 112–113.

180 Oaxaca

HAUVE

The Huave people have long inhabited the southeastern part of Oaxaca, bordering on the Pacific Ocean. From about 1970 to 1980, an anthropologist named Italo Signorini visited and studied the Huave. Their origin story included a reference to the Flood, which he summarized:

> The fear of floods, however, is not only due to the dramatic accumulated experiences, but also to a myth that refers to a flood (ndilihay, "world is turned around") of which only one man and two dogs were saved. These became the progenitors of the Huaves.[43]

Two Tzotzil Women on a Street in San Cristobal

181 Chiapas

TZOTZIL

The Tzotzils, cousins of the Tzeltals, live in the highlands of central Chiapas. They told the following tradition to Gary Hossen around 1968 or 1969. It appears that they adopted the term "our Father" from the Spanish, but preserved their own story:

> Our Father created the second man out of carved wood. When he was finished, he began to speak. Our Father gave him a bow for a mouth, a one-stringed instrument, but the man did not know how to touch it. Our Father broke his hands and feet and made new ones, and then the man began to dance a little. Our Father built a house, and the wooden men began to multiply little by little and become human beings. They did not know to do anything, not even how to speak. So our Father destroyed them in a flood. Only one man and one woman were saved, enclosing themselves in a box that floated. A buzzard came and ate at the end of the box. Then the waters began to retreat. The earth had sunk and the water began to emerge from submerged holes. Then hills, caves and valleys reappeared. The demons and snakes appeared. Then Our Father returned home and also the man and the woman arrived there. Our Father asked them if they wanted to stay with him and they said no, because he had almost killed them. So he put on them tails, turning them into monkeys. Thus did the second race of men disappear.[44]

Only one man and one woman were saved, enclosing themselves in a box that floated. A buzzard came and ate at the end of the box. Then the waters began to retreat.

Agua Azul Waterfall in Chiapas

43. Italo Signorini, *Los Huaves de San Mateo del Mar, Oaxaca* (Mexico: Institute Nacional Indigenista, 1979), p. 87.
44. Gary H. Gossen, *Los Chamulas en el Mundo de Sol* (Mexico: Instituto Nacional Indigenista, 1980), p. 398–399.

Hastéecöla Peaks
Near Kino Bay,
Sonora, Mexico

182 OPATA

Sonora

The Opata people live in the state of Sonora, which borders on Arizona and New Mexico. Natal Lombardo learned their language and wrote a manuscript in 1702, titled *Arte de la Lengua Teguima*. This manuscript preserves their origin story, which tells of a great flood long ago:

> Although the people of this nation do not have letters nor understand them, they have knowledge of the flood which occurred. They say that a few children, boys and girls, were put inside a hollow log the shape of a drum, in which they were saved. From these children the people are descended.[45]

…they have knowledge of the flood which occurred. … a few children, boys and girls, were put inside a hollow log the shape of a drum, in which they were saved. From these children the people are descended.

183 TLAHUICA

Mexico State

The Tlahuica people, who live in the hills about 40 miles southwest of Mexico City, have passed down a tradition of the Flood, according to Reyes Rabela. They say that long ago, the hill on which they lived was split apart by a great flood which changed the earth. They say this flood separated them from their brothers, whose part of the hill was carried far away.

> The flood happened and the earth changed. . . . The oldest hill was split. . . . Who knows where it is? . . . All the trees that are here, they are there too. And all our brothers who speak like us, they are there.[46]

Fabela suspects that they refer to the Matlatzincas, a group that has occupied the Matlatzinca Valley west of the capital, and who speak a related language of the Oto-Pamean group.

Tlahuica's Xochicalco Pyramid

45. Natal Lombardo, *Arte de la Lengua Teguima Vulgarmente Llamada Opata* (Mexico: 1702). Edward E. Ayer Manuscript Collection, Newberry Library, Chicago. Ayer MS 1641, p. 231.
46. Reyes Luciano Alvaro Fabela, *Tlahuicas* (Mexico: Comision Nacional para el Desarollo de los Pueblos Indigenas, 2006), p. 12. Tradition recorded in 2000.

184 LACANDON

Chiapas

Lacandon Jungle Ruins

The Lacandon are an isolated tribe from the jungles of southern Chiapas, near the border with Guatemala. They told a legend of the Flood to Didier Boremanse in the 1970s:

> Hach Ak Yum (one of the gods) said to his son-in-law, Ah K'in Chob, that he should build a boat, in which they should enclose one man and one woman of every lineage, and samples of all types of animals, and seeds of all trees and plants of the forest. Then, the red wind blew and carried away all the vegetation that existed. Then it began to rain without stopping. It was a deluge. People ran to their canoes, but these transformed into crocodiles. All mankind perished, except those who were in the boat. When the waters went down, the land was still soft. So the gods sent fire to burn and dry the land. Once the land was firm and dry again, Ah K'in Chob planted new trees and plants, and in little time the forest grew again.
>
> The people and animals multiplied, and food abounded. Ah K'in Chob protected mankind. Disease and death did not exist at that time. After that, the gods no longer lived in Palenque, but they appeared at Yaxchilan.[47]

...that he should be a boat, in which they should enclose one man and one woman of every lineage, and samples of all types of animals, and seeds of all trees and plants of the forest.

185 GUARIJIO

Chihuahua and Sonora

The Guarijio (also spelled Warihio) were a little-known tribe of northwest Mexico when Howard Gentry visited them in 1934. They have a tradition which mixes the memory of the Creation and the Flood, which is also a common characteristic of many "earth diver" accounts found in North America. Note the sending of a dove on a mission, as in the Genesis Flood.

> In the beginning of things the world was a "laguna," a plain of water. Tata Dios sang for three days and three nights. From the bottom he took a handful of sand and scattered it before him. These began to grow into hard land. At the end of three days he sent out a little white dove to see if the world had not grown hard in some part. The dove went to the farthest corners three different times. The last time it returned and said the world had grown to land.[48]

Then it began to rain without stopping. It was a deluge. ... All mankind perished, except those who were in the boat.

Other Texts (See Appendix A on page 241)

186 **Yaqui (Northwest Mexico)**

187 **Kiliwa (Baja California)**

47. Didier Boremanse, "Ortogenesis en la Literatura Maya Lacandona," *Mesoamerica*, vol. 10, no. 17 (Guatemala: 1989), p. 70–71.
48. Howard Scott Gentry, "The Warihio Indians of Sonora-Chihuahua: An Ethnographic Survey," *Bureau of American Ethnology Bulletin*, vol. 186 (Washington: GPO, 1963), p. 133.

Traditional Cabécar House

Section XI

GUATEMALA TO PANAMA

Further south, the nations of Central America all have an account of the Flood, including the K'iché, Miskito, Sumo, Pipil, Nicaraguans, and many others. The Jacalteks of Guatemala told that after the Flood a vulture was sent to search for land, but the bird shirked its mission and ate from the floating corpses. The Achi tribe of Guatemala had ancient paintings of the Flood, which the Spanish priests destroyed as idolatrous. The natives of Panama told the early Spanish colonizers that one man escaped the Flood, together with his wife and sons, and later they repopulated the earth.

Regional Tribes

188. K'iché (Guatemala)
189. Achi (Guatemala)
190. Jakaltek (Guatemala)
191. Miskito and Sumo (Nicaragua and Honduras)
192. Southern Mayas (Honduras)
193. Pipil (El Salvador)
194. Nicaragua Tradition
195. Guatuso (Costa Rica)
196. Cabecar (Costa Rica)
197. Panama Tradition
198. Kuna (Panama and Colombia)
199. Guaymi (Costa Rica and Panama)
200. Emberá (Panama and Colombia)
201. Bribri (Costa Rica)
202. Dorasque (Costa Rica and Panama)

188 K'ICHÉ

Guatemala

The K'iché (or Quiché), one of the Mayan peoples, had a powerful civilization in Guatemala at the time of the Spanish invasion. The Popol Vuh, or "Book of the People," is a document from about 1550 which contains their old traditions and beliefs. However, this document was secretly guarded until around the year 1700, when Francisco Ximenez befriended them and received a copy,. which he promptly translated from K'iché to Spanish. The text contains an account of an ancient flood, which they said took place in the previous creation, when the gods made men out of wood:

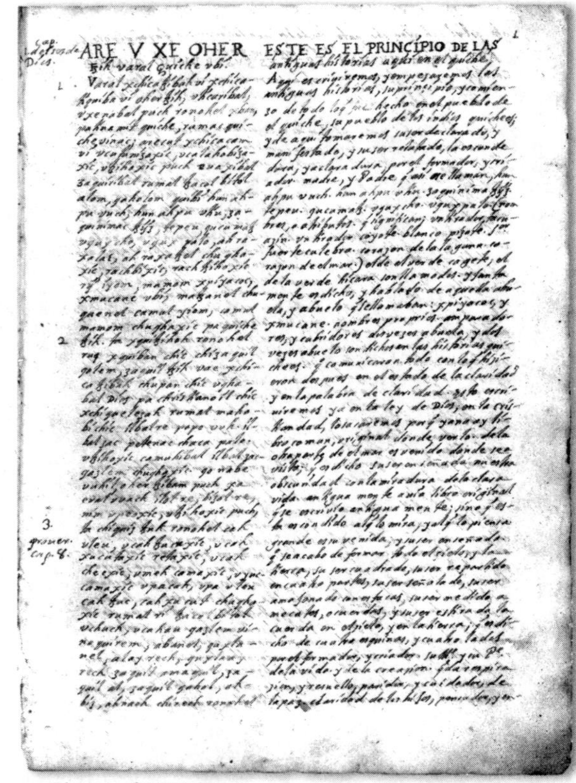

Photo of 1701 Ximenez manuscript of *Popol Vuh*, in parallel Quiche and Spanish

> Instantly the figures were made of wood. They looked like men, talked like men, and populated the surface of the earth. They existed and multiplied; they had daughters, they had sons, these wooden figures; but they did not have souls, they did not remember their Creator, their Maker; they walked on all fours, aimlessly.
>
> They no longer remembered the Heart of Heaven and therefore they fell out of favor . . . they no longer thought of their Creator nor their maker, nor of those who made them and cared for them. These were the first man who existed in great numbers on the face of the earth. Immediately the wooden figures were annihilated, destroyed, broken up, and killed.
>
> A flood was brought about by the Heart of Heaven; a great flood was formed which fell on the heads of the wooden creatures. . . . But those that they had made, that they had created, did not think, did not speak with their Creator, their Maker. And for this reason they were killed, they were deluged. A heavy resin fell from the sky.[1]

They no longer remembered the Heart of Heaven and therefore they fell out of favor . . . they no longer thought of their Creator. . . . A flood was brought about by the Heart of Heaven; a great flood was formed which fell on the heads of the wooden creatures. . .

The Popol Vuh also includes an account reminiscent of the Tower of Babel:

> . . . the three groups of Quichés were not divided. Three were they who were truly great in their nature: Tohil, Auilix, and Hacavitz.
>
> Then all the nations entered therein — the Rabinals, the Cakchiquels, and the Ah Tziquinahas, along with the Yaqui people, as they are called today. It was there that the languages of the nations were changed. Their languages came to be different. They did not hear each other clearly when they came from Tulan, thus they split apart.[2]

A reference to the K'iché Flood tradition is found also in Juan de Torquemada's work, *Monarquia Indiana*, published in 1615. Torquemada's sources included earlier records from the first Franciscan missionaries, as well as interviews he conducted personally.

1. *Popol Vuh*, trans. Delia Goetz and Sylvanus Griswold Morley (Los Angeles: Plantin Press, 1954), p. 43–46.
2. Brasseur de Bourbourg, *Popol Vuh: Le livre sacré et les mythes de l'antiquité américaine* (1861), p. 217.

In the kingdom of Guatemala, whose residents say they have knowledge of the Flood, some say they worshipped as gods the Great Father and Great Mother who are in heaven, just as they also worshipped these before the Flood.[3]

Tikal Temple I, Guatemala

189 ACHI

Guatemala

The Achi Indians are a Mayan people of Guatemala, who speak a language related to K'iché. Geronimo de Mendieta published a historical work in 1595 which mentioned the Achi flood history, depicted in their ancient paintings. However, none of this has survived due to the scorched-earth policy of the Spanish.

> What they said about the flood was also witnessed in Guatemala, the Achí Indians affirming that they have this flood painted among their antiquities. The friars, with their spirit and zeal to destroy idolatry, took and burned these things, counting them suspicious.[4]

What they said about the flood was also witnessed in Guatemala, the Achí Indians affirming that they have this flood painted among their antiquities.

190 JAKALTEK

Guatemala

The Jakalteks were also part of the pre-Columbian Mayan culture which stretched across Guatemala and the Yucatan Peninsula of Mexico. The Jakalteks live in the highlands of northwestern Guatemala. Around 1975, Victor Montejo — a Jakaltek man himself — collected traditions from a tribal elder named Antun Luc, the last living descandant of the Xuan Kanil clan. He shared a rather remarkable tradition of the Flood:

> In the ancient culture, our Mayan ancestors speak of a great deluge that covered and destroyed the world. They say: "Then the waters went up, up, and up, flooding all the mountains and highest hills and killing all that had life on the earth. Only one house had been raised over the waters, which had covered all the species of animals.
>
> For a long time the waters covered the land and very slowly they went down, and down, and down, until the land was again free from those turbulent, destructive waters. When that house was still on the waters, Ho Choc the clarinero (great-tailed grackle) was sent to observe the horizon. As the water was still high, the grackle soon returned to report its completed mission.
>
> After some time had passed, Usmij the vulture was sent to observe how far the water had fallen. This messenger went flying from the house, doing several turns in the air. Then it went to one of the hills that was now above the water, where it landed hungry. It found there a great quantity of dead and rotten animals and, not caring about its mission, began to eat of their corpses until it satisfied its wild appetite.

Then the waters went up, up, and up, flooding all the mountains and highest hills and killing all that had life on the earth. Only one house had been raised over the waters, which had covered all the species of animals.

3. Juan de Torquemada, *Monarquia Indiana*, vol. 2 (Madrid: Franco, 1723), Book 6, Chap. 26, p. 53.
4. Geronimo de Mendieta, *Historia Eclesiastica Indiana*, Book 4, Cap. 41, p. 532.

After this, it sought to return to give a report of its observations, but when it came to the house it was not allowed to land among the others because its stench was unbearable. As a judgment for its disobedience, Usmij was condemned to eat of every dead animal and to be the master of nauseating. Since then, they call the vulture 'the bird who cleans the world,' for its new function of cleaning with the beak all that contaminates the world."[5]

Miskito Hut in Nicaragua

MISKITO AND SUMO

191 Nicaragua and Honduras

The Sumo and Miskito, two closely related tribes, inhabit the eastern coast of Nicagarua and Honduras. They recounted a legend of the Flood to Eduard Conzemius in 1921. He wrote:

> The Miskito and Sumo, like many Indian tribes of America, have a tradition of a great catastrophe in which a whole country was submerged, only a few people being able to escape to the mountain tops.[6]

...like many Indian tribes of America, have a tradition of a great catastrophe in which a whole country was submerged, only a few people being able to escape to the mountain tops.

The legend tells of two brothers — Suko and Kuru — who went out fishing on a tributary of the Rio Oconguasto. They caught a gigantic river catfish, and Suko wanted to eat it, but Kuru objected, warning him that it was a spirit of some sort. Suko would not listen, however, and ate a piece of the fish which he roasted. He was transformed into a gigantic boa constrictor and became very thirsty. He began to drink incessantly, but the more he drank the thirstier he became. Kuru returned home and did not tell anyone what had happened, but some neighbors went to look for his brother Suko.

> Arrived at the fishing ground, they found the boa constrictor on the branches of a very high ceiba or silk-cotton tree. But hardly had they perceived him when a big flood came which inundated the whole country. Everyone was drowned with the exception of Suko and the latter's wife and children.[7]

Group of Miskito People

5. Victor D. Montejo, "Cuentos Traditionales de Jacaltenango," *Mesoamerica*, vol. 6, no. 10 (Guatemala: 1985), p. 417.
6. Eduard Conzemius, "Ethnographical Survey of the Miskito and Sumo Indians of Honduras and Nicaragua," *Bureau of American Ethnology Bulletin*, no. 106 (Washington: GPO, 1932), p. 130.
7. Ibid., p. 131.

Echoes of the Garden of Eden?

The above Flood tradition is representative of what we may call the "forbidden meat" motif, often involving a serpent. There are many tribes with related Flood stories, including the Jivaro and Chamacoco in South America, the Iban of Malaysia, and the Pai Yao in China. Importantly, there may be a memory here of the Garden of Eden, and the Serpent that induced Eve to eat of the forbidden fruit. With the confusion of languages that occurred at Babel, and the resulting loss of information, it is understandable that the memory of the Garden of Eden and the Flood got conflated together.

Equally reminiscent of the first chapters of Genesis are the "woman ravished by monster / serpent while bathing" stories, such as we find among the Lengua and Nivakle of Paraguay, the Moseten of Bolivia, other tribes of South America, and even the Kootenay of British Columbia.

There are other variants of the Flood tradition which could be related to the previous version, including the "forbidden item stolen" motif (the Taino, Andoque, Pemón, Yabarana, and Kraho tribes, for example), and the "arrow shot at monster" (e.g., the Menominee, Potawatomi, and Sinkyone tribes in North America, and the Murata in South America for example). A further analysis of these commonalities could point to a shared history of tribes across the world.

SOUTHERN MAYAS

192 **Honduras**

Other Mayan peoples, living in southern and central Honduras, told a unique Flood tradition to an archeologist named J. Eric Thompson in 1927:

> Often when hunting in the forest one comes upon old rubbing stones that have no legs. They are not really rubbing stones, although our people often take them home and use them as such. They are the boats of the tiny folk — the P'us. Long ago these little people lived very happily, for they possessed a magic chest, from which issued an inexhaustible supply of everything that they needed. On account of this they forgot to worship God. God sent a flood to destroy them. They knew beforehand that there was going to be a big flood, but they did not know when it would come. Accordingly they made themselves little stone boats, so that they would not rot in the wet season, as might have happened if they had made them of wood. When the flood came, they got into their stone boats, but they were all drowned as the stone would not float. There they lie to this day in the woods, often near holes in the ground where they sank when the big flood swept everyone away.[8]

Mayan Ruins at Copan, Honduras

…they forgot to worship God. God sent a flood to destroy them. They knew beforehand that there was going to be a big flood, … but they were all drowned…

8. J. Eric Thompson, "Ethnology of the Mayas of British Honduras," *Field Museum of Natural History Anthropological Series*, v. 17, no. 2, (Chicago, 1930), p. 166.

193 **El Salvador**

PIPIL

About 1,000 years ago, the Pipil tribe migrated south from Mexico to El Salvador — or Cuscatlán, as they called it. Miguel Espino was able to record several oral traditions from the tribe in his 1919 work, *La Mitología de Cuscatlán*. Their creation story preserves a memory of the Flood.

San Andres Ruins in El Salvador

> Afterwards [after the creation of the earth], their tradition tells how man was created, from the clot of a cactus that became muddied. From this created man came a lineage of evil men, who outraged the creator. A furious rain broke out on them, and the hurricane whistled, breaking apart the mountains. All died except for Coscotagat and Tlacatixitl, our common parents. After that disaster, humanity has been making progress little by little.[9]

From this created man came a lineage of evil men, who outraged the creator. A furious rain broke out on them, and the hurricane whistled, breaking apart the mountains. All died except for Coscotagat and Tlacatixitl, our common parents.

194 **Nicaragua**

NICARAGUA TRADITION

We have a very early reference to the existence of a Flood legend in Nicaragua, although we possess few details. This comes from an interview conducted on September 28, 1528, by a Spanish priest, with natives of a village in Nicaragua named Teola:

> **Bobadilla:** "Do you know, or have you heard, whether the world perished after the creation of the world?"
>
> **Native:** "From my parents I have heard that long ago, the world perished through water."
>
> **Bobadilla:** "Did all people drown?"
>
> **Native:** "I do not know, except that the gods (Famagoztad and Cippatonal) remade the world with more people and birds and all things."
>
> **Bobadilla:** "How did the gods (Famagoztad and Cippatonal) escape? Was it on some high place or canoe or boat?"
>
> **Native:** "I do not know, except that they are gods."[10]

9. Gonzalo Fernandez de Oviedo y Valdez, *Historia General y Natural de las Indias, Islas y Tierra-Firme del Mar Oceano*, ed. Jose Amador de los Rios, Part 3, Book 4 (Royal Academy of History: Madrid, 1855), p. 40.
10. Miguel Ángel Espino, *Mitología de Cuscatlán* (San Salvador: Concultura, 1996), p. 12.

195 GUATUSO

Costa Rica

The Guatuso of northern Costa Rica were able to remain isolated and undisturbed by the Spanish during Colonial times, due to the dense forests and their isolated location. They suffered heavy losses, however, in the second half of the 19th century, at the hands of rubber tappers from Nicaragua who invaded their land.

A linguist named Adolfo Umaña visited them in the 1970s and learned their language and most sacred traditions, including one concerning the Flood. This narrative is set to verse and is quite long. I share it in an abbreviated form:

> In ancient times, when they (the gods) sent the catastrophe, people behaved in this way: It is said that once there were people, our ancestors, who were seeking destruction. With their sisters, with their sisters, they had children. They even had children with the very aged. And man fornicated with men. So it is said that they lived. . . . And others fornicated with their mothers, and had children by them.[11]

In ancient times, when they sent the catastrophe ... the animals came to them, out from the forest, and warned that that destruction was coming.

Next, it says that animals came to them, out from the forest, and warned them that destruction was coming. First, the sloth, then the tapir, then the jaguar warned them, but the people did not listen. The flood was caused when the gods hurled large rocks at the sources of the rivers, which caused the rivers to grow and flood the entire earth:

> And it is said that, after a short time the world was drowned. . . . All the reprobates lost their faces. All died in the water. . . . [The gods] threw rocks at the soil. It is said that the rivers grew higher until they all joined together. The water mounted over everything, toward the sky.[12]

Umaña then tells that "The people were annihilated, with the exception of one righteous man, who is pulled out of the water by order of Him of the Nharine (River)."[13] This god then lamented having caused the flood, and proceeded to create mankind and the animals anew. Having created them, they come forth from a cave called Arefe.[14]

The notion of survivors coming out from a cave at the end of the Flood is not exclusive to the Guatuso, but is told also by the Incas of Peru, the Yuracaré of Bolivia, and even Santals of northern India, among others.

The people were annihilated, with the exception of one righteous man, who is pulled out of the water by order of Him of the Nharine (River).

196 CABECAR

Costa Rica

The Cabécar people of eastern Costa Rica have a rather interesting Flood history, which Rodrigo Salazar recorded in the 1970s.

> When the God Sibu commanded Sula Yaba to create the earth, he brought forth the first generation [of mankind]. There passed many days, nights, mornings, and evenings. Then one day, Sibu decided to visit his children on the earth. But when he saw that all the earth's inhabitants behaved very badly, that they forgot and denied that he was

11. Adolfo Constenla Umaña, *Laca Majifijica: la Transformacion de la Tierra* (San Jose: Editorial de la Universidad de Costa Rica, 1993), p. 145
12. Ibid., p. 146, 148.
13. Ibid., p. 51.
14. Ibid., p. 150, 152.

the one who had created them, Sibu said to them: "I will punish you and destroy this first generation, since you have disobeyed my commands!"

Sibu went up to the heavens and sent for Duluy Tami, who is the goddess of the sea, and told her to send a flood upon all the earth. Duluy Tami came, and with her, the sea was rising and covering everything in its path.

When the water rose to the point that it covered all the earth, Duluy Tami spoke to the inhabitants of the earth: "All of you who shall escape the flood are the ones who have kept the commands [of Sibu]. To that end, I will give you a task which, if you do it, Sibu will bless you and you will be part of the new generation of mankind."

At that time, the majority of the people had died, having drowned in the punishment.[15]

After that, a serpent bit Duluy Tami, and she was near the point of death. A toad tended to her, but became hungry and left for a moment to catch and eat insects. Then Duluy Tami's stomach grew, and out from it burst an enormous tree. Those who had thus far survived, with divine help, cut down the tree and built an enormous raft. They waited aboard the raft until the floodwaters subsided. The god Sibu came down and gave the survivors new commands, and warned them against behaving wickedly, lest he should find it necessary to punish them again.[16]

Those who had thus far survived, with divine help, cut down the tree and built an enormous raft. They waited aboard the raft until the floodwaters subsided.

197 PANAMA TRADITION

Panama

The natives of Panama told an account of the Flood to the early Spanish colonizers. Antonio de Herrera summarized this in his 1601 work, *Décadas*:

> The knowledge that they had was that when the Flood occurred, a man escaped in a canoe, with his wife and sons, and that from him the people of the world multiplied. And in heaven there was a Lord who made rain, and who caused all the other heavenly movements.[17]

Traditional Kuna House on Caledonia island

198 KUNA

Panama and Colombia

The Kuna tribe, who historically inhabited the forests and swamplands on the border of Panama and Colombia, shared their belief about the Flood with Mac Chapin in 1969. It is contained in a lengthy tradition, which ends as follows:

> The flood came and everything was destroyed. All the evil of the world was washed away by the flood. Aiban and his followers saved themselves at Tingwa Yala, which was so high in elevation that the waters did not reach them. They remained where they were four days, and when the waters descended they returned to the region where they lived before. The world looked as if it had been shaved. There were no plants, no animals, no people.[18]

The flood came and everything was destroyed. All the evil of the world was washed away by the flood. … There were no plants, no animals, no people.

15. Rodrigo Salazar, *Las Leyendas del Duchi* (San Jose: Departamento de Publicaciones del Ministerio de Educacion Publica, 1977), p. 25–32.
16. Ibid., p. 32–54.
17. Antonio de Herrera y Torsedillas, *Historia General, Década Quarta*, Book 1 (Madrid: Royal Office of Nicolas Rodriguez, 1726), p. 19.
18. Mac Chapin, *Pab Igala: Historias de la Tradicion Kuna* (Quito: Abya Yala, 1989), p. 109.

199 GUAYMI

Costa Rica and Panama

Flat-roofed Guaymi shelter

The Guaymi, or Ngabe, who live along the border of Panama and Costa Rica, related a memory of the Flood to Adrian de Ufeldre around the year 1622:

> The god Noncomala (who created the earth), having become angry with this province of Guaymi, of all the world, destroyed it with water, and killed all the people. And the particular god of the Guaymi, Nubu, took care to preserve the seed of man. And after the inundation and the anger of Noncomala had passed, he sowed the seed of man, and from the good part came forth men and women, and from the part that corrupted itself came monkeys.[19]

200 EMBERÁ

Panama and Colombia

In 1927, Erland Nordenskiöld visited the Emberá (or Choco) tribe of Panama and Colombia. His source on their traditions was a highly regarded medicine man of the tribe, Selimo Huacoriso, who spoke thus concerning the ancient Flood:

> It is said that the world was changed. There was a great river whose head was in the sea, and its mouth was up on the land. To change this, God caused a torrential rain to fall, and the world began to sink as the rain increased. A man went to where God was, to tell him that the world was going to drown because of the rising of the waters. Then the man warned the Chocos to save themselves on wooden rafts. This man who had gone to God arranged his house, and told the others to put rafts under their huts so they could float on the water. However, the people did not believe it. In order to have food, the man cut his bananas and sugar cane, and put these in his house. The others said that it was a lie that the man said that the world was going to sink, and they were drinking chicha when the waters began to rise. In three days, the world disappeared under the waters. The house of the man was carried on the surface of the waters, floating like a raft. All the hills collapsed except for the hill of Iya Mujarra (in San Juan), which was barely visible on the water. This hill was not covered with water because God made it grow.[20]

Next, a swordfish tried to cut the hill to drown the people. They sent, in succession, a gannet, a crow, and an otter, to kill the swordfish. The gannet failed. Likewise, the crow failed. But the otter killed the swordfish, brought it back, and received a blessing from God. For this reason it eats fish to this day.[21]

The god Noncomala (who created the earth), having become angry with this province of Guaymi, of all the world, destroyed it with water, and killed all the people.

God caused a torrential rain to fall, and the world began to sink as the rain increased. … In three days, the world disappeared under the waters. The house of the man was carried on the surface of the waters, floating like a raft.

19. Fray Adrian de Ufeldre, "Conquista de la Provincia de Guaymi," in *Tesoros Verdaderos de las Yndias*, ed. Juan Melendez, vol. 3, book 1 (Rome: 1682), p. 5.
20. Henry Wassen, "Cuentos de los Indios Chocos Recogidos por Erland Nordenskiold durante su Expedicion al Istmo de Panama en 1927," *Journal de la Societe des Americanistes*, vol. 25, no. 1 (Paris: 1933) p. 111–112.
21. Ibid., p. 112.

Other Texts (See Appendix A on page 241)

201 **Bribri (Costa Rica)**

202 **Dorasque (Costa Rica and Panama)**

Reconstruction of a Taino Village , Zapata Peninsula, Cuba

CARIBBEAN ISLANDS

The native tribes of the Caribbean Islands also have their Flood traditions. These include the Carib tribe, and the Taino tribe of Cuba, who told that "an old man, knowing that the Flood was to come, made a great boat. He placed inside it many animals, along with his family. He sent out a raven, which did not return, because it ate from the dead floating corpses. Then he sent a dove, which returned singing and carrying a twig with a leaf."

Tribes of the Region

203. Carib (Lesser Antilles)
204. Taino (Greater Antilles)

203 Lesser Antilles

CARIB

The Caribbean Sea and its islands are named after the Carib people, who live on the small islands known as the Lesser Antilles, which dot the sea between Puerto Rico and Venezuela. We have a record of their Flood tradition from the manuscript of a French missionary, Father De la Borde. His manuscript was included in a compilation published in 1684, but was probably written much earlier.

> What they say of the origin of the sea, and of creation, and generally of all the waters, relates in some manner to the deluge. The great Master of Spirits, who makes the good spirits, became angry at the Caribs of that time who were very wicked, and who would no longer offer to him Cassavas, nor Ouicou. So he caused it to rain for several days so great a quantity of water, and only a few saved themselves in small boats, and on the mountain Piragues, which at that time was the only one. It is this deluge of the hurricane which made the Mornes, the Pitons, and the cliffs which we see. The Mornes are hills, and the Pitons are high pointed rocks or mountains in the form of sugar loaves. It was he who separated the islands from the mainland.[1]

The great Master of Spirits, who makes the good spirits, became angry at the Caribs of that time who were very wicked, a… So he caused it to rain for several days so great a quantity of water, and only a few saved themselves in small boats…

Also, a French pastor named Charles de Rochefort wrote of their Flood tradition in a work published in 1658:

> Formerly they worshiped the sun, and had their priests whom they called Yaouas, who were very superstitious in rendering to the sun all the service which they had invented to his honor. They believed that the rays of the sun gave life to all things, that it dried the earth, and that, when the sun had remained for four hours in eclipse, the earth had been inundated. And the great lake, which they called Theomi, had pushed its waters as far as the summit of the highest mountains which surround them. But the sun, returning from its eclipse, had by its presence turned the waters back to their abysses. That the only mountain which is dedicated to its honor, and in which was its temple, was preserved from this deluge. And that their predecessors, and all the beasts who are now in the woods and on the earth, having gone to that mountain for refuge, were preserved to then repopulate the whole earth.[2]

Carib Group of Men

204 Greater Antilles

TAINO

The Taino people were the primary group that lived in the large islands of the western Caribbean Sea — the greater Antilles — from Cuba to Puerto Rico.

Juan de Torquemada (1562–1624) published an early Flood tradition of the Taino living in Cuba, told to the earliest Franciscan missionaries:

> The Indians of Cuba had a keen knowledge of the Deluge, and that the world had perished due to the great quantity of water. The old people, of more than seventy and eighty years (back when our [Spanish] people first came to that island) said that an old man, knowing that the Flood was to

The Indians of Cuba had a keen knowledge of the Deluge, and that the world had perished due to the great quantity of water.

1. De la Borde, "Relation de l'origine, Moeurs, Coustumes, Religion, Guerres, & Voyages des Caraibes," *Recueil de divers voyages faits en Afrique et en l'Amerique* (Paris: 1684), p. 7.
2. Charles de Rochefort, *Histoire naturelle et morale des iles Antilles de l'Amerique* (Rotterdame: 1658), p. 363–364.

come, made a great boat. He placed inside it many animals, along with his family. He sent out a raven, which did not return, because it ate from the dead floating corpses. Then he sent a dove, which returned singing and carrying a twig with a leaf.[3]

We Are All Brothers

*T*orquemada also relates an incident in which one Gabriel de Cabrera, a Spanish official in Cuba, was laughing at an old native man, over seventy years old, and called him "Perro" (dog). The man responded:

"Why do you laugh at me, and call me Perro? For we are all brothers. Are you all not descendants of one of the sons of that man who built the great boat to escape the waters, just as we are descendants of the other son?"[4] (They believed he had two sons and not three.)

How much cruelty and iniquity the world could have been spared, if we acknowledged the implications of the Flood: that we are all blood-relatives, that God created us, and that He will judge us after death?

In 1493, a monk named Ramon Pané accompanied Christopher Columbus on his second voyage to the Americas. He wrote the oldest ethnographic work about the Americas, dealing with the Taino tribe. According to Pané, the islanders at Hispaniola attributed the Flood to the theft of a forbidden calabash long ago, which ruptured and burst with water. They say this was the origin of all the world's oceans.[5]

... an old man, knowing that the Flood was to come, made a great boat. He placed inside it many animals, along with his family...

War Canoes and Talking Leaves

The Taino are the main tribe that historically inhabited the Caribbean Islands. Joseph Riverwind, a Taino chief and author, told that his forefathers passed down an ancient oral tradition which foretold strange things. Each generation waited to see if it would be fulfilled in their time. Specifically, this prophecy told that three strange war canoes would come to their shores, and that these war canoes would be filled with pale-faced, bearded men who were "covered like turtles" [heavily armed]. They would carry with them "Talking Leaves," which would bring further knowledge of the Creator. However, along with these Talking Leaves, there would come a great destruction of their people and way of life.[6]

Beginning in 1492, this prophecy was fulfilled, when three war canoes — La Nina, La Pinta, and La Santa Maria — landed at one of the Caribbean Islands. The Spanish colonizers brought with them the Bible, and in denial of the faith of the Bible, they callously committed crimes and atrocities against the native peoples.

3. Juan de Torquemada, *Monarquia Indiana*, vol. 2 (Madrid: Franco, 1723), Book 14, Chap. 19, p. 571.
4. Ibid., p. 571–572.
5. Ramon Pané, *Relacion acerca de las antiguedades de los indios*, ed.Jose Juan Arrom (America Nuestra, no date), p. 28–30.
6. RiverWind, *That's What the Old Ones Say*, p. 26–29.

Volcanic Landscape of Sierra Negra Mountain

COLOMBIA, VENEZUELA, AND THE GUYANAS

Proceeding to South America, we find ubiquitous testimony of the Flood. Among these, the Kágaba tribe of Colombia told that God "opened the doors of the sky, so that it would rain for four entire years." But a chief built a magical boat and placed all kinds of animals and provisions inside it. The man entered the magical boat and closed the door. So it rained for four entire years, and at last the boat came to rest on the peak of the Sierra Negra. The Arawaks of Guyana related that their ancestor named Marerewana, a righteous man, foresaw the coming Flood and prepared a great canoe to save himself and his family. The Ashaninkas of Peru, along with the Tamanacs, Achagua, Muiscas, Warao, Piaroa, and many other tribes, have noteworthy traditions of the Great Flood, which we will explore in the pages which follow.

Tribes of the Region

205. Muisca (Colombia)
206. Catío (Colombia and Panama)
207. Patángora (Colombia)
208. Wounaan (Colombia)
209. Cubeo (Colombia)
210. Ashaninka (Peru and Brazil)
211. Sikuani (Colombia and Venezuela)
212. Witoto (Colombia and Peru)
213. Chimila (Colombia)
214. Kágaba (Colombia)
215. Akawoio (Venezuela and Guyana)
216. Arawak (Venezuela, Guyana, and Suriname)
217. Warao (Venezuela and Guyana)
218. Achagua (Venezuela and Colombia)
219. Pemón (Venezuela, Brazil, and Guyana)
220. Girara and Airico (Venezuela and Colombia)
221. Tamanac (Venezuela)
222. Maipure (Venezuela)
223. Piaroa (Venezuela)
224. Guajiro (Colombia and Venezuela)
225. Yupa (Venezuela)
226. Yaruro (Venezuela and Colombia)
227. Macusi (Guyana and Brazil)
228. Wapishana and Taruma (Guyana and Brazil)
229. Ataroi (Guyana)
230. Ye'kuana (Venezuela and Brazil)
231. Cuiva (Colombia and Venezuela)
232. Mesaya (Colombia and Brazil)
233. Yabarana (Venezuela)
234. Wajapi (French Guiana, Suriname, and Brasil)
235. Palikur (French Guiana and Brazil)
236. Nukák (Colombia)
237. Yukpa (Venezuela)
238. Tatuy (Venezuela)
239. Baniwa (Venezuela, Colombia, and Brazil)
240. Wayana (Suriname, French Guiana, and Brazil)
241. Trio (Suriname and Brazil)
242. Matapi (Colombia)
243. Andoque (Colombia)
244. Tanimuka (Colombia)
245. Yagua (Colombia and Peru)
246. Desana (Colombia)

205 MUSCA

Colombia

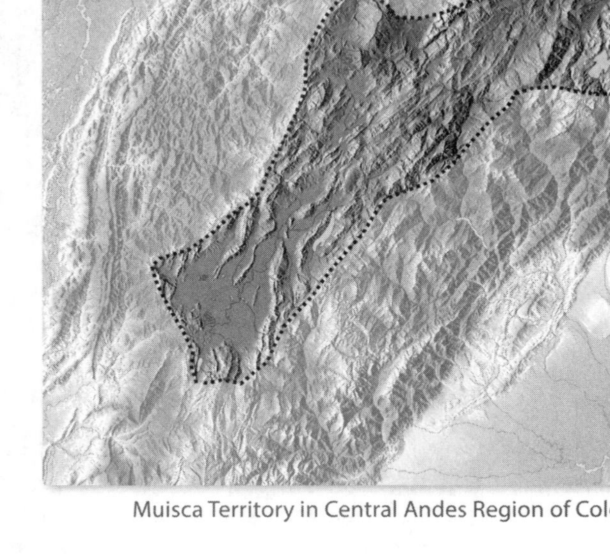
GNU Free Documentation License, Version 1.2: Dr Brains

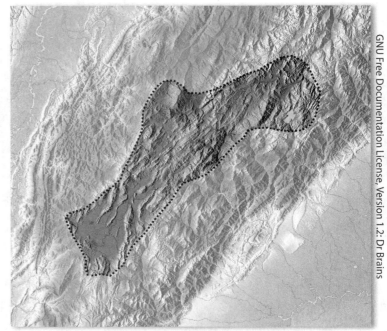

Muisca Territory in Central Andes Region of Colombia

The Muiscas (or Chibchas), who possessed one of the greatest civilizations in the pre-colonial Americas, had a Flood tradition associated with their two main deities, Bochicha and Chibchachum. A Franciscan missionary named Pedro Simón arrived in Colombia in 1603, and learned this tradition from the Muiscas:

> For certain things that Chibchachum committed against the people, the Indians murmured against him and offended him in secret and in public. This angered Chibchachum, who tried to punish them by flooding the lands. To accomplish this he created, or perhaps brought from other places, the two rivers of Sopo and Tibito, with the result that the waters of the valley rose so high that the greater part of the valley was swallowed up by the water. This had never happened before, when these two rivers did not come into the valley, for the water would be used up in the farming with no need of drainage. So universal and complete was this punishment by Chibchachum, and the inundation kept rising higher and higher so quickly each day, that they no longer had any hope of a remedy, nor of being able to supply their needs for food, for they had nowhere to sow their seeds. Also, the people were very numerous.
>
> So they took council and decided to take their complaint and their petition to the god Bochica, offering in his temple cries, sacrifices and fasting. After this, one evening, the sun reverberated in the sky, a loud noise came toward the mountain of Bogota, and a rainbow appeared in the sky. Seated on its top was Bochica, appearing in the form of a man, with a golden wand in his hand. And he called to the leading chiefs, to come quickly with all their vessels. And he said to them from on high, "I have heard your prayers, and I have compassion for you, and I know you are right in your complaint against Chibchachum. I have come to help you since you have honored me.[1]

… the Indians murmured against him and offended him in secret and in public. This angered Chibchachum, who tried to punish them by flooding the lands … So universal and complete was this punishment by Chibchachum, and the inundation kept rising higher and higher so quickly each day, that they no longer had any hope of a remedy…

Then Bochicha raised up a mountain to divert the floodwaters, and threw a golden wand toward Tequendama, which formed a rocky gorge for the waters to empty. Then Bochicha punished Chibchachum by making him carry the weight of the world on his shoulders, which formerly had been supported on great wooden pillars. This is why earthquakes occur from time to time, when Chibchachum shifts the weight from one shoulder to the other.[2]

1. Pedro Simón, *Noticias Historiales de las Conquistas de Tierra Firme en las Indias Occidentales,* Vol. 2 (Bogota: Medardo Rivas, 1891), Noticia, 4, Ch. 4, p. 289.
2. Ibid., p. 289–290.

206 CATIO

Colombia and Panama

The Catío people occupied northwestern Colombia and parts of Panama. Pedro Simón mentioned a Flood tradition he heard from them during his travels in the early 1600s:

> They have a tradition of the flood, although confused, in which many people were saved in an ark. They recognize a god of justice, a great monarch of the heaven and of the earth, and that he is the origin of all things.[3]

They have a tradition of the flood, although confused, in which many people were saved in an ark.

Around 1944, Milciades Chaves met with a Catío shaman, who shared many of the tribe's oral traditions. He said that the Flood occurred because the god Karagabi became angry with the people for their behavior. This Karagabi "killed all the Indians with the flood. He only left alive one man and one woman in a canoe, and from these the world has been populated."[4]

207 PATÁNGORA

Colombia

The Patángoras historically lived on the eastern slopes of the Central Cordillera mountains in Colombia. A Franciscan missionary named Pedro de Aguado visited them in the 1570s, and wrote thus about their account of the Flood:

> And what the Pátangoras say about the deluge is, that from their elders they have learned and understood, that generally the whole world was covered with water. The waters had drowned the people of that time. Neither men nor women escaped, with the exception of one man. This man, after the waters had gone down and the earth was no longer covered, walked upon the earth eating leaves and fruits of wild trees. At that time Am — that person which they imagine lives in heaven — came down from heaven and brought a stick wrapped in a mat. With this he made a small hut, and placed in it the man who had escaped the flood. With him, Am placed a hollow bamboo stick and a jug. The man went to sleep, and in the morning he found that the bamboo stick had turned into a woman. She then took the jug and went for water, and she began to serve the man.[5]

The waters had drowned the people of that time. Neither men nor women escaped, with the exception of one man.

208 WOUNAAN

Colombia

From ancient times the Wounaan people have lived along the San Juan River in northwestern Colombia, which outlets to the Pacific Ocean. Their language is related to Emberá, which is the only other extant language of the Choco group.

For the Wounaan Flood story, I am indebted to Ron Binder, a missionary who has lived among the Wounaan since the early 1970s. Binder obtained this legend in written form from Chindío Peña, an elder Wounaan man who is considered the authority on the tribe's oral traditions. This remarkable oral tradition of the global Flood is as follows:

...the whole world was covered with water. The waters had drowned the people of that time. Neither men nor women escaped, with the exception of one man.

> The origin of our people, the Wounaan, is attributed to Hẽwandam, Creator God, who created us on the huge stretch of beach along the Pacific coast of Colombia at the mouth of the Baudó River. Since there was only salt water there, the people went in search of fresh water, and

3. Pedro Simón, *Noticias Historiales de las Conquistas de Tierra Firme*, Vol 3, Noticia 4, Ch. 24, p. 327.
4. Milciades Chavez, "Mitos, Tradiciones, y Cuentos de los Indios Chami," *Boletin de Arqueologia*, vol. 1, no. 2 (Bogota, 1945), p. 153–154.
5. Fray Pedro de Aguado, *Recopilación Historial*, Book 10, Chap. 17.

after several years settled on the San Juan River, which they named and was known later in the region as Döchaar "the True River." The God of the universe, Hẽwandam, communicated with His creation via dreams and visions. He chose to reveal Himself to those who walked straight (correctly). His message at that time was the following:

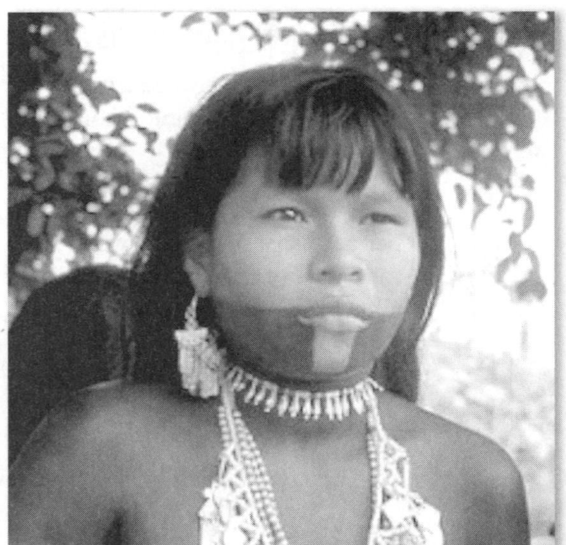

Natilda K'ipaar, a Wounaan Woman

"A torrential downpour of rain is going to hit the headwaters of the Döchaar River, and from there the mother of all waters (a huge flood) will come charging down the river as a great wave. Along with this a huge spinning top-shaped figure, Wäk'ärrmie, will be raging down the river with the voice of thunder like the sound of a huge waterfall. The world is going to sink under a flood that will drown our people and erase our culture. Start cutting down balsa wood and secure the beams of your houses to withstand the raging river. Place the balsa beams under your houses so that you can float to survive the flood.

Wäkärrmie is going to be corralling and separating the bad families from the good families to face Hẽwandam's judgment. For others He will extend long vines from the shores of Durr Hak Durr (the great mountain) so that you can grab onto them and make it safely to the mountain to survive. It will be the only mountain that will not be covered by the waters. Even if the bad people grab onto the vines they will not be saved. The vines will break and they will be swept downriver. They will be converted into dolphins and other species of fish as the punishment for their sins."

[God's] message at that time was ... "The world is going to sink under a flood ... start cutting down balsa wood ... Place the balsa beams under your houses so that you can float to survive the flood."

Well, everything happened that the people were warned about. The water covered the world and a grand number of the people, the sinners, to the furious current of water and were turned into dolphins and other species that have human characteristics. That is why we now have dolphins in the ocean. For us, dolphins are our relatives. We must help them if they get stranded in tidal pools or have other needs.

The Durr Hak Durr mountain still exists alongside the San Juan River. God caused the mountain to grow when the floods came and now it is a smaller version of what it was at that time. The people were afraid that the world would be permanently inundated with water, so to know if the water was receding, they chose someone to stay submerged in the water up to his neck. But the water was so cold, he couldn't stay in it very long. He was replaced by another called Iguana. After some days the people saw that the level of the water was lower than Iguana's neck. He stayed in the water for a long, long time, and as the water receded, the foam in the river left successive marks which stayed there as green stripes on Iguana's body all the way down to the tip of his tail. These can be observed today on iguanas.

... everything happened that the people were warned about. The water covered the world and a grand number of the people

This flood changed the world for our ancestors as they knew it. The flood changed the whole river system, causing the headwaters to switch places with the outlets of the rivers, resulting in all the rivers running in the opposite direction. Even to this day we remember this because of the chontadura fruit and the avocado. These fruits have seeds that are in a shape opposite the shape of the fruit itself. Besides all this we look at iguanas today. They are still named after Iguana and forever bare the strips from the receding river on their bodies. After the flood he was turned into an iguana. We all know the story.[6]

6. Personal communication with Ron Binder in January 2018.

209 CUBEO

Colombia

The Cubeo people live along the Vaupez River, a tributary of the Amazon River. Irving Goldman summarized a tradition they told him in 1939 or 1940:

> Dios was angry at the people because the abuhuwa, cannibalistic monsters living in the forest, had been killing many people and so he sent the flood. Those who were able fled to a high hill in the region and survived, but a great many people and many abuhuwa died. As a result there are fewer abuhuwa today than formerly.[7]

He sent the flood. Those who were able fled to a high hill in the region and survived, but a great many people and many abuhuwa died.

210 ASHANINKA

Peru and Brazil

In the early 1980s, the Ashaninka tribe shared their Flood tradition with Ronald Anderson. It is a detailed tradition, which is somewhat shortened as follows:

> There was a shaman who lived back when the world was inundated. One night, he had a dream in which he was warned of a coming flood, and that he should build a great raft with a house on it. The next morning, he told his grandsons to cut wood, make nails, and build the raft. His grandsons soon completed the raft, although some were lazy and refused to help.

Ashaninka Boys

> Next, the shaman told his grandsons, "The flood is coming soon. Therefore, we must hurry." Then they built a little house on the raft, where they would be able to live. "When the shaman saw that everything was finished, he saw that a tapir was coming to get on the raft. He saw all types of animals come as well." He told his grandsons to store up bananas and other foods on the raft.

> But there were other grandsons who were making merry and playing their instruments. These said to the other grandsons who were ready, "Look at our grandfather. From where will this flood come that is going to fill the earth?" Then the old man said, "Do not call me a liar. Thus I was warned in a dream the other day. You yourselves have seen the animals come to the raft. You come also."

> Not long after this, the Flood began. "A strong rain fell and began to fill the earth with water. . . . The raft continued floating higher and higher upon the waters. Next, they looked at the hill called Thamirivaca where a man named Tzincotsiite had lived. The raft kept climbing toward the sky."

A strong rain fell and began to fill the earth with water. … The raft continued floating higher and higher upon the waters. … The raft kept climbing toward the sky.

> The shaman wondered what prevented the Flood from subsiding. He said to his wife and children, "Stay here while I go into the water to see who has covered the hole where the water drains." He dove into the water, turned himself into an otter, and swam down to the place where

7. Irving Goldman, "Cosmological Beliefs of the Cubeo Indians," *Journal of American Folklore*, vol. 53, no. 210 (American Folklore Society, 1940), p. 244.

the water drains. There he found an enormous crab. The shaman ripped off one of the crab's claws, which allowed the water to drain. Over the course of many days, the water level fell and trees became visible.

When the earth dried a little, the animals left the raft. But finding nothing to eat upon the earth, they returned to the raft, for the earth was not yet dry enough. When the shaman came back out of the water, he was still in the form of an otter, and he could not convert himself back into a man. . . . When the earth had dried out from the flood, the children of the shaman dispersed in every direction. They also married among themselves, for there were no other women. So the people multiplied to the numbers which we have today. If it had not been for that shaman, we would not exist today. So is the tradition of the inundation of the earth.[8]

Ashaninka Men

SIKUANI

211 **Colombia and Venezuela**

The anthropologist Claude Levi-Strauss mentioned a Flood legend of the Sikuani.

When the earth had dried out from the flood, the children of the shaman dispersed in every direction.

The Sikuani of the plains of Venezuela attribute many nasalized vowels to their neighbors, the Saliva, who according to myths took refuge in a clay furnace when the flood came, while the Sikuani managed to float on a raft, and have many oral vowels.[9]

Our knowledge of the Sikuani was quite limited until Riena and Victor Kondo, of the Summer Institute of Linguistics (SIL), began working among them in 1963. They also recorded two different Flood traditions from the Sikuani, sometime prior to 1974. The first version went as follows:

Before our time the earth was flooded. All the people perished. Even though they went in canoes, they drowned. One family called Jomaenawi went in rafts of moriche palm-leaf stems. All the animals, such as jaguars and deer, died of the cold.

Then the wonito toad lifted the Jomaenawi people with his back onto a mountain. That was how they escaped.[10]

The second version went as follows:

After God destroyed the earth, there was nothing left, because he destroyed with water everything throughout all the land. At that time just a few people escaped the waters on top of a mountain. The place to which they escaped is called Maini Mountain. Another mountain is called Copipitone Mountain. Another is called Manuelaba Mountain. There we escaped inside of our ancestors (our generations were preserved).[11]

A Sikuani Chief Playing a Siku (Pan Flute)

8. Ronald J. Anderson, *Cuentos folkloricos de los Asheninca*, vol. 1 (Lima, 2008), p. 143–155.
9. Claude Levi-Strauss, *A Oleira Ciumenta* (Sao Paulo: Editora Brasiliense, 1985), p. 16.
10. Riena Louise Weidman Kondo manuscript, in *Folk Literature of the Sikuani Indians*, p. 114.
11. Ibid., p. 115.

212 WITOTO

Colombia and Peru

Between 1975 and 1977, two Witoto brothers named José and Lorenzo Soto Flórez shared their tribe's Flood legend with Maria Rodriguez de Montes. As she summarized it:

> The whole world was ordered to ascend the hill called Anequi because the earth was about to be drowned by a flood. A man named Guinadoma payed no attention to this word, but made a little cave which was well-sealed, and he went inside it.
>
> The people who went up to the top of the hill suffered many difficulties and sacrificed a child so that the water would abate. However, the water did not recede. Finally, an elderly man appeared, and he made the water recede through his prayers and his miraculous staff. When the deluge was over, the people heard the cries of Guinadoma, calling to his people for help, but he died there, buried under great amounts of mud which the flood had pulled down.[12]

... the water did not recede. Finally, an elderly man appeared, and he made the water recede through his prayers and his miraculous staff.

213 CHIMILA

Colombia

The Chimila were described as one of the most prominent tribes of pre-colonial northern Colombia. During his expedition in 1944, Gerard Reichel-Dolmatoff heard their legend of the Flood:

> One time it began to rain, and rain and rain, more and more, day and night. The sun and the moon themselves were drowned. At that time, the whole world was inundated, and there were no longer any rivers or creeks. The water grew higher and higher until all the earth was covered. There was no sowing and no food, and so all the Indians died.
>
> A single family remained alive. The man built a great house of stone under the earth — just like a house around ourselves, but with many rooms — but with one on top of another. So the man, together with his family, stayed there in the highest room while the rain came down outside, but none of the water entered.
>
> Then one day a woman said, "It has been years since I have seen the sun, and I am weary. I want to see a little light."
>
> After saying this, she got up and opened a hole in the roof. . . . Then, a rush of water entered in the house and everyone almost died. Then the man said, "Cursed woman! Someone could have died for your error! Now, when it stops raining, you will go out and be turned into an owl!" So it was, and when the rain stopped, the woman turned into an owl. Since then, the owl sings at night and wants to see the sun, but it can never see it.
>
> Then the man and the other women went down to another room and waited for the flood to be over. The waited many years, and finally they came out.
>
> Then the man said, "Now if all the animals die, what will we do?" But it did not happen thus. On a very high ridge was a calabash tree, and this tree grew much higher when it began to rain. The karau bird and the

The water grew higher and higher until all the earth was covered. ... A single family remained alive.

12. Maria Luisa Rodriguez de Montes, *Muestra de Literatura Oral en Leticia, Amazonas* (Bogota: Caro y Cuervo, 1981), p. 66, 122–124.

possum went up this tree. . . . When the flood ended, the two animals came down, and from these proceed all the animals of the world.

So the great rain passed, but in many parts the world was still not dry. Then two men said, "Let us dry the land!" They made a fire on a mountain, but it was very windy and so the mountain was burned, and with it all the sowed fields and houses. So it was that almost all the Indians died again.[13]

When the flood ended, the two animals came down, and from these proceed all the animals of the world.

214 Colombia

KÁGABA

The Kágaba or Kogi people live in the Sierra Nevada de Santa Marta mountains of northern Colombia. As told to Konrad Preuss in 1914 or 1915, one of their most ancient traditions includes an account of the Flood:

A Kogi Woman and Child, at the Ruins of Cuidad Perdida, Colombia

> After many centuries had passed, this world produced men with unnatural inclinations, of such a type that they cohabited with all types of animals. Mothers had lust for their sons, and fathers lusted for their daughters, and so did brothers for their sisters. The god Zantana saw this and opened the doors of the sky, so that it would rained for four entire years.
>
> The chiefs saw that he was going to do this. Then Chief Seizankua build a magical boat and put all types of animals and other things inside it: four-footed animals, the birds, and all types of plants. After this, the older brother Mulkueikai entered the magical boat and closed the door.
>
> Then, it began to rain with water red and green in color. It rained for four years. The rain extended, here in this world, forming lakes everywhere.
>
> The older brother Mulkueikai was at that time in the magical boat, which had come to rest on the peak of the Sierra Negra [a mountain to the east of Villanueva). There, he went out, not far, to the surrounding area and stayed on the mountain nine days.
>
> After these nine days, it took nine centuries until the lakes had dried, as the chiefs have passed down to us.[14]

After many centuries had passed, this world produced men with unnatural inclinations … Mulkueikai was at that time in this magical boat, which had come to rest on the peak of the Sierra Negra.

215 Venezuela and Guyana

AKAWOIO

Around 1840, when the missionary William Brett (1818–1886) visited the Akawoio and other tribes of interior Venezuela and Guyana, most of the European colonists had settled on the coast of South America without venturing too far into the thick jungles of the interior.

The Akawoio creation story includes an account of the Flood, but it is also noteworthy for its clear parallel with the Garden of Eden account. This tradition tells that in the beginning, all the animals were created by Makonaima, "the great spirit whom no man hath seen." They all lived in harmony together, under the

13. Gerard Reichel-Dolmatoff, "Mitos y Cuentos de los Indios Chimila," Boletin de Arqueologia, vol. 1, no. 1 (Bogota, 1945), p. 6–7.
14. Manuela Fischer and Konrad Theodor Preuss, *Mitos Kogi* (Quito: Abya-Yala, 1989), p. 39–40.

gentle rule of Sigu, the son of the creator. Each day, the animals, who had the gift of speech, went into the forests to feed. On their return, each animal brought back a portion as an act of respectful homage to its protector and lord.

Kaieteur Falls in Guyana

But there was a magical tree in the forest, with all sorts of fruits and vegetables growing on it and around it. One day it was found. Sigu, the master of the animals, determined it best that the tree be chopped down, and upon doing so it provided seeds for all kinds of foods. Then Sigu sent all the animals and birds to cultivate the fields with these seeds, and they began the work.

"All assisted willingly except Iwarrika (the monkey) who being very lazy and full of mischief, avoided his share of the labour, and by his tricks thwarted the efforts of the others." Seeing this, Sigu sent the monkey to fetch water, so that he would no longer cause harm.

But there was a magical tree in the forest, with all sorts of fruits and vegetables growing on it and around it. One day it was found.

Now the stump of the magical tree remained, and it was connected to a gigantic, subterranean fountain. One day it began to overflow, but Sigu capped it with a basket, and through some magical power it remained tightly secure.

However, the monkey abandoned his task of carrying water, and found the magic stump. Imagining that Sigu was hiding for himself the choicest fruits in it, the monkey removed the basket-seal, intending to eat what he might find within, while no one was near.

> So he hastily forced up the magic cover, and the next instant was gasping and struggling in abject terror and astonishment, being overturned and nearly drowned by a mighty torrent which burst forth, and from a rapidly enlarging aperture overspread the earth around.
>
> Gathering his little flock together to save them from the rising waters, Sigu led them to the highest spot of land, on which grew some enormous Cocorite palms. Selecting the tallest of these, he made the birds and climbing animals ascend. The animals which could not climb, and were not amphibious, he placed in a cave with a very narrow entrance. This he carefully closed, and sealed with wax, after giving the inmates a long thorn with which to pierce the wax, and ascertain whether the waters were above their level or no. What they did for air we are not informed.
>
> Sigu, having thus done his best for the safety of all, climbed the Cocorite; being driven by the rising water to the topmost branches. A terrible night, or rather period of darkness and storm equal in length to many days and nights, then ensued, during which all suffered intensely from cold and hunger. . . .
>
> The good Sigu, anxious for the safety of all, patiently endured this and every other discomfort, and from time to time dropped the seeds of the Cocorite into the water, that he might judge by the sound of

...being overturned and nearly drowned by a mighty torrent which burst forth, and from a rapidly enlarging aperture overspread the earth around.

its elevation. At length the periods which elapsed before the splash was heard became longer and longer. Then at last was heard the dull sound of the seeds striking the soft earth, and at the same time the birds, each with its own peculiar note, began joyfully to hail the approach of day.[15]

An Arawak Village

216 Venezuela, Guyana, and Suriname

ARAWAK

The Arawak, who lived along the Atlantic Coast from the Guyanas to Suriname, told William Brett their Flood legend sometime around 1850:

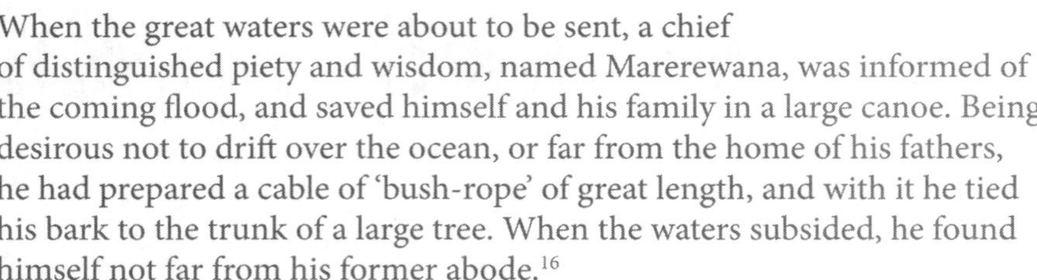

> When the great waters were about to be sent, a chief of distinguished piety and wisdom, named Marerewana, was informed of the coming flood, and saved himself and his family in a large canoe. Being desirous not to drift over the ocean, or far from the home of his fathers, he had prepared a cable of 'bush-rope' of great length, and with it he tied his bark to the trunk of a large tree. When the waters subsided, he found himself not far from his former abode.[16]

When the great waters were about to be sent, a chief of distinguished piety and wisdom, named Marerewana, was informed of the coming flood, and saved himself and his family in a large canoe.

217 Venezuela and Guyana

WARAO

William Brett made a passing reference to the Warao tribe's tradition about the Flood:

> The Warau traditions of the flood are of little interest. They differ from those of other tribes chiefly in the circumstance that the survivors saved themselves by a large woodskin, and made trial of various kinds of trees ere they decided on the bark fittest for their purpose.[17]

218 Venezuela and Colombia

ACHAGUA

The Achagua tribe, living along the Upper Orinoco River in southern Venezuela and eastern Colombia, related a Flood tradition to Juan Rivero in the 1720s, which he described thus:

View Over the Orinoco River

> They also have a tradition, passed from fathers to sons, about the Universal Flood, which they call "Catana" in their language. The truth is they err on the mode, although not on the substance. They say their forebears told them how the world was flooded long ago with a very heavy rainstorm which covered the earth, and caused everything to perish. But, one of our ancient grandfathers (so they refer to Noah), seeing that the world was being inundated, climbed up a very high mountain with his family, in order to escape with their lives. There, the waters could not reach them, and so they were saved.[18]

… their forebears told them how the world was flooded long ago with a very heavy rainstorm which covered the earth, and caused everything to perish.

15. William Henry Brett, *The Indian Tribes of Guiana: Their Condition and Habits* (London: Bell and Daldy, 1868), p. 378–382.
16. Ibid., p. 398–399.
17. Ibid., p. 393.
18. Juan Rivero, *Historia de las Misiones de los Llanos de Casanare y los Rios Orinoco y Meta* (Bogota: Silvestre y Compañia, 1883), p. 113.

219 **Venezuela, Brazil, and Guyana**

PEMÓN

Pemón Child

The Pemón people group (also known by other names including Arekuna or Taulipang) live in the southeastern tip of Venezuela and adjacent Brazil and Guyana. Around the year 1940 they told their Flood tradition to Cesareo de Armellada. This tradition, similar to that of the Akawoio, tells of a magical tree that was cut down, and which had a spring in its trunk containing all kinds of fish. A mischievous monkey unstopped the cover of this spring, causing water to burst forth and to flood the entire earth:

> The Makunaima, fleeing from the inundation, also sought places to climb up and shelter themselves. Chiké climbed up a palm tree called maripá, and his brother climbed a palm tree called warumá. They spent one winter atop the palm trees, feeding on the trees' fruits.
>
> . . . The Makunaima could tell that the waters were lowering from the distinct sound made by the discarded seeds from the fruits they were eating. When they knew that the seeds were not falling in water, they went down with caution, and went down little by little from the hills. . . .
>
> When the Makunaima went down from the palm trees and the hills, the earth and the same rocks were very soft. And in those times they entertained themselves making whimsical stones and waterfalls. And on many stones we still see their footprints.[19]

The Makunaima, fleeing from the inundation, also sought places to climb up and shelter themselves

Theodor Koch-Grünberg recorded a similar version in 1911.[20]

220 **Venezuela and Colombia**

GIRARA AND AIRICO

The closely associated Girara and Airico tribes inhabited the plains of northeastern Colombia and western Venezuela. They told Juan Rivero their history of the Flood when he met them around 1730:

> They do not adore idols, but confess that there are two gods who are brothers — one older and one younger. Of the elder brother deity, they say that he created everything from nothing, and that he destroyed all people with a Flood, in punishment for their sins. But after this the younger god came down from the heavens to earth and propagated the human lineage that perished in the flood, and that he lived in the world being emperor of all things. To this god they attribute earthquakes, saying that he moves the earth with the impact of his arm.[21]

…that he destroyed all people with a Flood, in punishment for their sins. But after this the younger god came down from the heavens to earth and propagated the human lineage that perished in the flood…

19. Cesareo de Armellada, *Tauron Panton: Cuentos y Leyendas de los Indios Pemón*, 2nd edition (Quito: Abya-Yala, 1989), p. 55–56.
20. Theodor Koch-Grünberg, *Vom Roraima zum Orinoco*, vol. 2 (Stuttgart: Verlag Strecker and Schroder, 1924), p. 33–38.
21. Rivero, *Historia de las Misiones de los Llanos*, p. 116.

221 Venezuela

TAMANAC

Alexander von Humboldt

The scientist and explorer Alexander von Humboldt (1769–1859) traveled the interior of South America from 1799 to 1804. He met the Tamanacs along the Cuchivero River, which is a southern tributary of the Orinoco River in Venezuela. He later wrote about what they told him about the ancient Flood:

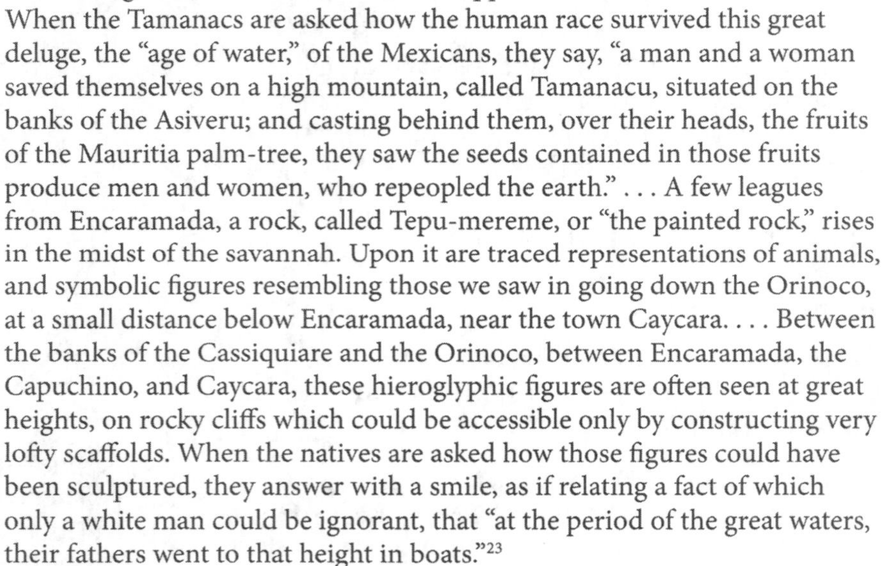

> I cannot quit this first link of the mountains of Encaramada without recalling to mind a fact that was not unknown to Father Gili,[22] and which was often mentioned to me during our abode in the Missions of the Orinoco. The natives of those countries have retained the belief that, "at the time of the great waters, when their fathers were forced to have recourse to boats, to escape the general inundation, the waves of the sea beat against the rocks of Encaramada." This belief is not confined to one nation singly, the Tamanacs; it makes part of a system of historical tradition, of which we find scattered notions among the Maypures of the great cataracts; among the Indians of the Rio Erevato, which runs in to the Caura; and among almost all the tribes of the Upper Orinoco. When the Tamanacs are asked how the human race survived this great deluge, the "age of water," of the Mexicans, they say, "a man and a woman saved themselves on a high mountain, called Tamanacu, situated on the banks of the Asiveru; and casting behind them, over their heads, the fruits of the Mauritia palm-tree, they saw the seeds contained in those fruits produce men and women, who repeopled the earth." . . . A few leagues from Encaramada, a rock, called Tepu-mereme, or "the painted rock," rises in the midst of the savannah. Upon it are traced representations of animals, and symbolic figures resembling those we saw in going down the Orinoco, at a small distance below Encaramada, near the town Caycara. . . . Between the banks of the Cassiquiare and the Orinoco, between Encaramada, the Capuchino, and Caycara, these hieroglyphic figures are often seen at great heights, on rocky cliffs which could be accessible only by constructing very lofty scaffolds. When the natives are asked how those figures could have been sculptured, they answer with a smile, as if relating a fact of which only a white man could be ignorant, that "at the period of the great waters, their fathers went to that height in boats."[23]

The natives of those countries have retained the belief that, "at the time of the great waters, when their fathers were forced to have recourse to boats, to escape the general inundation, the waves of the sea beat against the rocks of Encaramada."

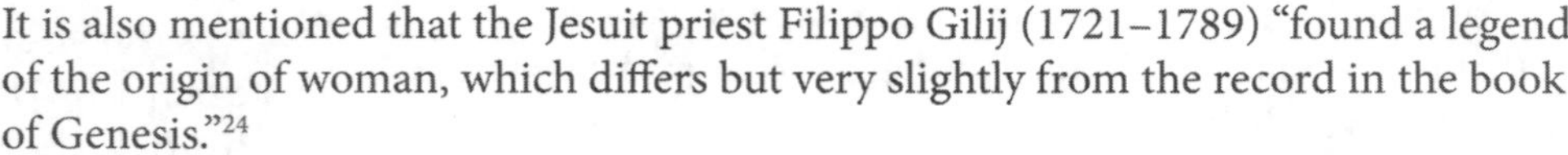

It is also mentioned that the Jesuit priest Filippo Gilij (1721–1789) "found a legend of the origin of woman, which differs but very slightly from the record in the book of Genesis."[24]

22. See: Filippo Salvatore Gilij, *Saggio de Storia Americana*, Vol. 3, Book 1, Ch. 4 (Rome: 1782), p. 19.
23. Alexander von Humboldt, *Personal Narrative of Travels to the Equinoctial Regions of the New Continent during the Years 1799–1804*, trans. and ed. Thomasina Ross, vol. 2 (London: George Bell and Sons, 1876), p. 182–183.
24. John Muehleisen Arnold, *Genesis and Science; Or the First Leaves of the Bible* (London: Longman, Green, & Co., 1875), p. 154.

222 MAIPURE

Venezuela

The explorer Robert Schomburgk heard a Flood tradition from the Maipure while surveying British Guyana between 1840 and 1844. Their tradition is very similar to that of the Tamanacs:

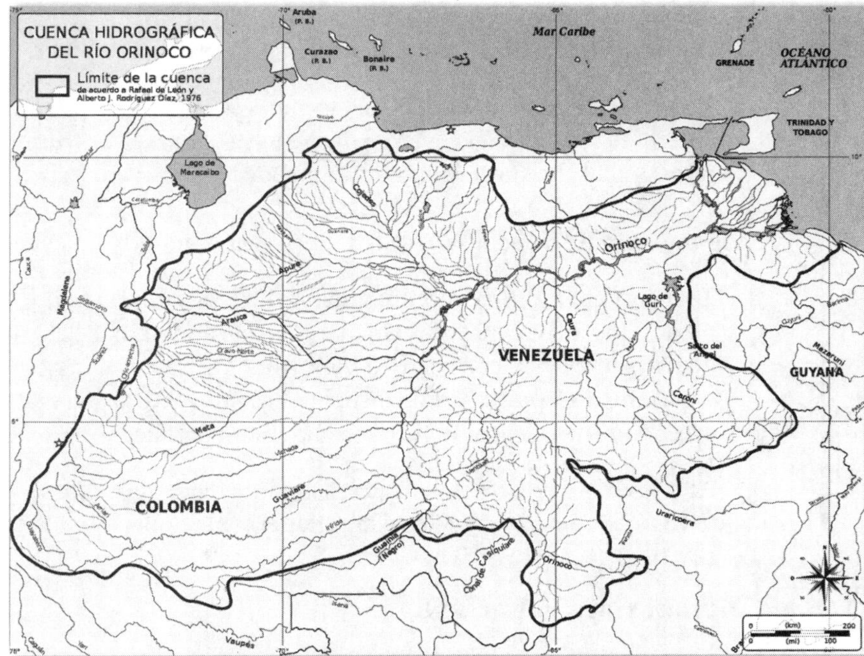

Drainage Basin of the Orinoco River, the World's Fourth Largest River by Discharge Volume

> The Maipuri again, and according to Alexander von Humboldt the Tamanacs also, have a legend that once upon a time the whole earth was flooded with water. Only two people, a man and a woman, saved themselves on the summit of the high mountain Tamanaku. As they wandered round and round in deep misery at the loss of their friends, they heard a voice instructing them to throw the Mauritia fruit over their shoulders behind their backs: this done, the fruits that the man threw became men, and those that the woman threw, women.

Only two people, a man and a woman, saved themselves on the summit of the high mountain Tamanaku.

223 PIAROA

Venezuela

The Piaroa people (also known as De'Aruwa) live along the Orinoco River in Venezuela. The Catholic missionary Cesareo de Armellada (1908–1996) studied the tribes of Venezuela from the 1940s through the 1970s. The Piaroa told him their Flood legend, that long ago there was a very good man named Poman-Ichaj, with a good and hard-working wife named Jiudej. One day an angelic sunbird, representative of the Sun, appeared to the woman and said to her:

A Piaroa Hut

> "The people are very evil. They murder each other with arrows, and they forget about the Sun. They no longer burn the holy fire in the morning in my honor, except for your husband Poman-Ichaj. The sun has sent me — I am his bird — to save you and your husband Poman-Ichaj. Build your hut up high, very high, on the mountain of Guanary, just as I make my nest very high, where the waters cannot reach it" And having said this, he disappeared.
>
> The woman could not wait for her husband to return before telling him, but ran in search of him toward the hill. On the road

she found him very happy with his "stones that sing." There she told him what the bird "Newaj" had told her, and the orders she had received.

Pimon-Ichaj replied, "Very well, tomorrow we will go up to the summit and there we will make a large house to save ourselves from the great rainfall that the sunbird has announced to us."[25]

The next day after they had finished their work, the rain began. It rained day after day without stopping. All the people were drowned…

After the couple offered a sacrifice to the Sun and built their shelter, the Flood began:

They worked for three months and finished their round house, situated on the peak of the hill Guanay and Guanary, beside a stream of clear water. . . . The next day after they had finished their work, the rain began. It rained day after day without stopping. All the people were drowned, as were all the animals except for the Capybara, the tapir, and the water dog, because these swim.

After a century, the waters receded, and the Parawi (Orinoco River) returned to its bed. Then, Poman-Ichaj and Jiudej came down from the peak.[26]

GUAJIRO

224 Colombia and Venezuela

The Guajiros believed that it was a punishment from God, who was angry. It began to rain… raining without ceasing.

The Guajiro or Wayuu people live on the northern sections of the Colombia/Venezuela border. The anthropologist Johannes Wilbert recorded their Flood legend, which he published in 1962:

There was an epoch when the Guajiros were not social with each other. Whenever they encountered others, they would argue, fight, and kill one other. Everyone lived in isolation from others, in his own house, forming isolated little groups with his relatives. No one could step out of their house. If anyone did so, they ran the risk of death, or that their women would be assaulted.

. . . One day, it began to thunderstorm. The moon and the sun were eclipsed. The Guajiros believed that it was a punishment from God, who was angry. It began to rain. At first they thought it would be a passing rain shower, but it was not so. Days and months passed, and it continued raining without ceasing. The water of the sea began to rise, and all the rivers overflowed their banks and began to invade the land.

In sight of this, they began to seek the highest elevations of the Guajiro. In that epoch there was a mountain range that was called Cosina or Cosineta. This sank beneath the waters. Everything was nullified by the water, but there remained one peak of a little hill, and everyone climbed up on it.

On this peak were gathered groups of various races, but the water began to invade this peak as well. The women began to cry, as did the children. All the world cried. They prayed to the god Mareiwa to save them, to not let them die.

Then it happened that the land started to rise. It ascended in elevation, but despite this the water would rise as well. The water continued rising until, finally, when there was but a small area of the peak not submerged, all of the people were huddled tightly together. Some animals were there too, which had been able to save

Guajiran Artisans

25. Cesáreo de Armellada and Carmela Bentivenga de Napolitano, *Literaturas Indígenas Venezolanas* (Caracas: Monte Avila, 1991), p. 319.
26. Ibid., p. 320.

themselves. This peak is called Epitsi, and in Spanish it is called "Cerro de la Teta" (Hill of the Teat).

Some days after it had ceased to rain, the sun appeared, and by night the moon was seen. The water began to descend, and also the people went down from the hill, until finally the water returned to its normal level.[27]

Map of Lake Maracaibo

225 YUPA

Venezuela

The Yupa historically lived in the lowlands of Venezuela west of Lake Maracaibo. Fleeing from Spanish and German colonizers, they migrated westward into the Sierras. Two elderly women of the tribe shared their traditions with Johannes Wilbert in May 1960. Their account of the Flood runs thus:

> A long time ago a great flood arose, from which only twenty pairs of human beings and a few animals were able to save themselves on top of a high mountain. One day a Yupa declared that he was truly the bird woodpecker, and would fly off to ascertain the extent of the flood. He found out that it was a gigantic sheet of water bordered all about by a wall of mud. Now the cayman wanted to determine the depth of the water. So he threw in a big wild boar first, and then a tapir, and then all the other animals one after the other — all of which drowned without exception, so deep was the water. Finally the crab decided to dive in; four days and four nights passed before he came up again. Now the cayman was a tuano (medicine man) who could dive that deeply without danger. He ordered the turtle and the armadillo to swim with him to the sand wall. Once there he dove under the water with the turtle to dig at the wall from below. The armadillo meanwhile was to work from above. Soon the wall gave way, and the water broke through. A good deal of sand remained lying on the backs of the armadillo, the turtle, and the cayman. Even today one can still see sand on their backs.[28]

A long time ago a great flood arose, from which only twenty pairs of human beings and a few animals were able to save themselves on top of a high mountain.

226 YARURO

Venezuela and Colombia

The Yaruro or Pumeh tribe live along the Capanaparo and Sinarucos Rivers, which are tributaries of the Orinoco River. They narrated their Flood tradition to Vincenzo Petrullo in 1934, which told that four people escaped the Flood and repopulated the human race:

> After the people were created and had lived on this earth a long time they began to forget to do the right thing. They no longer believed that Kuma is the mother of water and the entire universe and everything there is in it. So Kuma, in order to show them that she was the creator of the universe and everything therein, caused a rain to begin which continued until everything was covered over with water except a tree on the upper Capanaparo, and the top of a hill. A man and his sister took refuge on the very topmost branches of the tree, and a man with his aunt saved themselves by staying on top of this hill.[29]

After the people were created and had lived on this earth a long time they began to forget to do the right thing. They no longer believed…

27. Johannes Wilbert, in Separata de la Memoria de la Sociedad de Ciencias Naturales La Salle, vol. 12, no. 62 (Caracas: 1962), p. 102–103.
28. Johannes Wilbert, *Yupa Folktales* (Los Angeles: UCLA Latin American Center, 1974), p. 78.
29. Vincenzo Petrullo, "The Yaruros of the Capanaparo River, Venezuela," in "Anthropological Papers," *Bureau of American Ethnology Bulletin*, vol. 123 (Washington: GPO, 1939), p. 245–246.

227 MACUSI

Guyana and Brazil

The Macusis live in southern Guyana and northern Brazil, where they were historically a powerful, peace-loving, and orderly nation.[30] A German explorer named Robert Schomburgk met them between 1840 and 1844. He gave a bare mention of their Flood tradition:

> According to the myths of the Macusi the only man who survived the general flood threw stones behind him, and by that means populated the world afresh.[31]

Robert Schomburgk

228 WAPISHANA AND TARUMA

Guyana and Brazil

William Farabee and a team from the University of Pennsylvania Musuem visited the Wapishana, Taruma, and other tribes of southern Guyana from 1913 to 1916. The Flood tradition they narrated to him is similar to that of the Akawoio, attributing the Flood to a magical tree that was cut down. The reader will notice similarities to the Genesis account of the Garden as well.

According to the Wapishana and Taruma, a god named Duid used to feed the people with all the foods that grew at this magical tree. However, the people discovered the tree and decided to serve themselves from it. Furious at their insubordination, the creator god cut down the tree, and the waters of the deluge burst from its stump.

> When Tuminkar had the tree cut down the waters of the tree burst forth in a tremendous flood, which gradually rose and covered the face of the whole earth except Serriri, a three-peaked mountain, the highest in the region, located about forty miles northward between the Rupununi and Takutu Rivers. When the waters began to rise some of the people, in order to prevent the extinction of the race, caught a "bai," or wild Muscovy duck (Cairina muschata), cut off his upper mandible, which they used as a canoe, and floated to the top of the mountain. After twenty days the waters began to subside. The survivors were very hungry and wondered how soon the land would again appear, so they threw off rocks towards the north to determine the depth of the water and thus the small round-topped mountain nearby was built up. The duck's bill is frequently used today as a spoon, or worn suspended from a necklace as an amulet.[32]

> … the waters of the tree burst forth in a tremendous flood, which gradually rose and covered the face of the whole earth except Serriri…

> … which they used as a canoe, and floated to the top of the mountain. After twenty days the waters began to subside."

30. Schomburgk, *Travels in British Guiana* p. 246.
31. Ibid., p. 254.
32. William Curtis Farabee, "The Central Arawaks," *University of Pennsylvania Museum Anthropological Publications*, vol. 9 (Philadelphia: University Museum, 1918), p. 121.

229 ATAROI

Guyana

The Ataroi tribe had been recently absorbed by the Wapishana tribe when William Farabee visited them in 1913. Nevertheless, the knowledge of some of their oral traditions had not yet been lost, but was still preserved by the older members. They told him a Flood tradition, which he described this way:

He took a ball of beeswax, made himself a house of it and floated about until the water subsided.

> The accouri [a type of rodent] was the only animal saved at the time of the flood. He took a ball of beeswax, made himself a house of it and floated about until the water subsided. The evidence of this is that the back part of his lower hind leg has no hair and looks like wax because he sat on his legs so long in his wax house. Moreover, he has no tail, but a little wax stump instead.[33]

230 YE'KUANA

Venezuela and Brazil

The Ye'kuana or Maquiritare people told many of their legends to Marc de Civrieux in the 1950s, including this one pertaining to the Flood:

> The clouds rose slowly and began to rain terribly. Immediately, the water grew in all the rivers and it gradually flooded the earth, putting out the fire. In very little time, the water covered the whole surface of the earth, sweeping away all the people who had managed to save themselves from the fire.

Iureke, in the face of this general deluge, took shelter in the sky, climbing up to the top of a high palm…

> Iureke, in the face of this general deluge, took shelter in the sky, climbing up to the top of a high palm in the region of the Antabari river. He stayed there for a long time, eating the fruits of the palm in the middle of the night that covered all the earth, because the sun was hidden behind the thick clouds. It kept raining incessantly. Iureke thought that no one was going to escape death on earth. He did not know that a few animals — Tosede (a bird), Hauhi (the Pauxi bird) and Huakia (the tapir) — had been saved by having gotten inside large gourds that floated like boats on the waters. The waters began to go down and the earth began to dry.[34]

231 CUIVA

Colombia and Venezuela

Little was known about the Cuiva people, who inhabit a portion of eastern Colombia and western Venezuela, until Isabel Kerr visited them in 1965. A Cuiva man told her a tradition of the Flood, which went like this:

"My people, I'm calling you; in a short while there will be flooding." The people joked about it. "Maybe Namon is lying to us," they said. He commanded the people to make a raft.

> Long before our time, all the people died even though Namon called to them. He told them a story, saying: "My people, I'm calling you; in a short while there will be flooding." The people joked about it. "Maybe Namon is lying to us," they said. He commanded the people to make a raft. "Make yourselves canoes and rafts," he said, "or all of you may drown."

33. Ibid., p. 135.
34. Marc de Civrieux, "Leyendas Maquiritares," *Memoria de la Sociedad de Ciencias Naturales la Salle*, vol. 20, no. 56 (Caracas, 1960), p. 124–125.

Namon had one small area of dry ground. It was before our time when he said to the people: "I have one piece of dry ground; it's a high mountain. There is a naxaerabo tree standing on it." It was sufficient for all of us gathered together. Namon had one piece of dry land and one naxaerabo tree standing on it. He alone had food. He was not hungry and he did not drown.

All the people in the canoes were destroyed. It was not so with those on the raft. They survived and did not drown. The raft floated with all the people on it. On all sides there was water.[35]

232 Colombia and Brazil

MESAYA

The Mesaya lived along the Japura and Apaporis Rivers in southeastern Colombia and the Amazonas state of Brazil. They practiced cannibalism, but only toward their arch-enemies, the Miranha tribe. They told their Flood tradition to the explorer Paul Marcoy in 1846:

> The tradition of a deluge exists among these men. In very distant times, the water having covered the earth, the Mesayas of that period, whose stature rivalled that of the largest trees, escaped the general inundation by squatting under a "canahua" — canoe — the concave part of which they had turned towards the ground.[36]

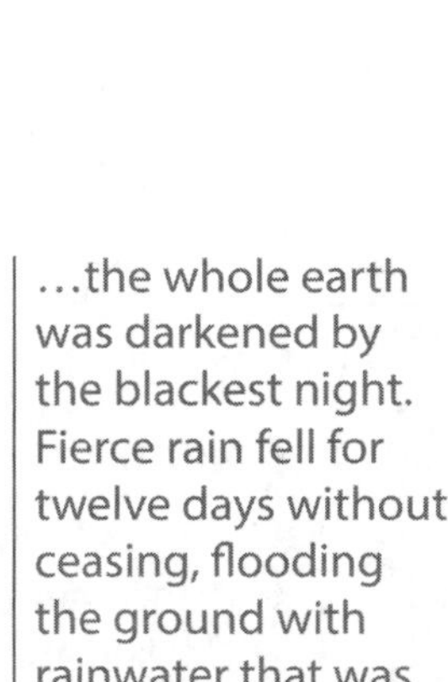

Mesaya Man

233 Venezuela

YABARANA

Around 1960, the Yabarana tribe told Johannes Wilbert an oral tradition which contains a reference to the Flood. They said the Flood was triggered by the opening of a magical box, which they had been warned not to open:

> Despite his recommendations, Ochi opened the basket. The sunbird flew away, its harmonious song became a horrible shriek, the clouds piled up, the sun disappeared and the whole earth was darkened by the blackest night. Fierce rain fell for twelve days without ceasing, flooding the ground with rainwater that was salty, black, cold, and infected.
>
> The two humans were about to perish. They were saved by a hill that emerged.
>
> . . . Years passed. Finally, Mayowoca sent the bird to look for the sun. . . . The wind took him to the end of the earth. Miracle! There was the sun, like a burning ball. Indeed, tired of being locked in the box, the sun had fled to the zenith and since then it has been running from end to end of the world, but without being able to escape further. Thus appeared the alternation of day and night.
>
> . . . Mayowoca then set about organizing the world, which the flood left uninhabitable. By the sheer force of his thought he made the trees grow, the rivers flow, the animals born. He opened a mountain from which emerged a new humanity to whom he taught the arts of civilization, religious ceremonies and the preparation of fermented beverages that allow communication with heaven. Finally, he rose to the clouds, from a place where the footprint of his two feet can still be seen.[37]

...the whole earth was darkened by the blackest night. Fierce rain fell for twelve days without ceasing, flooding the ground with rainwater that was salty, black, cold, and infected.

35. Johannes Wilbert, Karin Simoneau, and Bernard Arcand, *Folk Literature of the Cuiva Indians* (Los Angeles: UCLA Latin American Center, 1991), p. 55–56.
36. Marcoy, *A Journey Across South America*, vol. 2, part 2, p. 444.
37. Johannes Wilbert, Indios de la Region Orinoco-Ventuari (Caracas: Fundacion La Salle de Ciencias Naturales, 1963), p. 150–156. As quoted in Claude Levi-Strauss, Mitologicas III: El Origen de las Maneras de Mesa, trans. Juan Almela (Mexico: Siglo Veintiuno Editores, 1970), p. 133–135.

234

WAJAPI

French Guiana, Suriname, and Brazil

The Wajapi, a tribe living in northern Brazil, French Guiana, and Suriname, told their Flood legend to a doctoral student named Lilian Abram Dos Santos around the year 2000:

> Long ago, the ancients did not believe what God said about the flood that was going to come. But they said that God was lying and the flood was not going to happen. Still, some of the ancients believed what God said. Then, God made a great canoe, just like a [modern] ship for the people who believed him, so that they could stay inside this great canoe and not die in the flood. This was not only for those people, but also for the animals — birds great and small, snakes and other animals. God placed these in the great canoe. And the ancients who did not believe God, they all died in the waters of the deluge, because they did not believe what God had said about the flood, that is why.
>
> After the flood, the earth dried slowly. When it finished God released the vulture to go look for the people, to see whether they had died or were living. Then the vulture went and ate the dead.[38]

Long ago, the ancients did not believe what God said about the flood that was going to come… Then, God made a great canoe, just like a [modern] ship for the people who believed him…

235

PALIKUR

French Guiana and Brazil

The Palikur live in southeastern French Guiana and in the state of Amapá in Brazil. They told Artionka Capiberibe their creation story sometime prior to 2009, which contains an account of the Flood:

> One day a man was working on a canoe when he heard the singing of a bird, a Ticua. He was entertained by his service when the bird stopped and left. A short time later the man heard the noise of someone walking through the woods and soon saw a man, in fact, an Indian, dressed in a kamis (cloth), an outfit similar to the Wajãpi. The Indian said to the man, who was the Ticuan and who had brought a disagreeable and somewhat sad news, but that this novelty was sad only for those who do not know and do not understand. For one who understands, it was very good news because the person would live once again. That Ticuan had been sent by God to tell the man to put aside the canoe he was making, for it would not save him.
>
> He was to go home and call his wife, his children, his relatives, his friends, all the men and women on earth for five hundred years, to build a large clay pot that would serve to save them all. Because, once the pot was ready, God would destroy the world with water. Ticuan also said that when the pot was ready, they had to put around them ten bamboos. God would stick these bamboos and put the kanatru (reed) inside them. The flutes made with bamboo would be to warn when the waters were down. That is because, after the rain, there will be no one else, no one who can warn when the land dries up.
>
> Everyone who was called came to make the pot. They worked on it for three hundred years. But one day, people got tired, started

…to build a large clay pot that would serve to save them all. Because, once the pot was ready, God would destroy the world with water… with the staff he could call the animals, a couple of each species, to enter the pot. Then he ordered those who had built the pot to enter it, and finally locked the door outside.

After the flood, the earth dried slowly. When it finished God released the vulture to go look for the people, to see whether they had died or were living. Then the vulture went and ate the dead.

38. Lilian Abram Dos Santos, 2011, "Modos de Escrever: Tradição oral, letramento e segunda lingua na Educação Escolar Wajapi," Ph. D. Thesis (Universidad Estadual de Campinas, Campinas), p. 133.

> complaining and left the service. Only the man, the one who had spoken directly with Ticuan, and his seven sons-in-law, continued to work. After five hundred years, the pot was finally ready. Ticuan reappeared, gave the man a stick and said that with the staff he could call the animals, a couple of each species, to enter the pot. Then he ordered those who had built the pot to enter it, and finally locked the door outside. The rain fell, and the people outside the pot began to laugh at the man. But after thirty days, it began to rain. At first it was just a drizzle. Little by little the drizzle was thickening and the rain did not stop. In a fortnight, all the islands sank. When a mountain like Cajari sank, people finally believed the man and went to the pot, but he could not open the door.

Traditional Palikur Dance

> . . . When the water subsided and the pot sat on the ground again, the Turés touched. The man looked through a small window and saw that the water was low. The man sent a pigeon to see if the mountain was really dry. At that time, the pigeon, which we call Galician, was a vulture. When the pigeon arrived on the mountain, it found a pile of dead people. Instead of taking a grain of sand to carry the man, he decided to eat those dead who were already rotten. When he returned, he lied to the man, saying that the land was not dry yet. The man decided to send the vulture to check. The vulture gathered a grain of sand in its beak and returned to show the man that the mountain was dry. Because the pigeon had deceived him, the man decided to turn him into a vulture. And turned the vulture into a pigeon. The buzzard was cursed and condemned to eating only rotten meat. After that, the man came down from the pot and began to walk on the dry land.[39]

The man decided to send the vulture to check. The vulture gathered a grain of sand in its beak and returned to show the man that the mountain was dry.

We see that in South America, so far away from Israel, we still find the memory of Noah's dispatch of the two birds.

39. Artionka Capiberibe, 2009, "Nas Duas Margens Do Rio," Ph. D. Thesis (Universidade Federal do Rio de Janeiro), p. 75–76.

236 NUKÁK

Colombia

The Nukák live in the northwestern Amazon basin, in the Colombian state of Guaviare. They are located between the Guaviare and Inirida Rivers. The anthropologist Gabriel Cabrera visited and studied the Nukák people from 1991 to 1995 and was able to record their origin story. Their story tells that their ancestor and hero Mauro led the people to safety from the great flood in which everything was covered by water. He led them to live in caves in the high mountains, just like the bats do, but with the entrances sealed off from the water. Then Mauro and the people with him painted the hills as the water descended.[40]

The Cerros de Mavecure on the Inírida River

A 1993 New Tribes Mission report records a similar account.[41]

In order to punish the men, he opened great storehouses in the heavens and all the earth was drowned.

Venezuela

The Yukpa (or Yukko) told Adolfo de Villamañan told a tradition of both the Flood and the subsequent confusion of languages:

237 YUKPA

> The Yukpa and all the people were continually assaulting and robbing women. Kemoko was always counseling them to live in peace, but they did not listen to him. In the festivals, they fought heavily and many of them were killed by the women. Kemoko saw this from heaven. In order to punish the men, he opened great storehouses in the heavens and all the earth was drowned. The only ones who survived were those who took shelter on Tetare, above the river Atapshi by Manastara, very high up. When they were recovering they built up a great mountain of clay to save themselves, but Kemoko opened another of the storehouses of heaven and the mountain of clay was destroyed. Then they all dispersed and went back to fighting amongst themselves. The ants changed their languages, and they no longer understood each other, because they talked like animals. Before this everyone spoke the language of the Yukpa. The people continued doing the same things: fighting like animals as they spoke in different languages.[42]

Mountains of Northwest Venezuela,
Seen from Ayapaina, a Yukpa Community

40. Gabriel Cabrera, Carlos Franky, and Dany Mahecha, *Los Nukak: Nomadas de la Amazonia Colombiana* (Bogota: Unibiblos, 1999), p. 62–63.
41. Associacion Nuevas Tribus, “Informe de actividades Octubre-Noviembre-Diciembre” (Bogota: Direccion General de Asuntos Indigenas, 1993), no page numbers.
42. Adolfo de Villamañan, “Introducción al Mundo Religioso de los Yukpa,” *Antropologica*, vol. 57 (Caracas: Fundacion La Salle, 1982), p. 15.

238 TATUY

Venezuela

The Tatuy are a tribe that since ancient times has lived in the Sierra Nevada de Mérida mountains at the south end of Lake Maracaibo. Indeed, the word Tatuy means "most ancient." Closely related is the word "Taita," which means "father" or "grandfather," and represents the Tatuy view of themselves as ancestral to the other tribes of America.[43] They shared their knowledge of the Flood with a professor named Andrés Carrero:

> They believed in a universal flood. On the origin of the lagunas it is said that one day a man and a woman carrying a pitcher left the lagoon of Santo Domingo. As they reached places in the Cordillera, they let drops of water fall, forming lagoons, until they reached Lagunillas [likely Lake Maracaibo], the place they chose to found their nation. Here the pitcher burst, leaving behind the massive lake and their settlement, and the couple disappeared.[44]

239 BANIWA

Venezuela, Colombia, and Brazil

The Baniwa live on the border of Venezuela, Colombia, and Brazil along the Içana River and its tributaries. Robin Wright met this tribe and learned of their Flood legend during his doctoral thesis work in the late 1970s:

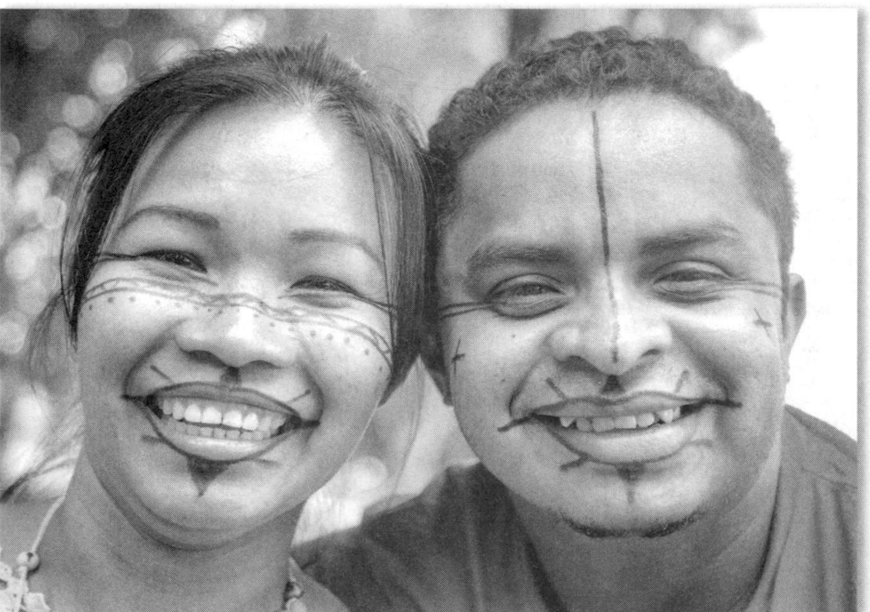

Modern Baniwa Couple

> In a myth which follows the beginning of Iaperikuli, the hero tries to kill Dzauikwapa, the chief of animals and poison. He made the world as dark as the night and the rivers rose in a flood, forcing the animals to climb an Abiu tree in the middle of the river. Iaperikuli made a lightning bolt break the tree in the middle, and the animals are devoured by piranhas in the waters. All were devoured except the Dzauikwapa who had perceived Iaperikuli's plan and escaped death within a dried fruit, floating in the waters until the "end of the world."[45]

All were devoured except the Dzauikwapa who had perceived Iaperikuli's plan and escaped death within a dried fruit, floating in the waters until the "end of the world."

43. Andrés Márquez Carrero, *Tatuy, raza aborigen del Estado Mérida, la civilización hija del sol* (Mérida, Venezuela: Consejo de Publicaciones de la Universidad de los Andes, 1985), p. 8.
44. Ibid., p. 35.
45. Robin M. Wright, "Aos que vão nascer: uma etnografia religiosa dos indios baniwa," manuscript dated January 1996. Accessed via www.researchgate.net. See also Cosmos, Self, and History in Baniwa Religion by Wright (Austin: University of Texas Press, 1998), p. 94.

240 WAYANA — Suriname, French Guiana, and Brazil

The Wayana live in French Guiana and bordering areas of Suriname and Brazil. In December 1975, a Wayana chief narrated their creation story to Daniel Schoepf — a 75-minute narration. He told that in most ancient times, a flood was unleashed by two twin brothers, Kuyuli and Kutumo, in revenge for the murder of their mother. The waters destroyed their enemies and continued to rise higher and higher without relenting. Through great difficulty, the brothers survived by floating on makeshift vessels.[46]

Trio Man and Boy

241 TRIO — Suriname and Brazil

The Trio or Tareno are a small tribe living in southern Suriname and bordering parts of Brazil. In the late 1970s or early 1980s, a 60-year-old former shaman of the tribe, named Temeto, narrated dozens of the oral traditions to Cees Koelewijn, who tape-recorded and later translated them into Dutch and English.

A remarkable tradition passed down by the Trio priests told that long ago, a terrible flood came which destroyed most of the people of the world. The flood came because the people acted wickedly. They were sexually promiscuous, they gossiped, lied, cursed, and murdered.

But before the flood came, an old shaman foresaw what was to happen, and he warned the people of the coming calamity. Next, all of the tortoises came to the village of the shaman. Upon seeing this the people grew more terrified and wondered what this could mean. Then snakes beyond number came to the village as well. Then all the land animals came, close together, side by side. Finally, the spirit beings came to the village as well.

But before the Flood came, an old shaman foresaw what was to happen, and he warned the people of the coming calamity.

'We will perish!' the people said. 'We will perish. We will be wiped out. Where shall we go?'

Leaders of other tribes came near as well. A valiant leader of the Pireujana people, named Maruwaike, went away and found the mountain Kantani. He told the shaman about this mountain, saying that it is the highest of all places and is suitable as a place to take refuge from the coming flood.

So all the people who listened to the shaman went and set up camp at the top of Mount Kantani. After three days, the flood came. There they were safe above the waters, which rose and covered all the earth, except for the top of Mount Kantani.

But many people disbelieved and did not heed the warning. They perished when the flood came, especially those of the Maraso tribe.

After much time of hardship, darkness, and cold, and seeing that the water level did not diminish at all, the people wondered and said to one another, 'What will happen now? What shall we do?' A cuckoo bird offered to fly in search of land. After much flying he could do so no longer, and he fell and drowned. Then the red macaw attempted it, and suffered the same fate. So too, the blue macaw after that.

Then the pigeon went, and he too flew without getting tired, but he found no end of the water.

Then the woodpecker went. He flew with stamina and survived, though he found no end of the water. Then the pigeon went, and he too flew without getting tired, but he found no end of the water.

46. Daniel Schoepf, "Le récit de la création chez les Wayana-Aparai du Brésil," *Bulletin Annuel du Musée d'Ethnographie de la Ville de Genève* (1986), p. 126.

Finally, the waters abated after the people offered of a few of themselves in sacrifice to the monster in the waters. Then the people were able to come down from the mountain, and they dispersed again to live in different places. The shaman warned the people that the flood had come because of their wickedness, and they should not behave that way again.[47]

But many people disbelieved and did not heed the warning. They perished when the flood came, especially those of the Maraso tribe.

The tradition also refers to nephilim or fallen beings in the pre-Flood world. "At that time all sorts of beings came down from the sky. One of them was a giant human being called Kenekenekeime. They all came down from the sky, also those who are known to be cannibals. Only the shaman was strong. (He protected his people from these evil beings)"[48]

MATAPI

Colombia

The Matapi creation story contains a vague memory of the Flood. As told by an elderly man who was considered the tribe's authority on their oral traditions:

> ...After this time [after creation] the earth and its features began to change. That is when the flood came, and brought to an end all those living at that time. . . . The flood went on for a long time. Then the flood gradually diminished until the earth dried up again. The first beings left something like a very fertile seed here on earth. On the earth they created themselves again through this seed.[49]

Other Texts (See Appendix A on page 241)

243 **Andoque (Colombia)**

244 **Tanimuka (Colombia)**

245 **Yagua (Colombia and Peru)**

246 **Desana (Colombia)**

---

47. Cees Koelewijn and Peter Riviere, *Oral Literature of the Trio Indians of Suriname* (Providence, RI: Foris Publications, 1987), p. 149–154.
48. Ibid., p. 152.
49. Carlos Matapi and Uldarico Matapi, *Historia de los Upichia* (Bogota: Tropenbos, 1997), p. 24.

Incan Ruins at Machu Picchu

ECUADOR, PERU, AND BOLIVIA

The Incans, one of the most powerful nations of the New World, had a well-known tradition of the Flood, but instead of the ark their means of shelter was a high cave inside a mountain. Instead of birds, a pair of dogs was sent out to search for dry land. When they returned muddy instead of wet, the people discerned that the Flood was almost over. Among the other tribes of Ecuador, Peru, and Bolivia, the knowledge of the Flood is also attested to, as we will see in the following pages.

Tribes of the Region

247. Incas (Peru)
248. Cuzco Area Traditions
249. Chincha (Peru)
250. Aymara (Peru, Bolivia, Chile)
251. Cañari (Ecuador)
252. Guaraní (Brazil, Uruguay, Paraguay, Argentina)
253. Peruvian Tradition
254. Huanca (Peru)
255. Maina (Peru and Ecuador)
256. Jivaro (Ecuador and Peru)
257. Shuar (Ecuador and Peru)
258. Cashibo (Peru)
259. Murata (Ecuador and Peru)
260. Secoya (Ecuador and Peru)
261. Machiguenga (Peru)
262. Moseten (Bolivia)
263. Urarina (Peru)
264. Yuracaré (Bolivia)
265. Chané (Bolivia)
266. Orejone (Peru)
267. Ese Ejja (Peru and Bolivia)
268. Iskonawa (Peru)
269. Piros (Peru)
270. Chayahuita (Peru)
271. Amahuaca (Peru and Brazil)
272. Waorani (Ecuador)
273. Cocama (Peru)
274. Tacana (Bolivia)
275. Quijos-Quichua (Ecuador and Peru)
276. Kashinawa (Peru and Brazil)
277. Cofán (Ecuador and Colombia)
278. Pauserna (Bolivia and Brazil)

247

INCAS

Peru

Regarding the Incan nation of Peru, one of our earliest records of their Flood tradition comes from Jose de Acosta (1539–1600), who arrived in Peru in 1570 and wrote an important work, *Historia Natural y Moral de las Indias*. In this he wrote:

Llamas Wandering the Mountains of Rural Peru

> The title with which they (the Incans) conquered, and became masters of all that land, was in telling that after the universal flood — of which all these Indians had knowledge — that these Incas had replenished the world — seven of them coming forth from the Cave of Pacaritambo. And that is why all other people owed tribute and vassalage to them, as to their predecessors.[1]

A more detailed account of their belief regarding the Flood comes from Gregoria de Garcia, a missionary and ethnographer who in 1607 wrote *Origen de los Indios del Nuevo Mundo*. From his interviews of the native peoples living around what is now the city of Lima:

> The Indians say that, in order to escape the flood, they all went into certain caves of very high mountains. And to keep the water from entering where they were, they built doors to close off the mouths of the caves. They had brought in much provision, and many animals of that land for sustenance as well as service. When they felt that it was no longer raining and the flood had ceased, they sent out two dogs. These returned wet and not dirty as from mud, which gave a sign that the waters had not yet diminished. So it was not right or safe to go outside. Then they sent out other dogs, and when they returned muddy and not wet, they knew that the Flood had ceased, and they could leave. And so they went out to populate the earth, in which there was much work, nuisance and impediment in the multitude of large snakes. These had bred in the humidity and dampness caused by the flood, and these are also found to this day. When the people had killed them, they were able to live secure.[2]

When they felt that it was no longer raining and the flood had ceased, they sent out two dogs. These returned wet and not dirty as from mud, which gave a sign that the waters had not yet diminished.

George Stanley Faber on the Seven Survivors

Is there significance to the number of survivors (seven) reckoned by the Incans? The theologian and scholar George Stanley Faber (1773–1854), who wrote several volumes on world religions and mythology, concluded: "The number of persons, whom they supposed to have been thus saved, is seven. But this is the precise number of the Noetic family, exclusive of its head: whence that number became so famous in the diluvian mythology of the ancients. The Peruvian seven are doubtless the same as the seven Cabiri, the seven Titans, the seven Hindoo Rishis, and the seven arkite companions of the British Arthur."[3]

1. Joseph de Acosta, *Historia Natural y Moral de las Indias*, Vol. 2, Book 6, Chap. xix (Madrid: 1894), p. 200.
2. Gregorio Garcia, *Origen de los Indios del Nuevo Mundo e Indias Occidentales*, p. 334–335.
3. George Stanley Faber, *The Origin of Pagan Idolatry Ascertained from Historical Testimony and Circumstantial Evidence*, vol. 2 (London, 1816), p. 142.

248 Cuzco

Incan Site of Moray

The Incan peoples living around Cuzco had the following tradition, which the early historian Herrera mentioned in *Historia General* (published in 1615):

> Others of the mountains affirm that all people perished in the deluge, except for six people who were saved in a raft. These six repopulated the world. And there has been one particular flood, one can believe, because all the people of the provinces are in agreement on this flood.[4]
>
> What was referred to (of the first rulers of the Incans) is the tradition told by the oldest Indians of Cuzco. Others of the region agree in that the first Incan was Mangocapa, and they say that he came forth from a cave after the Flood, six leagues from Cuzco. And (they say) that he gave origin to two lineages of Incans, founded in the city of Cuzco. One was called Anancuzco, and the other Urincuzco. From the first came two rulers who conquered the land. The first who was head of this lineage was Incaroca, who founded the family of Vizaquirao.[5]

…that all people perished in the deluge, except for six people who were saved in a raft. These six repopulated the world. And there has been one particular flood, one can believe, because all the people of the provinces are in agreement on this flood.

During the 1570s, the explorer Sarmiento de Gamboa interviewed many Cuzco natives and elders well-informed on their tribal history, in order to write his *History of the Incas*. This record they told him contains several striking parallels, not only to the Genesis Flood account, but to the Creation account:

> The natives of this land affirm that in the beginning, and before this world was created, there was a being called Viracocha. He created a dark world without sun, moon or stars. Owing to this creation he was named Viracocha Pachayachachi, which means "Creator of all things." And when he had created the world he formed a race of giants of disproportional greatness painted and sculptured, to see whether it would be well to make real men of that size. He then created men in his likeness as they are now; and they lived in darkness.
>
> Viracocha ordered these people that they should live without quarrelling, and that they should know and serve him. He gave them a certain precept which they were to observe, on pain of being confounded if they should break it. They kept this precept for some time, but it is not mentioned what it was. But as there arose among them the vices of pride and covetousness, they transgressed the precept of Viracocha Pachayachachi and falling, through this sin, under his indignation, he confounded and cursed them. Then some were turned into stones, others into other things, some were swallowed up by the earth, others by the sea, and over all there came a general flood which they call "unu pachacuti," which means "water that overturns the land." They say that it rained 60 days and nights, that it drowned all created things, and that there alone remained some vestiges of those who were turned into stones, as a memorial of the event, and as an example to

They say that it rained 60 days and nights, that it drowned all created things.

4. Antonio de Herrera y Torsedillas, *Historia General, Década Quinta*, Book 3, p. 60.
5. Ibid., p. 63–64.

the posterity, in the edifices of Pucara, which are 60 leagues from Cuzco.[6]

From the manuscript of Cristoval Molina (1529–1585), we learn that there was a temple to the Sun, called Poquen-Cancha, located near Cuzco, which had a painting memorializing the deluge. The tradition associated with it was narrated to him this way:

> In the life of Manco Ccapac, who was the first Inca and from whom they began to be called Children of the Sun and to worship the Sun, they had a full account of the deluge. They say that all people and all created things perished in it, in as far as the water rose above all the highest mountains of the world. No living things survived except a man and a woman, who remained in a box, and when the waters subsided, the wind carried them to Huanaco, which will be over seventy leagues from Cuzco, a little more or less.[7]

Temple of the Sun at Machu Picchu, which Contains a Painting Memorializing the Flood

No living things survived except a man and a woman, who remained in a box, and when the waters subsided, the wind carried them to Huanaco.

Pedro Sarmiento de Gamboa (1532–1592) also mentioned:

> Some of the nations, besides the Cuzcos, also say that a few were saved from this flood to leave descendants for a future age, of how their first ancestors were saved from the waters of the deluge. . . .
>
> But the Incas and most of those of Cuzco, those among them who are believed to know most, do not say that anyone escaped from the flood, but that Viracocha began to create men afresh, as will be related further on.[8]

Flood accounts connected to this deity Viracocha were collected by other early historians as well.[9]

249 CHINCHA

Peru

The Chincha people lived near what is now the city of Lima. A priest named Francisco de Avila recorded a tradition of the Flood in his manuscript written in 1608. This version has similarities to that of the Tlapanecs and Huichols of Mexico:

Bronze relief of Pedro Sarmiento de Gamboa

> What I have to mention here is a saying of the Indians which is more ancient than the eclipse. They relate that there was nearly an end to the world, which happened in the following way: An Indian was tethering his llama in a place where there was good pasture, and the animal resisted, showing sorrow and moaning after its manner,

6. Pedro Sarmiento de Gamboa, ,trans. Clements Markham, *The History of the Incas* (Cambridge: Hakluyt Society, 1907), p. 28–30. See also a summarized account in: Joseph de Acosta, *Historia General y Moral de las Indias*, vol. 1 (Madrid: Juan de Leon, 1894), p. 113.
7. Christoval de Molina, “An Account of the Fables and Rites of the Yncas,” trans. Clements R Markham, *Narrative of the Rites and Laws of the Yncas* (New York: Burt Franklin, 1873), p. 4.
8. Pedro Sarmiento de Gamboa, “Historia de los Incas,” trans. Clements Markham (Cambridge: Hakluyt Society, 1907), p. 30–31.
9. Joseph de Acosta, *Historia General y Moral de las Indias*, vol. 1 (Madrid: Juan de Leon, 1894), p. 113. Acosta lived from 1540 to 1600. Also: Antonio de la Calancha, Coronica Moralizada (Barcelona: Pedro Lacavalleria, 1639), Book 2, Ch. 10, p. 366–367. In that account, Calancha quotes from an earlier writer, Juan Polo de Ondegardo (1500–1575).

which it does by crying yu' yu'. The master, who happened to be eating a choelo, observing this, threw the core (which they call coronta) at the llama, saying, "Fool, why do you moan and refrain from eating? Have I not put you where there is good pasture?" The llama thus replied: "Madman! What do you know, and what can you suppose? Learn that I am not sad without good cause, for within five days the sea will rise and cover the whole earth, destroying all there is upon it." The man, wondering that his llama should speak, answered it by asking whether there was any way by which they could save themselves. The llama then said that the man must follow it quickly to the summit of a high mountain and that he might thus be saved. The man did as he was told, carrying his load on his back and leading the llama, and he arrived on the summit of the mountain, where he found many different kinds of birds and animals assembled. Just as he and his llama reached the top the sea began to rise, and the water filled the valleys and covered the tops of the hills, except that of Villca-coto; but the animals were crowded together, for the water rose so high that some of them could hardly find foothold. Among these was a fox, whose tail was washed by the waves, which they say is the reason that the tips of foxes' tails are black. At the end of five days the waters began to abate, and the sea returned to its former bounds; but the whole earth was without inhabitants except that solitary man, from whom, they say, descend all the people who now exist.[10]

> ... here is a saying of the Indians which is more ancient than the eclipse. They relate that there was nearly an end to the world, which happened in the following way...

> "Learn that I am not sad without good cause, for within five days the sea will rise and cover the whole earth, destroying all there is upon it."

250

AYMARA

Peru, Bolivia, Chile

The Aymara tribe lived in the mountainous area of southeastern Peru, northern Chile, and western Bolivia. We have a brief reference to this people's Flood tradition from Pedro de Cieza de Leon (1520–1554), the Spanish conquistador and historical writer, in his 1553 *Chronicle of Peru*, First Part:

> Many of these Indians recount that their ancestors told of a great flood that occurred long ago, and of the manner that I describe in the third chapter of the Second Part (of this work). And it demonstrates that the antiquity of their nation is great.[11]

Aymara Girl

Sadly, the section of his Second Part that he refers to is lost.[12]

> "Many of these Indians recount that their ancestors told of a great flood that occurred long ago"

10. Francisco de Avila, "A Narrative of the Errors, False Gods, and Other Superstitions and Diabolical Rites in which the Indians of the Provinces of Huarochiri, Mama, and Chaclla Lived in Ancient Times," *Narrative of the Rites and Laws of the Yncas*, ed. and trans. Clements R. Markham (New York: Hakluyt Society, 1883), p. 132–133.
11. Pedro de Cieza de Leon, *La Cronica del Peru* (Madrid: Calpe,1922), p. 314.
12. Cieza de Leon, *The Second Part of the Chronicle of Peru*, trans. and ed. Clementes R. Markham (London: Hakluyt Society, 1883), p. xvii–xviii. The manuscript upon which our modern copies are based, and which is housed in the royal Library of the Escorial, is missing pages containing the first three chapters, apart from a fragment at the end of Chapter Three.

251 CAÑARI

Ecuador

Cristoval de Molina (1529–1585) spent much time living among the native peoples of Peru and Ecuador, learning their traditions and languages. His manuscript written around 1575 describes the Cañari tradition of the Flood:

> In the kingdom of Quito (Ecuador), there is a province called Cañaribamba, and the Cañari Indians are so named from their province. These Cañaris say that, at the time of the deluge, two brothers escaped to a very high mountain called Huaca-ynan. As the waters rose the hill also increased in height, so that the waters never reached them. After the flood had subsided, their store of provisions being ended, they came forth and sought for food in the hills and valleys. They built a very small house in which they dwelt, living on herbs and roots, and suffering much from hunger and fatigue.[13]

The account then tells that the men went on to repopulate the world with two birds that had the faces of beautiful women.

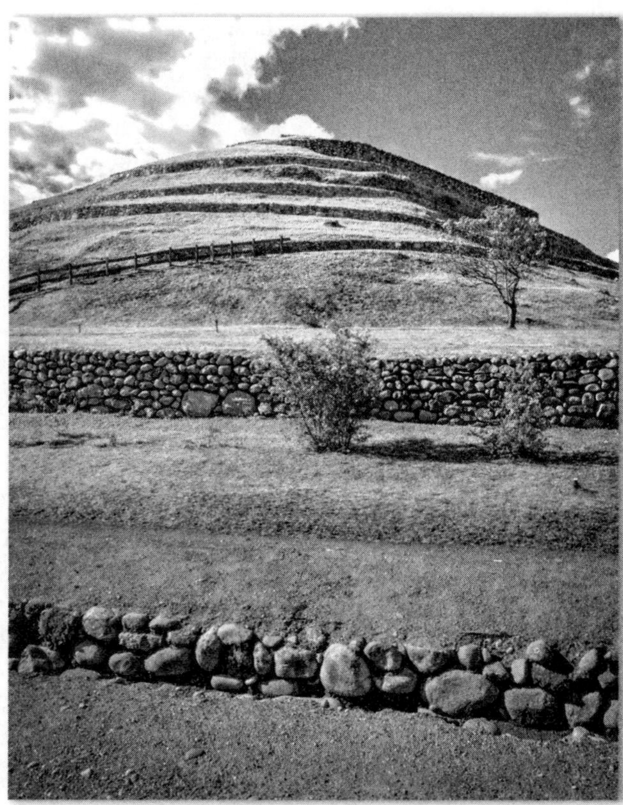

Ancient Ruins of Pumapungo in Cuenca, Ecuador

252 GUARANÍ

Brazil, Uruguay, Paraguay, Argentina

In the 1890s, Bernardino de Nino heard a Flood tradition from the oldest members of the Guaraní tribe. According to this, the evil god Aguara-Tunpa rebelled against the true god and creator, and sought to kill mankind. He sent a fire upon the fields and pasturelands to destroy their food source, but they fled to the rivers to fish. Then he changed his plan:

> He caused torrents of water, called Ipoca, to fall from the sky in order to annihilate the Chiriguana race, drowning all of them in the waters. He nearly succeeded in destroying all the Chiriguanos, but these, acting on a word from the true god, Tunpacte, sought out a large mate leaf, which they called Choguao. And they placed two small children on it — a male child and a female child from the same woman — and left them to float in it upon the surface of the waters. The rain continued to fall in all its impulsiveness, and the waters continued to rise upon the earth, climbing to great heights. All the Chiriguanos were drowned, except the two children on the Choquao or great mate leaf, who survived the catastrophe.[14]

He caused torrents of water, called Ipoca, to fall from the sky in order to annihilate the Chiriguana race, drowning all of them in the waters. He nearly succeeded … but these, acting on a word from the true god, Tunpacte, sought out a large mate leaf … And they placed two small children on it…

After this, they sought how to recover the knowledge of fire, which had been extinguished by the Flood. A toad had guarded the last remaining fire underground. "When he knew that the water was no longer covering the earth, he took up the burning coals in his mouth and came up from the earth. He sought out the children, and showed them the fire. So they were able to cook the fish and to warm their cold bodies." From these children the human race repopulated.[15]

13. Christoval de Molina, "An Account of the Fables and Rites of the Yncas," *Narrative of the Rites and Laws of the Yncas*, p. 8–9.
14. Bernardino de Nino, *Etnografia Chiriguana* (La Paz: 1912), p. 131–132.
15. Ibid., p. 132–133.

It is said that a true Guaraní never kills a toad for the compassion that the toad showed the human race after the deluge.[16]

Mantaro Valley, Peru

253 PERUVIAN TRADITION

Peru

In 1648, a priest named Fernando de Avendano published a work which alluded to a Flood legend of a local tribe. This tradition states that three eggs were dropped out of heaven after the Flood, giving rise to the current population. These were a gold egg, giving rise to the priests, a silver egg, producing the warriors, and a copper egg, which produced the common people. Avendano mocked their tradition as ludicrous, but it is noteworthy that they acknowledged the Flood.[17]

Others of the mountain people affirm that all mankind perished in the Flood, except for six people who were saved in a boat, who later repopulated that country.

254 HUANCA

Peru

The Huanca people inhabit the Mantaro Valley of central Peru, and they aided the Spanish in overthrowing the Incan Empire. The historian Herrera, relying on the early Spanish records, told of the Huanca people's Flood tradition in his Décadas (published 1615):

> The very old Indians say, by tradition of their ancestors, that long before there were Incas, when the whole earth was well-populated with people, there was a great flood. So great was this flood that the sea abandoned its limits, and the earth became covered with water, and thus all the people perished. Regarding this, the Guancas (Huancas), who inhabit the Valley of Xuaxa (Juaja), and those of Chiquito, in the altiplano, say that some people sheltered themselves in the caves and hollows of the highest mountains and then returned to repopulate the earth. Others of the mountain people affirm that all mankind perished in the Flood, except for six people who were saved in a boat, who later repopulated that country.[18]

255 MAINA

(Peru and Ecuador)

The Maina people (also known as Kandoshi) live along the Marañon River — the main tributary of the Amazon River, in Peru and southern Ecuador. Julian Steward and Alfred Metraux heard a few differing Flood legends from them:

Valley of the Marañón River

> We have three fragments of Maina flood legends. (1) The flood was caused by a god whom people had thrown into a dirty pit because he was covered

16. Ibid., p. 67.
17. Don Fernando de Avendano, *Sermones de los Misterios de Nuestra Santa Fe Catolica* (Lima: Jorge Lopez, 1648), p. 111. Translation provided by F.L. Hawks in Peruvian Antiquities by Mariano Edward Rivero and John James von Tschudi (New York: George Putnam, 1858), p. 113–114.
18. Antonio de Herrera y Torsedillas, *Historia General, Década Quinta*, Book 3 (Madrid: 1728), p. 60.

with sores; the only survivor was the man who rescued him and cleaned him. (2) A man and woman took refuge on a zapote tree, which grew up to the sky. They ate its fruits until the flood subsided. (3) A flood of the Rimachuma Lagoon destroyed all mankind except one man who lived in a hut where he found food prepared daily; he discovered that it came from two parrots who flew to his house and became women, one the mistress, the other her servant; he married the mistress, hence women are now lazy.[19]

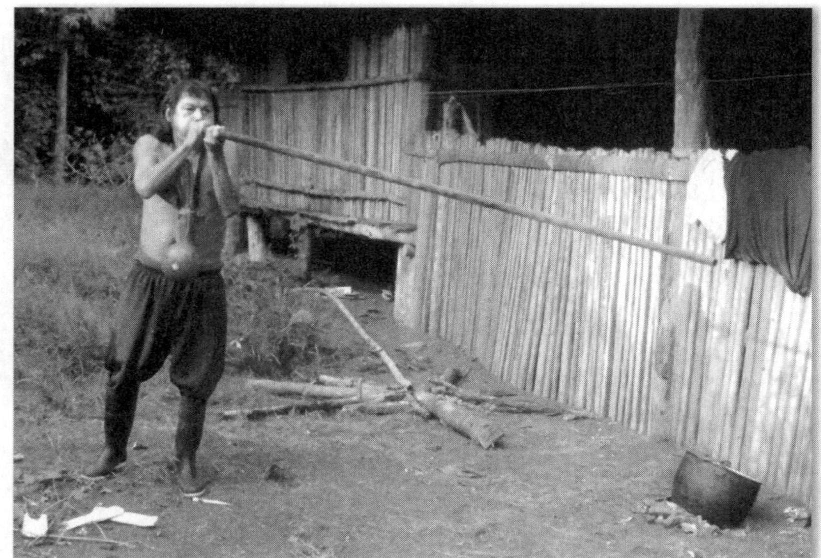

Jivaro Man with a Blowgun

256 JIVARO

Ecuador and Peru

The Jivaros were headhunters, and had a reputation for shrinking the heads of their victims in boiling water. Rafael Karsten visited them along the Marañon River, from 1916 to 1919, and heard their account of the ancient Flood. This account also seems to contain a mixed memory of the serpent and the forbidden fruit of the Garden of Eden.

This tradition tells that the Jivaro were about to have a festival, and they sent two young men to hunt food for the people. As they were hunting, their food kept disappearing while they were gone. They came to realize that their food was being stolen by the "pangi" — the great serpent, that is, the boa constrictor, which is the archdemon of their spiritual world. They found the snake and burned its hiding spot. Later, one of the two men ate the snake meat, which is forbidden since it is considered an evil demon. The man became struck with an unquenchable thirst, as he drank all the water he could find. Then he slowly turned into a monstrous snake, like the pangi.

The great serpent, the archdemon of their spiritual world … They killed it and one man ate the serpent meat, which is forbidden. The man was struck with an unquenchable thirst, and was transformed.

His companion returned and found him turned into a pangi. "Go quickly to save yourself. I no longer have power to respect you, but will only devour you. Go back to where our people are, and tell them what has happened. Warn them that the water is going to grow more and more, and that it will inundate the land. Tell them to go up on the highest hills, and upon the trees that grow on those hills. Otherwise, they will drown in the flood which will cover the earth. And you, put food in your canoe of palm wood, and with this go up to the highest hill. If the water covers even that hill, go up on the tallest tree of that hill to save yourself."[20]

The other man did so, and went to his people and warned them of these things. However, they did not believe him, saying, "What nonsense is he speaking? He has killed the other man." So this man fled by himself, taking food in his canoe. The Flood came, the waters rose, and lifted his canoe to the highest hill. Finally, the hill too was covered, except for a tall tree on that hill, which he climbed.[21]

So this man fled by himself, taking food in his canoe. The Flood came, the waters rose, and lifted his canoe to the highest hill. Finally, the hill too was covered, except for a tall tree on that hill, which he climbed.

19. Julian H. Steward and Alfred Metraux, "Tribes of Peruvian and Ecuadorian Montana," in "Handbook of South American Indians," ed. Julian Steward, vol. 3, in *Bureau of American Ethnology Bulletin*, vol. 143 (Washington: GPO, 1948), p. 649.
20. Rafael Karsten, *Mitos de los Indios Jibaros del Oriente del Ecuador* (Quito: Sociedad Ecuatoriana de Estudios Historicos Americanos, 1919), p. 4–5.
21. Ibid., p. 5–6.

All the other Jivaros, who did not wish to save themselves, drowned in the waters. This man alone was saved, remaining in the palm tree for many days, before finally the water began to subside. To see if the water level had fallen and the earth had dried, he dropped seeds from the palm tree. When he heard them hit ground, he knew the water had gone down, and he came down from the tree.[22]

Shuar Group in Logroño, Ecuador

257 SHUAR

Ecuador and Peru

The Shuar people have an interesting Flood story, related to the Jivaro version above, and which seems to contain a memory of the Garden of Eden in addition to the Flood. Parallels to the Akawoio, Pemón, Wapishana, Taruma, and Yabarana traditions cited above are also evident. Their oral tradition, passed down from grandparents to their grandchildren, told of a mysterious being or spirit named Tsunki, which sought to communicate its powers to mankind. It took the form of a beautiful woman, and captured the heart of a married man. However, to remain undiscovered, Tsunki took the form of a snake during the day, and the married man hid her in a covered basket. At night, she would lay with the man, wrapping him with a layer of water so they would remain undiscovered. When he went hunting, he would severely prohibit his family members from opening the basket.

The mysterious being or spirit named Tsunki captured the heart of a married man. During the day it took the form of a snake.

However, one day, his first wife opened the basket and found the snake. Tsunki tried to escape, but the woman chased and killed it. Then the sky darkened, the earth shook, and turbulent waters came out from the earth and covered even the mountains. All humanity succumbed to the waters and the monsters of the abyss. Only the married man and his oldest daughter escaped by climbing the tallest tree on a mountain. They came together and repopulated the earth. As divine punishment, Tsunki could not have offspring with men nor communicate her spiritual powers to mankind.[23]

258 CASHIBO

Peru

The Cashibo or Unia are a historically isolated tribe living along the Aguaytia River, a headwater of the Amazon. The version of the Flood that they told Erwin Frank, during his visit between 1980 and 1984, went like this:

> This is what was told to me about the time when a great storm came upon our people. Not long after the creation of the world, our ancestors kidnapped a beautiful woman. She was so gentle and hard-working, and her fragrance was like the fruit of the pineapple tree. But her master, a wizard, became very angry and sent the deluge to punish them.[24]

Another version, narrated around 1960 by a man named Poliponte Odicioold, went as follows. Animals of all sorts began acting strangely. Then they

22. Ibid.
23. "El mítico relato del diluvio en la etnia shuar" (17 May 2020) retrieved from: https://www.eltiempo.com.ec/noticias/intercultural/1/el-mitico-relato-del-diluvio-en-la-etnia-shuar.
24. Erwin H. Frank, Villacorte Bustamante, Villacorte Mea, and Santiago Mea, *Los Pueblos Indios en sus Mitos* (Quito: Abya-Yala, 1993), p. 78–79.

disappeared altogether. Even their tracks in the mud disappeared. All the people became frightened.

Next, a man came running from a downriver tribe. He shouted and warned the people that a great flood was destroying everything below them in elevation, and that the flood was coming here too and would consume the entire earth. He told them to pack plantain and manioc, and to prepare balsa rafts to float upon.

San Pablo Lake and Imbabura Volcano, Ecuador

Then the flood came, and it covered the entire earth. "Our ancestors tied their canoes higher and higher on the tree trunks, as the water rose right up to the top of the mountains." After a long period, the waters subsided, and they saw turtles and tapir eating among the decaying bodies of people buried by the flood.[25]

259 **Ecuador and Peru**

MURATA

The Murata, a subtribe of the Andoa, numbered about 5,000 people when Jorge Von Hassel visited them around the year 1900. The Flood story they told him went like this:

> A Murato man went to fish at a lagoon of the Pastasa River, and a young alligator ate the bait. So the fisherman killed the alligator. The mother of the young alligators became angry, and with her tail struck the water so hard that it flooded everything around the laguna. Everyone drowned except for one man, who climbed up a pivai palm tree. He remained there several days amidst perpetual darkness. From time to time he would drop a fruit from the pivai tree, but he would always hear it fall into the water. But one day, he heard it hit dry ground. So he came down from the tree, and built a dwelling and a farmhouse. And from a piece of his flesh planted in the ground grew a woman. And he lived with her and had many children.[26]

Everyone drowned except for one man … He remained there several days amidst perpetual darkness. From time to time he would drop a fruit from the pivai tree, but he would always hear it fall into the water. But one day, he heard it hit dry ground. So he came down from the tree…

260 **Ecuador and Peru**

SECOYA

In 1983, Maria Cipolletti traveled to the village of San Pablo, Ecuador, where the majority of remaining Secoya people live today. The aged members of the tribe told her a lengthy creation story, which contains a memory of the Flood. It tells of a quarrel that took place between the gods, when they were together at a dinner, on account of jealousy over their wives. Two of them died, and one of the wives, who lost her husband, retaliated by causing the Flood:

> The earth was drowned — all, all this. And afterward, at the place where God was standing remained a little earth. . . . And while God was standing at the place where he was, he saw that all of this was still inundated — every direction which he saw was pure water. The land no longer existed; every direction which he saw was only water. After this he saw some bubbles come up from the water and he thought it must be an animal. And he thought, "Let it come up," that is, out of the water. And the animal that came up was the armadillo. God made it go down into the water and bring up some earth. The animal returned with mud that it had put on its

25. Lila Wistrand-Robinson, *Cashibo Folklore and Culture* (Dallas: SIL, 1998), p. 12–14.
26. Jorge M. Von Hassel, "Las Tribus Salvajes de la Region Amazonica del Peru," *Boletin de la Sociedad Geografica de Lima*, vol. 17 (Lima: Oficina Tipografica de La Opinion Nacional, 1905), p. 68.

> back. God took this mud and with it reconstructed the earth afresh.[27]

Moon Valley Near La Paz, Bolivia

This tradition is noteworthy for its "earth diver" motif, which is widespread in North America but less so in South America.

261 MACHIGUENGA

Peru

In the 1930s, the Machiguenga people of southeastern Peru told Secundino Garcia their ancient traditions, including one touching upon the Flood.

This account, which is clearly related to the Muisca version (see page 172), tells of a malevolent god named Yabireri who tried to exterminate the people with a flood. However, the god Berenakoni caught him and punished him, by nailing him down to several tree trunks, somewhere outside of this physical earth. If he were to test the strength of these nails, the world itself would shake violently.

They also believe that disease and death did not exist until the punishment and nailing down of Yabireri, and would not exist now if that had not occurred.[28] It seems that this tradition combines a memory of both the Flood and the punishment in the Garden of Eden.

> The land no longer existed; every direction which he saw was only water.

262 MOSETEN

Bolivia

The Moseten people live north of La Paz in Bolivia. In the 1500s, they were being invaded by the Incas, who aborted their conquest when they received word of the landing of the Spanish.

They had a memory of the Flood, which they told Erland Nordenskiold (1877–1932) in the first decade of the 1900s:

> A man seduced a girl while she was bathing in a river. She became pregnant and bore a child with long hair. The father wanted his child but could not find him. Becoming angry, he caused the rivers to flood the country. Only a few men on top of a mountain were saved.[29]

263 URARINA

Peru

> Becoming angry, he caused the rivers to flood the country. Only a few men on top of a mountain were saved.

The Urarina people live along the Chambira River, one of the headwaters of the Amazon in northeastern Peru. Bartholomew Dean recorded their flood legend from them on tape in 1991, and then had it translated from their native language.

They tell that there is a father god, Kana Najca, and a mother god, Kana Neba. They had a son, Kuanra Kajlaui. A flood was caused when evil men attempted to kill the divine son. However, he was rescued by a group of good men. Then he warned them of a coming flood:

---

27. Maria Susana Cipolletti, *Aipe Koka: La Palabra de los Antiguos: Tradicion Oral Siona-Secoya* (Quito: Abya-Yala, 1988), p. 54–58.
28. Secundino Garcia, "Mitologia de los Salvajes Machiguengas," *Actas y Trabajos Cientificos del XXVIIo [27th] Congreso internacional de Americanistas* (Lima: 1939), vol. 2, p. 234–236.
29. Erland Nordenskiold, *Forschungen und Abenteuer in Sudamerika* (Stuttgart: 1924), p. 151.

"A massive storm is about to break. My father is going to avenge me, all the world is going to be destroyed, drowned in a torrential downpour."

One of the good men instructed his family to rapidly cook the fish, and then the fish were eaten. Afterwards, the good man was told to find something that wouldn't be covered by water. He was told to climb up the cudi tree before the world was lost, before the big flood began. The man and his family climbed up the cudi tree to a branch above the flood-line. The man's pregnant wife was transformed into a termites' nest, and she remained stuck in the middle of the tree. Then the rains came and it became very dark. The evil people, those who had buried the son of god, were all drowned. But those who had climbed up the cudi tree were saved. . . .

They say it took more than a month for the flooded river to go down. To test if the waters had receded, they dropped the tree's fruits. When the fruit hit the water below, it made the sound "tolon . . . tolon . . . tolon." It was still dark, and only the flood-lands, or tahuampa, could be seen below. . . . The man then sent his son down the tree to see if the water was drying up. The son exclaimed, "Yes, the flood waters are receding," and he was then transformed into an Iraru, a white heron. The man's other one was also sent down the tree, and he too turned into a bird, a coro coro. The coro coro flew off. That's why the father himself had to climb down the tree.[30]

Urarina Shaman

264 YURACARÉ

Bolivia

The Yuracaré have a creation story with an account of the Flood, in reference to two ancient men, Tiri and Karu.

Another bird invited them (Tiri and Karu) to drink chichi. The magical vase filled itself as it was being emptied. Tiri, surprised, wanted to see where the flow would stop. He struck the vase, and the liquor came out in such abundance that it flooded the whole earth and made his friend (Karu) drown. When the earth dried up, Tiri looked everywhere for his friend. He finally found the bones and resuscitated him.[31]

The man then sent his son down the tree to see if the water was drying up. The son exclaimed, "Yes, the flood waters are receding," and he was then transformed into an Iraru, a white heron. The man's other one was also sent down the tree, and he too turned into a bird…

The next tradition from the Yuracaré is even more interesting. It has several similarities to the Genesis Flood account, only that "water" is replaced with "fire."

The world began in the dark forests inhabited by the Yuracares. An evil demon named Sararuma or Aima Sune, set the whole world on fire. No tree, and no living being, escaped from this conflagration. One man alone escaped the universal disaster, who had taken the precaution of digging a very deep underground dwelling, where he had withdrawn with provisions for the duration of the fire. To see whether the flames still burned hot, he stuck a long branch out. Twice, when he pulled the branch back it was aflame, but the third time it was cold. He waited four more days to come out from underground. Walking sadly across this desolate land, without food or shelter, he lamented his sad fate. But then, coming from far off lands, Sararuma, all dressed in red, appeared to him and said to him, "Though I am the cause of all the evil, I still have compassion on you."

30. Bartholomew Dean, "The Poetics of Creation: Urarina Cosmogony and Historical Consciousness," *Latin American Indian Literatures Journal*, vol. 10, no. 1 (1994), p. 25–26.
31. Alcide Dessalines d'Orbigny, *Voyage dans l'Amérique méridionale*, vol. 3, part 1 (Paris: Chez V. Levrault, 1844), p. 215.

> Then he gave him a handful of the seeds of plants most necessary for human life, ordering him to sow them. These he planted, and a magnificent forest was soon formed as by magic.[32]

What are we to conclude from the two above-mentioned texts? It seems to me that they confused the memory of the Garden of Eden and the Noahic Flood — a pattern that we have noticed in several South American versions, such as the Miskito / Sumo, Wapishana, Shuar, and Machiguenga. Indeed, the first text has evidence of being related to the version told by some of these tribes. It appears rooted in a memory of the Garden of Eden, with mixed up details of the Flood grafted on. The second text is derived from a memory of the Flood event, and of Noah's tests to see whether it is safe to come out — but with "fire" inserted in place of "water." Perhaps this comes from the memory of Noah's fire by which he made burnt offerings to God. This text is one of several from South America where "fire" is injected into a clearly Noahic Flood story. See the topical index at the back of this volume for more.

265 CHANÉ

Bolivia

In his expedition from 1908 to 1909, Erland Nordenskiold visited several tribes in the Gran Chaco and eastern Bolivia, including the Chané. A Chané chief named Vocapoya told him the following tradition of the Flood:

El Fuerte de Samaipata, Chané ruins

> A young man had gone into the forest and seen in a pool the image of a beautiful girl, whom he followed. He stayed with her for a long time — a month — and his mother thought he was dead and cut off her hair. She thought he had been bitten by a snake or the like. One day, however, the son came home and told her that he had found a pretty girl with whom he had married. The mother told him he was going to fetch her, and brewed a mass of corn beer to celebrate their arrival.
>
> The boy came with his wife, and she was beautiful and well-dressed. During the festival, she changed and became very ugly. Over it, the betrothed man made a remark, and she became angry and left him, and went angrily to where she had come from, declaring that she was going to avenge herself. She said, however, that only a boy and a girl should be placed in a large clay pot. A brother and a sister were placed in a clay pot together with the seeds of corn, pumpkin, and beans, and the pot was well covered. When this happened, it started to rain terribly. Houses and everything were covered with water. The large pot, however, floated upon the waters. All mankind and animals drowned in the rising water. For a long time, the clay pot floated around, and the boy and the girl started to grow up.
>
> The water then sank, but when they got out, the ground was still swampy, and they had to wait for it to dry. When they came out of the clay pot, they sowed corn, pumpkin and beans from the seeds they had taken with them.[33]

It started to rain terribly. Houses and everything were covered with water. The large pot, however, floated upon the waters. All mankind and animals drowned in the rising water. For a long time, the clay pot floated around, and the boy and the girl started to grow up.

32. Ibid., p. 209–210.
33. Erland Nordenskiold, *Indianerleben: El Gran Chaco (Sudamerika), trans. Carl Auerbach* (Leipzig: Albert Bonnier, 1912), p. 253.

266 **Peru**

OREJONE

Ese Ejja Village

The Orejone, living along the Napo River in northern Peru, told a tradition of the Flood to the explorer and painter Paul Marcoy in 1846. Notice that they replace the floating ark with an underground box:

> The tradition of a deluge exists among them, only instead of the ark or vessel which in the cosmogonies of various peoples floats on the surface of the waters, we find among the Orejones a large open box, coated with the local pitch, which their ancestors buried deep in the ground, with its open part downwards, and under which, supplied with solid and liquid provisions, they remained nearly a month, while the deluge covered the earth.[34]

267 **Peru and Bolivia**

ESE EJJA

The Ese Ejja, also known as the Huarayo, told their Flood tradition to one Jose Alvarez during the 1930s:

> Now the story which they have told me many times, concerns the flood. It is at Tambopata that this event took place, according to them. It was a great day of celebration. Men, women, and children had given themselves completely to this time of celebration with the greatest joy. Suddenly, they were surprised by such a huge and expanding flood of all the rivers at once. In a moment they were all carried away by the flood into the middle of the waters, and among violent swirls when the waters collided against each other, with the result that none could be saved. Only one man ("Noija") with his wife, were able to climb the summit of a lofty hill — the only one left uncovered by the waters. Some who wanted to follow him were instantly buried by the continuous collapses of water that made them roll to the middle of that turbulent swell, in which they drowned inescapably.[35]

Suddenly, they were surprised by such a huge and expanding flood of all the rivers at once. … none could be saved. Only one man ("Noija") with his wife, were able to climb the summit of a lofty hill — the only one left uncovered by the waters.

268 **Peru**

ISKONAWA

In 1959, two missionaries named Clifton Russell and James Davidson discovered a previously unknown, isolated group of indigenous people along the headwaters of the Rio Ucayali in Peru. The group was identified as the Iskonawa ("people of the oriole"), or Isco. They numbered just 25 when they were found. This tribe had never had peaceful contact with white men.[36]

The adult members of the tribe told Russell and his interpreter the following tradition:

> Many years ago there was a great flood. The waters rose and the people cried out and all were drowned except two named Majo rabe (meaning

Many years ago there was a great flood. The waters rose and the people cried out and all were drowned except two…

34. Paul Marcoy, *A Journey Across South America*, vol. 2, part 2 (London: Blackie, 1878), p. 325.
35. Jose Alvarez, "Mitologia, tradiciones y creencias religiosas de los salvajes hurayos," *Actas y Trabajos Cientificos del XXVIIo [27th] Congreso internacional de Americanistas* (Lima: 1939), vol. 2 (Lima: Gil, 1942), p. 160.
36. Louis Whiton, Bruce Greene, and Richard Momsen, "The Isconahua of the Remo," *Journal de la Société des Américanistes* (Paris: 1964), vol. 53, p. 85.

two Majos) who swam away resting at times on a floating log. After many days they came to where people were and men started living again in the world. The animals were saved because they turned into birds during the flood.[37]

Huallaga River in Peru

269 **Peru**

PIROS

The Piros narrated a lengthy tradition to Ricardo Alvarez when he met them in the 1950s. To summarize, it tells of a young woman who united with a serpent (an echo of the Garden of Eden?), and gave birth to a child through this union. One day, the boy's grandmother entered the house and found him surrounded by a brood of serpents. Shocked at the discovery, she seized him and threw him into the fire. However, the boy's mother came and rescued him.

In revenge, the serpents determined to unleash a deluge which would destroy all life. The child felt compassion for his mother, so he secretly went and warned her of the coming disaster. He told her to plant a seed of the Genipa tree, and to prepare food. The tree rapidly grew overnight. When the flood came, the woman and her sister went up into it, and the tree continued to grow taller as the flood waters rose.

> The two sisters saw a torrent of water coming ... The inundation covered the houses, the highest trees, and the hills. They all drowned.

> The two sisters, from the viewpoint of the tree, saw a torrent of water coming through the river which was covering the trees of the mountain. They warned their mother, but the old woman did not believe them. They pounded the tree so that it grew higher, and they rose above the waters. The inundation covered the houses, the highest trees and the hills. The people swam about, crying and yelling, hopelessly. There were no trees for them to cling to, nor hills on which to find refuge. They all drowned. The old woman drowned also.[38]

270 **Peru**

CHAYAHUITA

The Chayahuita people, known to themselves as the Kanpopiyapi, live along the Huallaga River in central Peru. In the 1980s, a witch-doctor of the tribe told Nancy Siguas their account of the Flood:

> When the Flood happened, the people succumbed to the waters and died. Only one person survived. This person is considered as a god and is called Konpanama. When the water covered all the earth, Konpanama climbed to the highest part of a hill while the water was yet rising.[39]

37. Ibid., p. 94.
38. Ricardo Alvarez, *Los Piros* (Lima: Instituto de Estudios Tropicales Pio Aza, 1960), p. 42.
39. Nancy Ochoa Siguas, "El Mito del Diluvio y la Creación de la División Sexual entre los Kanpopiyapi de la Amazonía Peruana," *Journal de la Société des Américanistes*, vol. 72, part 2 (Paris: 1992), p. 164.

271 Peru and Brazil

AMAHUACA

We have a fragmentary reference to the Amahuaca tribe's belief concerning the Flood, from Gertrude Dole's field work between 1960 and 1961:

> In their myths the great flood was attributed to the cutting down of burnt stumps and to the giant serpent of the river.[40]

Confluence of the Tambo River and Urubamba River, forming the Ucayali River

272 Ecuador

WAORANI

The Waorani (or Huaorani) tribe of Ecuador gained a degree of fame through the ministry of Jim and Elizabeth Elliott, and the associated publications such as *Through Gates of Splendor* and *End of the Spear*. An elder of the tribe, almost 100 years old, gave a passing reference to their Flood story when Rogelio Rioverde met him in the 1990s:

> "We are now in the fourth world," he told me, "and the great flood was the last of the stages of destruction. Before that, there was only one chonta spear. The families had run out of spears. Then Nenquihuenga, the son of the sun, arrived and taught a Huaorani how the chonta spears were made. Before that, people had been destroyed by fire and only two families who lived correctly were saved. This was in very old times. There are many, many stories."[41]

273 Peru

COCAMA

The Cocama were greatly feared in the 17th century as river pirates, living along the Ucayali River.[42] We have a bare mention of the Flood, from what two tribal authorities told Juan Abaurre:

> Jara created the world, when there was the Deluge, with a small arrow. When the arrow fell right, the river remained right. When it fell at an arced path, the river curved. Afterwards, he put upon the earth all things, animals, and plans. After putting everything in order, he went up to the world in heaven.[43]

Jara created the world, when there was the Deluge, with a small arrow.

40. Gertrude E. Dole, "Los Amahuaca," *Guía Etnográfica de la Alta Amazonía*, vol. 3 (Quito: Abya-Yala, 1998), p. 257.
41. Rogelio de los Campos Rioverde, "Los Huaorani," *Ecuador: Terra Incognita*, vol. 3 (Quito: Ecuador Terra Incognita, 1999). Retrieved from: http://www.terraecuador.net/revista_3/3_huaorani.htm.
42. Alfred Metraux, "Tribes of the Middle and Upper Amazon River," in *Handbook of South American Indians*, vol. 3, p. 687.
43. Juan Carlos Ochoa Abaurre, 2002, "Mito y Chamanismo: El mito de la tierra sin mal en los Tupí-Cocama de la Amazonía Peruana," Ph. D. Thesis (Universidad de Barcelona), p. 125.

274 **Bolivia**

TACANA

The Tacana tribe, relatives of the Ese Ejja, told this account of the Flood to Ida de Ottaviano in the 1970s:

> In the beginning there was a deluge which covered everything. . . . The entire mountain was covered, and all the people drowned. Only two young people, a brother and sister, survived by climbing a palm tree. They stayed in the tree until the earth dried. The water remained upon the earth for a long time — 20, 30, 40, or 50 days. From the tree, they could not see any part of the mountain, nor any other tree. Theirs was the only tree which remained above the waters: this was done by God.[44]

The tradition proceeds to tell that they dropped fruits from the treetop to see whether the earth had dried. After they came down, they recovered the knowledge of fire from a toad. "That event [the Flood] was the last judgment, and God saved two people in the royal palm tree.[45]

Quijos Preparing Barbasco, a Fishing Technique

Other Texts (See Appendix A on page 241)

275 **Quijos-Quichua (Ecuador and Peru)**

276 **Kashinawa (Peru and Brazil)**

277 **Cofán (Ecuador and Colombia)**

278 **Pauserna (Bolivia and Brazil)**

In the beginning there was a deluge which covered everything… all the people drowned. Only two young people, a brother and sister, survived by climbing a palm tree.

44. Ida de Ottaviano, *Textos Tacana* (Riberalta, Bolivia: Instituto Linguistico de Verano, 1980), p. 71–74.
45. Ibid., p. 75–76.

An Oca, or Indigenous Brazilian House, Serving Several Families

BRAZIL

In Brazil, the Ticuna told that a man was forewarned of the coming Flood, and prepared a great canoe to save himself and his family. They landed at Mount Vaipi and waited there until the waters abated. Likewise, the Tupinamba say that a wise man foresaw the coming Flood, and escaped the calamity with his family. The Juruna tribe told how their ancestor Sinaá warned his people of the Flood, and constructed a great canoe. Then the Flood came and "only the top of the mountains remained above the water. Everything was water." "The animals died. Even the high mountains were under water," said the Yanomami tribe. "Almost all of mankind was destroyed with a flood because the people were foolish and would not cease to do evil," said the Xavante tribe of Mato Grosso. "A torrent of water burst forth! A flood that went over all the world," said the Krahó tribe of northeastern Brazil. Dozens of other tribes of Brazil and the Amazon basin likewise have their ancient accounts of the Flood.

Tribes of the Region

279. Ticuna
280. Tupinamba
281. Amniapa and Guaratagaja
282. Nambicuara
283. Arua
284. Mura
285. Aré
286. Caingang
287. Caraya
288. Kayapo
289. Paumari, Abederi, and Kataushi
290. Juruna
291. Barasana
292. Arawete
293. Canella and Sherente
294. Kraho
295. Yanomami
296. Apapocuva
297. Xavante
298. Bacairi
299. Apinaje
300. Bororo
301. Aymore
302. Camacan
303. Mundurucu
304. Enawene Nawe
305. Zo'e
306. Asurini
307. Katawishi
308. Paraviana
309. Kaxuyana
310. Tariana
311. Waimiri-Atroari
312. Aikewara
313. Tapirapé
314. Ipurina
315. Kaiwa

279 Brazil, Peru, Colombia

TICUNA

The Ticuna live along the Amazon River near the border of Brazil and Peru. Between 1941 and 1942, they told Curt Nimuendajú their Flood tradition:

The Tupinamba People Once Lived on the São Francisco River

> An Indian once owned a dog. One day the animal began to speak in the human language, saying that there would be a great flood; that he, the dog, was going to Mount Vaipi and his master had better accompany him if he wished to save himself. The master, however, did not wish to go, for he did not know where the dog was going to lead him. Then the animal advised him to have a great canoe ready to save himself and his family in the hour of the flood. So saying, the dog departed for Vaipi.
>
> The waters burst boiling out of the earth and flooded the entire surface. The Indian and his family embarked in the canoe that had been prepared and moored to a tree by a very long liana vine. However, the waters steadily rose, and the current pulled the canoe this way and that, so that they were obliged to lengthen the liana repeatedly and had by then long lost track of where they were. But finally they landed on Mount Vaipi, where they remained until the waters subsided. They abandoned their canoe on the mountain — where, it is said, it may still be seen today — and, guided by their lengthened vine, returned to their former home.[1]

One day the animal began to speak in the human language, saying that there would be a great flood; … Then the animal advised him to have a great canoe ready to save himself and his family in the hour of the flood.

280 Coastal Brazil

TUPINAMBA

The Tupinamba are a people group that occupied vast stretches of the Brazilian coast prior to European colonization. An explorer named Jean de Lery visited Brazil in 1557, where he met a group of the Tupinamba. They told him their ancient tradition of a great flood that covering the whole earth. Only two brothers escaped, along with their wives, by climbing very tall trees.[2]

Around the same time period, a Tupinamba group told Andre Thevet a similar account of the Flood.[3]

A priest and historian named Simam de Vasconcellos also heard of the Flood from them. He wrote in 1668:

> [They] tell that before the flood arrived. there was a man of great knowledge, whom they called the Paye (which means magician or diviner or prophet), whose name was Tamanduara, or Tupa, which means superior excellence. This man came to be at the same level with God, spoke with him, and discovered his secrets. And among others he told him that there was to be a flood upon the earth, caused by the waters of the earth, and

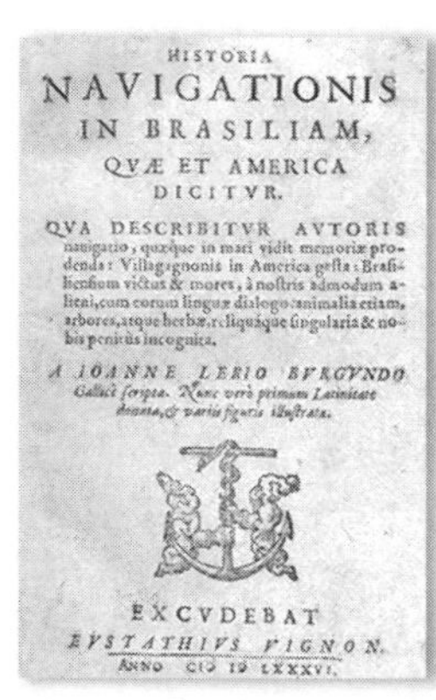

HISTORIA
NAVIGATIONIS
IN BRASILIAM,
QVÆ ET AMERICA
DICITVR.
QVA DESCRIBITVR AVTORIS navigatio, quæque in mari vidit memoriæ prodenda: Villagagnonis in America gesta: Brasiliensium victus & mores, à nostris admodum alieni, cum eorum linguæ dialogo: animalia etiam, arbores, atque herbæ, reliquaque singularia & nobis penitùs incognita.
A IOANNE LERIO BVRGVNDO
Gallicè scripta. Nunc verò primùm Latinitate donata, & variis figuris illustrata.
EXCVDEBAT
EVSTATHIVS VIGNON.
ANNO CIϽ IϽ LXXXVI.

Cover of *Historia Navigationis in Brasiliam*

1. Curt Nimuendaju, "The Tukuna," ed. Robert H. Lowie, trans. William D. Hohental, *University of California Publications in American Archaeology and Ethnology*, vol. 45 (Berkeley and Los Angeles: 1952), p. 141.
2. Jean de Lery, *Historia Navigationis in Brasiliam, quae et America dicitur* (Geneva: 1586), p. 238.
3. Andre Thevet, *La Cosmographie Universelle*, vol. 2 (Paris: 1575), p. 914.

that the whole world was going to be flooded, and no mountain or tree would escape it, no matter how tall. . . . God will leave his palm tree of great height, which was on the top of a certain hill, and the clouds were turned, and the tree gave fruit like coconuts. This palm was appointed by God to save him and his family from the flood. And the prophet passed to this mountain, which was for the salvation of him and his house. And that, being in this place, one day it came to pass that it began to rain heavily, and the waters grew higher, little by little, until they flooded all the earth.

And when the water began to cover the mountain where he was, he climbed the appointed tree, with his family. They remained in this tree all the time that the flood lasted, sustaining themselves by the tree's fruits. When the flood ended, they came down, multiplied, and again inhabited the land. This was the fabulous account of those natives.[4]

The prophet passed to this mountain, which was for the salvation of him and his house. . . . it began to rain heavily, and the waters grew higher, little by little, until they flooded all the earth.

281 AMNIAPA AND GUARATAGAJA

Brazil and Bolivia

The Amniapa and Guaratagaja are two closely associated tribes living along the Guapore River, which forms part of the border of Bolivia and Brazil. Emil Snethlage reported that they "admit cannibalism and eat not only the barbecued bodies of their enemies but even their own tribesmen and women who are put to death for a crime."[5] According to their Flood history, Snethlage wrote that "the mythical being, Barabassa, is held responsible for the great flood from which only one couple survived to repopulate the world."[6]

Bridal Veil Waterfall in Mato Grosso, Brazil

282 NAMBICUARA

Mato Grosso State

The Nambicuara (or Nambikwara), a small tribe from the state of Matto Grosso in Brazil, met the anthropologist Claude Levi-Strauss in the early 1940s. They had a belief about the Flood:

> The only legend recorded by Levi-Strauss is a flood tale relating to the destruction of human life and its re-creation through several incestuous marriages between the offspring of an old woman, who was the only being who escaped the disaster.[7]

4. Simam de Vasconcellos, *Noticias Curiosas do Brasil* (Lisbon: Ioam da Costa, 1668), p. 78–79.
5. Emil Heinrich Snethlage, *Atiko y: Meine Erlebnisse bei den Indianern des Guapore* (Berlin: Klinkhardt & Biermann, 1937). As quoted by Claude Levi-Strauss in "Tribes of the Right Bank of the Guapore River," *Handbook of South American Indians*, ed. Julian Steward, vol. 3 (Washington: GPO, 1948), p. 375.
6. Ibid., p. 378–379.
7. Claude Levi-Strauss, "The Nambicuara," *Handbook of South American Indians*, vol. 3, p. 369.

283 **Rondônia State**

ARUA

The Arua, a tribe from the state of Rondonia in western Brazil, told Emil Snethlage their Flood tradition when he met them in the 1930s:

> Two mythical brothers were regarded by the Arua as creators of the world and bringers of darkness and of fire. Disguised as birds, they stole fire from the old man who was its keeper. When the brothers were old, a flood threatened to destroy mankind, but their sister saved two pairs of children from the best families by putting the children afloat in wooden troughs.[8]

When the brothers were old, a flood threatened to destroy mankind, but their sister saved two pairs of children from the best families by putting the children afloat in wooden troughs.

284 **Rondônia State**

MURA

Curt Nimuendajú met the Mura tribe in the state of Rondônia sometime around 1940. What they told him about the Flood went as follows:

> Men escaped the rising flood in canoes and found a high rock, where they gathered, subsisting on the animals which also had taken refuge there. After the deluge had passed, they could not find their way home until a shaman took them there.[9]

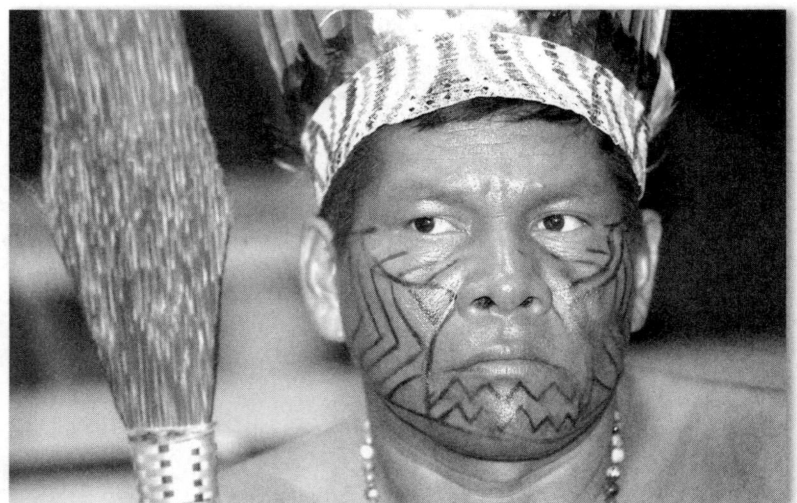

Mura Chief

285 **Paraná State**

ARÉ

According to the Aré tribe of southern Brazil, whom Telêmaco Borba met in the late 1800s:

> In other times there was a great rain, which flooded the lands we inhabited. One of our tribe, who was swimming in the water, saw the top of a palm tree emerging from the water. He approached it and got on a branch which broke because it was dry. He continued to swim, supported by the branch. At dusk he saw the top of another palm tree. He approached it, and took hold of a green branch, by which he was able to secure himself on top of the branches, and there he was for many days suffering hunger and cold. Then the fruit of the palm tree began to ripen, and he ate and fed on them.
>
> One day he heard in the distance the sound of the sapacurú (a kind of ibis bird of our rivers), which approached him. "Stay there. I will bring some land for you." Later, a female ibis came and landed on the palm tree and said, "There is land here, why not go there?" He said, "I cannot. I'm very weak. If I leave the palm tree, I will surely die." Then the female ibis said, "I'm going to get land." And she and the male ibis would bring soil in the beaks and spread it through the drying water. In the places where the male bird put the earth, as his beak was bigger, the earth was elevated forming mountains. Before this rain, the land we inhabited was flat. And the water

One day he heard in the distance the sound of the sapacurú [an ibis bird], which approached him. "Stay there. I will bring some land for you." … She and the male ibis would bring soil in the beaks and spread it through the drying water.

8. Emil Heinrich Snethlage, *Atiko y Meine Erlebnisse bei den Indianern des Guapore*. As quoted by Claude Levi-Strauss in "Tribes of the Right Bank of the Guapore River," *Handbook of South American Indians*, vol. 3, p. 379.
9. Curt Nimuendajú, "The Mura and Piraha," *Handbook of South American Indians*, vol. 3, p. 265.

disappeared, and the man descended from the palm tree, and lived on the fruits and roots of the trees.[10]

Brazilian Kaingang Man

286 CAINGANG

Southern Brazil

In the late 1800s, Telêmaco Borbas visited the Caingang or Coroado people who live in the states of Paraná, Santa Catalina, and Rio Grande do Sul in southern Brazil. A "cacique" or chief named Arakxo told Borbas their tradition of the Flood. Arakxo had learned this in his youth from his great-grandmother, who in turn had learned it from her predecessors. It is similar to the Aré tribe's tradition, cited above.

> In times past, there was a great flood that was submerging all the land inhabited by our ancestors. Only the summit of the Crinjijinbê remained above the waters. The Caingangs, Cayurucrês, and Camés swam toward the mountain, carrying firewood in their mouths. The Cayurucrès and Camés became tired and drowned; Their souls went to live in the center of the mountain. The Caingangs and a few of the Curutons reached the Crinjijinbê peak. There they stayed on the ground, and others, for lack of space, used the branches of trees. Several days passed without the waters lowering and without eating. They were prepared to die when they heard the singing of the saracura birds, who were carrying earth in baskets, throwing it into the water that was slowly withdrawing. The people shouted at the saracuras to hurry, and they did so, also adding to the song and inviting the ducks to aid them.[11]

Several days passed without the waters lowering and without eating. … [then] they heard the singing of the saracura birds, who were carrying earth in baskets, throwing it into the water that was slowly withdrawing.

When the flood subsided, the Caingangs went down and settled at the foot of the mountain. The souls of the Cayurucres and Cames, who had drowned, began to burrow their way out of the mountain in which they were imprisoned. After much time they came out and kindled a fire. Out of the ashes of the fire one of the Cayurucres molded jaguars, tapirs, aardvarks, bees, and many other animals. And he brought them to life and told them what they should eat.[12]

Edon Schaden also heard of the Flood from a Caingang chief's family, during his visit in 1947:

> Many Indians died in the great Flood that swept through these remote lands. Those who escaped were only two young children, who were siblings. They were from the Kamé group. Those little ones swam and swam, and eventually came to a very high mountain range, which is called Krim-Takré. The two climbed to the top of the mountain, and were clinging to the leaves of the trees. When the waters of the flood went down, they too went down. Then the two of them married — brother and sister — and the Indians increased again. They made fire, for they already knew the vine that gives fire.[13]

Many Indians died in the great Flood that swept through these remote lands. Those who escaped were only two young children, who were siblings.

10. Telêmaco Morocines Borba, "Observações sobre os indígenas do Estado do Paraná," *Revista do Museu Paulista*, vol. 6 (Sau Paulo, Typographia do Diario Official, 1904), p. 61–62.
11. Ibid., p. 57–58.
12. Ibid., p. 58–59.
13. Egon Schaden, "A Origem dos Homens, o Diluvio e Otros Mitos Kaingang." *Revista de Antropologia*, vol. 1, no. 2 (São Paulo, 1953), p. 140.

287 Tocatins, Pará, Matto Grosso States

CARAYA

The Carayas (or Karajas) live along the Araguaya River, a major southern tributary of the Amazon. In 1887 or 1888, an old man of the tribe told Paul Ehrenreich a tradition of the Flood. This tells that one day, the Carayas were on the hunt and drove animals into a hole. They began to pull them out and kill them one by one. But then they found a man, who was a powerful magician, inside the earth. His name was Anatiua. He had a thin body but a big belly. They brought him into their village. However, they did not understand the language he spoke, and were terrified by his strange behavior. They fled from him with their wives and children, and Anatiua became angry:

> He turned himself into a great piranha and pursued them. He carried with him many gourds full of water. He yelled to the Karayas to stop, and when they did not yield, he smashed one of the vessels, and the water began to rise. But the Karayas continued to flee, and so he also broke the second vessel, and the water rose even higher. And then he broke another, and another, and another, until at last all the land was flooded, and only the mountains at the mouth of the Tapirape River stood above the flood. The Karaya took refuge on the two peaks of this mountain range. Then Anatiua called all the fish to draw the people down into the water. The Jahu, the Pintado, and the Pacu tried to do this, but none of them succeeded. At last, the bicudo (a fish with a long beak-shaped snout) was able to climb the mountain from behind and to pull down the Karayas. A great lagoon still marks the location where they fell. Only a few of the people remained on the mountain, and they descended when the water had run off.[14]

…all the land was flooded, and only the mountains at the mouth of the Tapirape River stood above the flood. The Karaya took refuge on the two peaks of this mountain range.

288 Pará and Mato Grosso States

KAYAPO

The Kayapo tradition is similar to that of the Carayas, but they replace the buried magician with a buried artery:

Kayapo Tribesmen

> An armadillo hunter, digging, discovered what he thought was a thick lump. The vine was the artery of the Earth and, when cut, spouted water in such a quantity that the world was flooded. The anemones died, but the Indians climbed on the tallest trees that were not submerged. The waters took a long time to go down and the survivors were so thin and weak that they could not go down. But they did not die. They became hornets and termites that, to this day, make their homes on the tops of the trees, revealing their human origin.
>
> From the flood, as from universal fire, only one family was saved. An old woman closed herself, with a couple of children, inside a large pestle, sealing the opening with a wax. And several seeds were kept in small cages tied to the pestle.[15]

An old woman closed herself, with a couple of children, inside a large pestle, sealing the opening with a wax. And several seeds were kept in small cages tied to the pestle.

14. Paul Ehrenreich, *Beiträge zur völkerkunde Brasiliens* (Berlin: W. Spemann, 1891), p. 40–41.
15. Horace Banner, "Mitos Dos Indios Kayapo," *Revista de Antropologia*, vol. 5, no. 1 (São Paulo: 1957), p. 49–50.

289 PAUMARI, ABEDERI, AND KATAUSHI

Amazonas State

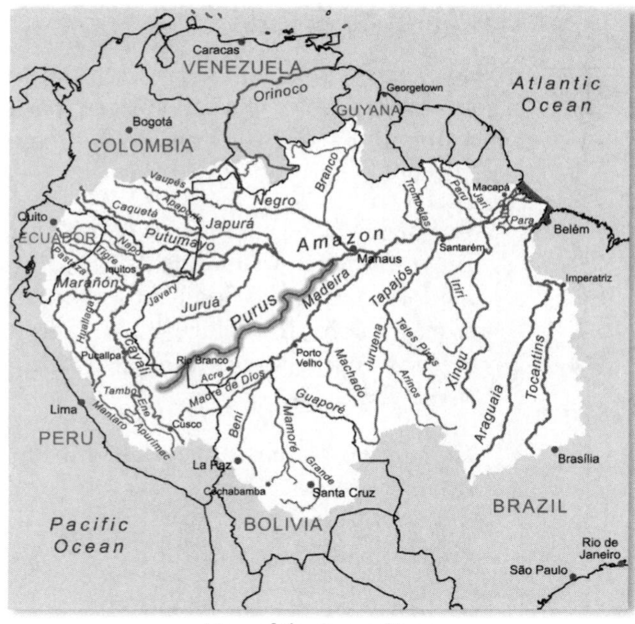

Map of the Purus River

The Paumari, Abedery, and Kataushy live closely together along the Purus River in southwestern Brazil. They shared their oral tradition of the Flood with a Dr. Barbosa around the year 1900:

> They also tell us that at one time in the ancient past, the world really was destroyed. First, they heard a roar over and under the earth. It is said that the sun and the moon, as a sign, became red, blue, and yellow, and the wild animals mingled among the humans, without fear. A month later, they heard a more powerful roar. They then saw that darkness rose from the earth to the sky, with a thundering and a great rain destroying the day and the earth. Some people got lost, others died, without knowing why. Everything was in a fearful confusion. The waters then rose very high, and they said that the earth went down into them, and only the branches of the tallest trees stood out. People had gone up there for refuge, and they died of hunger and cold, as it was raining and dark the whole time. Only Uassu and his wife were saved.[16]

290 JURUNA

Pará and Mato Grosso States

The Juruna people told Orlando and Claudia Boas many of their oral traditions in 1946, including one regarding the Flood:

> The Juruna had everything. When the waters began to rise with the rains, Sinaá warned his people that the water of the rivers was going to rise and cover the forests, the fields, and the hills. He was saying, "The rain is not going to stop until everything is filled and covered by water. We need to build a great canoe in order to sow within it."
>
> Sinaá made the canoe, a great canoe, in which many people could fit. In the middle of the front of the boat he put soil and planted cassava, millet, yams, and everything else. The waters kept rising higher and higher. The rivers overflowed and covered the forests. Only the top of the mountains remained above the water. Everything was water. The tapirs, pigs, and insects swam from here to there, but could find no land on which to stand. In the end they drowned.[17]

Sinaá made the canoe, a great canoe, in which many people could fit. … Only the top of the mountains remained above the water. Everything was water.

The tradition adds that after the Flood, "Sinaá gave each group that was leaving a different language."[18]

16. Carl Teschauer, "Mythen und alte Volksagen aus Brasilien," *Anthropos*, vol. 1 (1906), p. 739.
17. Orlando Villas Boas and Claudia Villas Boas, "Xingu," *Los Pueblos Indios en sus Mitos*, vol. 17 (Quito: Abya-Yala, 1993), p. 233.
18. Ibid., p. 234.

291 BARASANA

Brazil and Colombia

We have two accounts of the Flood from the Barasana or Yepa-Masa tribe who live in southeastern Colombia and adjacent parts of Brazil. As they told Stephen Hugh-Jones around the year 1968, a great flood took place long ago, caused by the female deity Romi Kumu:

> She made a door on the edge of this earth, the Door of Water, in the east. There was much water outside of it, and when she opened the door, the water rushed in and flooded the earth. . . . The people made canoes in order to escape the deluge, but only those who were in a canoe made from the wood of the Kahuwu tree survived. All the other people and all animals were drowned.
>
> The survivors came to the peak of the hill called Ririho, near the Pirá-Paraná (River).[19]

Only those who were in a canoe made from the wood of the Kahuwu tree survived. ... The survivors came to the peak of the hill called Ririho

This tradition adds that a fire broke out after the flood and destroyed everything again.

Another version, which tribe members told Acacio Camargo de Piedade during the 1990s, went like this:

> The great snake Sepiro did not let the population of Indians increase, because it had the power to flood the world and thus to eat the defenseless Indians. Sepiro was the serpent of the flood. One day, the world had been flooded by Sepiro, but there was a tall mound that was not underwater, the mount Patí. All the Indians swam there, but there was no room for them, as the mountain was already full of animals. Yepa-oakihi sought to kill Sepiro with a blowpipe. He blew the blowpipe four times and wounded the snake the last time. . . . Sepiro is still alive. He can no longer cause a flood, but can still kill Indians.[20]

[The great serpent] Sepiro is still alive. He can no longer cause a flood, but can still kill Indians.

292 ARAWETE

Pará State

The Arawete were historically one of the most isolated tribes of Brazil. They had no known contact with westerners until the 1960s, and no meaningful contact until the 1970s. Eduardo Castro wrote an ethnography of the Arawete, containing a tradition they told him which has interesting Genesis parallels:

Arawete Group on a Boat Ride

> Humans are defined as those who were left behind, the forsaken ones. Before that, humankind and the future gods (Maï) lived together on the earth, a world without work or

19. Stephen Hugh-Jones, *La Palma y las Pleyades* (Bogota: Universidad Central, 2011), p. 333.
20. Acácio Tadeu de C. Piedade, 1997, "Musica Yepa-Masa," Ph. D. Thesis (Universidade Federal de Santa Catarina, Florianopolis), p. 181.

death, but also without fire or cultivated plants. Then, as a result of being insulted by his wife Tadide, the god Aranami decided to leave, exasperated with humans. . . . The ascent of the heavens unleashed a catastrophe. Deprived of its stone foundation, the earth dissolved under the waters of a flood that, according to some versions, was caused by a river or, according to others, by heavy rains. Pako aco and Yicire aco, the monstrous piranha and alligator, devoured the humans. Only two men and a woman (no one could tell me their names) saved themselves by climbing a bacaba palm. They were the tema ipi, the "origin of the creeping vines," the ancestors of current humankind.[21]

Two Indigenous Men from Brazil

The ascent of the heavens unleashed a catastrophe ... the earth dissolved under the waters of a flood... Only two men and a woman saved themselves by climbing a bacaba palm.

293 CANELLA AND SHERENTE

Goiás State

The Canella and Sherente tribes told their tradition to Curt Nimuendajú in the early 1930s. In this version, the sun and moon were said to have walked on the earth as friends during ancient times. The flood occurred when the moon made the mistake of picking up a turtle, which they were forbidden from touching. This turtle burst forth with torrents of water:

> At the bottom of the creek the acangapara turtle was lying buried in the sand, the water only bubbling up over her nose. "Leave it alone!" Sun warned, but his companion (Moon) went there and raised it a little. Immediately a torrent of water burst forth from under the animal, so that he set it down again in alarm. But when through with bathing, he again went and lifted its entire body. Now the water came rushing forth in such quantity and with such force as to carry everything away. The current seized Moon and carried him off, while from the bank Sun vainly tried to fish out his comrade with a long burity stick he extended to him. At last the current carried him under the branches of an inga tree, by which he pulled himself out. After a while he reached Sun with his belly burnt. The spots are still to be seen on the moon's belly.[22]

Now the water came rushing forth in such quantity and with such force as to carry everything away. The current seized Moon and carried him off...

21. Eduardo Viveiras de Castro, trans. Catherine V. Howard, *From the Enemy's Point of View* (Chicago: University of Chicago Press, 1992), p. 58–59.
22. Curt Nimuendaju, "The Eastern Timbira," *University of California Publications in American Archaeology and Ethnology*, vol. 41 (Berkeley: University of California Press, 1946), p. 243–244, 232.

294 KRAHO

Maranhão and Tocantins

The Krahó tribe have a very similar Flood story to that of the Canella and Sherente tribes. When Pudlere (the moon) picked up the forbidden turtle, "a torrent of water burst forth! A flood that went over all the world and carried off Pudlere." With difficulty, Pud (the sun) extended a palm branch into the water, and managed to save his friend from drowning.[23]

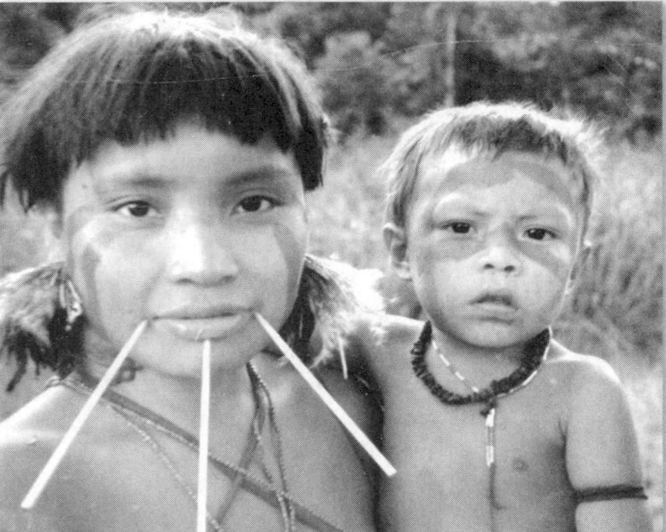

Yanomami Woman and Child

295 YANOMAMI

Brazil and Venezuela

The version told by the Yanomami tribe is clearly related to that of the above-mentioned tribes:

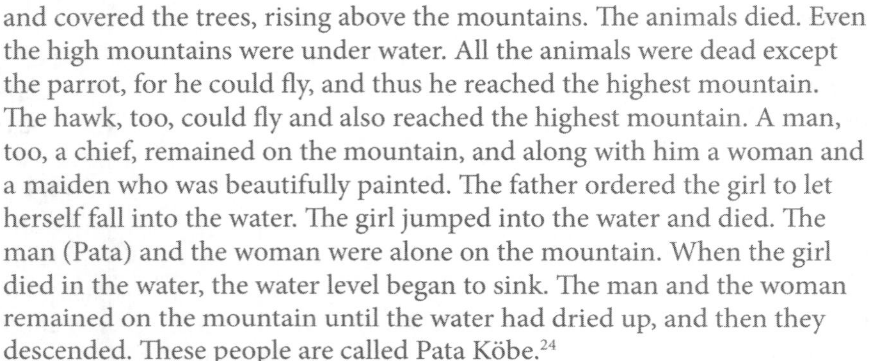

> Mauñene was looking for crabs. He pulled a stone out of the earth, whereupon water flowed out, first only a little, a small stream, then more and more. It flooded the earth and covered the trees, rising above the mountains. The animals died. Even the high mountains were under water. All the animals were dead except the parrot, for he could fly, and thus he reached the highest mountain. The hawk, too, could fly and also reached the highest mountain. A man, too, a chief, remained on the mountain, and along with him a woman and a maiden who was beautifully painted. The father ordered the girl to let herself fall into the water. The girl jumped into the water and died. The man (Pata) and the woman were alone on the mountain. When the girl died in the water, the water level began to sink. The man and the woman remained on the mountain until the water had dried up, and then they descended. These people are called Pata Köbe.[24]

It flooded the earth and covered the trees, rising above the mountains. The animals died. Even the high mountains were under water… The man and the woman remained on the mountain until the water had dried up, and then they descended.

296 APAPOCUVA

Mato Grosso do Sul, Paraná, and São Paulo

It was from the Apapocuva tribe of southeastern Brazil that the German ethnologist Curt Unckel received his honorary last name, Nimuendajú, which means "one who has made himself a home." They told him the following tradition of the Flood around the year 1913:

> [Guyraypoty said] "But now make a house for yourselves. Make a house for yourselves out of planks. Otherwise, they say that when the water comes, it will destroy the house. Nanderuvusu tells me so."
>
> And Guyraypoty said to Yyperu, "Give help to my children!"
>
> "I will not help. I want to make a canoe."
>
> To the wild duck he said, "Help my children to build the house!"
>
> "Neither will I help them. Rather, I will fly."
>
> He said to the Suruva, "Will you also not help my children with the house?"

23. Harald Schultz, "Lendas dos Indios Krahó," *Revista do Museu Paulista*, vol.4 (new series, (Sau Paulo, 1950), p. 56.
24. Franz Knobloch, *Die Aharibu-Indianer in Nordwest-Brasilien* (St. Augustin bei Bonn: Verlag des Anthropos-Instituts, 1967), p. 148. As quoted in *Folk Literature of the Yanomami Indians*, eds. Johannes Wilbert and Karin Simoneau (Los Angeles: UCLA Latin American Center, 1990), p. 78.

"Neither will I."

"Then do as you will. You will see how you will fare when the water comes."

The children made a house out of planks. They finished it, and danced again. "Do not fear when the water overflows its limits, because it is said that the water comes in order to cool the earth's supports." "Dance for three years, it was said, when the waters came and overflowed." "Take care that you do not fear."

The house spun and elevated over the water, and rose higher and higher. They came to the entrance to the heavens, and the water rose to just below their level.

The waters came and overflowed. And Yperu cried out, "Bring me an ax of stone. I want to make a canoe for myself." He cried and the spray of the water flew over his head. The wild duck tried in vain to fly. The animals of the water devoured him. The Suruva also cried, "The water comes indeed!" The water went in his mouth, and his soul passed to the place of the birds.

. . . And the water covered the house. The wife of Guyraypoty said to her husband, "Come up to the house!" . . . And Guyraypoty sung. And the house began to move. The house spun and elevated over the water, and rose higher and higher. They came to the entrance to the heavens, and the water rose to just below their level.[25]

297 XAVANTE

Mato Grosso State

We have only a fragmentary reference to the Flood from the Xavante tribe of eastern Mato Grosso. Around the year 1970, the oldest living member of the tribe, a man named Jeronimo, stated that their god destroyed almost all of mankind with a flood because the people were foolish and would not cease to do evil.[26]

Aerial View of an Amazon Tributary River, Mato Grosso

298 BACAIRI

Mato Grosso State

The Bacairi (or Bakairi), a tribe living in Mato Grosso, told their creation story to a historian named Joao Capistrano de Abreu around the year 1890. This creation story contains a Flood account which is very similar to Genesis:

The Brazilians' grandparents dreamed. "At the next moon the sea will swell," the spirits told them. When he told his people they said, "You are lying." Then he took his ax. He made a great canoe, tall as a house. Into the canoe he took his food. At night, with only his wife and children, he embarked. When he entered the sea, he went up, and up, at night. Then all the people died.

Then he took his ax. He made a great canoe, tall as a house. Into the canoe he took his food. At night, with only his wife and children, he embarked.

25. Curt Nimuendaju, *Los Mitos de Creación y de Destrucción del Mundo como Fundamentos de la Religión de los Apapokuva-Guaraní*, ed. Juergen Riester G. (Lima: Centro Amazónico de Antropología y Aplicación Práctica, 1978), p. 173–176.
26. Bartolome Giaccaria, *Mitología Xavante* (Quito: Editorial Abya-Yala, 1991), p. 320–321.

> When the sea rose it made the sand. After a year the sea came down, and the sand became a stone. Then the heavens and the earth were changed. The earth went to the sky, and the sky came to earth with the stars.[27]

299 Tocantins State

APINAJE

The Apinaje, or Apinaye, told a Flood legend to Curt Nimuendajú around the year 1930:

> The big snake Kane-roti came up from the sea and made the Rio Tocantins and the Rio Araguaya. He left to his smaller companions the task of making the lesser streams and creeks. Then it rained for many days. All the watercourses overflowed their banks; the flood waters of the Tocantins joined those of the Araguaya. For two days the whole world was flooded. Many Apinaye fled to the Serra Negra, a mountain behind Sao Vicente, toward the Araguaya, which for that reason is called Ken-klimati (mountain of the meeting). Others took refuge in high Jatoba trees, still others clung to big bottle gourds, drifted hither and yon, and finally perished.
>
> One married couple took three gigantic gourd bottles, put manioc cuttings, maize and other seeds inside, stopped the orifices thoroughly with wax, and tied the three vessels together. Then the two sat down in the middle and allowed themselves to drift on the water. The current drove their craft close to the Serra Negra, but it resisted the powerful whirlpool.
>
> On the Serra Negra the water was already up to people's knees; quite suddenly at night it fell again. Those perched on the high Jatoba trees were now unable to get down and finally turned into nests of Chope bees and termites. When the water had ebbed away, the couple with the three gourds looked for a dwelling site and started a farm there.[28]

For two days the whole world was flooded… One married couple took three gigantic gourd bottles, put manioc cuttings, maize and other seeds inside, stopped the orifices thoroughly with wax, and tied the three vessels together.

300 Brazil and Bolivia

BORORO

Herbert Baldus visited the Bororo tribe in 1934, and they told him their tradition of the Flood. This version seems to be another example of the theme in which a hunter kills a forbidden animal — by shooting an arrow — and which retaliates by sending the Flood.

Bororo Man from Mato Grosso

> One day, a long time ago, the men had set up fishing nets from their fishing boats. One of them went to see if there was fish in his. Fixing his gaze, he saw inside his net the three Jacomos spirits: one yellow, one red, and the third black. Targeting the yellow, he shot the arrow and injured him.

27. João Capistrano de Abreu, "Os Bacaeris," *Ensaios e Estudos* (Critica e Historia), vol. 3 (Rio de Janeiro: Sociedad Capistrano de Abreu, 1938), p. 246–247.
28. Curt Nimuendaju, *The Apinaye*, trans. Robert H. Lowie (Washington: Catholic University of America Press, 1939), p. 183.

When the spirit was struck, the waters began to rise and overflow their limits. Immediately the man sought to save himself, but it seemed that they pursued him, because where he sought refuge, the waters rose and overtook him.

Fleeing, he met other men and advised them to flee as well, for the waters kept increasing. Finally, he arrived at the village and urged the inhabitants to flee quickly because the waters did not give them time to delay. Taking a burning ember, he set off toward the mountain.

At the warning of the companion, some attempted to flee promptly, but were not swift enough to evade the waters. While they followed the man who had warned them, they went up the mountain but drowned and perished. And those who did not believe the man's words, but quietly stayed in the village — they too were destroyed.

... they went up the mountain but drowned and perished. And those who did not believe the man's words, but quietly stayed in the village — they too were destroyed.

The one who had wounded the spirit reached the mountain. He turned his eyes everywhere and saw that the fields, the jungles, the ravines, and the hills were all covered with water. He saw no animal, for all had perished. And the waters grew continually until they reached the man, who, sitting on the top of the mountain, watched that stupendous flood.

He felt lost. What could he do? Suddenly he obeyed an inspiration. With the burning ember he had brought, he warmed a stone, crushed it, and threw the fragments on the four sides, so that the waters would subside. So the waters did.

When the waters had gone down, the survivor came down from the mountain and ran to the place where the village was. Nothing else was found. He whistled and whistled to call his companions. Not getting an answer, he said: "Woe is me! I'm alone; No one else lives!"[29]

The story goes on to tell how he found one living thing — a deer — and with this deer he repopulated the world.

301 AYMORE

Espíritu Santo State

The Aymore occupied the state of Espíritu Santo in eastern Brazil. Historically, they were referred to by the Portuguese as Botocudos (from *botoque*, a plug) for the wooden plugs they wore in their ears and on their lower lip.

We have only a mention of their Flood tradition. The explorer Prince Maximillian of Wied met them during his expedition between 1815 and 1817. He wrote: "They [the Botocudos] also have a tradition of a great flood, like the majority of the earth's people."[30]

Prince Maximillian of Wied

29. Herbert Baldus, *Ensaios de Etnologia Brasileira*, p. 176–177.
30. Maximillian Prinz zu Wied-Neuwied, *Reise nach Brasilian in den Jahren 1815 bis 1817*, vol. 2 (Frankfurt: 1821), p. 59.

302 CAMACAN

Bahía State

The Camacan are a small tribe from the state of Bahía in eastern Brazil. Albert Metraux and Curt Nimuendajú studied this tribe during the 1930s and 1940s and mentioned the existence of a Flood tradition among them but did not provide details.[31]

Portrait of Chief Camacan Mongoyo

303 MUNDURUCU

Pará State

The Mundurucu live along the Tapajos River, a southern tributary of the Amazon. William Farabee visited them during his Amazon expedition between 1913 and 1916. They have a tradition of an ancient cataclysm, remarkably similar to that of Genesis where Noah releases birds to search for land — only that a flood of water is replaced with fire. Farabee tells:

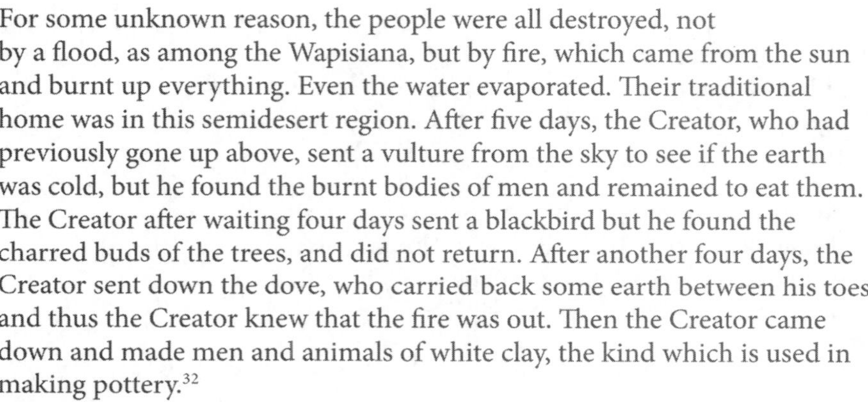

> For some unknown reason, the people were all destroyed, not by a flood, as among the Wapisiana, but by fire, which came from the sun and burnt up everything. Even the water evaporated. Their traditional home was in this semidesert region. After five days, the Creator, who had previously gone up above, sent a vulture from the sky to see if the earth was cold, but he found the burnt bodies of men and remained to eat them. The Creator after waiting four days sent a blackbird but he found the charred buds of the trees, and did not return. After another four days, the Creator sent down the dove, who carried back some earth between his toes and thus the Creator knew that the fire was out. Then the Creator came down and made men and animals of white clay, the kind which is used in making pottery.[32]

The Creator after waiting four days sent a blackbird … After another four days, the Creator sent down the dove, who carried back some earth between his toes and thus the Creator knew that the fire was out.

304 ENAWENE NAWE

Mato Grosso State

The Enawene-Nawe lived in isolation in the state of Mato Grosso and were not contacted until 1974. Marcio Silva met them in the mid-1990s and mentioned their account of the Flood:

> The Enawene-Nawe says they are descendants of a single surviving couple from a flood caused by a deluge in time immemorial, which practically extinguished the population. Only a pair of young virgins escaped death from drowning, taking refuge on the top of a hill. With the return of the waters to normal levels, this couple had many children, who are the ancestors of the present population.[33]

The Banks of the Tapajos River In Pará, Brazil

31. Alfred Metraux and Curt Nimuendaju, "The Camacan Linguistic Family," in "Handbook of South American Indians," vol. 1, p. 547.
32. William Curtis Farabee, "The Amazon Expedition. The Tapajos," *The Museum Journal of the University of Pennsylvania*, vol. 8 (Philadelphia: 1917), p. 133.
33. Marcio Silva, "Demografia e antropologia em contraponto: os Enawene-Nawe e suas derivas matrimoniais," *Revista Brasileira de Estudos de População*, vol. 33, no. 2 (August 2016), p. 359.

305 ZO'E

Pará State

The Zo'e or Poturu tribe live along the Cuminapanema River, a northern tributary of the Amazon. In 1992, a man well-informed on his tribe's traditions narrated the account of the Flood. According to this, the Zo'e perished in the ancient Flood and were recreated by the god Jipohan. "That was when the flood swallowed us, when the great waters came and swallowed us." Another race known as the Kirahi, or white people, survived by floating in gourds.[34]

Enawene Nawe Man

306 ASURINI

Pará State

The Asurini tribe, from the state of Pára in northern Brazil, shared a fragmentary but nonetheless significant tradition with Lucia Andrade around the year 1990. Notice the parallel to the Genesis creation:

> It was not possible to collect complete narratives about the events of this time, only scattered information. There seems to have been a first creation of the universe and then a flood, when the earth ended, and it became soft. From this destruction only one man survived, sheltered in the top of a palm tree. It was then that Mahira [the creator god] called the tapir so that the animal would harden the surface of the earth. Mahira also removed his own rib, transforming it into a woman, which allowed the human population to increase. It was not possible to know Mahira's relationship with the first creation of the universe and with the deluge sometimes associated with Mahira's irritation with men.[35]

Mahira also removed his own rib, transforming it into a woman…

307 KATAWISHI

Amazonas State

The Katawishi (or Katawixi) inhabited a part of the southwestern Amazon basin, but no longer exist as a distinct tribe. Prior to that time, the Catholic missionary Constantin Tastevin visited them in the early 1920s. The Flood story they told him, like Genesis, has a particular notion about the rainbow:

> The Katawishi recognize two rainbows: Mawali to the west, and Tini to the east. They were twin brothers. After the splitting of the Amazon, which left the two brothers apart, it was Mawali who created women anew. Tini and Mawali provoked the flood that inundated all the world and which killed all living things, except two young women whom they saved in order to take them as their companions. One must not look at either rainbow. To look at Mawali will condemn one to become dumb, lazy, cursed in the hunt and in fishing. To look at Tini will make one so stupid that he cannot go out without stumbling and wounding his foot on all obstacles of the road, nor take up a sharp instrument without cutting himself.[36]

Tini and Mawali provoked the flood that inundated all the world and which killed all living things, except two young women

34. Carlos Alberto Ricardo, ed., *Povos Indígenas no Brasil* 1996/2000 (São Paulo: Instituto Socioambiental, 2000), p. 37.
35. Lucia M. M. de Andrade, 1992, "O corpo e o cosmos: relações de gênero e o sobrenatural entre os Asurini do Tocantins," Masters Thesis (Universidade de São Paulo), p. 117.
36. Constantin Tastevin, "La légende de Bóyusú en Amazonie," *Revue d'Ethnographie et des Traditions Populaires*, Year 6, No. 22 (Paris: 1925), p. 191.

308 PARAVIANA

Roraima State

The Paraviana (or Paraviyana) no longer exist as a separate tribe, but have been absorbed by the Wapishana.[37] However, in 1774 or 1775, a government official named Francisco Sampaio met them during his expedition. They told him a brief account of the Flood in connection with their deity named Mauari. "They say that he had escaped from the universal deluge, that when he found himself alone he created a woman for his company. He formed this woman from the resin of a tree."[38]

Sunset on the Amazon River

309 KAXUYANA

Pará State

In 1970, a Polish ethnologist named Protasio Frikel met the Kaxuyana tribe along the Cachorro River, which is a northern tributary of the Amazon. The tribe's religious leader, a man named Amekpuru, told him an account of the Flood, which he said destroyed their remotest ancestors. As Frikel summarized:

> There came a great flood that flooded and drowned everything. A remnant of the population escaped to the top of a mountain, where they were saved. . . . When Tuná-imó (the Flood) was over, the people who were left came down from Toronori [the mountain] and spread.[39]

After this, the Kaxuyana replace the Tower of Babel event with a devastating fire, which they say happened shortly after the Flood. This sent the people fleeing back up the mountain.[40]

There came a great flood that flooded and drowned everything. A remnant of the population escaped to the top of a mountain, where they were saved…

310 TARIANA

Brazil and Colombia

The Tariana tradition is very similar to that of the Kaxuyana.[41]

Lower Basin of the Apaporis River

37. John Gillin, "Tribes of the Guianas and the Left Amazon Tributaries," in *Handbook of South American Indians*, vol. 3, p. 810.
38. Ribeiro de Sampaio, "Relação Geographica Historica Do Rio Branco," p. 254.
39. Protasio Frikel, "Os Kaxuyana: Notas Etno-historicas," *Publicaçoes Avulsas*, vol. 14 (Belem, Brazil: Museu Paraense Emilio Goeldi, 1970), p. 26.
40. Ibid.
41. Alexandra Y. Aikhenvald, Tariana Texts (München: Lincom Europa, 1999), p. 52–53.

311 **Roraima and Amazonas States**

WAIMIRI-ATROARI

The Waimiri-Atroari, a tribe of northern Brazil in the states of Roraima and Amazonas, shared their oral traditions with Cláudia Espinola in the early 1990s. They attribute the Flood to the falling of the sky, caused by the god Mawa. She recorded this at the village Cacau in 1993:

> Mawa . . . lived after the sky descended and killed Kinja, then came the water, that is, the flood, and left a couple.[42]

> The sky descended and killed Kinja [one of their gods] and left a couple, then came water and left Mawa and his wife.[43]

...then came the water, that is, the flood, and left a couple... then came water and left Mawa and his wife

312 **Pará State**

AIKEWARA

The Aikewara or Suruí tribe of the state of Pará possess a tradition of the Flood, but the source document is currently unavailable to me.[44]

Canaima National Park, Roraima

Other Texts (See Appendix A on page 241)

313 **Tapirapé (Brazil)**

314 **Ipurina (Brazil)**

315 **Kaiwa (Brazil)**

42. Cláudia Voigt Espinola, 1995, "O Sistema Medico Waimiri-Atroari; Concepções e Práticas," Masters Thesis (Universidade Federal De Santa Catarina, Florianópolis), p. 198, 83.
43. Ibid., p. 198.
44. Clarisse do Carmo Jabur, 2001 "Aikewara ispenheim: comparação do mito do dilúvio Aikewara (Suruí) com os demais grupos Tupi-Guarani," Masters Thesis (Universidade de Brasilia: Brasilia).

Paraguayan Native Village

THE SOUTHERN CONE

(CHILE, ARGENTINA, PARAGUAY, AND URUGUAY)

Traveling south from Brazil, the tribes of Argentina, Paraguay, Uruguay, and Chile all testify to the Flood. The Tehuelche of Chile told that "in the remote past, people acted very wickedly. The sun-god sent torrential and continuous rain, the springs opened, and the ocean overflowed. All mankind and all animals were swept away." Later, the sun-god sent a hawk and a dove to search for dry land, and the dove returned with blades of grass in its beak, a sign that the earth was drying. According to the Mbaya of Paraguay, "When the flood came, Tupa went into a boat with his family."The Puelche tribe of Argentina said, "After the flood which covered all the earth except the Sierra de la Ventana, the people came out of caves in the mountains and the world was populated again." The Ayoreo tribe of Paraguay tell that one man foresaw the Flood and took refuge in his house. His house "floated slowly on the water. . . . all the people around him drowned." The Chamacoco tribal elders said, "It rained without ceasing, day and night…Only one man remained. He built a great house and, together with his wife, fought against the stormy waters, rescuing the animals. . . . Soon, the waters lowered so that the mountain became visible." Even at the southernmost limits of this continent, we find the knowledge of the Flood.

Regional Tribes

316. Chamacoco (Paraguay)
317. Tehuelche (Argentina and Chile)
318. Chile Flood Tradition
319. Guayaki (Paraguay)
320. Guarayú (Paraguay)
321. Lengua (Paraguay)
322. Chorote (Bolivia, Paraguay, and Argentina)
323. Mataco (Argentina, Paraguay, and Bolivia)
324. Mbaya (Paraguay, Bolivia, and Brazil)
325. Mocoví (Argentina)
326. Vilela (Argentina)
327. Puelche (Argentina, Uruguay, and Brazil)
328. Ayoreo (Paraguay)
329. Yahgan (Tierra del Fuego)
330. Selk'nam (Tierra del Fuego)
331. Alacalufe (Chile)
332. Nivaklé (Paraguay)
333. Toba and Pilaga (Argentina)

316 CHAMACOCO

Paraguay

The Chamacoco or Ishir tribe live in the grasslands and forests of Paraguay. While surveying this region in the 1920s, the cartographer Juan Belaieff spent time among the Chamacoco. They narrated to him a tradition which, like many other versions we find across South America, contains a memory of both the Flood and the Garden of Eden:

> In the past our ancestors the Eshiporio lived peacefully and ate only fruit, roots, and honey. They did not eat meat or kill anything.
>
> But one day, the Eshiporio committed a crime. He killed the great creature, Mbusu, and ate its meat. And the great Tatu Cornudo,[1] in its anger, caused the inundation, "Amormalata," the worldwide flood.
>
> It rained without ceasing, day and night. The waters climbed in the rivers and in the lakes. Everyone and everything disappeared beneath the waters. The Eshiporio drowned. Only one man remained. He built a great house and, together with his wife, fought against the stormy waters, rescuing the animals which were struggling to survive in the waves.
>
> The storm ended, and the waters began to recede. Soon, the waters lowered so that the mountain became visible. At its bank he formed a tent and shared it with all the families of animals.[2]

Mulato, a Tehuelche Chief

Only one man remained. He built a great house and, together with his wife, fought against the stormy waters, rescuing the animals which were struggling to survive in the waves.

317 TEHUELCHE

Argentina and Chile

The Tehuelche are a tribe of skillful hunters who have inhabited central Argentina, living off the meat of guanaco, rhea, armadillos, skunk, and other animals. A Scottish man named W.M. Hughes wrote a book in 1927 about Patagonia (the southern part of South America). This contains a few oral traditions from the Tehuelche, including this remarkably well-preserved memory of the Flood:

> At a remote time in the past, the earth was inhabited also by people other than those created by the sun-god. They were very bad and fought among themselves all the time.
>
> When the sun-god saw this he decided to annihilate these people and to create another population in their stead. To destroy the bad people, the sun-god sent torrential and continuous rain, the springs opened, and the ocean overflowed. In the deluge all mankind and all animals were swept away.
>
> Within several days, the sun-god sent a carancho hawk to find out whether the water had subsided. But the carancho could not make the return trip because it had gorged itself on meat. So the sun-god sent the dove, which returned with blades of grass in its beak, proving thereby that it had

…the springs opened, and the ocean overflowed. In the deluge all mankind and all animals were swept away.

1. Belaieff indicates this is likely a Glyptodon (a relative of the armadillo), the bones of which are found in this part of South America.
2. Juan Belaieff, "Los Indios del Chaco Paraguayo y su Tierra," *Revista de la Sociedad Cientifica del Paraguay*, vol. 5 (Asuncion: 1941), p. 41–42.

found dry land. Then the sun-god decided to create new people. First he made a man, then a woman, and finally a dog to keep them company. Later he created the guanaco and the rhea as food for the couple he had brought forth. The sun-god visited the man and the woman who had many children. And that is how the earth was populated once more.[3]

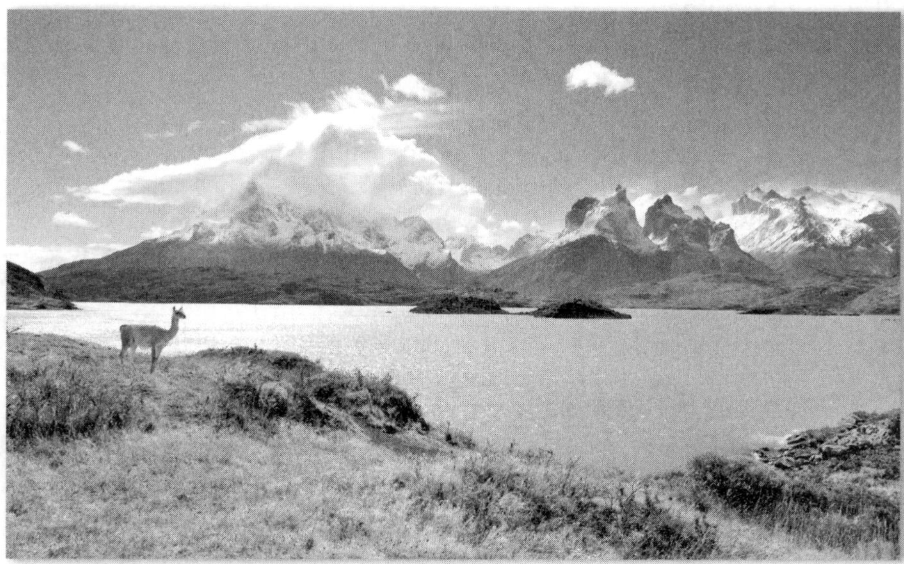

Lake Pehoe at Torres del Paine State Park in Southern Chile

CHILE FLOOD TRADITION

318 **Chile**

The native peoples of Chile possessed an oral tradition of the Flood, which was well-attested from all across this nation. The following text is from one of the earliest historians of Chile, Diego de Rosales (1601–1677), which he recorded around the year 1640. I have abbreviated it due to length:

> And it is widely believed that when the sea abandoned its limit and swallowed up the earth in ancient times, without knowing when (because the Indians have no historical record of times or years), some Indians escaped on the summits of a few high mountains which they call Tenten. These mountains are to them a sacred thing. And in all the provinces there is some Tenten, a mountain greatly revered, as it is believed that upon it their ancestors were saved from the general Deluge. . . . They add to this, that before the flood and the rise of the sea (which they imagine), they were warned by a man. He was poor and humble, and because of this they did not pay any attention to him. . . . They say that the animals, having more keen instincts than men, and knowing the times and movements of the earth better, and knowing of the coming flood, hastened to climb Tenten and so to escape from the rising waters. So they climbed the mountain before the people, due to the incredulity of the people, of whom only few survived at the top of the mountain. . . . some say that two men and two women were saved on Tenten, along with their children. Others say that only one man and woman were saved.[4]

…due to the incredulity of the people, of whom only few survived at the top of the mountain…some say that two men and two women were saved on Tenten, along with their children. Others say that only one man and woman were saved.

They add that, to placate the anger of the lord of the sea, they needed to sacrifice one of their children and cast him into the sea. So they did, and so the sea descended to its former level. As the sea lowered, the mountain lowered as well — just like the floating ark. "And they say that the serpent Tenten and its mountain remain famous and of great religious importance among these Indians."[5]

3. W.M. Hughes, *Ar Lannaur Gamwy Im Mhatagonia* (Liverpool: 1927), p. 69. As quoted in Folk Literature of the Tehuelche Indians, eds. Johannes Wilbert and Karin Simoneau (Los Angeles: UCLA Latin American Center, 1984), p. 104.
4. Diego de Rosales, *Historia General de el Reyno de Chile*, ed. Benjamin Vicuña Mackenna (Valparaiso: 1877), p. 4-6.
5. Ibid.

319 GUAYAKI

Paraguay

The Guayaki, living in the forests of eastern Paraguay, were described by Alfred Metraux and Herbert Baldus as one of the least-known tribes of South America.[6] The botanist Moises Bertoni heard an account of the Flood from them sometime around the year 1900, of which we have a brief reference:

> Long ago, when there was a big flood, men climbed on Pindo palms and lived on the fruits, but they threw the stones of the fruit into the water, thus causing it to rise until most of them were drowned.[7]

Guarayú Woman at Gran Chaco, Paraguay

320 GUARAYÚ

Paraguay

The Guarayú tribe inhabited Paraguay but migrated west into Bolivia in the early 1520s, fleeing from Portuguese conquistadors. A text written in Latin in 1591 by the Jesuit missionaries provides valuable information on the Guarayú and Guaraní peoples. This text does not give us a detailed Flood account, but merely states that they had a Flood tradition in connection with one of their gods, named Candir.[8]

321 LENGUA

Paraguay

The missionary Wilfrid Grubb (1865–1930) planted churches in the Paraguayan Gran Chaco region among isolated tribes. Around the turn of the century, he recorded this Flood legend from the Lengua people. Like several South American texts, it also seems to contain a memory (albeit distorted) of when the Serpent deceived the woman in the Garden.

> In a certain Chaco river, a monster was supposed to live, who had the form of half-man and half-fish. He was held in great terror by the people, and few dared to approach the river. A woman one day unthinkingly went down to draw water, and met the fish-man, who fell in love with her, and asked her to become his wife. She, out of fear, consented, but begged leave to first return to the village with her water-jar. Her request was granted. For a long time she was afraid to return to the river, but eventually she had to go, as there was no other water obtainable. As she was dipping in her jar, the fish-man again appeared, and was very angry with her for having deceived him. Seizing her by the hand, he insisted on taking her to his home beneath the water, and making her his wife. She, however, bit his hand, and, as he drew it away in pain, she ran off. In revenge he caused the water of the river to flood, with the result that nearly all her people were drowned.[9]

A woman one day unthinkingly went down to draw water, and met the monster…

6. Alfred Metraux and Herbert Baldus, "The Guayaki," in "Handbook of South American Indians," ed. Julian H. Steward, vol. 1, in *Bureau of American Ethnology Bulletin*, vol. 143 (Washington: GPO, 1946), p. 435.
7. Moises Santiago Bertoni, *Los Guayakies* (Asuncion: Guaraní, 1941), p. 24.
8. Alfred Metraux, "Un ancien document peu connu sur les Guarayu de la Bolivie orientale," *Anthropos*, vol. 24 (Vienna: St. Gabriel-Modling, 1929), p. 924. For the Latin original, see: *Annuae Litterae Societatis Iesu Anni MDLXXXIX* (Rome: 1591), p. 426–427.
9. Wilfrid Barbrooke Grubb, *A Church in the Wilds* (New York: E.P. Dutton & Co., 1914), p. 60–61.

322 CHOROTE

Bolivia, Paraguay, and Argentina

Around the year 1980, the Chorote people told the anthropologist Maria Verna their Flood tradition:

> Long ago there were people. Then came heavy rains which killed all those people. Afterward the water subsided, and when it was gone other people arrived, lots of them, from above. When they came, the earth was completely dry. Then all of us new people appeared here. There was a man who gave birth to a girl from his hand. He had to marry her himself. After they got married there began to be people. There were men and women; all were there.[10]

Paraguay River

323 MATACO

Argentina, Paraguay, and Bolivia

The Mataco tribe, who occupy part of the Gran Chaco region, shared a fragment of a Flood legend to Alfred Metraux around 1933:

> The rainbow doesn't like menstruating women. Once a menstruating woman was killed and eaten by the rainbow. As a consequence there were heavy rains and a great flood. When the water receded large pools remained as witnesses of that flood.[11]

324 MBAYA

Paraguay, Bolivia, and Brazil

The Mbaya or Guaycuru were a fierce and powerful nation, occupying territory in modern-day Paraguay, Bolivia, and parts of Brazil. Today their descendants are known as the Caduveo. Franz Muller heard their tradition of the Flood sometime between 1910 and 1924.

> According to the flood story, Tupa once lived on earth until the flood came as a result of his son's bloodshed; Thereupon, Tupa went into a boat with his family "in the heaven beyond." Since that time, Tupa has been called "the one who orphaned us."[12]

Map of Argentina

10. Manuscript by Maria Alejandra Verna. As quoted in *Folk Literature of the Chorote Indians*, eds. Johannes Wilbert and Karin Simoneau (Los Angeles: UCLA Latin American Center, 1985), p. 38.
11. Alfred Metraux, *Myths and Tales of the Matako Indians* (Gothenburg, Sweden: Walter Kaudern, 1939), p. 10.
12. Franz Muller, "Beiträge zur Ethnographie der Guarani-Indianer im östlichen Waldgebeit von Paraguay," *Anthropos*, vol. 29 (St. Gabriel-Mödling: Vienna, 1934), p. 186.

325 MOCOVÍ

Argentina

The Mocoví, another tribe of the Gran Chaco region, told an account of the Flood to Robert Lehmann-Nitsche, sometime around 1910:

Sierra de La Ventana Mountains

> Long ago there was a large boat so well enclosed that it had only a single opening or window. It was called Nehcotá, a name subsequently used for every boat.
>
> A very heavy rain had extinguished the Mocoví's fire and had made it impossible to light it again, for the sticks used for making fire were wet. While the Mocoví were pondering their dilemma, a vulture appeared in their country with a firebrand in its beak, from which all took some fire. The vulture was never to return to the boat, for he would have enough to do to find fire for the Mocoví. The tribe was extremely grateful for the favor. Although they hunt and shoot down all birds, not letting a single one escape, they never shoot at the vulture, not even the boys in sport.[13]

326 VILELA

Argentina

The Vilela no longer exist as a distinct tribe, but have been absorbed into the nearby Toba tribe. Sometime prior to 1910, one Professor Llamas was able to record their Flood tradition from the remaining tribe members:

> The sky became covered with clouds and began to rain. Many mosquitoes arose in great numbers, and sucked the blood of the big father and the big mother. . . . Afterwards it still rained. All the land of the Chaco was covered with much water that continued to grow much more, drowning everything. Many flies ate the multitude of animals that had died by water. The water continued to grow and killed everyone. Everything drowned.
>
> Our old parents, with all their innumerable children, escaped by running swiftly many days to the side of the falling sun (west). They reached high ground and thus did not drown. The air was stinking and all the other people died.[14]

All the land of the Chaco was covered with much water that continued to grow much more, drowning everything. . . . The water continued to grow and killed everyone. Everything drowned.

327 PUELCHE

Argentina, Uruguay, and Brazil

The Puelche are a tribe from the grassy plains, *La Pampa*, of northern Argentina and its neighboring countries. In the 1740s, they told their tradition of the Flood to a Catholic missionary named Joseph Labrador. His manuscript is inaccessible to me, but John Cooper summarized it in his article in *Handbook of South American Indians*:

> There was a tradition of a very high tide, and also of a flood. After the flood which covered all the earth except the Sierra de la Ventana, the people came out of caves in the mountains and the world was populated again.[15]

13. Robert Lehmann-Nitsche, "Mitología Sudamericana XII: la Astronomía de los Mocoví," vol. 2, *Revista del Museo de la Plata*, vol. 30 (Buenos Aires, 1927), p. 147.
14. Robert Lehmann-Nitsche, "Mitologia Sudamericana: La Astronomia de los Vilelas," *Revista del Museo de La Plata*, vol. 28 (1924), p. 211–212.
15. John Cooper, "The Patagonian and Pampean Hunters," in "Handbook of South American Indians," vol. 1, in *Bureau of American Ethnology Bulletin*, vol. 143 (Washington: GPO, 1946), p. 168.

328 AYOREO

Paraguay

The Ayoreo, or Moro, told this version to Mario Califano in the 1970s:

> Lightning was the only one who knew that it was going to rain and he took refuge in his little house. There was no time for the others to build houses. So Lightning stayed quietly in his house. While the rain lasted the others, Lightning's relatives, also wanted to take refuge in his house, but he would not let them in. "No, you are bad people. You do not love me or my family. So my family does not love you either. Stay outside my little house."
>
> Then the people were transformed. They were changed into animals, all kinds of animals that live in the river, toads and frogs. Lightning's house floated slowly on the water. When the water rose, his little house rose with it. Finally all the people around him drowned. They were transformed into frogs. They are the frogs that are found in the rivers now.[16]

Beagle Channel, Tierra del Fuego

Lightning was the only one who knew that it was going to rain and he took refuge in his little house. There was no time for the others… Lightning's house floated slowly on the water. When the water rose, his little house rose with it.

329 YAHGAN

Tierra del Fuego

The Yahgan or Yamana people are the southernmost tribe of the world, inhabiting Tierra del Fuego at the southern tip of South America. This archipelago is so named for the many fires that European sailors saw on the islands, which the natives used to warm themselves. The Yahgan told an account of the Flood to an Anglican missionary named Thomas Bridges in the 1870s:

> They have a tradition of the flood. . . . Their tradition on the flood is very fanciful and unclear. The sun was submerged in the sea, the waters rose in tumult, and all the lands were submerged except a very high mountain on which a small number of individuals found shelter.[17]

330 SELK'NAM

Tierra del Fuego

The Selk'nam people live on the main island (*Isla Grande*) of the Tierra del Fuego archipelago. During one of his visits between 1918 and 1924, Martin Gusinde heard about the Flood from the Selk'nam peoples:

> Once in the old days there came so much water that our whole country was flooded. The water rose higher and higher, eventually even covering the mountains. The people saw the great water approaching. To save themselves they ran out on the rocks, some turning into sea lions and others into birds. Afterward all the water subsided. That is why the sea lions and the birds today like to sit on rocks and sandbanks.
>
> All this water had come because the shamans of those days had not paid attention soon enough when the water drew near. They should have stopped it and pushed it back.[18]

Once in the old days there came so much water that our whole country was flooded. The water rose higher and higher, eventually even covering the mountains. The people saw the great water approaching.

16. *Folk Literature of the Ayoreo Indians*, eds. Johannes Wilbert and Karin Simoneau (Los Angeles: UCLA Latin American Center 1989), p. 52.
17. Thomas Bridges, "Mœurs et coutumes des Fuégiens," *Bulletins de la Societe d'anthropologie de Paris*, ed. G. Masson, vol.7 (Paris: 1884), p. 181.
18. *Folk Literature of the Selknam Indians: Martin Gusinde's Collection of Selknam Narratives*, eds. Johannes Wilbert and Karin Simoneau (Los Angeles: UCLA Latin American Center 1975), p. 73.

331 **Chile**

ALACALUFE

The Alacalufe or Halakwulup people live on the western islands of the Tierra del Fuego archipelago. In 1975, a tribesman named Jose Tonko Wide told the following tradition to Oscar Aguilera. It bears resemblance to other Flood traditions found across North and South America, only that here they replace the monster with a coypu (a beaver-like rodent).

Tierra del Fuego National Park, Patagonia

> In the past there was a young man who, while his father was hunting coypu and birds, went out and found a coypu and killed it. . . . A moment later, a wind and storm began to roar, as the legend goes. Then a great ocean wave covered the earth. The young man who killed the coypu survived and ran to save his life. He ran to the peak of a hill. He stayed at the top of the hill. Then the tide went down. Seeing that the water was now low, he went down from the hill. He found the bodies of his brother, mother, and father, who had all drowned. When he returned he also saw animals, orcas, and whales strewn across the forest. Then, the young man went, with his wife, and built a hut. . . . The man slept and in his dream had a premonition. . . . He woke up his wife and said to her, "Listen, go and bring a burning stick. For I had a dream, and a coypu is going to come in, and you have to strike it with the stick and kill it." Then he went back to sleep. The next moment, a pack of coypu entered. The woman went about killing them with the stick, one by one, according to the legend.[19]

Then a great ocean wave covered the earth. … He ran to the peak of a hill. He stayed at the top of the hill. Then the tide went down.

Other Texts (See Appendix A on page 241)

332 **Nivaklé (Paraguay)**

333 **Toba and Pilaga (Argentina)**

19. Oscar Aguilera and Maria Eugenia Brito, "Analysis de un texto Kawesqar," *Boletin de Filologia de la Universidad de Chile*, vol. 21, no. 1 (1980), p. 315–316.

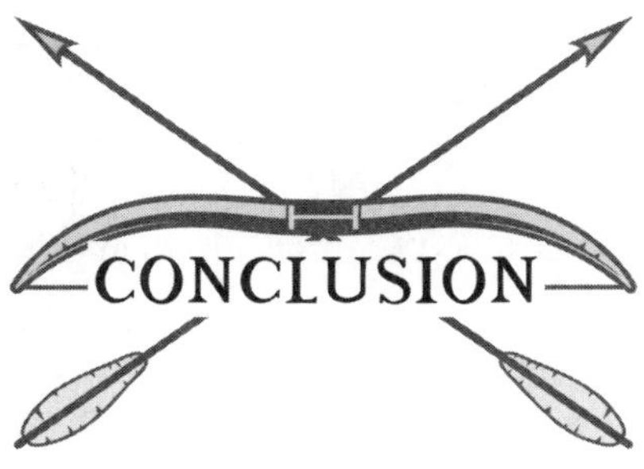

The Courtroom

It is fitting to conclude this volume with an analogy. We find ourselves in a courtroom, and we are the jurors. We must listen carefully to a wide variety of witness testimonies and then make our judgment on a very important case.

Dozens and dozens of witnesses are brought forward, one after the other, to give their testimonies. In some aspects their stories conflict. Some of the testimonies are incomplete and far from perfect, yet they all agree on several particular details. They are all consistent with one another on this common thread of details that runs through the testimonies of all of them.

From these ubiquitous common details, we, the jury, must determine the facts of the case and reach a verdict.

The Verdict?

Likewise, we have heard the testimony of over 300 tribes from North and South America. From the Ute people of the slopes of the Rockies, to the jungles of South America — from the Inuit people of the northern Arctic coasts, to the Yaghan tribes of the southernmost parts of the hemisphere — all of these tribes have given their testimony. Although their stories differ in many ways, they all agree on the fact that a great Flood happened long ago. When we examine the recurring details — the forewarning (almost always given to an old man), the great canoe, the saving of pairs of animals, the landing on a high mountain, the raven and the dove sent in search of land, the freshly plucked leaf, the sacrifice, the rainbow, and the godless ways of man that provoked the Flood — they all match those of the Genesis Flood account.

Now, as one of the jurors, you must make up your own mind and give your verdict. What will you do with the information you have heard?

The Ultimate Verdict

We now possess conclusive and overwhelming evidence that the Genesis Flood account is true. The Flood is a revolutionary fact of history which has wide-ranging implications for us as a society and as individuals. It supersedes the man-centered, atheistic, evolutionary views in vogue today and establishes a God-centered, Bible-centered paradigm.

Consider the weighty implications of this. Think about the Flood for a moment. God sent the global Flood upon the ancient world in punishment for sin. Every last person that was not on board Noah's Ark perished. Yet He lovingly saved Noah—a faithful, God-fearing man—along with his whole family through that Ark. By His strong hand He protected and guided them, and provided a future for them, and their children, and for us.

Yet, as massive as this is, there is something even more massive than the Ark. The Ark pointed forward to something greater. As the Apostle Peter explained, the Ark was a foreshadowing of Jesus Christ (there are many foreshadowings of Jesus in the Old Testament). Jesus is the ultimate Ark. He is the true Savior, and the living God, who saves those who put their trust in Him.

In the past, God sent a Flood in judgment for sin. It nearly annihilated the human race, but He provided a means of rescue for Noah and his seven family members with him. In the future, God will again judge the world for sin. It will be a violent flood of judgment. Our very souls are at risk, and we are in peril because of our sins and disobedience against God.

But God has provided an Ark, the perfect Savior. Jesus came to earth to offer His life, his perfect righteousness in atonement for sin. Then He rose from the dead because He is God. For all who trust in Jesus, His perfect legal righteousness is credited to you. He will give you forgiveness, a new heart, the Holy Spirit's presence, and eternal life. He is the one we must place our hope and confidence in so that we will experience salvation today, every day, and on Judgment Day.

In the next volume, we will turn to the tribes of Asia, Africa, Europe, the Middle East, and the Pacific Isles, as we explore their history and their traditions of the Flood.

APPENDIX A

EXPANDED TEXTS: NORTH AMERICA

Coos (Oregon):

When one day the flood-tide came, there was no ebb-tide. Everything was full of water. Not long afterwards the water reached its full mark. The earth was entirely filled with people. There were too many people, and they looked at the water as it reached its full mark.

Some people had big canoes, and some had small canoes. All kinds of people crowded in when they settled down on the earth. Some people had stored away braided ropes. So they quickly went into the canoes. All people became thus scared.

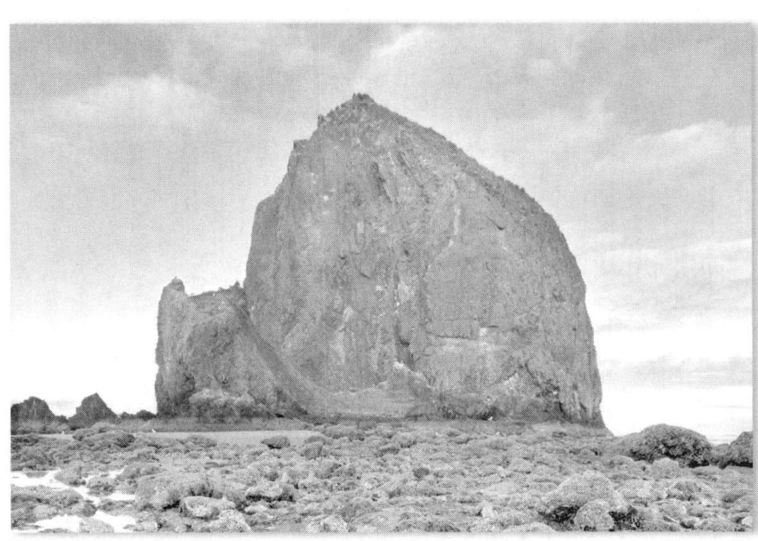

Haystack Rock in Cannon Beach, Oregon

The earth sank into the water. Wherever a small piece of land was sticking out, there they went. A small piece of land was sticking out. There the people assembled. All kinds of animals came there in pairs. All kinds of little birds, all came there in pairs. All kinds of things came there in that manner. They were mixed up there with the people. It seemed as if no one knew the other, when they were thus mixed up with the people. Wherever the top of a fir tree was sticking out, there they fastened their canoes to it. Some people had no braided ropes. Some people drifted far away. Many people had braided ropes. They no longer knew each other.

> So they quickly went into the canoes. All people became thus scared. . . . . The water would carry them away. One-half of the people thus scattered. They no longer knew one another.

The small piece of land kept on floating. This was the name of the small river, "Qalal" (Kentuck Slough). This one was sticking one. There the people assembled. There all kinds of things came together. All kinds of animals were among the people. All kinds of birds mixed in there in pairs. Nobody knew the other one. People were afraid. The thing that was sticking out disappeared. They were scattered everywhere, the people who drifted far away. The water carried them far away. As soon as night came on, the people had their canoes fastened. They were watching their canoes. They were watching the canoes when they were made fast. Some people had short ropes. Suddenly they would let them loose, and they would drift away. The water would carry them away. One-half of the people thus scattered. They no longer knew one another.

A Makah Woman

When evening came, the water ran down. Everywhere people had one canoe that was fastened. They did not know how to take care of the canoes when the water went down. Whenever a canoe was caught on a limb, they would let it loose. Some people did not watch the canoes. They did not watch them, and the canoes would consequently tip over whenever they caught on a limb. This caused their canoes to tip over when night came on. Thus they were working. They could not sleep while they were watching their canoes. When the earth became dry again, the people dropped down to the ground with their canoes. So again they severally came back there. Everywhere they settled down individually — one man with one woman. Thus they settled down. The animals, too, came back ashore when the earth became dry. And the little birds did likewise. The little birds went everywhere in pairs. They did not know the place where they dropped down, and the people started to go far away. They did not know where they dropped down. Thus the people became scattered.[1]

Makah (Washington State):

When the earth became dry again, the people dropped down to the ground with their canoes.... Thus the people became scattered.

"A long time ago," said my informant, "but not at a very remote period, the water of the Pacific flowed through what is now the swamp and prairie between Waatch village and Neeah Bay, making an island of Cape Flattery. The water suddenly receded, leaving Neeah Bay perfectly dry. It was four days reaching its lowest ebb, and then rose again without any waves or breakers, till it had submerged the Cape, and in fact the whole country, excepting the tops of the mountains at Clyoquot. The water on its rise became very warm, and as it came up to the houses, those who had canoes put their effects into them, and floated off with the current, which set very strongly to the north. Some drifted one way, some another; and when the waters assumed their accustomed level, a portion of the tribe found themselves beyond Nootka, where their descendants now reside, and are known by the same name as the Makahs in Classet, or Kwenaitchechat. Many canoes came down in the trees and were destroyed, and numerous lives were lost. The water was four days regaining its accustomed level."[2]

Swan commented that he did not believe this to be a reference to the Noahic Flood, but rather to a local flood. Myron Eells disagreed with Swan's assessment, and rightly so, for Swan's view cannot account for the description that the flood covered the mountains. Eells wrote:

Neah Bay, Washington

It is the opinion of Hon. J.G. Swan that this was simply a rising of the tides, and has no reference to the Deluge of Noah. I suggest, however, that if they had preserved any tradition of the flood in their migrations, when they settled at Neah Bay, where

1. Leo J. Frachtenberg, "Coos Texts," *Columbia University Contributions to Anthropology*, vol. 1 (New York: Columbia University Press, 1913), p. 45–49. Frachtenberg recorded this account of the Flood from the only known member of the tribe who could still articulate the traditions of his people.
2. James G. Swan, *The Indians of Cape Flattery* (Washington: Smithsonian Institute, 1870), p. 57.

nearly all of their floods, though smaller, were caused by the rising of the tide, that they would naturally, in a few generations, refer it to the same cause. The natives of the Sandwich Islands, where floods are caused in the same way, have a tradition of a great flood, but refer it to the rising of the tide.[3]

Traditional Plank House of the Indigenous Peoples of the Pacific Northwest

Kathlamet (Washington State):

The Kathlamet Flood tradition spoke of a marriage between a woman and the Beaver (many Native American traditions either personify animals or do not distinguish them from humans). The woman had been advised by the Blue Jay to marry the Panther, which she intended to do, but she married the Beaver by mistake. One day, the Beaver said to her, "Go and take my trout, woman." So she went and found his canoe at the beach, but instead of trout she found willow branches. This upset the woman, and one night she left the house while he slept. She went on to marry the Panther, whom she was supposed to marry in the first place. When the Mink told the Beaver that she was in bed with the Panther, the Beaver cried and cried for five days. His tears caused a great flood that covered all the land and the houses. All the animals headed to their canoes. The flood reached almost to the sky, and was high for one year. The animals began trying to dive into the water in search of some earth, and proceeded one by one, beginning with the Blue Jay. Finally the Muskrat dove, and some flags came up. The water began to recede, summer came, and the canoes came to rest on the ground. As they jumped out of the canoe, the Bear struck his tail against the boat and lost it. That is why they have short, stubby tails to this day.[4]

"I will destroy the earth." … A third one released the waters in the north and the earth was deluged. The water rose to his sweat-house.

Kathlamet (Washington State):

Nom-hleyus-tawa was the creator. At Waiyel-nomil-tos, eight miles above the hatchery on McCloud River, or, as some say, at Waiyel-puiyel-tos, he created a tree. He was looking down from above and watching the tree, when beside it appeared a man the size of an ant. One by one others came out.

At Chuyikhlul (Stillwater Creek) after many years he saw, as he looked down from the sky, the arm of some person pounding acorns with the elbow. The person was inside a house. The hand would reach out to Mohmas (on Sacramento River opposite Redding) and bring back sand for leaching the meal. He continued to watch. After a while a woman came out and went down the trail to the river with a basket. When she stooped to get water, he saw a long tail stretching out behind her. She was abhorrent to him.

He said: "That does not suit me. I will destroy the earth." His uncle Takut begged him not to do so. Nevertheless he made a sling, took three large rocks, and threw them with his left hand, one to the east, one to the west, one to the north. A third one released the waters in the north and the earth was deluged. The water rose to his sweat-house.

3. Myron Eells, "Traditions of the Deluge among the Tribes of the North-west," p. 72.
4. Franz Boas, *Kathlamet Texts* (Washington: GPO, 1901), p. 20–25.

His uncle reproached him: "You would not listen to me. Now the water is running into our house." Then Nom-hleyus-tawa went out and lay across the north side of the house, and the water was divided into two streams by his body. At last the water ran off, and the earth remained, a bare, level rock.

Reflections of Mount Shasta on the Lake

His uncle said: "I told you not to destroy this country. You should not have done it." Nom-hleyus-tawa said nothing. He sat there rubbing his palms together, wondering what to do, while his uncle upbraided him. After a while a moist bit of cuticle was rolled up in his hand. He regarded it thoughtfully between his thumb and fingers. Then he stepped outside and dropped it downward. It became Bulit [Mount Shasta],, as its shape today shows the pinching between the creator's thumb and fingers. Without further effort on his part other hills began to spring forth. All the people had been drowned except the tailed woman Hakamin-takona, whom he had desired to destroy. She was now wading in the ocean, which came up only to her knees. Across the ocean she walked into the next land.

Again the creator planted a tree, and again, as he watched, the people appeared, one after another, just like ants. These were the ancestors of the present race.[5]

He went back to his first piece of land, and told the water to overflow the land he had created out of the five cakes of mud. Some time afterwards he ordered the water to recede, and looked again.

Chemetunne (Oregon):

The new land was soft, and looked like sand. Xowalaci stepped on it, and said, "I am going to see if the great land has come;" and as he stepped, the land grew hard.

Then Xowalaci looked at the sand, and saw a man's tracks. They seemed to have come from the north, disappearing in the water on the south. He wondered what that could mean, and was very much worried. He went back to his first piece of land, and told the water to overflow the land he had created out of the five cakes of mud. Some time afterwards he ordered the water to recede, and looked again. This time he saw the tracks coming from the west, and returning to the water on the north side. He was puzzled, and ordered the water to cover up his new land once more. Five times he repeated this process. At last he became discouraged, and said, "This is going to make trouble in the future!" and since then there has always been trouble in the world.[6]

5. Curtis, *North American Indian*, vol. 14, p. 173.
6. Livingston Farrand and Leo J. Frachtenberg, "Shasta and Athapascan Myths from Oregon," *Journal of American Folklore*, vol. 28 (Lancaster and New York: American Folklore Society, 1915), p. 224–225.

Chimariko (Northern California):

> Dog and Coyote were traveling eastwards. Dog said, "It is going to rain, it is going to blow. Hold tight to a live-oak tree." It blew, and Coyote was blown away. Dog stood there and called, "Come back, you shall be strong." Coyote did not wish to, for he was angry with Dog. The latter said, "Let us fight," but Coyote declined. After some discussion they agreed to travel about, and get married. A flood was coming on, in which they believed they would be drowned, so they tried to make a house, but it fell down. Water came, it rained and snowed, and all people were starved and lost. Frog was floating in a canoe, and Otter and Mink floated on the water. Frog found the rib of one of those who had been drowned. At sunset it became a baby, which was put in a basket. The girl baby grew up, and married Frog, and to them a child, a boy, was born, and by and by there were many people. There was an abundance of food then, and people went about eating and dancing, and living as they do now.[7]

A flood was coming on, in which they believed they would be drowned, so they tried to make a house, but it fell down. Water came, it rained and snowed, and all people were starved and lost.

Achomawi (Northern California):

The Achomawi told Roland Dixon, when he met them around the year 1900, the Flood was caused by a shaman named Hawk-man, who was angered that his two wives left his home and went to that of another man. Seeing that there was no way to stop the rising Flood, other than to interrupt the shaman's ritual of dancing and singing, one man from among the people went over and killed Hawk-man, and the Flood was ceased.[8]

There is also a "fire-fetching" episode reminiscent of some of the Flood traditions of Southeast Asia and the Pacific. "After Hawk had been killed, and the flood had subsided, people found that all fires were put out all over the world. Nothing could be cooked, but for a time people did not trouble about it. Then after a few days they began to talk about it, and sent Owl to Mount Shasta to look all over the world and see if he could find any trace of fire." Several animals in succession tried to go and retrieve fire from a sweat-house in the distance — Owl, Lizard, Coyote, and Dog. Finally the dog was able to retrieve fire. "So people got fire again."[9]

An Achomawi Man

Wukchumni (California):

> There was water everywhere. Everyone had been drowned except a few people in a high place. Eagle and Cougar both wanted to make the world, but Eagle had more power than Cougar. They picked out three little ducks. They tied strings to their legs and told them to dive down to the bottom. They tried to reach bottom but they were dead when they returned to the surface. Then Turtle had a string tied to his leg and down he went. When he came up he was nearly dead but he had a few grains of earth under his fingernails. Dove collected this earth and took it to Eagle.
>
> Eagle then talked a long time to the earth and it became this world. Blue Jay and Crested Jay and Coyote ran all around planting trees. Soon there were many people. Then Eagle sent Wolf far to the south. He

There was water everywhere. Everyone had been drowned except a few people in a high place.

7. Roland B. Dixon, "The Chimariko Indians and Language," *University of California Publications in American Archaeology and Ethnology*, vol. 5, no. 5 (Berkeley: 1910), p. 346.
8. Roland B. Dixon, "Achomawi and Atsugewi Tales," *Journal of American Folklore*, vol. 21, no. 82 (Boston: Houghton Mifflon, 1908), p. 164–165.
9. Ibid., p. 165.

was to stay there, and he was to howl when the world became old and sick. His howling would cure it. The animals now are all living far to the east at a place called Metyakao (big rock).[10]

Hopi (Northeast Arizona):

The Hopi emergence story tells of a great flood that destroyed everything in the third world, with the exception of a small group of good people who were saved by floating in hollow reeds:

> Sotuknang came to Spider Woman and said, "There is no use waiting until the thread runs out this time. Something has to be done lest the people with the song in their hearts are corrupted and killed off too. It will be difficult, with all this destruction going on, for them to gather at the far end of the world I have designated. But I will help them. Then you will save them when I destroy this world with water."
>
> "How shall I save them?" asked Spider Woman.

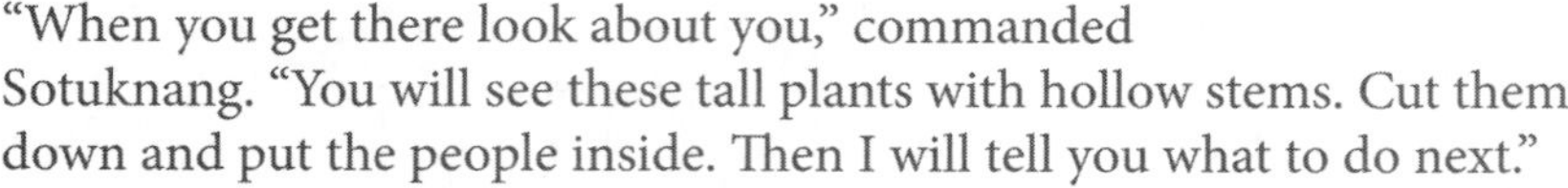

Four Hopi Women in Front of Pueblo Buildings

> "When you get there look about you," commanded Sotuknang. "You will see these tall plants with hollow stems. Cut them down and put the people inside. Then I will tell you what to do next."
>
> Spider Woman did as he instructed her. She cut down the hollow reeds; and as the people came to her, she put them inside with a little water and hurusuki (white cornmeal dough) for food, and sealed them up. When all the people were thus taken care of, Sotuknang appeared.
>
> "Now you get in to take care of them, and I will seal you up," he said. "Then I will destroy the world." So he loosed the waters upon the earth. Waves higher than mountains rolled in upon the land. Continents broke asunder and sank beneath the seas. And still the rains fell, the waves rolled in. The people sealed up in their hollow reeds heard the mighty rushing of the waters. They felt themselves tossed high in the air and dropping back to the water. Then all was quiet, and they knew they were floating. For a long, long time — so long a time that it seemed it would never end — they kept floating. Finally their movement ceased. The Spider Woman unsealed their hollow reeds, took them by the tops of their heads, and pulled them out.[11]

"…and I will seal you up," he said. "Then I will destroy the world." So he loosed the waters upon the earth. Waves higher than mountains rolled in upon the land. Continents broke asunder and sank beneath the seas. And still the rains fell, … sealed up in their hollow reeds heard the mighty rushing of the waters

The story went on to discuss how they sent many kinds of birds out to look for land, but with no success. They paddled in their reeds, which they used as canoes, until they came to the fourth world.

Another Hopi tradition of the Flood was told by the chief of the Water clan in Walpi, a village east of the Grand Canyon. Victor Mindeleff presented this in the *8th Annual Report of the Bureau of Ethnology*:

> In the long ago the Snake, Horn, and Eagle people lived here (in Walpi), but their corn grew only a span high, and when they sang for rain the cloud god sent only a thin mist. My people then lived in the distant Pa-lat

10. Anna H. Gayton and Stanley S. Newman, "Yokuts and Western Mono Myths," *University of California Anthropological Records*, vol. 5 (Berkeley: University of California Press, 1940), p. 20.
11. Frank Waters, *Book of the Hopi* (New York: Penguin Books, 1963), p. 18.

Kwa-bi in the South. There was a very bad old man there, who, when he met anyone, would spit in his face, blow his nose upon him, and rub ordure upon him. He ravished the girls and did all manner of evil. Baholikonga got angry at this and turned the world upon its side, and water spouted up through the kivas and through the fireplaces in the houses. The earth was rent in great chasms, and water covered everything except one narrow ridge of mud; and across this the serpent deity told all the people to travel. As they journeyed across, the feet of the bad slipped and they fell into the dark water, but the good, after many days, reached dry land. While the water was rising around the village the old people got on the tops of the houses, for they thought they could not struggle across with the younger people; but Baholikonga clothed them with the skins of turkeys, and they spread their wings out and floated in the air just above the surface of the water, and in this way they got across. They were saved of our people Water, Corn, Lizard, Horned Toad, Sand, two families of Rabbit, and Tobacco. Wearing these turkey-skins is the reason why old people have dewlaps under the chin like a turkey; it is also the reason why old people use turkey-feathers at the religious ceremonies.[12]

Hopi Village of Walpi, Arizona

The earth was rent in great chasms, and water covered everything except one narrow ridge of mud…

Washoe (Lake Tahoe Area):

Long before these mountains were lifted up so very high as they now are, the Digger Indian possessed the whole earth, and was a great people. . . . But the time arrived when a new people, unlike our fathers, only in being more warlike and powerful, though speaking a different language, came down from the north and began a terrible war, destroying our homes, our wives and our children. Though unaccustomed to war, our fathers made a long and determined resistance; but after years of troublesome warfare, they were at length all driven away, or made the slaves of their conquerors, for life. . . . But at length the Great Spirit put a stop to this by destroying alike our people and their oppressors. A great wave like a mountain came up from the sea, and swept away all of them, and they were seen no more — all but a few Digger slaves and their masters. They were the great spirits or teachers of their people; and as there were no mountains then, they had to assemble on the top of a great temple that our people had been compelled to rear, and where they worshipped the column of perpetual fire; and thus was a remnant of our fathers and mothers saved, together with a few of their task-masters.[13]

A Washoe Woman

12. Victor Mindeleff, "A Study of Pueblo Architecture, Tusayan and Cibola," *Eighth Annual Report of the Bureau of American Ethnology* (Washington: GPO, 1891), p. 31.
13. Ed. James Hutchings, "The Spirit's Lodge," Hutchings' *Illustrated California Magazine*, vol. 2 (San Francisco: Hutchings & Rosenfield, 1858), p. 357.

Navajo:

The Navajo had an emergence story, a story that told that the earliest population passed through a series of worlds, coming up from underground to finally reach the fifth and current world. A great flood occurred in the first and fourth worlds. The first world, in which the people flew like insects, was destroyed by a flood because of their evil deeds:

Navajo Woman with Baby

> They committed adultery, one people with another. Many of the women were guilty. They tried to stop it, but they could not. . . . When again they sinned and again they quarreled, Tieholtsodi in the east, would not speak to them; Blue Heron, in the south, would not speak to them; Frog, in the west, would say nothing; and White Mountain Thunder, in the north, would not speak to them. . . . At dawn Tieholdsodi began to talk. "You pay no attention to my words. Everywhere you disobey me; you must go to some other place. Not upon this earth shall you remain." Thus he spoke to them. . . . At the end of the fourth night, in the morning, as they were rising, something white appeared in the east. It appeared also in the south, the west, and the north. It looked like a chain of mountains, without a break, stretching around them. It was water that surrounded them. Water impassable, water insurmountable, flowed all around. All at once they started. They went in circles upward till they reached the sky. It was smooth. They looked down; but there the water had risen, and there was nothing else but water there. While they were flying around, one having a blue head thrust out his head from the sky and called to them, saying, "In here, to the eastward, there is a hole." They entered the hole and went through it up to the surface (of the second world)."[14]

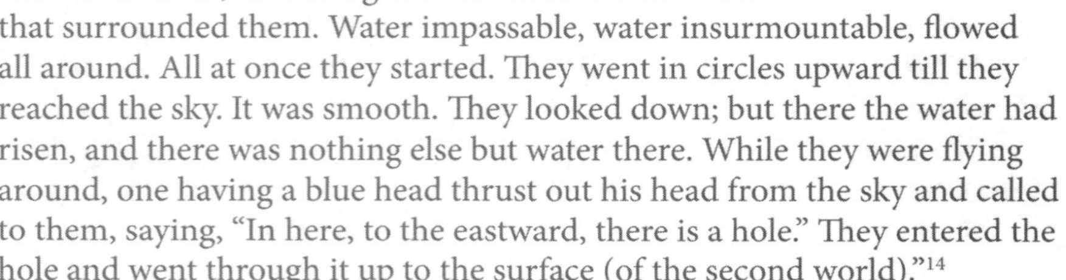

In the fourth world, a similar flood occurred. The people survived by entering a giant reed, similar to the ark (and reminiscent of many other Native American legends):

It looked like a chain of mountains, without a break, stretching around them. It was water that surrounded them. Water impassable, water insurmountable, flowed all around.

> On the morning of the fourth day, when the white light rose, the people observed in the east a strange white gleam along the horizon, and they sent out the Locust couriers to see what caused this unusual appearance. The Locusts returned before sunset, and told the people that a vast flood of waters was fast approaching from the east. On hearing this the people all assembled together, the Kisani with the others, in a great multitude, and they wailed and wept over the approaching catastrophe. They wept and moaned all night and could not sleep.
>
> When the white light arose in the east, next morning, the waters were seen high as mountains encircling the whole horizon, except in the west, and rolling on rapidly. The people packed up all their goods as fast as they could, and ran up on a high hill nearby, for temporary safety. . . . One of the approaching men was old and gray-haired; the other, who was young, walked in advance. They ascended the hill and passed through the crowd, speaking to no one. . . . The elder took out seven bags from under his robe and opened them. Each contained a small quantity of earth. he told the people that in these bags he had earth from the seven sacred mountains.

14. Washington Matthews, *Navaho Legends* (Boston and New York: American Folklore Society, 1897), p. 64–65.

There were in the fourth world seven sacred mountains, named and placed like the sacred mountains of the present Navajo land. "Ah! Perhaps our father can do something for us," said the people. "I cannot, but my son may be able to help you," said the old man. Then they bade the son to help them, and he said he would if they all moved away from where he stood, faced to the west, and looked not around until he called them; for no one should see him at his work. They did as he desired, and in a few moments he called them to come to him. When they came, they saw that he had spread the sacred earth on the ground and planted in it thirty-two reeds, each of which had thirty-two joints. As they gazed they beheld the roots of the reeds striking out into the soil and growing rapidly downward. A moment later all the reeds joined together and became one reed of great size, with a hole in its eastern side. He bade them enter the hollow of the reed through this hole. When they were all safely inside, the opening closed, and none too soon, for scarcely had it closed when they heard the loud noise of the surging waters outside.[15]

When they were all safely inside, the opening closed, and none too soon, for scarcely had it closed when they heard the loud noise of the surging waters outside.

The giant floating reed continued rising dangerously higher, and the people sought safety. They sent out the Locust, who found the opening to the next world, but had to pass the test that the Grebes, or people of that world, imposed. The Locust passed the test, the people reached the hole but found it too small to pass through. They sent the Badger to dig and widen the hole. Then First Man and First Woman led the way and all the others followed them, and they climbed up through the hole to the surface of this — the fifth — world.[16]

Once again, it is interesting to note that the survivors sent out animals to determine whether or not the world was ready, a detail that has been almost universal.

Monument Valley, Arizona

15. Ibid., p. 74–76.
16. Ibid., p. 76.

Owens Valley Paiute (Nevada and California):

> Drake and Duck lived together. Something kept killing Drake, but every time he was killed, Duck found herself a new mate. Drake was killed by Hawk. After Drake had been killed many times, Duck became angry. She went off to the ocean, swallowed it, and brought it back in a little bag. She hung the bag on a limb. Coyote ran around one day under the limb from which the bag hung. Every time he passed under it, he said, "Something feels cold. I wonder what this thing is that feels cold?" Then he found the bag hanging on the limb. He seized it and threw it down. "This is what makes it cold every time I pass under here."
>
> The bag began to drip and drip and the water ran out. In a little while there was a pond there. It became deeper and deeper, and after a while it almost covered Coyote. He said, "I can swim, too. I am just as good a swimmer as anybody." When the water was up to his neck he began to swim. But soon he was exhausted and drowned. There were some Indians living near this place. When the flood rose, they went up to Mount Tom and other high places to live. The marks of fires which they built on these summits could be seen a few years ago by hunters who went up there.
>
> When the flood died down, those who had wings flew straight up and looked down at the earth from the sky. Crane' looked down, and said to Eagle,' "You see that thing there near the edge of the lake?" Eagle said, "No, I don't see anything." Crane said, "Well, it is a fish." Crane dropped down from the sky, got the fish from the pond, and brought it back. He showed it to Eagle. Then Eagle, in order to make things even, said, "You see that thing down there by the bush?" Crane said, "No, I don't see anything." Then Eagle flew straight down, brought back a rabbit, and showed it to Crane. One could see the fish and the other could see the animal. That is the way the birds are.[17]

Once the whole world was flooded. Wolf, who was the strongest and greatest man in the world, was alone in a boat in which he paddled around for a long time.

They also have this tradition of the creation of the earth:

> Once the whole world was flooded. Wolf, who was the strongest and greatest man in the world, was alone in a boat in which he paddled around for a long time. He was lonely and wanted somebody with him. He made Coyote and called him brother. Wolf said, "We can't paddle around all the time. We must have some earth." He took a handful of earth and placed it on the water. It stayed there. At first it was very shaky, but later it became solid. Then he added more and more earth until he had a little round place. They got out on the earth.[18]

The following is from a creation story told by one Jack Stewart of Big Pine.

> The world was once nothing but water. The only land above the water was Black mountain. All the people lived up there when the flood came, and their fireplaces can still be seen. . . .[19]

The Sierra Nevada Mountains Seen from the Owens River Valley

17. Julian H. Steward, "Myths of the Owens Valley Paiute," *University of California Publications in American Archaeology and Ethnology*, vol. 34, no. 5 (Berkeley: University of California Press, 1936), p. 372.
18. Ibid., p. 363.
19. Ibid.

Acoma Pueblo (New Mexico):

Acoma Pueblo, New Mexico by Ansel Adams

After the Twins stole these staves they said to the katsina, "Go on sleeping. We have everything with which you work and we can use them as well as you. We will do so. We are going to take them and plant them in the ground and we challenge you to dig them up. If you can do that, we will believe in you." This was also a mistake on the part of the Twins. They had made the katsina angry. . . .

The Twins did not get far from where they had buried the staves before a large cloud appeared that was followed by a cloudburst. Lightning tried to strike them, but they shielded themselves with the buckskin shirts their father had given them. . . . They traveled back toward the village and all the way it was raining. When they reached the village they found the lake had overflowed and driven out the people. Many people had been struck by lightning and killed. When they returned, they stretched their buckskins so as to shield all the people, so no more were struck. So the spirits who rule in the four directions said, "We give up. I guess we cannot kill them." But they let the snake follow their instructions.

It continued to rain. The people were completely driven from their homes and were able to take with them only the altars and the things they needed most. The people moved on south to a high mountain. All the chaianyi worked [magic], and Country Chief and Antelope Man prayed for it to stop raining. But no one listened to them. There were many animals driven to this mountain and many different peoples. Some spoke different languages, others spoke similarly. All were shielded under the buckskin. The world began to fill with water and the dashing waves almost swept them from the mountain. So the Twins, seeing the large waves, said, "That must be Water Snake. He is coming to kill us." They had never used the four arrows their father had given them and they said, "Perhaps this is where we are to use these arrows." So they watched carefully until they saw the biggest wave coming up. They said, "This is where his heart is." Each shot an arrow into it. After they had done this the waves came slower and became a huge snake which wrapped itself around the mountain where the Twins killed it, using up the rest of the arrows, each shooting four times. So everything became calm and there was no more rain. The water started to recede, but very slowly. It is said that formerly the mountains were beautifully smooth and rounded. But this flood and the receding waters cut canyons and gullies and made it rough.

When things began to get dry, they separated again, not being able to understand each other.

It is not known how long they camped on this mountain, but they always had food, and the animals that were saved were increasing. When things began to get dry, they separated again, not being able to understand each other.[20]

20. Matthew W. Stirling, "Origin Myth of Acoma and Other Records," *Bureau of American Ethnology Bulletin*, vol. 135 (Washington: GPO, 1942), p. 77–78.

Tubatulabal (Southern California):

Kern River in Southern California

> It is raining all the time. Then the water filled this earth. Then everyone, they ran away toward the mountain. "We get slaughtered," says Coyote. Then they went and arrived on top of the mountain. Coyote is ready to die; his food (is) nothing. Coyote then said, "Let someone dive there; he will make earth appear; who will make earth appear there?" Then from there they dived, but Mud-Diver is sitting to one side. Then they have brought up nothing. "So we get slaughtered," says Coyote. "You (are) next," (Coyote) says to Mud-Diver. Then Mud-Diver dived and, after a while, Mud-Diver came out from there to here. Mud-Diver is coming and holding very little (earth). Then everyone saw it. Then Coyote says, "Again, once again." Coyote is in a hurry. Then Mud-Diver dived again. Mud-Diver had been gone a long time. Coyote is circling about. Already, in the evening, Mud-Diver came out from there to here. Coyote came and ran first. Mud-Diver is coming holding earth in his own hand. Then Coyote says, "There it is, there it is, there it is." Then from there Mud-Diver put the earth in the middle of the water. Mud-Diver made the earth appear. There it is ended.[21]

It is raining all the time. Then the water filled this earth. Then everyone, they ran away toward the mountain. "We get slaughtered," . . . .

Yellowstone Valley Tradition (Wyoming):

Hap Gilliland (1918–2017) was a professor at Montana State University and an adventurer who collected flood legends on six continents. One very rainy day, sometime prior to 1950, an old man told him the tradition which follows. Gilliland was not able to find out what tribe this man was from, though Crow, Cheyenne, and Shoshone were likely candidates:

> For many winters the people lived at peace with the animals and with the land. When they killed a buffalo, they thanked the Great Spirit, and they used every part of the buffalo. It took care of every need. Then other people came. They did not think of the animals as brothers. They killed, even when they did not need food. They burned and cut the forests, and the animals died. They shot the buffalo and called it sport. They killed the fish in the streams. When the Great Spirit looked down, he was sad. He let the smoke of the fires lie in the valleys. The people coughed and choked. But still they burned and they killed.
>
> So the Great Spirit sent rains to put out the fires and to destroy the people. The rains fell, and the waters rose. The people moved from the flooded valleys to the higher land. . . . Still the rains fell, and the waters rose. The people moved from the flooded plans to the hills. . . . Still the rains fell, and the waters rose. The people moved from the flooded hills to the mountains. Still the rains fell. Like all rawhide, the buffalo skin stretched when it was wet. Spotted Bear stretched it out over the village. All the people who were left crowded under it. All the rains fell, the medicine

So the Great Spirit sent rains to put out the fires and to destroy the people. The rains fell, and the waters rose. The people moved from the flooded valleys to the higher land.... Still the rains fell, and the waters rose.

21. Charles F. Voegelin, "Tubatulabal Texts," *University of California Publications in American Archeology and Ethnology*, vol. 34, no. 3 (Berkeley: University of California Press, 1935), p. 210–211.

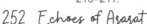

men stretched the buffalo skin across the mountains. Each day they stretched it father. Then Spotted Bear tied one corner to the top of the Big Horn Mountains. That side, he fastened to the Pryors. The next corner he tied to the Bear Tooth Mountains. Crossing the Yellowstone Valley, he tied one corner to the Crazy Mountains, and the other to Signal Butte in the Bull mountains.

The rain had stopped and a rainbow arched across the Yellowstone Valley.

The whole Yellowstone Valley was covered by the white buffalo skin. Though the rains still fell above, it did not fall in the Yellowstone Valley. The waters sank away. Animals from the outside moved into the valley, under the white buffalo skin. The people shared the valley with them. . . . The Great Spirit saw that the people were living at peace with the earth. The rains stopped, and the sun shone. As the sun shone on the white buffalo skin, it gleamed with colors of red and yellow and blue. As the sun shone on the rawhide, it began to shrink. The ends of the dome shrank away until all that was left was one great arch across the valley. The old man's voice faded away; but his hands said "Look," and his arms moved toward the valley. The rain had stopped and a rainbow arched across the Yellowstone Valley. A buffalo calf and its mother grazed beneath it.[22]

Bannock (Idaho):

An old Bannock man named Sunni White Bear Navo told his tribe's creation story to a Professor Sven Liljeblad in 1941. To their Flood memory they add the idea that there was a fire before the Flood:

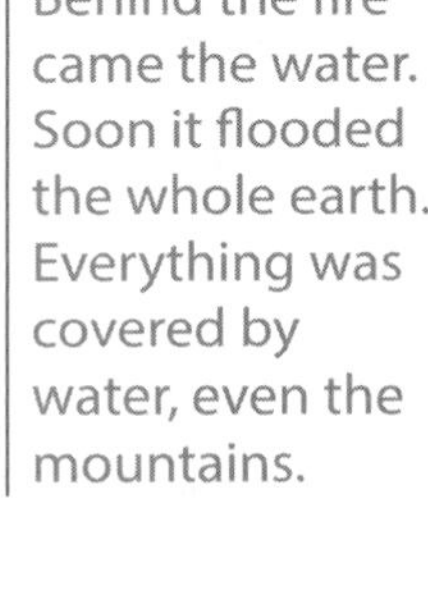

Behind the fire came the water. Soon it flooded the whole earth. Everything was covered by water, even the mountains.

Behind the fire came the water. Soon it flooded the whole earth. Everything was covered by water, even the mountains. The Father and his son made themselves very small, so that they could ride on the foam on top of the water. There they remained for a long time, on the water-foam.

Thinking about the earth where he had lived, the Father knew he would like to have it back again. He used to wonder, "How can I get the earth back again?" For many years water stayed like that. At last the Father knew that it would not go down or dry up. He stayed there on the water-foam another winter. During the time they lived on the water, the Father made his son part of himself. Now they could get the earth back again.

"How can I get help?" he wondered.

He thought of the water-people. "I could ask them to help me get earth," he said to himself. "They must be somewhere around here."

Then he called out, "Water-people, where are you? Come. Let us smoke and hold council."

. . . Then they said to Muskrat, "You dive to the bottom of the water and bring up earth." . . . Under Muskrat's fingernails, they found bits of mud. The Father took these bits of mud and formed them into a little ball.[23]

Bannock People in Idaho

22. Hap Gilliland, *The Great Flood*, p. 42–45.
23. Ella Clark, *Indian Legends of the Northern Rockies*, p. 172–174.

Hidatsa (North Dakota):

Formerly there existed water only, and no earth. A large bird, with a red eye, dived. The man who does not die, or the lord of life (Ehsicka-Wahaddish, literally the first man), who lives in the Rocky Mountains, had made all, and sent the great bird to fetch up earth. Another being, worthy of veneration, is the old woman whom they call grandmother, and who roams about all over the earth. She, too, has some share in the creation, though an inferior one, for she created the sand-rat and the toad. She gave the Manitaries [Hidatsa] a couple of pots, which they still preserve as a sacred treasure, and employ as medicines, or charms, on certain occasions. She directed the ancestors of these Indians to preserve the pots, and to remember the great waters, from which all animals came cheerful, or, as my old narrator expressed it, dancing. The red-shouldered oriole came, at that time, out of the water, as well as all the other birds which still sing on the banks of the rivers. The Manitaries [Hidatsa], therefore, look on all these birds as medicine for their plantations of maize, and attend to their song. At the time when these birds sing, they were directed by the old woman to fill these pots with water, to be merry, to dance and bathe, in order to put them in mind of the great flood. When their fields are threatened with a great drought they are to celebrate a medicine feast with the old grandmother's pots, in order to beg for rain: this is, properly, the destination of the pots. The medicine men are still paid, on such occasions, to sing for four days together in the huts, while the pots remain filled with water.[24]

. . . they were directed by the old woman to fill these pots with water, to be merry, to dance and bathe, in order to put them in mind of the great flood.

. . . he threw himself with greater force upon the waters and they began to ebb. A third time the mighty elk threw himself to the earth and again the waters were lowered.

Osage (Missouri):

After the people acquired souls in the first upper world, the Hun-ka began to talk with each other. They talked about going below to the earth. . . . Realizing that none of them knew the way, they asked Hun-ka-Ah-tut-un to search out a way. He led the people downward through the four heavens. Four times he soared in wide circles and then without pause he dived downward through the standing clouds. He came in sight of the tops of seven trees, where he waited. The people alit in the tops of the trees and firmly gripped the branches with their feet. All the earth below the branches was covered with water. The people became desperate and they begged Hun-ka-Wa-tse-ka-wa to help them. He went to seek help from spider-like, water spider; black bean-like, water beetle and whitleather-like, white leech; who offered to seek help, but furnished no solution. At last, Radiant Star came to Opon-Tun-ka, the Big Elk. To help the Little Ones, he threw himself violently on the earth. Huge waves radiated away from the impact. Again he threw himself with greater force upon the waters and they began to ebb. A third time the mighty elk threw himself to the earth and again the waters were lowered. For the fourth time the noble elk threw himself down and the soil of the earth appeared, to become dry and habitable. Big Elk then called for the four winds, the breath of Wa-kon-ta, to come dry the land. . . .[25]

Osage Chief Black Dog

24. Prince Alexander Philipp Maximillian Wied, trans. H. Evans Lloyd, *Travels in the Interior of North America* (London: Ackermann and Co., 1843), p. 398.
25. Louis F. Burns, *Osage Indian Customs and Myths* (Tuscaloosa: University of Alabama Press, 1984), p. 179–180.

Menominee (Wisconsin):

> Hiawatha, or Manabo, having incurred the enmity of the Prince of Serpents, a very Typhon in character, who held sway in the basin of Lake Superior, the spirit permitted the ice to break in during the winter season, while Chibiabos, his grandson was crossing from one point to another. The following summer, the demi-god watched along the shore to find the sandy bay, where the serpents came out to bask; and having consulted with a kingfisher as to the precise spot, he took his station on shore, and transformed himself into the semblance of a high stump of a tree, broken off by the wind. As soon as the Prince of the Serpents and his court appeared, and had sunk into repose on the sand, he drew his bow, and shot an arrow into his enemy's heart. The serpents fled, screaming, into the depths of the sea; but, in revenge for this act, caused the waters to rise, which overflowed the forests, and pressed on, after the fleeing demi-god, until all the land was submerged. The benevolent god, who assumes in these latitudes the name of Manabo, ascended a high mountain, and climbed to the top of a tree; but the waters rose to his feet. He then commanded the tree to stretch upward, and it obeyed him. But the waters still rising to his feet, he again bade the tree to grow taller, which it did, and finally it became stationary. The waters having risen to his neck, the amphibious animals and water-fowl were playing around him; for they were his brothers. He first directed the loon to dive down for some earth; but when it rose to the surface it was dead. He then told the beaver, the otter, and the mink to attempt the same feat; but none of them found the bottom. At last he sent the muskrat; "for your ancestors," he said, "were always famous for grasping the muddy bottoms of pools with their claws." The animal succeeded in bringing up a morsel of earth in its talons; and from this new chaotic mass the Algic deity recreated the earth.[26]

Amiskquew, a Menominee Warrior

As soon as the Prince of the Serpents and his court appeared... he drew his bow, and shot an arrow ... The serpents in revenge caused the waters to rise...

Missouri Tradition:

In 1824, a medicine man of a tribe local to Perryville, Missouri narrated a tradition concerning the origin of his people. His tribal identify was not recorded, but he was most likely either Illini, Quapaw, or Osage. The Catholic missionaries of the Lazarist Order summarized what he told:

> In general it is hard to get from Indians precise details even of the little which they profess to know. They are afraid of being laughed at. Like other Indians, they generally believe in God and in subordinate gods, good and bad, vague parodies, perhaps, of our good and bad angels; in future rewards and punishments, in which the Catholic view of a threefold state are distinguishable. Their old tradition is that they came from the cold North; that the first remembrance their fathers had was of their floundering on the surface of a vast lake; that a god in white approached them from the south; one in red from the north; one in motley colors from the west. The god in white was the superior.

A bird was sent to discover land, but without result. Different animals then followed. One returned with its feet besmeared with mud.

26. Henry Rowe Schoolcraft, *History of the Indian Tribes of the United States*, Part VI (Philadelphia: J.B. Lippincott & Co., 1857), p. 571–572. A similar text can be found in: Alanson Skinner and John V. Satterlee, "Folklore of the Menomini Indians," *Anthropological Papers of the American Museum of Natural History*, vol. 13, part 3 (New York: American Museum of Natural History, 1915), p. 255–258.

A bird was sent to discover land, but without result. Different animals then followed. One returned with its feet besmeared with mud. The god in white led them towards the point whence the animal had returned. Land was found. They knelt to thank and adore the god in white. "No, children," he said; "I am sent by the Great Spirit; Him you must adore." He then predicted their victories over all the nations they should encounter, till they reached the sunny South, and that, in the lapse of ages, they would see white men, children of the god in white, whom they should never injure for the sake of their guide.

Strange gestures and wild episodes accompanied the account, of which the above is an abridgment. From their tradition it seems that besides some vague recollections of the earlier revelation, they retained some remembrances of the deluge, and of Noah's trials to know whether it had ceased.[27]

...they retained some remembrances of the deluge, and of Noah's trials to know whether it had ceased.

Caddo (Texas to Arkansas):

An additional Flood tradition from the Caddo was collected by Richard Erdoes and Alfonso Ortiz. This told of a woman who once gave birth to four monsters. She was warned to kill them, but she refused, saying they would turn out alright. However, they did not turn out alright, but became giant, sinister monsters. They kept growing. Eventually they put their backs together — one facing north, one south, one east, and one west — and they grew into one terrible monster, whose heads surpassed the clouds and reached the sky.

Then the man who could see into the future heard a voice telling him to set up a hollow reed and plant it in the ground. The man did, and the reed grew bigger and bigger very fast. In no time it rose to touch the sky. The man heard the voice again, saying: "I will make a great flood. When the signs of bad things coming appear, you and your wife climb up inside this hollow cane. Be naked as you were born, and take with you a pair of all the good animals in order to save them." The man asked: "What sign will you be sending?" "When all the birds in the world — birds of the woods, the sea, the deserts, and the high mountains — form up into a cloud flying from north to south, that will be the sign. Watch for the cloud of birds."

The man heard the voice again, saying: "I will make a great flood. When the signs of bad things coming appear, you and your wife climb up inside this hollow cane. Be naked as you were born, and take with you a pair of all the good animals in order to save them."

One day the man looked up and saw a big cloud made up of birds traveling from north to south. At once he and his wife moved up into the hollow reed, taking with them all the animals they wished to save. Then it began to rain and did not stop. Waters covered the earth and kept rising until only the top of the hollow

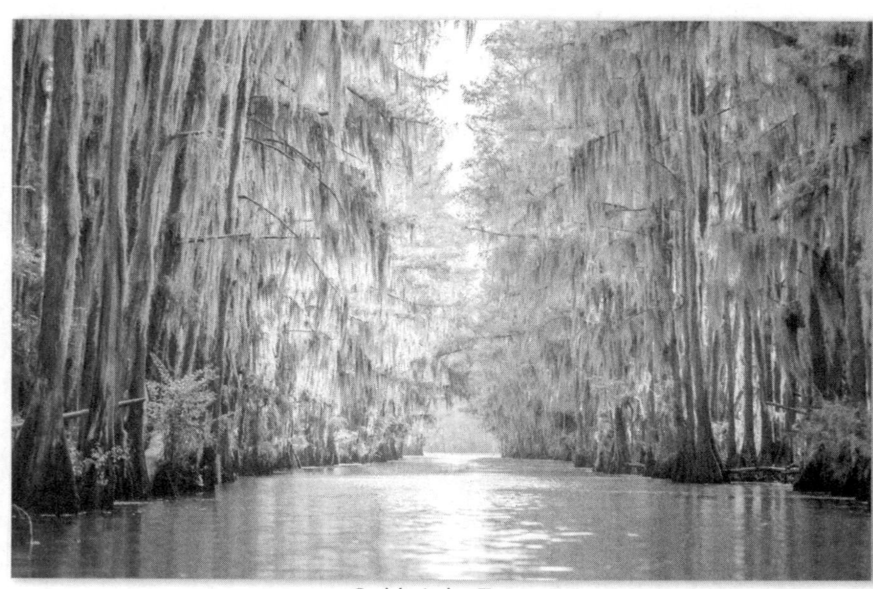

Caddo Lake, Texas

27. J.M. Lucey, "Missionary Labors of Lazarist Priests in Arkansas from 1818 to 1844," *Donahoe Magazine*, vol. 27 (Boston: Pilot, 1892), p. 152.

cane and the heads of the monsters were left above the surface. Inside the hollow reed, the man and his wife heard the voice again: "Now I shall send Turtle to destroy the monsters."

The monsters' heads were saying to each other: "Brothers, I'm getting tired. My legs are weakening. I can't keep standing much longer." The floods swirled around them with strong currents that almost swept them away. Then the Great Turtle began digging down underneath the monsters' feet. It uprooted them, and they could not keep their footing but broke apart and toppled over. They fell down into the waters, one sinking toward the north, one toward the east, one toward the south, and one toward the west. Thus the four directions came into being.

After the monsters had drowned, the waters subsided. First the mountaintops reappeared, then the rest of the land. Next came hard-blowing winds that dried up the earth. The man climbed down to the bottom of the hollow reed and opened the hole at its foot. He looked. He stuck out his hand and felt around. He said to his wife: "Come out. Everything is dry." So they emerged, followed by all the animals.[28]

Next came hard-blowing winds that dried up the earth. The man climbed down to the bottom of the hollow reed and opened the hole at its foot. He looked. He stuck out his hand and felt around. He said to his wife: "Come out. Everything is dry." So they emerged, followed by all the animals.

The voice then told the woman to plant corn, saying that by it they would be able to live and form a new generation.

Alabama Tribe:

Once, long ago, before the time of the oldest people, water covered everything. The only living creatures above the water were some small animals and birds who occupied a log raft drifting about on the great ocean. Nothing else could be seen above the surface of the water. Each day the occupants on the large raft looked in all directions, but all they saw was water and the sky. The birds would fly out from the raft hoping to find land, but always there was just water. Soon the occupants of the raft grew restless and began talking about how to find land. They chose Horned Owl to be their council chief. During their discussion one day, Horned Owl said, "Land is somewhere beneath the water. We must make it appear or we will starve. Who will look for land?" . . . Now, Crawfish has a wide tail which he can use as a scoop. When he reached the bottom of the water, he used his tail to scoop mud into a great chimney. He worked rapidly, building it higher and higher, until the top of the mud chimney stuck up above the water, where it began to spread and form a mass of soft earth. The birds and animals on the raft looked at the new earth and agreed that Crawfish had done a good job, but they thought the earth was too smooth. So Horned Owl sent Buzzard out to shape the earth's surface. . . . When he swung his wings down, he made valleys and mountains. During the time that Buzzard glided along without flapping his wings, he made level country and plains.

Each day the occupants on the large raft looked in all directions, but all they saw was water and the sky. The birds would fly out from the raft hoping to find land, but always there was just water.

After the earth had hardened, the animals and birds left their raft and make homes in the new land, each according to his needs.[29]

28. Richard Erdoes and Alfonso Ortiz, *American Indian Myths and Legends*, (New York: Pantheon Books, 1984), Google Play version, p. 134–135.
29. Howard N. Martin, *Folk-tales of the Alabama-Coushatta Indians* (Jacksonville, TX: McFarland Publishing, 1945), p. 2–3.

EXPANDED TEXTS: CENTRAL AND SOUTH AMERICA

Yaqui (Northwest Mexico):

Yaqui People

The following tradition, collected by Ruth Giddings in 1942 from an older Yaqui man, shows evidence of a degree of Spanish influence. It is impossible to tell the extent of that influence, and what the original version was. Nevertheless, their Flood story has a core of content which is surely native:

> Yaitowi, in his time, walked with Dios when came to pass the days when waters rose over the earth to destroy all living things, alike beneath the sky, on the earth, and living in the water — even the birds who fly over the earth in the open expanse of the sky. It so happened that on the seventh day of February the flood waters covered the earth. In this time of Yaitowi, in the year 614, the day of the 17th of that same month of February, it rained all over the world. This continued for fourteen days and fourteen nights. Since the blessed end, everything that had been alive, and all life substance was thus finished. The waters increased hugely over all the earth, destroying all living things, after the days of men and women were terminated. And on the seventeenth of the month of July the waters were receding until the first of October, when the tops of the hills showed. And the first day of November, the water retired from the world's surface. Yaitowi and thirteen others as well as eleven women were saved on the hill of Parbus, which today is called Maatale. And on the hill of Jonas, eleven souls and one woman called Emac Dolores were saved.[30]

Kiliwa (Baja California):

> The flood took place in San Felipe Desert, south of Amu Wey. There was a shaman called Kemey Juwilu. He killed a jack rabbit. He took the lomitas and put them to one side. They grew larger and became people. They were his sons. Then there was a fire-circle hunt for rabbits, and the boys went out to join it. The boys went ahead and the old man stayed behind. The people had ordered the badger, mejwapikuyak, to make a hole in the ground. They covered the hole with branches. The people began closing in the circle, and ordered the two boys to sit on the branches over the hole. The boys fell into the hole and were killed, and the people filled up the hole with earth. Menuikunama had killed them: the people in the hunt were his people. They killed the boys because the old man used to come and kill one rabbit, not more; then he made the boys, and the boys killed very many rabbits. This made the people angry, and they made the trap to kill the boys.
>
> The boys' father came up and was looking for them everywhere but could not find them. He had killed a rabbit. And when he was looking about, a

30. Ruth Warner Giddings, *Yaqui Myths and Legends* (London: Forgotten Books, 2008), p. 101–102. Originally published 1959.

bird told him who had killed his sons. Then he opened the rabbit and took out parts of the rabbit and threw them in the four directions. Then summer clouds formed above the upper part of Jankil Arroyo, beyond Kay Sipukwin, and it rained, and all the people of Maikwiak were killed. The people were killed by the sheer violence of the storm, the wet, and the cold.

Sea of Cortez near San Felipe, Baja California

The shaman and his people stayed in a cave in Jankil Canyon. The name of the cave was Metailunaipai, "world-cave-people." Thus they escaped the rain. The animals all went into the cave. They had names: cogau, jamsiluk, cutol, chimkal (a bird), seman (a bird). Satemu, a little blue bird . . . was left behind when the others went into the cave. He was killed, and became a bird afterward. (All the animals in the cave were people.) . . .

> The shaman and his people stayed in a cave in Jankil Canyon. … Thus they escaped the rain. The animals all went into the cave.

After the flood, the people all went back to the places where they lived. . . . After the flood, Metailkwaipaiv went to Jankil and married two sisters there, the other side of Ja-il. . . .

According to Emiliano, when the flood occurred all the people went north, perhaps to California, and stayed there in the cave until the flood was over. When they came back, the first place at which they stopped was Japok. One man stayed there and the others went to other places.[31]

Bribri (Costa Rica):

A long time ago lived in Bribri a tribe called Tuléski . . . They had very strange customs . . . If someone visited them and they fed them, they had to eat everything . . . If they asked for a plant, they had to take it all. . . . Once, a Usékol [tribe] boy went to fetch firewood, cut a dry tree, took home only what he needed, and left the rest. . . . The Tuléski looked for him and beat him, leaving him half dead. The Usékol decided to take revenge.

When the Usékol had their revenge plan ready, he ordered the good people to leave immediately. "It will rain all night and everyone will drown." It was midnight, the Usékol made it thunder and rain heavily. The rivers overflowed, all the Tuléski perished. . . . In the morning, there was not even one alive. That was how that evil tribe perished.[32]

Traditional House of the Bribri

31. Peveril Meigs, III, *The Kiliwa Indians of Lower California* (Berkeley: University of California Press, 1939), p. 67–68.
32. Elena F. Raid, "La Leyenda de los Tuleski," *Tradicion Oral Indígena Costarricense*, eds. Maria Eugenia Bozzoli, Carmen Cubero V., and Adolfo Constenla Umaña (Universidad de Costa Rica: Vicerrectoria de Acción Departamento de Antropología), vol. 3, no. 3. As quoted in *Enrique Margery, El Mito del Diluvio en la Tradición Oral Indoamericana* (Abya-Yala: Quito, 1997), p. 66, 193.

Dorasque (Costa Rica and Panama):

The Lost Waterfalls Trail, Boquete, Panamá

The following is a summary of the tradition told to Beatriz Cabal, due to length:

> A very long time ago there was an Indian village situated on a certain river. And at a point along the river was a very strange pond. This pond was very large and deep, and people avoided going there because strange and horrifying creatures came out of it. But the people noticed that a young woman of the village frequently went to this pond to bathe. Her father followed her one day from afar, and saw her seated in the pond with the head of a hideous monster on her knees. He did not think that he had been seen, and he told the villagers. But afterward his daughter told him that she saw him, and furthermore she was pregnant, and that they needed to build a dark tent of seven layers to keep out all light, and she commanded them that no one could see the baby that was to come.
>
> However, six young men and six young women pressed forward and burst through the tent and saw, to their horror, that she had given birth to a hideous snake. She reproached them for finding out her secret, and told them that they should not be surprised at what will happen to them.
>
> The next night, the great demonic serpent, which was the father, came and carried the woman and the young serpent back with it to the river. What followed were days of rain, without sun and with much torment. It sounded like a noise of distant thunder came up from the river. All the people were terrified at the disaster which seemed to be coming upon them. A hurricane roared and came out from the river. The water of the pond rose higher and higher, and the houses of the people were torn down and the people could not find a place to protect themselves. On a hill, an old man and six children took refuge, and the rest of the village was destroyed.[33]

The Dorasque tradition attributes the Flood to the union of a young woman with the great demonic serpent…

Andoque (Colombia, Brazil, and Peru):

The Andoque people live between the Caqueta and Putumayo Rivers, which encompass border areas of Brazil, Colombia, and Peru. The linguist Jon Landaburu led a visit to the Andoques in 1969 and recorded several oral traditions from the tribal elders, including one of the Flood, which is summarized due to length.

A man named Huevo de Chupaflor gave a feast at the center of town, and the people ate and drank. He sent two subordinates to toss the bones in the river, commanding them not to lick the bones, because there was unquenchable water inside the bones. However, the younger man saw meat on the bones and decided to taste it. The older man warned him, but the younger man tasted anyway. When he did so, water burst out from the bone and would not stop. He held the bone to his mouth but could take no more. Finally, they stuck the bone in the ground, but it continued to gush water all the more. Next, the sky darkened and it began to rain. And it rained and rained. Huevo de Chupaflor saw it and said, "See! This people is very disobedient. I told them not to lick the bone!"

Next, the sky darkened and it began to rain. And it rained and rained. … "See! This people is very disobedient."

33. Beatriz Miranda de Cabal, *Un Pueblo Visto a traves de su Lenguaje* (Panama: 1974), p. 17–18.

The water level climbed and climbed, and it drowned the entire earth. Some children took refuge atop the hill called Site of Crying. Finally, a knifefish swam down and broke the seal which had prevented the water from draining, and this allowed the water to recede.[34]

Tanimuka (Colombia):

When it (the sloth) still had the human form, it climbed to the top of a tree and then ascended to the sky through a vine. It hung in the sun and blocked its light. The earth plunged into darkness and began to rain: it was the old Sloth who was urinating. The flood spread everywhere, there was nothing left to eat. A fruit of Micrandra fell into the water and started to boil. The old Sloth was bombarded with projectiles, and ended up being cut in half. A fish fell into the water and turned into a water bird, and the other, caught between two branches, turned into the Two-toed Sloth. The sun brightened again.[35]

The earth plunged into darkness and began to rain: … The flood spread everywhere, there was nothing left to eat.

Yagua (Colombia and Peru):

Very long ago, Nawa, the river, started to swell. When the dry season came, the people saw that the river kept on rising. Then they knew that there would be a great flood. They left their houses, which were on the lowlands of the forests, and built new houses on the higher places. Still the water came and the forest got very wet. All the people walked in water up to their knees. They strung the hammocks high in the house, but still the river grew.

Iwaoi, who was a very clever man, went to hunt. He hunted for a long time. During this time he ate very little, but collected all the meat he hunted, and his wife smoked it so that it would keep. When Iwaoi finally returned from the hunt, he cut down many balsa trees and made a big and very strong raft. His wife collected all the manioc she could gather, and put it on the raft. The people were now walking in water up to their necks.

Rasacsun was a great shaman. He saw the raft that Iwaoi built and made evil magic against Iwaoi. Iwaoi died and Risacsun took the widow as his woman. They boarded the raft and had all the food Iwaoi had collected. The other people wanted to get on the raft, but Risacsun killed some of them by magic, and then nobody tried any more.

Rasacsun was a great shaman. He saw the raft that Iwaoi built and made evil magic against Iwaoi.

The rainy season started, the water rose, and a great many of the people drowned. Others climbed trees, but most of these died there from hunger. Risacsun was on the raft,

A Yagua Tribeman Demonstrating the Use of a Blowgun

34. Jon Landaburu and Roberto Pineda, *Tradiciones de la Gente de Hacha* (Bogota: Instituto Caro y Cuervo, 1984), p. 73–78.
35. Claude Levi-Strauss, *A Oleira Ciumenta* (Sao Paulo: Editora Brasiliense, 1985), p. 105–106.

and ate well and slept. The river rose, and one day the raft broke away from the tree to which it was tied. Risacsun and his wife tied all their bundles to the middle of the raft, as there was too much movement and shaking. They floated on the water for a very long time. Everything around them was under water, and even the tree tops were overrun.

> One day a heron came to roost and Risacsun saw that its feet were muddy with clay. Risacsun then knew that there was dry land near, so he steered the raft in the direction from which the heron had come ...

As Risacsun ate too much, all the food Iwaoi had collected was soon gone, and then they were hungry. The birds had no place to roost, so they came to the raft and sat down. Rasacsun waited until the birds had fallen asleep, then killed them and ate well. One day a heron came to roost and Risacsun saw that its feet were muddy with clay. Risacsun then knew that there was dry land near, so he steered the raft in the direction from which the heron had come, and found there was land covered with mud. Risacsun tied the raft to a tree and went on to the land. He found dry land, and with the aid of his wife built a house on it.

The rainy season ended, and the waters went down. Risacsun and his wife then walked many days until they got back to the place where they came from. There they found very few people, as most of them had died in the flood, but the manioc grew well in the mud that remained on the ground when the water receded. The people had a lot to eat, they grew very fat, and had many children.[36]

Desana (Colombia):

When the Sun saw that the Creation was suffering and that there were so many bad things, he decided to go down to earth to take control and eliminate the beasts. First, he sent a great flood and all the beasts drowned. Then he sent a very hot summer and everything caught fire and burned. Only those who lived towards the Eastern Plains were saved. Only the armadillo was saved because it made a cave and hid, but its tail that was once big and hairy was burned. Of the birds, only the boru was saved, a white bird that sings in the afternoon and is of good omen, and also the hen of the mountain. Then life came again. Another time came.[37]

Quijos-Quichua (Ecuador and Peru):

In the opinion of many, it seems that a great flood occurred in most remote times, which dragged down from the mountains those stones that, being crushed in the rolling among the boulders, separated the gold, which is found scattered in small, flat particles subrotonda.[38]

Aguarico River, Ecuador

36. Paul Fejos, "Ethnography of the Yagua," *Viking Fund Publications in Anthropology*, no. 1 (New York: Johnson Reprint Corp., 1943), p. 99–100.
37. Gerardo Reichel-Dolmatoff, *Desana: simbolismo de los indios tukano del Vaupés* (Bogotá: Procultura, 1986), p. 60–61.
38. Gaetano Osculati, *Esplorazione delle regioni equatoriali lungo il Napo ed il fiume delle Amazzoni* (Milan: Presso I Fratelli, 1854), p. 125.

Kashinawa (Peru and Brazil):

The Kashinawa attribute the destruction of the world and its first inhabitants to excessive rains, to flooded rivers, and to a general fire caused by a spark fallen from the sky. Some versions add that the sky crashed down and changed places with the earth.[39]

Kashinawa Village in Acre, Brazil

Cofán (Ecuador and Colombia):

The world was destroyed by an earthquake. When the earth shook everything ceased to exist, and the people also died. When the people died only three men survived, and no women survived. Then everything was turned into a river, and one man left for here and the others left for there. But the one that remained alone survived first. All of them collected planks of wood in order to float. Assembling a raft, they went forth on the water. The first man thought to himself, "I am alone." Then when the waters went down from the earth, he went about walking and searching. There was no forest, but everything was sand. There was no solid ground, but everything was wiped clean. It was not dry, but muddy. Everything was muddy. When he went about searching, he found another man. After this another man came too. Only three had survived, but they did not have leaves to build houses.[40]

Then everything was turned into a river, and one man left for here and the others left for there. … All of them collected planks of wood in order to float. Assembling a raft, they went forth on the water.

Pauserna (Bolivia and Brazil): (also known as the Guarasug'we)

This tribe is said to have an account of the Flood. However, the source is currently unavailable to me.

39. Alfred Metraux, "Tribes of the Jurua-Purus Basins," in "Handbook of South American Indians," ed. Julian Steward, vol. 3, in *Bureau of American Ethnology Bulletin*, vol. 143 (Washington: GPO, 1948), p. 684.
40. Enrique Criollo and M.B. Borman,,"Folklore Cofan," *Cuadernos Etnolinguisticos*, vol. 12 (Quito: Instituto Linguistico de Verano, 1991), p. 15.

Tapirapé (Brazil):

In point of time, the Tapirape consider the present as the third world. Twice people were destroyed, once by flood and once by universal fire. Before these catastrophes, there were pre-Tapirape called Karanjuntuwere. These people lacked the many refinements which were later brought to the Tapirape by their culture heroes. They ate several varieties of wild seeds, they did not have maize, manioc or any modern garden plants, and they lacked the bow and arrow. The Tapirape are not certain whether the Karanjuntuwere lived before or after the flood, but when the great deluge came, one man and one woman climbed a small palm tree which grew as rapidly as the water rose, carrying them above the flood. After they had been there some time the man began to spear fish and snakes which swarmed in the waters, using the long narrow palm leaves as spears. As he killed a fish or snake, the waters gradually diminished and finally ran back into the river beds.

When the great deluge came, one man and one woman climbed a small palm tree which grew as rapidly as the water rose, carrying them above the flood.

Four ancestors escaped the second destruction of people — the universal fire. These ancestors took the form of birds: there were two jacu which were men, and one parakeet and one mutuum, both women. These escaped underground and from the union of the two couples came "men" or ampa awa, as modern Tapirape call themselves.[41]

Ipurina (Brazil):

In the sun there was a large cauldron with boiling water. Countless storks were busy around it. Some of the storks were flying around the world, collecting everything that was there to throw it into the cauldron. Only the indestructible hardwood "parakuba" did they leave alone. The storks surrounded the kettle and waited for something to be cooked, and then they snapped it up. Now the chief of the storks—indeed, the creator of all birds—was Mayuruberu. When the water in the kettle got low, he cast a round stone into it. The kettle fell, the hot river flowed to earth, and destroyed everything, the forest, and even the water. Only the people survived, and of plants only the marimari (cassia).

The ancestor of the Ipurina was the sloth. He climbed the cassia tree to provide fruit for the people who had nothing to live on. On earth it was dark. The sun and moon were hidden. The sloth picked off the fruit and threw down the kernels. The first fell on hard earth, the second already in water, the third in deep water, and so forth. At the fall of the first kernel, the sun appeared again, but was very small, barely an inch in diameter. At the fall of the second, it was bigger; at the third, it was an arms length, and so forth, until it finally reached its present dimension.[42]

41. Charles Wagley, "World View of the Tapirape Indians," *Journal of American Folklore*, vol. 53, no. 210 (American Folk-lore Society, 1940), p. 254. For a similar account: Herbert Baldus, Ensaios de Etnologia Brasileira (Sao Paulo: 1937, Companhia Editora Nacional), p. 223.
42. Paul Ehrenreich, *Beiträge zur völkerkunde Brasiliens*, p. 71–72.

Kaiwa (Brazil):

It was all the more surprising for me to find among the Kaiwa a little myth about a third technique of creating fire — that of flint — a technique which is completely absent from their culture. The narrative of an old Indian priest, from the village of Dourados, takes as its starting point the Universal Fire, followed by the Deluge. Of this, they say that only a couple of children were saved, under a ladled pot, which was the beginning of humanity. "This couple," says the myth, "found the stone of fire [flint]. Beating pieces of it together, they obtained fire."[43]

Nivaklé Man Using a Spade

Nivaklé (Paraguay):

The parrot (Ekluéh) could talk, and he talked very well. There was a woman who was menstruating, and she went with her water jar to fetch water. But the animal that lived in the water became very angry, so the woman went back home. Soon thereafter a heavy rain and wind came up. What a wind! It began to rain heavily, it rained all night long and by four o'clock in the morning everything was inundated. All the children had drowned, they were dead, and the older people climbed on top of their houses. The horses and goats were stuck in the mud. Then the houses fell down and sank and were covered by the water. All the people drowned, they all died. However, one man seems to have been running all night long until he came to a spot where there was sand. Only one person was left.[44]

Toba and Pilaga (Argentina):

There was a menstruating woman who said, "I am thirsty, I wish to drink," but her mother did not bring her water. Being very thirsty, she went to a lagoon and drank. She returned home. Rainbow (a heavenly being) arrived. He is displeased when menstruating girls enter water, and for that reason he was angry. A strong wind arose, accompanied by whirlwinds and heavy rain. Rainbow caused the people to turn green and yellow and black. The water rose and rose. The people were drowned and all died. The white corpses of children floated over the water. A wak'ap bird (a sort of stork) came and attached a cloth to a stick. He struck the corpses with it and they were changed into pumas and birds. Some were green, some yellow, and some black. The word of Rainbow was accomplished. He who had destroyed the village made the wak'ap bird into a chief.[45]

The water rose and rose. The people were drowned and all died.

43. Egon Schaden, "A Origem e a Posse do Fogo na Mitologia Guarani," *Anais do XXXI Congresso Internacional de Americanistas*, vol. 1 (Sao Paulo: Kraus, 1954), p. 220.
44. *Folk Literature of the Nivaklé Indians*, eds. Johannes Wilbert and Karin Simoneau (Los Angelos: UCLA Latin American Center, 1987), p. 86–87.
45. Alfred Metraux, "Myths of the Toba and Pilaga Indians of the Gran Chaco," *Memoirs of the American Folklore Society*, vol. 40 (Philadelphia: 1946), p. 29.

APPENDIX B

THE HISTORICITY OF GENESIS, COMPARISONS WITH THE *EPIC OF GILGAMESH*, AND NORTH AMERICAN FLOOD TRADITIONS

Abstract

Some have dismissed the historicity of the Genesis account of the Flood by pointing to the Babylonian work known as the *Epic of Gilgamesh*. This work, a sprawling poem in the vein of "The Odyssey," contains an ancient Flood story with similarities to that of Genesis. It is alleged that Genesis borrowed the Flood story from this ancient work, or a related Mesopotamian source, and that the Genesis Flood is nothing more than a borrowed story.

We will demonstrate that, first, Moses used historical documents to write Genesis, and that Genesis records sober history. Second, we will demonstrate that there is evidence that the sources Moses used were recorded by the early patriarchs themselves (including Noah, Shem, Abraham, Isaac, Jacob, and Joseph). These sources therefore contain first-hand testimony of great antiquity.

Third, we will briefly survey many evidences outside of the Bible that confirm the events recorded in Genesis, which provide independent witnesses to the accuracy of Genesis. Finally, we will compare Genesis and the *Epic of Gilgamesh* directly, and also show that the oral traditions of the Flood from North America contained in this volume agree more with Genesis, and not the *Epic of Gilgamesh*. Indeed, Flood traditions from all over the world show remarkable similarity to the Genesis account. The only sensible explanation for this is that the Flood actually happened, and that Genesis accurately records how it happened.

The Historical Basis of Genesis

Whether one accepts Genesis to be true or not, it is at least apparent to the honest reader that its author, Moses intended Genesis to be understood as true history. It is not a work of fiction or poetry. It is a work that deals with history, and makes sober claims to fact. Historical statements are presented simply, yet with great detail. It contains chronologies, names, and genealogies.

We must first examine the question of where Moses got this information. Did he get it through a divine revelation? Did he make it up or steal ideas from preexisting Mesopotamian literature? What is the foundation upon which Genesis is based?

I submit to you that all the evidence points to this: that Moses possessed historical documents. Consider the following:

1. Genesis 5:1 says, "This is the book of the history (or generations) of Adam." The Hebrew word ספר (sepher) means "a book or writing." Here Moses plainly indicates

that he used a written source. If that were not enough, the text connected with this contains detailed genealogical facts on Adam, his descendants, and their lifespans. Both the content and format of this text demand a written source.

2. The verse above is one of 11 similar statements in Genesis (2:4, 5:1, 6:9, 10:1, 10:32, 11:10, 11:27, 25:12, 25:19, 36:1, 37:2) containing the Hebrew word תדלות (toledot), which is translated as "history, generations, record, or descent." For example, "This is the book of the history of Adam" (Genesis 5:1), "This is the record (or history) of Noah" (6:9), and "Now these are the generations of Terah." (11:27) **These toledot statements indicate a source was used.** They always follow the cited material, which itself provides evidence of being a source. This is seen in the great detail of the text, and the noticeable variation from one toledot (or section of Genesis) to another. They are also written in a terse style that reflects the use of a historical record. And again, one of the toledot statements (5:1) **explicitly says a book was used**.[1]

3. Moses explicitly quotes a tradition about Nimrod in Genesis 10:9, and in Numbers 21:14–15 he cites a "Book of the Wars of the Lord" for geographical information. This is further proof that Moses possessed and used sources in writing Genesis. By the way, divine inspiration and use of sources are not mutually exclusive! I believe that Moses used historical records in the same way that Luke and other scriptural authors did.

4. Genesis contains a **great deal of detail**, including genealogies,[2] lists of kings and chiefs,[3] records of battles,[4] geographical descriptions,[5] and transaction records.[6] The genealogies contain detailed family information, and often years, places, and other information. All of this detail is burdensome and unnecessary in a fictional work — which is what some imagine Genesis to be — and is very difficult to account for, unless Moses is using historical sources.[7] The very presence of this information demonstrates written sources. We will demonstrate later that these are the family records preserved by Noah, Shem, Abraham, Isaac, Jacob, and Joseph.

5. Shortly after Moses, we read of Joshua sending men of Israel to survey the land, and that "they described it by cities in seven divisions in a book" (Joshua 18:8–9). **Clearly they were literate!** Let us stop this pretentious nonsense about the men in biblical times being illiterate. We know that the practice of writing in clay tablets was common in Abraham's home country. The Ebla Tablets even show that writing was common hundreds of years prior to Abraham.[8]

6. The early generations of man knew how to write. Adam's son Cain built a city (4:17). Just seven generations after Adam, they had invented musical instruments including the lyre and piped instruments, as well as the forging of bronze and iron tools (4:21–22).[9] Evolutionary thought has misled us to think that early man was stupid and incapable of many things, but this is far from the truth.

7. There are many examples in which **Moses injects commentary or confirming data, such as geographical information, alternate names, or observations**. This is the sort of thing that one does in a historical, non-fiction work rather than a fictional work. For example, in Genesis 14:3 he writes of a battle that was fought in the "Valley of Siddim,"

---

1. This Tablet Model is to be distinguished from the Documentary (or JEDP) Hypothesis. For more information, see the following article by Bodie Hodge and Terry Mortenson. "Did Moses Write Genesis?" (June 28, 2011), Retrieved from: https://answersingenesis.org/bible-characters/moses/did-moses-write-genesis/.
2. For example, Adam through Noah (5:1–32); Shem, Ham, Japheth, and their descendants (10:1–32); Shem through Abraham (11:10–32); Jacob (35:22–29); Esau (36:1–43); and others.
3. For example, 14:1–9, 36:15–19, 36:31–39, 36:40–43.
4. 14:1–9.
5. For example, 12:5–9, 14:10, 23:19.
6. For example, 23:16–20, 37:25–28.
7. Moses is writing through the inspiration of God. But this level of detail and documentation is preserved, by God's design, to demonstrate the historical basis and the reliability of Scripture.
8. Joseph M. Holden and Norman Geisler, *The Popular Handbook of Archaeology and the Bible* (Eugene, OR: Harvest House, 2013), p. 86.
9. Hodge and Mortenson, "Did Moses Write Genesis?"

and then comments that this is now the Salt Sea (the Dead Sea). It was not yet a sea in Abraham's day, though it was muddy and a treacherous place to walk (see 14:10), no doubt due to the influx of water that was slowly turning this area into a lake.[10]

8. Moses was very well-educated. Acts 7:22 tells us he was a man of great learning, and that he benefited from the prestigious education afforded to the Egyptian elite. Josephus also says as much.[11] Genesis gives every impression to the reader of having been written by a master historian, someone who knew what he was talking about!

Historical Sources from the Patriarchs

Having shown that Moses had access to historical records that he used to write Genesis, let us now dig a bit deeper to truly understand how ancient these sources are and who wrote them. I believe the reader will find there is strong evidence that the records were preserved by the patriarchs themselves — including Noah, Shem, Abraham, Isaac, Jacob, and Joseph, or their close family members. Consider the following:

1. As discussed previously, Genesis 5:1 says, "This is the book of the history (or generations) of Adam." Moses is letting us know that he had a written source, which is also very evident by the nature of the account and the material it contains. But this text deals with the creation and the earliest generations of man. Therefore, this book must be very ancient.
2. Noah and his family were the only ones who survived the Flood. Anything not preserved by him would have been lost. The oldest sources, including that of 1:1 to 2:4, and the "book" (5:1) of 2:4 to 5:1, must have been preserved by Noah aboard the Ark.[12]
3. Moses, the author of Genesis, was the leader of the Israelite people at the time of the Exodus (around 1,450 B.C.). Moses' position, and the time in which he lived, coupled with his high level of education, afforded him access to all the treasured historical records and family histories of the Jews. Above all, this included records kept by, and about, Abraham, Isaac, and Jacob, as well as the sons of Jacob.[13] The elders of Israel would have been able to assist Moses obtain any information that he sought.
4. Considering that the majority of Genesis (chapters 12 to 50) deals with Abraham, Isaac, Jacob, and Joseph, it would not have been difficult for Moses to obtain this information, since it deals with events that had only happened a few hundred years earlier, and involving the most important patriarchs of the Jews. And we know how meticulous the Jews were in their QA/QC process whenever texts were copied and the reverence and faithfulness with which they preserved the Word of God.[14]
5. The Flood account in Genesis chapters 6 through 8 is very detailed and gives every indication of being a logbook recorded by Noah himself while he was on the Ark. Additionally, chapter 6 records the instructions that God gave Noah for the

---

10. For example, Genesis 10:9, 10:19, 10:30, 10:32, 14:2–3, 14:17, 23:19, 26:33, 32:32, 36:6–9, 35:19–20, 36:20–21, 36:24, 50:11, and 50:13.
11. Josephus, *Antiquities of the Jews*, 2.9.7.
12. Regarding the most ancient accounts in Genesis 1-4, an ancestor of Noah such as Seth or Enoch could have passed down records. Concerning the creation account in Genesis 1:1 through 2:4, it may be that God told Adam how He created the earth (Adam walked and talked with God in the Garden). Then it was written down by one of Adam's descendants. This view is supported by the existence of Genesis parallels from other cultures (see page 184).
13. If anyone doubts that Moses authored Genesis and the rest of the Torah, I highly recommend to you the fourth chapter of Joseph Holden and Norman Geisler's book, *Popular Handbook of Archaeology and the Bible*.
14. For example, Joseph Holden and Norman Geisler provide powerful analysis of the textual reliability of scripture in *Popular Handbook of Archaeology and the Bible*, including evidence from the Dead Sea Scrolls and a vast pool of other manuscripts for both the Old Testament and New Testament Scriptures.

construction and preparation of the ark. It was certainly in Noah's best interest to write these down, to make sure that he followed God's instructions perfectly, for the survival of himself and his family — to say nothing of the future of the human race and of the animals.

6. The logbook of the Flood and other written records of Noah would have passed to his godly son, Shem, and thus been preserved by Shem's descendants as family heirlooms.
7. Abraham, being a descendant of Shem, would have had access to the records passed down to Shem and his family. Indeed, the detail of the genealogy in 11:10–27 connecting Shem to Abraham's father Terah implies that Abraham had access to these records.
8. Abraham was a God-fearing man and did what any God-fearing man in his position would do: seek out the truths of God and preserve their memory. Josephus also describes Abraham as a man of learning and great knowledge of astronomy.[15] Genesis describes him as a man of great influence (14:14–17, 23:6) and one who was well-traveled (12:1–10). Abraham was more than capable of tracking down any records that he lacked, and had plenty of time to do so.
9. Many tribes around the world (including but not limited to North America and the Pacific Islands) have stories very similar to the events recorded in the early chapters of Genesis: God breathing the breath of life into clay to form the first man, the creation of the first woman from a rib, a deceitful serpent that introduced evil and death into the world, and others.[16] Borrowing from Christian or Jewish sources is not feasible. These people groups must have had this knowledge prior to the dispersion from the Tower of Babel. Given the "bottleneck" that occurred with the Flood, the source must have been Noah himself. And remember, Genesis 5:1 tells us there was a written source. Thus it survived the Flood and was passed down by many of the tribes of the world, whether orally or in written form, and with varying levels of accuracy in preservation over the ages.
10. There are very personal elements in the accounts in Genesis — for example, involving Jacob, Joseph, Isaac, and Abraham — which provide internal evidence that they came from eyewitness sources who directly participated in the events.
    a. For example, we read in Genesis 43:29–31 about how Joseph was overcome with emotion when he finally saw his younger brother Benjamin again (he had not yet revealed himself to his brothers). He hurried out of the room, looked for a place to weep, and went to his chamber where he wept. Then he washed his face, regained his composure, and returned back out to the dining room and said, "Serve the meal."
    b. Why is this sort of thing recorded in Genesis? Because the account came from an eyewitness (Joseph) who was also the primary participant in the event. Joseph remembered how he felt and how his heart was moved, and so it was preserved in the story. When people retell something that happened to them, their narration is often flavored by how they felt, which is what they remember the most. Often they go out of their way to give these personal details, involving their feelings, which are not strictly necessary from a historical perspective. There is no reason for Moses to write it this way if he is "making it up." The story is narrated in such a way as only Joseph would have recorded it — emotions and all — which testifies to its genuineness.
    c. Similarly, the section in chapter 29 where Jacob travels east and meets his future wife Rachel contains much personal content, and is told as only Jacob would have told it. Again, Moses didn't have to write it this way. But I'm glad he did. Genesis 24:67 contains a similar affectionate memory

Genesis is divinely inspired, like all Scripture. Ironically, it is the humanity of Genesis that provides one of the best witnesses to its genuineness and historical reliability.

There are very personal elements in the accounts in Genesis — for example, involving Jacob, Joseph, Isaac, and Abraham — which provide internal evidence that they came from eyewitness sources who directly participated in the events.

15. Josephus, *Antiquities*, 1.7.1–2.
16. See, for example, Theodor H. Gaster, *Myth, Legend, and Custom in the Old Testament*, and the topical index in Appendix G of this volume.

of Isaac's. Likewise, there is the dialogue between Jacob and Joseph in Genesis 48, and in 50:23. We are told that "the sons of Manassah were born on Joseph's knees." We are told that Joseph got to see his great-great-grandchildren. We are told the words that he said on his deathbed. Such narratives are highly personal, and are told in a way that only the direct participants would have told them. This shows these are first-hand, ancient, genuine sources which Moses used in writing Genesis.

Many narratives in Genesis are highly personal, and are told in a way that only the direct participants would have told them.

11. Again, several of the accounts in Genesis contain a level of detail that seems unnecessary to some, but which actually points to the use of a historical source containing first-hand information. For example, Genesis 24:22–23 says of Abraham's servant, when he found a wife for Abraham's son Isaac, "When the camels had finished drinking, the man took a gold ring weighing a half-shekel and two bracelets for her wrists weighing ten shekels in gold." Why all of this detail? It would have sufficed to say he gave her golden bracelets and a golden ring. But it is because the source used by Moses specified the weights. But who could have known the weights of these objects? Only those who participated in the event: mainly Isaac, possibly with input from Rebekah and his father's servant.

"I have long thought that the narrative in Gen. vii. and viii. can be understood only on the supposition that it is a contemporary journal or log of an eyewitness incorporated by the author of Genesis in his work. The dates of the rising and fall of the water, the note of soundings over the hill-tops when the maximum was attained, and many other details, as well as the whole tone of the narrative, seem to require this supposition, which also removes all the difficulties of interpretation which have been so much felt." —John William Dawson [17]

Additional Evidence for Genesis

1. Historical and archeological discoveries continually prove the accuracy of Genesis and the rest of the Bible and how faithfully these texts have been preserved. The archeologist Nelson Glueck writes,"It may be stated categorically that no archaeological discovery has ever controverted a biblical reference. Scores of archaeological findings have been made which confirm in clear outline or exact detail historical statements in the Bible."[18] It is beyond the scope of this book to delve into the historical, archeological, and scientific evidence confirming the Bible, but I would highly recommend several other resources to the reader.[19] And the evidence continues to pour in. Many biblical sites have been located and confirmed within the past several years, not least of which are Sodom and Gomorrah, and Mount Sinai.[20]

"It may be stated categorically that no archaeological discovery has ever controverted a biblical reference. Scores of archaeological findings have been made which confirm in clear outline or exact detail historical statements in the Bible."
— Archeologist Nelson Glueck

17. John William Dawson, *The Story of the Earth and Man* (London: Hodder and Stoughton, 1873), p. 290–291.
18. Nelson Glueck, *Rivers in the Desert: History of Negev* (New York: Farrar, Straus, and Cadahy, 1959), p. 31.
19. A few of the books I would recommend include: *The Popular Handbook of Archaeology and the Bible* by Norman Geisler and Joseph Holden; *New Evidence that Demands a Verdict* by Josh McDowell; *The Case for Christ* by Lee Strobel; *Evolution's Achilles Heels* written by nine Ph.D. scientists; and *The Genesis Flood* by Henry Morris. There is also a superb new book and documentary video, *Patterns of Evidence: Exodus*, by researcher and filmmaker Tim Mahoney. I would also highly recommend the detailed presentations from about 15 Ph.D. scientists in the 2017 *Is Genesis History?* Conference, associated with the documentary by the same name.
20. On the discovery of Sodom and Gomorrah, see *Discovering the City of Sodom*, by Stephen Collins. Dr. Collins regularly provides reports and updates on this ongoing excavation. On the discovery of the Red Sea Crossing location and Mount Sinai, see the book *The Lost Sea of the Exodus* by Glen Fritz, the doctoral thesis "The Biblical Significance of Jabal Al Lawz" by Charles Whittaker, and the film *Search for Mt. Sinai: Mountain of Fire* (2008), directed by Jim Schmidt. Researcher and filmmaker Tim Mahoney is currently working on a film and book documenting evidence for the Red Sea Crossing and Mount Sinai.

2. As to the fact of the global Flood and the existence of the ark atop a high mountain in Armenia, the historian Josephus (ca. A.D. 90) cites several more ancient historians, whose works are mostly unavailable to us today (though some are quoted by Eusebius):

> Now all the writers of barbarian histories make mention of this flood and of this ark; among whom is Berosus the Chaldean; for when he is describing the circumstances of the flood, he goes on thus: "It is said there is still some part of this ship in Armenia, at the mountain of the Cordyaeans; and that some people carry off pieces of the bitumen, which they take away, and use chiefly as amulets for the averting of mischiefs. Hieronymous the Egyptian, also, who wrote the Phoenician Antiquities, and Mnaseas, and a great man more, make mention of the same. Nay, Nicolaus of Damascus, in his ninety-sixth book, hath a particular relation about them, where he speaks thus: "There is a great mountain in Armenia, over Minyas, called Baris, upon which it is reported that many who fled at the time of the Deluge were saved; and that one who was carried in an ark came on shore upon the top of it; and that the remains of the timber were a great while preserved. This might be the man about whom Moses, the legislator of the Jews wrote."[21]

"Now all the writers of barbarian histories make mention of this flood and of this ark" — Josephus

3. As to the very long lifespans of the ancients, Josephus cites several ancient sources in confirmation. These sources are mostly unavailable to us today, but were to his readers:

> Now I have for witnesses to what I have said, all those that have written antiquities, both among the Greeks and barbarians; for even Manetho, who wrote the Egyptian History, and Berosus, who collected the Chaldean Monuments, and Mochus and Hestiaeus, and besides these, Hieronymous the Egyptian, and those who composed the Phoenician History, agree to what I here say: Hesiod and besides these, Ephorus and Nicolaus relate that the ancients lived a thousand years.[22]

4. Regarding the Tower of Babel, we will survey several confirming evidences from antiquity. One is an Assyrian tablet, marked K 3657, located in the British Museum. According to its translator, Chad Boscawen, it tells of "the building of some great temple tower, apparently by command of a kind. The gods are angry at the work, and so to put an end to it they confuse the speech of the builders."[23] Another is a Sumerian text, written in a series of cuneiform tablets, dated to the late third century B.C. It tells of a golden age in the past when all men worshipped the god Enlil in one tongue. But that "The leader of the gods, endowed with wisdom, the lord of Eridu, changed the speech in their mouths. [He brought] contention into it, into the speech of man that (until then) had been one."[24]
5. Josephus also cites an ancient record confirming the Tower of Babel:

> The Sibyl also makes mention of this tower, and of the confusion of the language, when she says thus: "When all men were of one language, some of them built a high tower, as if they would thereby ascend up to heaven; but the gods sent storms of wind and overthrew the tower, and gave everyone his peculiar language; and for this reason it was that the city was called Babylon."[25]

6. Douglas Petrovich has found archeological and historical support for locating the Tower of Babel at the site of Eridu.[26]

---

21. Josephus, *Antiquities of the Jews*, 1.3.6.
22. Josephus, *Antiquities of the Jews*, 1.3.9.
23. "The Legend of the Tower of Babel," trans. W. St. Chad Boscawen, Records of the Past, vol. 7 (London: Samuel Bagster, 1876), p. 129.
24. Samuel Noah Kramer, "The Babel of Tongues: A Sumerian Version," Journal of the American Oriental Society, vol. 88 (1968), p. 111.
25. Josephus, *Antiquities of the Jews*, 1.4.3.
26. Douglas Petrovich, Identifying Babel and Its Tower Lecture (video format), June 20, 2017. Retrieved from https://isgenesishistory.com/douglas-petrovich/.

7. Abydenus, in his *Assyrian History*, mentions the Tower of Babel. This ancient writing has not survived to the present day, but Eusebius quotes him:

> There are some who say that the men who first arose out of the earth, being puffed up by their strength and great stature, and proudly thinking that they were better than the gods, raised a huge tower, where Babylon now stands: and when they were already nearer to heaven, the winds came to the help of the gods, and overthrew their structure upon them, the ruins of which were called Babylon. And being up to that time of one tongue, they received from the gods a confused language.[27]

8. Moses of Chorene, the writer of the first Armenian history, also refers to the Tower of Babel. He quotes from an ancient Chaldean document, from the royal Assyrian library at Nineveh. "From the gods, it is there said, who inhabited the earth in the first ages, there sprang the race of giants of immense size, and of the strongest bodily frame. Full of insolent daring, they formed the ambitious design to build a lofty tower. But while they were employed in the erection, a dreadful tempest, raised by the gods, destroyed the huge edifice, and scattered among them unknown words, whence arose discord and confusion."[28]
9. Hundreds of oral traditions of the Flood have been found from tribes all over the world. As this work expands, it may be possible to get a more accurate total. No doubt, hundreds more have forever been lost, having disappeared before somebody could record them. And we have many oral traditions of the Tower of Babel as well! When this work is complete, we may have between 50 and 100 traditions from tribes across the world. This volume contains many of them (see the index in Appendix F). My second volume will document more of these.
10. Three Ph.D. scientists specializing in genetics research (Robert Carter, Stephen Lee, and John Sanford) have recently published an analysis of human Y chromosome and mitochondrial chromosome sequences. Among other insights, their analysis of both Y chromosome and mitochondrial chromosome data sets points to an original human pair that lived less than 10,000 years ago.[29] This is entirely consistent with Genesis but is a far cry from that required by the materialist worldview.
11. Darwinian evolution is a model in crisis, and many scientists have boldly expressed objections to it.[30] Many more keep their reservations quiet for fear of consequences. We are now a century and a half after Darwin, and evolutionists still cannot produce a single fossil that can withstand cross-examination and show evidence of transitions between animal kinds. Nor is there anything approaching a biological mechanism that can explain how macroevolution could happen. The field of genetics has brought to light a new world of information which has been especially devastating in this regard.[31]
12. One of the internal evidences to the accuracy of Genesis is that it records the flaws and indiscretions of the patriarchs. It would have been too easy to whitewash their sins and to present them as perfect people. But the fact that these unflattering details are preserved is best explained by the truth. The same is true of the Exodus. Why

Why would any people group make up the story that they were originally slaves in another land, or that they complained about being set free? Unless it were true. This confirms the reliability of the book of Exodus.

27. Eusebius, *Preparatio Evangelica*, trans. E.H. Giffford (1909), Book 9, Chapter 14.
28. E.F.C. Rosenmüller, *The Biblical Geography of Central Asia*, vol. 2, trans. N. Morren (Edinburgh: Thomas Clark, 1837), p. 67.
29. Carter, R.W., S.S. Lee, and J.C. Sanford, "An Overview of the Independent Histories of the Human Y Chromosome and the Human Mitochondrial Chromosome," in *Proceedings of the Eighth International Conference on Creationism* (Pittsburgh, PA: Creation Science Fellowship, 2018), p. 133.
30. See the "Scientific Dissent from Darwinism" petition, available at www.dissentfromdarwin.org.
31. See, for example, *Evolutions' Achilles Heels* by nine Ph.D. scientists; *Replacing Darwin* by Nathaniel Jeanson; *Greatest Hoax on Earth: Refuting Dawkins on Evolution* by Jonathan Sarfati; the detailed presentations from the 2017 Is Genesis History? Conference, on multiple fields of study, associated with the documentary by the same name; *Genetic Entropy* by John Sanford; and *Signature in the Cell* by Stephen Meyer.

would any people group make up the story that they were originally slaves in another land, or that they complained about being set free? Unless it were true.

Confirmation of Genesis in Oral Traditions from Other Cultures

1. Further confirmation that Genesis is more historically reliable than related traditions from other cultures is found in this: the accounts in Genesis are consistently simpler, soberer, and are not embellished or interwoven with what is clearly fictional or legendary material.
    a. For example, the Epic of Gilgamesh tells of the gods having a heated dispute among themselves after one of them realized mankind had escaped the Flood. This happened because the god Ea forewarned the man who built the ark, Uta-napishti, thus escaping the wrath of the god Enlil. Then Uta-napishti and his wife were given immortality and status as gods by Ea for having escaped the Flood.[32]
    b. This is the type of mythical content that characterizes the Epic of Gilgamesh, and other versions from around the world. In contrast to this we have the sober, simple, historical reporting in Genesis, which stands out as the accurate, original record.
    c. There is a directionality to myth. As stated by the esteemed Ancient Near East scholar Kenneth Kitchen:

> The common assumption that the Hebrew account is simply a purged and simplified version of the Babylonian legend (applied also to the Flood stories) is fallacious on methodological grounds. In the Ancient Near East, the rule is that simple accounts or traditions may give rise (by accretion and embellishment) to elaborate legends, but not vice versa. In the Ancient Orient, legends were not simplified or turned into pseudo-history (historicized) as has been assumed for early Genesis.[33]

"The common assumption that the Hebrew account is simply a purged and simplified version of the Babylonian legend ... is fallacious on methodological grounds. In the Ancient Near East, the rule is that simple accounts or traditions may give rise ... to elaborate legends, but not vice versa."
—Kenneth Kitchen

2. A comparison of all the alternate versions — whether we are talking of the Flood account or the creation of man, or other accounts in the first 11 chapters of Genesis — points to Genesis as the original, authentic version. Genesis demonstrates centrality and antecedence.
    a. When you take an autograph signature and have several people look at it and try to reproduce it, you end up with a bunch of signatures very different from one another. But they all share commonalities with the original. In the same way, Genesis preserves the authentic record preserved by Noah and passed down by the patriarchs to Moses. Therefore, it makes sense that we find that global Flood stories share more with the Genesis version than with any other version.
    b. When we actually study the variety of oral traditions found around the world, we can detect that the Genesis text is the authentic, original version from which all others are based. Each element of the Flood account in Genesis 6 to 8 can be found represented in the oral literature of at least some tribes. On the other hand, those tribes that lack that particular element of their Flood story (such as the rainbow) possess other parts of the story (such as the landing of the boat on a mountain and the sending of a raven and a dove).

32. "Epic of Gilgamesh," Tablet XI, verses 172–206.
33. Kenneth A. Kitchen, *Ancient Orient and the Old Testament* (London: Inter-Varsity Press, 1966), p. 89. In support of this, Kitchen refers to the legend of Sesostris in Egypt, progressive exaggerations in later traditions about the Hyksos kings of Egypt, the growth of traditions about Gilgamesh king of Uruk, and *Enuma Elish*.

3. Arthur Custance well observes that the Genesis Flood account stands out as perhaps the only one which admits the ark landed not locally, but in a faraway country.

> This is a quite exceptional circumstance. All other traditions report that the ark landed locally. In Greece on Mount Parnassus; in India the ark landed in the Himalayas; in America one story has it landing on Keddie Peak in the Sacramento Valley. And so it goes; everywhere the same — always a local mountain. This circumstance surely suggests that here in the Bible we have the genuine account. And it also underscores the great respect which the Hebrew people had for the Word of God and the requirement that they never tamper with it. It would surely, otherwise, have been most natural for them to land the ark on their most famous mountain, Mount Zion.[34]

Comparison with Epic of Gilgamesh

Reading the two accounts, we can observe that the *Epic* is full of obvious myth and embellishment — contrasted with the simple, sober, and credible account in Genesis. This strongly suggests that the Genesis account is the more ancient and more accurate record of the original events. Also consider the following differences listed in Table B-1.

Table B-1: Comparison of Genesis and *Epic of Gilgamesh* Texts	
1. Sacrifice after the Flood (note the mythical content in the *Epic of Gilgamesh*)	
Noah offered a sacrifice to God after he came out from the ark. It was pleasing to God, and God blessed him (Genesis 8:20–9:1).	"The gods gathered like flies" at the sacrifice that Uta-napishti offered, and then an argument arose between the gods when one of them discovered that mankind had escaped the Flood. (Tablet XI, verses 157–198)
2. Regarding the Flood itself, compare the journal entry language of Genesis with the mythical, poetic content of the *Epic*	
"In the six hundredth year of Noah's life, in the second month, on the seventeenth day of the month, on the same day all the fountains of the great deep burst open, and the floodgates of the sky were opened. The rain fell on the earth for forty days and forty nights" (7:11–12).	"There rose on the horizon a dark storm cloud, and bellowing within it was Adad the Storm God. The gods Shullat and Hanish were going before him, bearing his throne over mountain and land. The god Errakal was uprooting the mooring-poles, Ninurta, passing by, made the weirs overflow. . . . Even the gods took fright at the Deluge, they left and went up to the heaven of Anu, lying like dogs curled up in the open. . . . For six days and seven nights, there blew the wind, the downpour, the gale, the Deluge, it flattened the land. But the seventh day when it came, the gale relented, the Deluge ended. The ocean grew calm, that had thrashed like a woman in labour. The tempest grew still, the Deluge ended" (verses 98–103, 114–116, 127–133).
3. The ark is simpler in Genesis, and more developed in the *Epic of Gilgamesh*	
Genesis tells that the ark was built on land, and when the Flood came it was lifted up by the waters. It had no steering system. It was simply a floating vessel, as it had no place to go (7:17–18).	In the *Epic*, the boat is launched into the Gulf (of Persia) prior to the Flood, and Uta-napishti appoints a shipwright to oversee its navigation (verses 42, 80, 95).

34. Arthur C. Custance, "Flood Traditions of the World," *Symposium on Creation IV* (Grand Rapids, MI: Baker, 1972), p. 17.

Table B-1: Comparison of Genesis and *Epic of Gilgamesh* Texts	
4. Genesis reads like concise journal entries, the *Epic* contains poetic repetition	
"Of clean animals and animals that are not clean and birds and everything that creeps on the ground, there went into the ark to Noah by twos, male and female, as God had commanded Noah" (7:8–9). "In the seventh month, on the seventeenth day of the month, the ark rested upon the mountains of Ararat. The water decreased steadily until the tenth month; in the tenth month, on the first day of the month, the tops of the mountains became visible" (8:4–5).	"All I loaded aboard; All the silver I owned I loaded aboard; All the gold I owned I loaded aboard; All the living creatures I had I loaded aboard" (verses 81–86). "Mount Nimush held the boat fast and it did not budge; One day and a second, Mount Nimush held the boat and it did not budge; a third day and a fourth, Mount Nimush held the boat and it did not budge; a fifth day and a sixth, Mount Nimush held the boat and it did not budge" (verses 142–146).
5. Ut-Napisthtim becomes a god?	
Genesis honestly records one of Noah's flaws — 9:20–22 tells how he planted a vineyard and got drunk. He lay naked in his tent and was seen by his son Ham. There is little reason for this unflattering account about Noah unless it is true.	Uta-napishti and his wife are granted immortality and become gods as a reward for surviving the Flood (verses 203–206)

Table B-2 below summarizes several differences in the two Flood accounts.

Table B-2: Sample of Differences Between Genesis Flood Account and *Epic of Gilgamesh*

#	Genesis	Epic of Gilgamesh (and Related Babylonian Versions)
1	God sends the Flood due to man's wickedness, violence, and continual evil ways.	The gods send the flood because mankind is too noisy, making it impossible for the gods to sleep.[35]
2	Noah sends a raven out from the ark, followed by a dove. Later, the dove returns from a second flight with a freshly picked olive leaf in its beak.	Uta-napishti sends a dove, then a swallow, then a raven. None of the birds returns with anything in its beak.
3	God gives a rainbow as a sign of His promise never to destroy the world again with a flood.	No reference to the rainbow
4	The ark is built on land and is lifted up by the waters once the Flood comes.	Ark is launched out into the Gulf before Flood starts, and he assigns its navigation to his shipwright.
5	The ark is 300 cubits long, 50 cubits wide, 30 cubits high (a cubit is approximately 1.5 feet).	The ark is square: 120 cubits long by 120 cubits wide, and 7 levels.
6	The rains last for 40 days. Noah remains in the ark for 1 year and 10 days.	The Flood rains last 6 days, and the total duration of the Flood is unspecified.
7	8 persons enter the ark.	More than 8 persons enter the ark (Uta-napishti, his family, and "members of every skill and craft").
8	Noah is just a man, and his flaws are recorded.	Uta-napishti becomes a god and gains immortality as a reward for surviving the Flood.
9	Noah offers a sacrifice to God after he exits the ark, and God is pleased.	Uta-napishti offers a sacrifice, and the gods "gather like flies" over it, and an argument erupts between the gods when Enlil discovers man survived the Flood.

35. Implied in the *Epic of Gilgamesh*, but explicitly stated in the related Babylonian account of the Epic of Atrahasis. See *Epic of Gilgamesh*, trans. Andrew George (Penguin Books, 1999), p. xliii, xliv.

Comparison Based on North American Flood Traditions

Let us use the many Flood traditions from North America as a sample set for comparing Genesis and the *Epic of Gilgamesh*. When we study these, we find that the North American Flood traditions agree far more with Genesis than with the *Epic of Gilgamesh*. The best explanation for this is that the Flood truly happened, as all tribes around the world say it did, and that Genesis accurately recorded how it happened.

1. 18 North American Flood traditions confirm the Genesis account regarding the raven and dove being sent, with the dove returning with a fresh leaf in its beak. **Zero** agree with the *Epic of Gilgamesh*'s version, in which a raven, a dove, and a swallow are sent, but none returns (although even here, the *Epic of Gilgamesh* agrees with Genesis, in that birds were sent out to check for land).
2. 20 agree with Genesis regarding the cause of the Flood (God's judgment upon man's evil ways), and **zero** agree with the *Epic of Gilgamesh* (human noise making it impossible for the gods to sleep).
3. 27 agree with Genesis in that the ark was canoe-like in shape, and **zero** agree with the *Epic of Gilgamesh*'s square-shaped ark.

There are other areas of agreement/disagreement, but these three points alone are more than enough to make us pause and consider the historical accuracy of the Genesis account, as compared to the accuracy of the Gilgamesh Epic.

Conclusion

The evidence presented gives clear, multifaceted testimony to the accuracy of Genesis and to the God of the Bible. This study only scratches the surface of the evidence that confirms Genesis and the Bible. Even from North America, we see that the Flood traditions from the peoples of this land agree with Genesis and not with the *Epic of Gilgamesh*. Where Genesis and the *Epic of Gilgamesh* differ, agreement with Genesis is unanimous, and agreement with the *Epic of Gilgamesh* is nonexistent. That confirms that Genesis is the authentic, original history. Nevertheless, the *Epic of Gilgamesh* itself serves as a witness to the fact that the Flood occurred.

EARTH DIVER STORIES AND OTHER VARIANTS

Earth Diver Stories

If you have read my book all the way to this point, you have likely noticed that many North American tribes possess what are known as "earth diver" stories. In these stories, various types of animals are sent diving into the deep floodwaters in search of some clay, which is used to remake the earth. The details vary, but usually the animals are sent by an old man in a canoe. The animals also vary, but often include the muskrat, dove, raven, otter, and duck. See, for example, the Arapahoe version on page 94 and the Montagnais version on page 18. Earth diver stories are most common roughly east of the Continental Divide in the United States and Canada, especially among the Algonquian, Iroquoian, and Muskogean language families. Earth diver stories have even been found in South America (as documented in this volume) and in parts of Asia!

It is a natural question to ask then: what is the origin of these earth diver stories? And what is their relation to the Genesis Flood account, if any?

Let's answer those two questions in reverse order. First, it is very apparent from reading the earth diver stories contained in this volume, that they describe a global and destructive flood which occurred in the ancient past — just like the Genesis Flood. Second, they contain specific similarities with the Genesis Flood account. Among others, these similarities can include an old man in a boat sending animals in search of land, a raven or a dove (which are particular to Genesis), the animal returning with a leaf or other object in its mouth as an indication that the flood is abating, and the slow reemergence of land after the flood. Overall, the similarity to the Noahic birds account (from Genesis 8:6–12) is the most striking. That passage goes like this:

> Then it came about at the end of forty days, that Noah opened the window of the ark which he had made; and he sent out a raven, and it flew here and there until the water was dried up from the earth. Then he sent out a dove from him, to see if the water was abated from the face of the land; but the dove found no resting place for the sole of her foot, so she returned to him into the ark, for the water was on the surface of all the earth. Then he put out his hand and took her, and brought her into the ark to himself. So he waited yet another seven days; and again he sent out the dove from the ark. The dove came to him toward evening, and behold, in her beak was a freshly picked olive leaf. So Noah knew that the water was abated from the earth. Then he waited yet another seven days, and sent out the dove; but she did not return to him again (Genesis 8:6–12).

Again, there are many similarities between the earth diver stories and the Genesis Flood account. Here in Table C-1 is a sample of the similarities — looking only at the Noahic birds portion from Genesis 8 verses 6 through 12. Remember that these animals are often sent by an old man (Noah) in a canoe (the Ark) floating hopelessly on a featureless water-covered earth.

Table C-1: Similarities between Earth Diver Stories and Noahic Birds Account in Gen. 8:6–12	
1	In the Cree account (see page 18), the dove returns with a piece of clay in its legs (instead of an olive leaf in its beak).
2	The Chitimacha (page 123) replace the raven with a woodpecker, and then the dove returns with a grain of sand in its beak (instead of an olive leaf).
3	In the Arapaho account (page 94), the dove returns and reports that the waters still cover the earth. Then, God commands the turtle to dive for earth. The turtle returns with some mud in its mouth and tells that the earth is found beneath the sea. God then commands the waters to depart and the earth to rise.
4	According to the Eastern Shoshone (page 98), a raven (followed by other birds) was sent to get a piece of earth (instead of a leaf).
5	In the Montagnais version (page 18), a raven is sent to fly in search of earth, but it fails. Then, (instead of sending the dove) an otter and a muskrat are successively made to dive for earth.
6	In a second Cree account (page 18), a duck is sent (instead of the raven and dove). Like the raven and dove, it is sent in multiple attempts.
7	In the Beaver account (page 28), In the Beaver account (page 29), a buzzard eventually is able to make a successful dive to find earth, which is taken as a sign that the water level upon the earth is descending.
8	In the Lenape version (page 114), a bird dives into the water for earth, but does not find any. Later it flies far away and returns with some earth in its bill.
9	In the Wukchumni version (page 245), a turtle dives and fetches some earth, but a dove delivers it.
10	In the Iowa version, a muskrat dives and gets some earth, and a dove also returns to the canoe with a small branch and some leaves. Both elements are used to remake the earth. And the account of the Sauk and Fox tribes (page 108) is very similar.
11	In the Potawatomi version (page 106), the animals dive for earth, but there is a remnant of the raven being sent in flight for a special purpose too.
12.	According to the Tuskegee account (page 130), a dove is first sent to fly in search of earth, but it fails to find any. Then a crawfish dives into the water and manages to bring up some earth.
13	The Saulteaux Flood story includes earth-diving animals, and a remnant of the sending of the birds. For when the new earth had just been formed, he sends out a wolf, followed by a crow to determine its length. When the latter does not return, he concludes it is large enough to inhabit, and he and the animals get out of the boat.

Clearly, then, there is a connection between these earth diver stories and the Genesis Flood. They are inextricably tied. There is no trying to explain them as separate accounts which exist independently. One must have come from the other. So which one came first: the earth diver story, or the Flood account found in Genesis?

The Flood account found in Genesis came first.[1] For one thing, there is a directionality to myth. The pattern is that simple and sober historical accounts become more mythical over time — not the reverse. Fairy tales do not become sober historical accounts over time.[2] Genesis is simpler and soberer. Earth diver stories are more embellished, mythical, fanciful. Secondly, Flood stories from all over the world — different types of Flood stories — are much more similar to Genesis than to earth diver stories. This shows that Genesis contains the original version, to which all other different versions are the most similar. This is analogous to spokes of a wheel radiating in different directions, yet they all touch the hub.

So How Did the Earth Diver Story Come About?

Let's suppose — as Genesis says — that there was a Flood which caused a population bottleneck, and that Noah and the seven others with him repopulated the earth.

1. I do not mean that the tribes possessing earth diver stories got their story after reading the Book of Genesis, for that is implausible and absurd. I mean that they got their Flood story from Noah and his direct descendants, and then their Flood story changed over time to include this "earth diver" element.
2. Kenneth A. Kitchen, *Ancient Orient and the Old Testament*, p. 89.

Furthermore, the history of the world from Adam to Noah was preserved by Noah and his family. Next, after the human population grew over a few generations, people became puffed up and built a great tower as a refuge in case God should flood the earth again. God was not pleased and confused their language, resulting in the scattering of smaller groups according to their new languages.

Remember that prior to the confusion at Babel, the people had an understanding of history which they learned from Noah and his sons. This included the Flood, the creation, and some of the events recorded between Genesis chapters 1 and 8. However, much of this became *lost in translation* once they lost their original language. People groups scattered, they remembered what they could, and they passed it on to future generations as best they could.

Well, one thing that happens when your memory fails is that you mix up different events, and you cannot recall which one happened when. Thus, we should not be surprised if we find certain tribes that mixed up the memory of the serpent tempting Eve (Genesis 3) with the memory of the Flood (Genesis 6–8). This is exactly what we find in many tribes, from North America all the way down to South America, as noted in this book. Nor should we be surprised to find a conflation of the memory of the Flood and the confusion of languages at Babel. We find exactly this in the traditions of tribes scattered across the world, documented in this book.

Nor should we be surprised to find a conflation of the memory of a forbidden tree or fruit (Genesis 3) with the Flood. We find this in many tribes of South America, and other places. Nor should we be surprised if we find a conflation of the memory of God creating the sun and moon (Genesis 1) with the Flood. We find this in several jungle tribes of Brazil. Nor should we be surprised if we find a conflation of the memory of the Flood with a memory of God's judgment upon the serpent, woman, and man in the Garden (Genesis 3). We find this in Mexico and Central America, and to a degree in South America.

And finally, we should not be surprised if we find a conflation of the water-covered world from which land was created (Genesis 1) with the water-covered world of the Flood. This is what we find in the earth diver stories which are common in North America. There is clearly a creation element reminiscent of Genesis 1. At the same time, there are the distinct similarities with the Noahic birds account in Genesis 8, and other similarities with the Flood account in general.

Raven Stories

What about other Flood stories that we find in parts of the western United States? We find many raven stories. These include Flood stories where the raven returns with a leaf in its mouth, rather than the dove, or the raven replaces the dove entirely (see the Gros Ventres version on page 99). In other cases, we find accounts where the raven plays a special role in creation, or in remaking the earth after the Flood, such as the Gwich'in (page 43) and Potawatomi (page 106) accounts. We find accounts where the raven possesses supernatural, sometimes evil, powers (such as the Haida, Tahltan, and Tlingit traditions on pages 32, 37, and 44, respectively). It seems these trace their origin back to Noah and the memory of the Flood and of creation as well.

Recalling the raven's role in the Flood event, it is not surprising that some people decided (incorrectly) to exalt or attribute deity to a raven at some time in the past. It is, after all, one of only two animals mentioned by name in Genesis as having played a role in the Flood and the search for land afterward. Incidentally, the other animal, the dove, is well-represented in earth diver accounts and is likewise exalted in some of these.

Coyote and Other Stories

A similar thing seems to have taken place with the stories involving a coyote. In the Papago account (page 74), a coyote is sent repeatedly to find the border of the land and sea, similar to how Noah dispatched the raven and the dove. The Saulteaux version (page 26) is similar, but it is a wolf instead of a coyote, and it is sent along with a crow. In the Pomo account (page 67), the coyote takes the place of Noah and saves himself and several others from the Flood. A simple error in translation, such as occurred at Babel, or an error in transmission over the centuries which followed, could easily result in these changes. Thus, we begin to see how these divergent Flood stories could come about after Babel and certainly in the thousands of years that have passed since.

Conclusion

We find Flood stories of many different types around the world, including the "earth diver" type. When we find these variations, the correct way to think about it is to remember that the Flood was not the only historical event which our ancient ancestors were aware of at the time of the Tower of Babel. They had a memory of other events of early Genesis, including the creation, the serpent tempting Eve in the Garden, the Curse, and other things. These are exactly the themes we keep finding mixed up with the Flood, in stunning fashion, in the oral traditions of many tribes. It is no wonder that the memories got mixed up and distorted; it is because of the confusion of languages that happened at Babel. The earth diver story in particular contains a very distinct memory of Noah's dispatch of the raven and the dove after the Flood, but also a memory of creation week when God created land in the midst of only water. The history recorded in Genesis is the one account that makes sense of all the varying Flood traditions we find across the world. It really brings it all into clearer perspective. This points to Genesis as the original, authentic record of our past, confirming the reliability of this book.

NATURALISTIC EXPLANATIONS OF FLOOD TRADITIONS

Introduction

Now we must address the objections of our friends who hold to naturalism and a materialistic worldview. Whenever the subject of global Flood traditions is brought up, those of the materialist worldview have typically countered with the following objections: [1]

> **Objection 1:** That these Flood traditions arose by the influence of Christian missionaries (or others) upon the beliefs of the native tribes. In other words, that the tribes did not originally have these Flood traditions, but the missionaries got there early and influenced them.
>
> **Objection 2:** That these Flood traditions arose by environmental factors and/or human thought patterns, as an attempt to explain the world around them. In other words, that their resemblance to the Genesis Flood account is by chance.

Objections Answered

In truth, one of the main purposes in writing this book was to clearly demonstrate that the above objections are unsustainable. That they can no longer be entertained as plausible. That these objections, a barrier to accepting the truth of Genesis and the bearing of the Word of God upon one's life, have been raised for too long and finally need to be abandoned.

Objection 1 fails for the following reasons:

1. It does not account for the existence of written Flood histories from various cultures prior to the time of Christ.
    a. Josephus, quoted on page 272, cites several ancient historians, and alludes to many others, from various corners of the known world, each of which affirms the historical Flood.
    b. Nor are these ancient documents limited to that region. For example, in India the Rig Vedas and an ancient book of the Santal people of India affirm the historical Flood. The same is the case for the text of the Mayan Popol Vuh, and historical paintings of the Aztecs, which antedate the arrival of European powers by at least several centuries.
2. It ignores the early date of the recording of many Flood traditions. Many of the traditions in this volume, and other parts of the world (to be covered in the next volume), were recorded

1. See, for example, Sir James Frazer, *Folk-Lore In the Old Testament*, vol. 1 (London: Macmillan and Co., 1919), p. 104–106.

at or around first contact with the tribes. This rules out the possibility of Christians having influenced traditions prior to their recording.

3. It presumes that the First Nations peoples were easily influenced to abandon or alter their traditions upon contact with Europeans. This was far from the case and is frankly condescending toward the First Nations peoples. Their oral traditions were considered sacred and were guarded closely. Only under great existential difficulty and religious persecution — combined with a sufficient time for those who knew the traditions to die off (at the very minimum, approximately 75 years) — only in these conditions was it possible for their oral traditions to begin to be influenced by outsiders. And even then in many cases they still preserved their traditions with great integrity and perseverance.
4. It does not account for the finding of Flood traditions among very isolated tribes — those with great geographical, linguistic, and cultural barriers to outsiders.
5. It does not account for the clearly native material that characterizes these Flood traditions. There is a wealth of internal evidence in these traditions that demonstrates they are native, rather than the result of missionary teaching or influence. It is very obvious in cases where influence has taken place, and that is not the case with the Flood traditions presented in this volume.[2]
6. It does not account for the fact that I have already screened out versions where obvious Christian influence took place.
7. This objection requires special pleading. If missionaries influenced them, why do we not find several hundred versions of other well-known biblical accounts, such as the virgin birth, the Trinity, the death and Resurrection of Jesus, David and Goliath, the Exodus, and so forth?

With that established, **Objection 2** also fails for the following reasons:

1. It cannot account for similarities with the Genesis Flood on specific details. These include: the sending of the raven and the dove, with the dove returning with a leaf in its beak; the rainbow being given as a promise the earth will never be destroyed by another flood; a pre-Flood race of fallen beings; an old man being forewarned to prepare a great boat for the coming Flood; the godless ways of mankind that precipitated the Flood; and other factors.
2. It cannot account for the convergence of several elements of the Flood account that are similar to the Genesis Flood account. Perhaps one or two similarities could occur by chance, but the numbers of similarity that we find defy statistical odds.
3. There is no inherent reason for tribes to invent a flood story of the world's destruction — much less one that matches the Genesis account in so many particulars.

Summary

In short, naturalistic explanations cannot account for the global testimony of Flood traditions that we possess. If the world and its history is what materialist evolutionists say it is, we should not find such ubiquitous testimony of the Flood, in clear confirmation of the Genesis record. On the other hand, these Flood traditions are exactly what we should expect to find if Genesis is true.

The new and expanded collection of Flood traditions that we possess defies naturalistic explanations. They testify to the reality of the Genesis Flood and to the God who sent the Flood in righteous judgment.

2. For example, some recorded Flood traditions contain word-for-word quotes from Genesis, or contain the words "Noah," "Jesus," "the Trinity," etc. In cases where missionary influence took place, the signs are very easy to tell. Also, in any case where the phrase "forty days and forty nights" occurred, I discarded that Flood tradition.

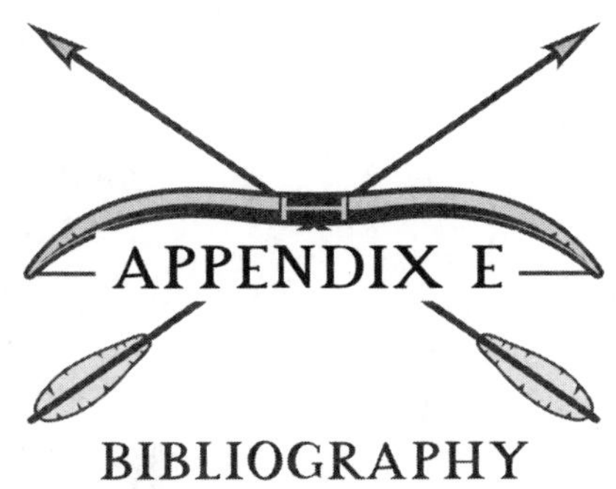

APPENDIX E

BIBLIOGRAPHY

Adamson, Thelma, *Folk-tales of the Coast Salish* (New York: American Folklore Society, 1934).

Alanson, Skinner, and John V. Satterlee, "Folklore of the Menomini Indians," *Anthropological Papers of the American Museum of Natural History*, vol. 13, part 3 (New York: American Museum of Natural History, 1915).

Anderson, Thomas G., "Narrative of Capt. Thomas G. Anderson, 1800–28," ed. Lyman Copeland Draper, *Collections of the State Historical Society of Wisconsin,* vol. 9 (Madison: State Historical Society, 1909).

Austin, Stephen A. "Nautiloid mass kill and burial event, Redwall Limestone (Lower Mississippian)," *Proceedings of the First International Conference on Creationism* (Pittsburgh: Creation Science Fellowship, 2003).

--------- and Roger W. Sanders, "Paleobotany Supports the Floating Mat Model for the Origin of Carboniferous Coal Beds," *Proceedings of the Eighth International Conference on Creationism* (Pittsburgh: Creation Science Fellowship, 2018).

--------- "Mount St. Helens and Catastrophism," *Proceedings of the First International Conference on Creationism* (Pittsburgh: Creation Science Fellowship, 1986).

Balikci, Asen. *The Netsilik Eskimo* (Garden City, NY: Natural History Press, 1970).

Bancroft, Hubert Howe, *The Native Races of the Pacific States of North America*, vol. 3, (New York: D. Appleton and Co., 1875).

Barrett, Samuel Alfred, "Pomo Myths," *Bulletin of the Public Museum of the City of Milwaukee*, vol. 15 (Milwaukee: Order of the Board of Trustees, 1933).

Beatty, Charles, *Journal of a Two Months Tour: With a View of Promoting Religion Among the Frontier Inhabitants of Pennsylvania, and of Introducing Christianity Among the Indians to the Westward of the Alegh-Geny Mountains* (London: William Davenhill, 1768).

Benedict, Ruth, "Tales of the Cochiti Indians," *Bureau of American Ethnology Bulletin,* vol. 98 (Washington: Smithsonian, 1931).

Blackburn, Thomas C., *December's Child: A Book of Chumash Oral Narratives* (Berkeley and Los Angeles: University of California Press, 1975).

Blackburn, Thomas C., and Lowell John Bean, "Kitanemuk," *Handbook of North American Indians*, vol. 8, ed. Robert F. Heizer (Washington: Smithsonian, 1978).

Boas, Franz, "Mitteilungen über die Vilzula Indianer," *Original Mittheilungen aus der Ethnologischen Abtheilung der Königlichen Museen zu Berlin* (Berlin: W. Spemann, 1885).

--------- "The Central Eskimo," *Sixth Annual Report of the Bureau of American Ethnology* (Washington: GPO, 1888).

--------- "Traditions of the Tsetsaut," *Journal of American Folk-lore*, vol. 9 (Boston and New York: Houghton, Mifflin and Co., 1896).

---------, *Kathlamet Texts* (Washington: GPO, 1901).

Boscana, Geronimo, *Chinigchinich,* translated by Alfred Robinson (New York: Wiley and Putnam, 1846).

Boscawen, W. St. Chad, "The Legend of the Tower of Babel," *Records of the Past,* vol. 7 (London: Samuel Bagster, 1876).

Burns, Louis F., *Osage Indian Customs and Myths* (Tuscaloosa: University of Alabama Press, 1984).

Bushnell Jr., David I., "The Choctaw of Bayou Lacomb, St. Tammany Parish, Louisiana," *Bureau of American Ethnology Bulletin*, No. 48 (Washington: GPO, 1909).

Byrd, William II, *Letter from William Byrd, Lincoln's Inn, London, to Dr. John Woodward, 1697 August 14.*

Manuscript X.c.50, Folger Shakespeare Library, Washington, DC.

Carter, Robert W., Stephen S. Lee, and John C. Sanford, "An Overview of the Independent Histories of the Human Y Chromosome and the Human Mitochondrial Chromosome," in *Proceedings of the Eighth International Conference on Creationism* (Pittsburgh, PA: Creation Science Fellowship, 2018).

Catlin, George, *The North American Indians*, vol. 1 (Edinburgh: Jon Grant, 1926).

--------- *North American Indians*, vol. 2 (Philadelphia: Leary, Stuart & Co., 1913).

--------- *Last Rambles Amongst the Indians of the Rocky Mountains and the Andes* (London: Sampson Low, Son, and Marston, 1868).

--------- *O-Kee-Pa: A Religious Ceremony and other Customs of the Mandans* (Philadelpha: J.B. Lippincott and Co., 1867).

Catcott, Alexander, *Treatise on the Deluge* (London: E. Allen, 1768).

Chamberlain, A.F., "Report on the Kootenay Indians of South-eastern British Columbia," in *Eighth Report of the Committee on the North-Western Tribes of the Dominion of Canada, in Report of the Sixty-Second Meeting of the British Association for the Advancement of Science Held in Edinburgh, 1892* (London: John Murray, 1893).

Clark, Ella E., *Indian Legends of the Pacific Northwest* (Berkeley: University of California Press, 1953).

--------- *Indian Legends of the Northern Rockies* (Norman, OK: University of Oklahoma Press, 1966).

Connelley, William Elsey, *Indian Myths* (New York: Rand McNally, 1928).

Cranz, David, *History of Greenland*, vol. 1 (London: 1767).

Culin, Stewart, "Games of the North American Indians," *Twenty-fourth Annual Report of the Bureau of American Ethnology* (Washington: GPO, 1907).

Curtin, Jeremiah, *Myths of the Modocs* (Boston: Little, Brown & Co., 1912).

Curtis, Edward S., *The North American Indian*, vol. 1 (Cambridge, MA: University Press, 1907).

--------- *The North American Indian*, vol. 5 (Cambridge, MA: University Press, 1909).

--------- *The North American Indian*, vol. 6 (Norwood, MA: Plimpton Press, 1911).

--------- *The North American Indian*, vol. 13 (Norwood, MA: Plimpton Press, 1924).

--------- *The North American Indian*, vol. 14 (Norwood, MA: Plimpton Press, 1924).

Cushman, Horatio Bardwell, *History of the Choctaw, Chickasaw and Natchez Indians* (Greenville, TX: Headlight Printing, 1899).

Cusick, David, *Sketches of the Ancient History of the Six Nations* (Lockport, NY: Turner & McCollum, 1848), part 1.

Custance, Arthur C., "Flood Traditions of the World," *Symposium on Creation IV* (Grand Rapids, MI: Baker, 1972).

Davidson, M.O., "Arizona Superintendency," *Annual Report of the Office of Indian Affairs for the Year 1865* (Washington: GPO, 1865).

Dawson, George M., *Report on the Queen Charlotte Islands* (Montreal: Dawson Brothers, 1880).

--------- "Notes and Observations on the Kwakiool People of the Northern Part of Vancouver Island," *Proceedings and Transactions of the Royal Society of Canada for the Year 1887* (Montreal: Dawson Brothers, 1888).

Dawson, John William, *The Story of the Earth and Man* (London: Hodder and Stoughton, 1873).

De Schweinitz, Edmund, *The Life and Times of David Zeisberger* (Philadelphia: J.B. Lippincott and Co., 1870).

Dean, James, "Mythology of the Iroquois; or, Six Nations of Indians," Document 13805. New York State Library, Albany.

Dixon, Roland B., "The Chimariko Indians and Language," *University of California Publications in American Archaeology and Ethnology*, vol. 5, no. 5 (Berkeley: 1910).

--------- "Shasta Myths," *Journal of American Folk-lore*, vol. 23, no. 87 (Boston and New York: Houghton Mifflin, 1911).

Dorsey, George Amos, *The Mythology of the Wichita* (Washington: Carnegie, 1904).

--------- *Traditions of the Arikara* (Washington: Carnegie, 1904).

--------- *Traditions of the Skidi Pawnee* (Boston: Houghton, Mifflin & Co., 1904).

--------- *The Cheyenne, Field Columbian Museum Publication 99*, vol. 9, no. 1 (Chicago: Field Columbian Museum, 1905).

--------- *Traditions of the Caddo* (Washington: Carnegie, 1905).

---------*The Pawnee*, vol. 1 (Washington: Carnegie, 1906).

Dorsey, James A., and Alfred L. Krober, *Traditions of the Arapaho* (Chicago: Field Columbian Museum, 1903).

Dorsey, James Owen, "Nanibozhu in Siouan Mythology," *Journal of American Folk-lore*, vol. 5, no. 19 (Boston and New York: Houghton, Mifflin and Co., 1892).

Du Pratz, Antoine-Simon Le Page, *L'Histoire de la Louisiane*, vol. 3 (Paris: 1758).

--------- *The History of Louisiana* (London: T. Becket, 1774).

DuBois, Constance Goddard, *The Religion of the Luiseño Indians of Southern California* (Berkeley: University of California Publications, 1908).

Eells, Myron, "Traditions of the Deluge Among the Tribes of the North-West," *The American Antiquarian and Oriental Journal*, vol. 1 (1878).

--------- "The Religion of the Indians of Puget Sound," *American Antiquarian*, vol 12 (Chicago: 1890).

Epic of Gilgamesh, translated by Andrew George (Penguin Books, 1999).

Erdoes, Richard, and Alfonso Ortiz, *American Indian Myths and Legends* (New York: Pantheon Books, 1984).

Eusebius, *Preparatio Evangelica*, translated by E.H. Gifford. 1909.

Faraud, Henri, "Missions de l'Amérique du Nord," *Annales de la Propagation de la Foi*, vol. 36 (Lyon: 1864).

Farrand, Livingston, and Leo J. Frachtenberg, "Shasta and Athapascan Myths from Oregon," *Journal of American Folklore*, vol. 28 (Lancaster and New York: American Folklore Society, 1915).

Fletcher, Alice C., and Francis La Flesche, "The Omaha Tribe," *Twenty Seventh Annual Report of the Bureau of American Ethnology* (Washington: GPO, 1911).

Fletcher, Jonathan E., "Origin and History of the Winnebagoes," *Information Respecting the History, Condition and Prospects of the Indian Tribes of the United States*, Part IV., edited by Henry Schoolcraft (Philadelphia: Lippincott, Grambo & Co., 1854).

Frachtenberg, Leo J., "Coos Texts," *Columbia University Contributions to Anthropology*, vol. 1 (New York: Columbia University Press, 1913).

--------- "Alsea Texts and Myths," *Bureau of American Ethnology Bulletin*, vol. 67 (Washington: GPO, 1920).

Frazer, Sir James George, *Folk-Lore In the Old Testament*, vol. 1 (London: Macmillan and Co., 1919).

Freeman, Thomas, and Peter Custis, *An Account of the Red River, in Louisiana, Drawn Up From the Returns of Messrs. Freeman and Custis to the War Office of the United States, Who Explored the Same, In the Year 1806* (Washington: 1806).

Garcia, Gregorio, *Origen de los Indios de el Nuevo Mundo, e Indias Occidentales* (Madrid: Francisco Martinez Abad, 1729).

Gatschet, Albert S., Leo J. Frachtenberg, and Melville Jacobs, "Kalapuya Texts," *University of Washington Publications in Anthropology*, vol. 11 (Seattle: University of Washington, 1945).

Gatschet, Albert S., "Some Mythic Stories of the Yuchi Indians," *American Anthropologist*, vol. 6, no. 3 (1893).

Gayton, Anna H., and Stanley S. Newman, "Yokuts and Western Mono Myths," *University of California Anthropological Records*, vol. 5 (Berkeley: University of California Press, 1940).

Gifford, Edward Winslow, and Gwendoline Harris Block, *Californian Indian Nights* (Glendale, CA: Arthur H. Clark, 1930).

Gilliland, Hap, *The Great Flood* (Billings, MT: Council for Indian Education, 2008).

Glueck, Nelson, *Rivers in the Desert: History of Negev* (New York: Farrar, Straus, and Cadahy, 1959).

Goddard, Pliny Earle, "Chilula Texts," *University of California Publications in American Archaeology and Ethnology*, vol. 10, no. 7 (Berkeley: University of California Press, 1914).

Goos, Anita, *The Legends*. N.D. Retrieved from: https://archive.org/details/ChumashFolkloreStories.

Gover, Kevin, "American Indians Serve in the U.S. Military in Greater Numbers Than Any Ethnic Group and Have Since the Revolution," December 6, 2015. Retrieved from https://www.huffingtonpost.com/national-museum-of-the-american-indian/american-indians-serve-in-the-us-military_b_7417854.html.

Grinnell, George Bird, *Pawnee Hero Stories and Folk-Talks* (New York: Charles Scribner's Sons, 1893).

--------- *Blackfoot Lodge Tales* (New York: Charles Scribner's Sons, 1908).

Gunther, Erna, "Klallam Folk Tales," *University of Washington Publications in Anthropology*, vol. 1 (Seattle: University of Washington Press, 1927).

Hall, Charles Francis, *Life with the Esquimaux*, vol. 2 (London: Sampson Low, Son, and Marston, 1864).

Hall, Frank, *History of the State of Colorado*, vol. 4 (Chicago: Blakely Printing Co., 1895).

Harris, Martha, *History and Folklore of the Cowichan Indians* (Victoria, BC: Colonist Publishing, 1901).

Henry, Alexander, *Travels and Adventures in Canada and the Indian Territories between the years 1760 and 1766*, Part 1 (New York: J. Riley, 1809).

Hewitt, John Napoleon Brinton, and Jeremiah Curtin, "Seneca Fiction, Legends, and Myths," *32nd Annual Report of the Bureau of American Ethnology* (Washington: GPO, 1918).

--------- *Iroquoian Cosmology*, Part 1 (Washington: GPO, 1904).

Hodge, Bodie, and Terry Mortenson, "Did Moses Write Genesis?" (June 28, 2011). Retrieved from: https://answersingenesis.org/bible-characters/moses/did-moses-write-genesis/.

Holden, Joseph M. and Norman Geisler. *The Popular Handbook of Archaeology and the Bible* (Eugene, OR: Harvest House, 2013).

Holm, Gustav, "Den Østgrønlandske Expedition udført I Aarene 1883–85," *Meddelelser om Grønland*, vol. 10 (Copenhagen: 1888).

Holmberg, H.J., "Ethnographische Skizzen über die Völker des Russischen Amerika," *Acta Societatis Scientiarum Fennicae*, vol. 4 (Helsingfors, 1856).

Hooper, W.H., *Ten Months Among the Tents of the Tuski* (London: John Murray, 1853).

Hutchings, James, "The Spirit's Lodge," *Hutchings' Illustrated California Magazine*, vol. 2 (San Francisco: Hutchings & Rosenfield, 1858).

Irvin, S.M., and William Hamilton, "Iowa and Sac Tribes," *Information Respecting the History, Condition and Prospects of the Indian Tribes of the United States*, part III. Edited by Henry Schoolcraft (Philadelphia: Lippincott, Grambo & Co., 1853).

James, George Wharton, *The Indians of the Painted Desert Region* (Boston: Little, Brown, and Co. 1903).

Jetté, J., "On Ten'a Folk-Lore," *Journal of the Royal Anthropological Institute*, vol. 38 (London: 1908).

Johnson, Elias, *Legends, Traditions, and Laws of the Iroquois, or Six Nations* (Lockport, NY: Union Printing and Publishing Co., 1881).

Johnson, Emily Pauline, *Legends of Vancouver* (Vancouver: David Spencer, 1911).

Jones, Peter, *History of the Ojebway Indians* (London: A.W. Bennett, 1861).

Josephus, *Antiquities of the Jews*. In *The Works of Josephus*. Translated by William Whiston (Peabody, MA: Hendrickson, 1987).

Josselyn, John, *An Account of Two Voyages to New England Made During the Years 1638, 1663* (Boston: William Veazie, 1865).

Kelly, Isabel T., "Northern Paiute Tales," *Journal of American Folk-lore*, vol. 51, no. 202 (New York: American Folk-lore Society, 1938).

Kitchen, Kenneth A., *Ancient Orient and the Old Testament* (London: Inter-Varsity Press, 1966).

Kramer, Samuel Noah, "The Babel of Tongues: A Sumerian Version," *Journal of the American Oriental Society*, vol. 88 (1968).

Kroeber, Alfred L., "Preliminary Sketch of the Mohave Indians," *American Anthropologist*, vol. 4 (new series), no. 2 (New York: G.P. Putnam's Sons, 1902).

--------- "Gros Ventre Myths and Tales," *Anthropological Papers of the American Museum of Natural History*, vol. 1 (New York: Order of the Trustees, 1907).

--------- "Indian Myths of South Central California," *University of California Publications American Archaeology and Ethnology*, vol. 4, no. 4 (Berkeley: University Press, 1907).

--------- "A Mission Record of the California Indians: From a Manuscript in the Bancroft Library," *University of California Publications in American Archaeology and Ethnology*, vol. 8, no. 1 (Berkeley: University Press, 1908).

--------- "Sinkyone Tales," *Journal of American Folk-lore*, vol. 32 (Lancaster and New York: American Folklore Society, 1919).

--------- *Yurok Myths* (Berkeley: University of California Press, 1976).

Kroeber, Alfred L., and Edward W. Winslow, *Karok Myths* (Berkeley and Los Angeles: University of California Press, 1980).

Le Jeune, Paul, "Relation of What Occurred in New France in the Year 1634," *The Jesuit Relations and Allied Documents,* ed. Reuben Gold Thwaites, vol. 6 (Cleveland: Burrow Brothers, 1898).

Leland, Charles Godfrey, *The Algonquin Legends of New England* (London: Sampson Low, Marston, Searle & Riverton, 1884).

Lowie, Robert Harry, *The Assiniboine* (New York: Order of the Trustees, 1909).

--------- "The Northern Shoshone," *Anthropological Papers of the American Museum of Natural History*, vol. 2, part 2 (New York, 1909).

Lowrie, Walter, and Matthew St. Clair Clarke, editors. *American State Papers, Class II: Indian Affairs,* vol. 1 (Washington: Gales and Seaton, 1832).

Lucey, J.M., "Missionary Labors of Lazarist Priests in Arkansas from 1818 to 1844," *Donahoe Magazine,* vol. 27 (Boston: Pilot, 1892).

Lynd, James W., "History, Religion, Legends, Language, and General Condition of the Dakota Nation." *James W. Lynd Papers*, Minnesota Historical Society Library, St. Paul, MN.

MacKenzie, Alexander, *Voyages from Montreal*, vol. 1 (Toronto: George Morang, 1902).

Marsh, Cutting, "Expedition to the Sacs and Foxes," *Collections of the State Historical Society of Wisconsin*, vol. 15 (Madison: Democrat Printing Co., 1900).

Martin, Howard N., *Folk-tales of the Alabama-Coushatta Indians* (Jacksonville, TX: McFarland Publishing, 1945).

Mason, John Alden, *The Ethnology of the Salinan Indians* (Berkeley: University of California Publications, 1912).

Masson, Louis Rodrigue, "George Keith Letters to Mr. Roderic MacKenzie," *Les Borgeois de la Compagnie du Nord-Ouest,* vol. 2 (Quebec: Imprimerie Générale a Coté et Cie, 1890).

Mather, Cotton, *The Ecclesiastical History of New England* (London: Thomas Parkhurst, 1702).

Matthews, Washington, *Navaho Legends* (Boston and New York: American Folklore Society, 1897).

Mayne, Richard Charles, *Four Years in British Columbia and Vancouver Island* (London: John Murray, 1862).

McBeth, Kate C., *The Nez Perces Since Lewis and Clark* (New York and Chicago: Fleming H. Revell Co., 1908).

McWhorter, Lucullus V., "Yakima Tradition of the Flood," *McWhorter Manuscript Collection,* Washington State University Library.

Meacham, Alfred Benjamin, *Wi-ne-ma (the Woman Chief) and Her People* (Hartford: American, 1876).

Merriam, Clinton Hart, *The Dawn of the World* (Cleveland: Arthur H. Clark Company, 1910).

Mindeleff, Victor, "A Study of Pueblo Architecture, Tusayan and Cibola," *Eighth Annual Report of the Bureau of American Ethnology* (Washington: GPO, 1891).

Mooney, James, "Die Tonkawas, der letzte Kannibalenstamm in den Vereinigten Staaten," *Globus,* vol. 82 (Brunswick, Germany: Friedrich Vieweg, 1902).

Morice, Adrien-Gabriel, "Three Carrier Myths," *Transactions of the Canadian Institute*, vol. 5 (Toronto: Canadian Institute, 1895).

Nelson, Edward William, *The Eskimo About Bering Strait* (Washington: GPO, 1900).

Olden, Sarah E., *Shoshone Folk Tales, as Discovered from the Rev. John Roberts, a Hidden Hero, On the Wind River Indian Reservation in Wyoming* (Milwaukee: Morehouse Publishing Co., 1923).

Opler, Morris Edward, "Myths and Tales of the Chiricahua Apache Indians," *Memoirs of the American Folk-lore Society,* vol. 42 (New York: 1942).

Pargellis,Stanley, "An Account of the Indians of Virginia," *William and Mary Quarterly*, vol. 16, no. 2 (Williamsburg, VA: Omohundro Institute of American History and Culture, 1959).

Bullchild, Percy, *The Sun Came Down: The History of the World as my Blackfeet Elders Told It* (New York: Harper & Row, 1985).

Parsons, Elsie Clews, "Tewa Tales," Memoirs of the American Folk-lore Society, vol. 19 (New York: American Folk-lore Society, 1926).

Petitot, Émile, *Monograph of the Dene-Dindjie Indians.* Translated by Douglas Brynner. 1878.

--------- *Traditions Indiennes du Canada Nord-ouest* (Paris: Maissonneuve Fréres, 1886).

Petrovich, Douglas, *Identifying Babel and Its Tower* (video lecture), 20 June 2017. Retrieved from https://isgenesishistory.com/douglas-petrovich/.

Powers, Stephen, *Tribes of California* (Washington: GPO, 1877).

Rasmussen, Knud, *The Netsilik Eskimos: Social Life and Spiritual Culture* (Copenhagen: 1931).

Reagan, Albert B., and L.V.W. Walters, "Tales from the Hoh and Quileute," *Journal of American Folklore*, vol. 46, no. 182 (Lancaster and New York: American Folklore Society, 1933).

Riggs, Stephen R., "Memoir of Hon. Jas. W. Lynd," *Collections of the Minnesota Historical Society*, vol. 3 (St. Paul: Minnesota Historical Society, 1880).

RiverWind, Joseph, *That's What the Old Ones Say* (Middletown, DE: Firekeepers, 2015).

Rosenmüller, E.F.C., *The Biblical Geography of Central Asia,* vol. 2, trans. N. Morren (Edinburgh: Thomas Clark, 1837).

Russell, Frank, "The Pima Indians," *Twenty-Sixth Annual Report of the Bureau of American Ethnology* (Washington: GPO, 1908).

Sapir, Edward, "A Flood Legend of the Nootka Indians of Vancouver Island," *Journal of American Folk-lore*, vol. 32 (Lancaster and New York: American Folklore Society, 1919).

--------- "Takelma Texts," *Anthropological Publications of the University of Pennsylvania Museum,* vol. 2, no. 1 (Philadelphia: University Museum, 1909).

Schoolcraft, Henry Rowe, *Notes on the Iroquois* (Albany, NY: Erastus H. Pease & Co., 1847).

--------- *Historical and Statistical Information Respecting the History, Conditions and Prospects of the Indians Tribes of the United States*, Part 1 (Philadelphia: Lippencott, Grambo & Co., 1851).

--------- *History of the Indian Tribes of the United States,* Part VI (Philadelphia: J.B. Lippincott & Co., 1857).

--------- and Thomas H. Benton, "Remarks on the Prints of Human Feet, Observed in the Secondary Limestone of the Mississippi Valley," *The American Journal of Science and Arts*, vol. 5 (New Haven, CT: S. Converse, 1822).

Shoemaker, Henry Wharton, "History of Tamarack Swamp: Another Page from Indian Antiquity," *Reading Times*, January 6, 1912.

Skinner, Alanson, "The Mascoutens or Prairie Potawatomi Indians, Part III, Mythology and Folklore," *Milwaukee Public Museum Bulletin*, vol. 6, part 3 (Milwaukee: Order of the Trustees, 1927).

Skinner, Charles Montgomery, *Myths and Legends of Our Own Land*, vol. 2 (Philadelphia and London: J.J. Lippincott, 1896).

--------- *Myths and Legends Beyond Our Borders* (Philadelphia and London: J.B. Lippincott, 1899).

Snelling, Andrew. *Earth's Catastrophic Past: Geology, Creation & the Flood*, 2 vols. (Green Forest, Arkansas: Master Books, 2018).

--------- *Earth's Catastrophic Past*, vol. 2, p. 497.

Speck, Frank G., "The Creek Indians of Taskigi Town," *Memoirs of the American Anthropological Association*, vol. 2 (Lancaster, PA: New Era Printing Co., 1907).

--------- "Catawba Texts," *Columbia University Contributions to Anthropology*, vol. 24 (New York: Columbia University Press, 1934).

Spence, Lewis, *The Myths of the North American Indians* (London: George G. Harrap, 1916).

Spencer, J., "Shawnee Folk-lore," *Journal of American Folk-lore*, vol. 22 (Lancaster, PA and New York, NY: 1909).

St. Clair, Harry Hull, "Shoshone and Comanche Tales," *Journal of American Folk-lore*, vol. 22, edited by Robert H. Lowie (Boston and New York: Houghton Mifflin, 1909).

Stevenson, Matilda Coxe, "The Sia," *Eleventh Annual Report of the Bureau of American Ethnology* (Washington: GPO, 1894).

Stevenson, Tilly E., "The Religious Life of the Zuñi Child," *Fifth Annual Report of the Bureau of American Ethnology* (Washington: GPO, 1887).

Steward, Julian H., "Myths of the Owens Valley Paiute," *University of California Publications in American Archaeology and Ethnology*, vol. 34, no. 5 (Berkeley: University of California Press, 1936).

--------- "Some Western Shoshoni Myths," *Bureau of American Ethnology Bulletin 136,* No. 31 (Washington: GPO, 1943).

Stirling, Matthew W., "Origin Myth of Acoma and Other Records," *Bureau of American Ethnology Bulletin,* vol. 135 (Washington: GPO, 1942).

Swan, James G., *The Indians of Cape Flattery* (Washington: Smithsonian Institute, 1870).

Swanton, John R., "Mythology of the Indians of Louisiana and the Texas Coast," *Journal of American Folklore,* vol. 20, no. 79 (Huffton Mifflin, 1907).

--------- "Indian Tribes of the Lower Mississippi Valley," *Bureau of American Ethnology Bulletin,* No. 43 (Washington: GPO, 1911).

--------- "Myths and Tales of the Southeastern Indians," *Bureau of American Ethnology Bulletin,* Vol. 88 (Washington: GPO, 1919).

--------- "Early History of the Creek Indians and their Neighbors," *Bureau of American Ethnology Bulletin,* No. 73 (Washington: GPO, 1922).

--------- *Tlingit Myths and Texts* (Washington: GPO, 1909).

Tache, Rev. Dr., "Hudson's Bay Missions," *Annals of the Propagation of the Faith*, vol. 13 (London: 1852).

Taylor, Alexander Smith, "The Indianology of California," *The California Farmer*, April 27, 1860.

Teit, James, *Traditions of the Thompson River Indians* (Boston and New York: Houghlin and Mifflin, 1898).

--------- "The Shuswap," *The Jesup North Pacific Expedition*, vol. 2, part 3, edited by Franz Boas (New York: G. E. Stechert, 1909).

--------- "Traditions of the Lillooet Indians of British Columbia," *Journal of American Folk-lore*, vol. 25 (Lancaster, PA, and New York, NY: 1912).

--------- "Folk-Tales of Salishan and Sahaptin Tribes," *Memoirs of the American Folk-Lore Society*, vol. 11, edited by Franz Boas (Lancaster and New York: American Folklore Society, 1917).

--------- "Kaska Tales," *Journal of American Folk-lore*, vol. 30 (Lancaster and New York: American Folklore Society, 1917).

--------- "Tahltan Tales," *Journal of American Folk-lore*, vol. 32, no. 124 (1919).

Thompson, David, *David Thompson's Narrative of his Explorations in Western America,* edited by J.B. Tyrell (Toronto: Champlain Society, 1917).

Turner, Sharon, *The Sacred History of the World, as Displayed in the Creation and Subsequent Events to the Deluge*, vol. 2 (London: Longman, 1834).

Twiss, Richard, *One Church, Many Tribes* (Minneapolis: Baker Publishing, 2000).

Waters, Frank, *Book of the Hopi* (New York: Penguin Books, 1963).

Wetmore, Helen Cody, *Last of the Great Scouts: The Life Story of Col. William F. Cody ("Buffalo Bill") as Told by His Sister Helen Cody Wetmore* (Chicago: Duluth Press, 1899).

Whitney, Ernest, *Legends of the Pikes Peak Region* (Denver: Chain & Hardy Co., 1892).

Wied, Prince Alexander Philipp Maximillian, *Travels in the Interior of North America,* translated by H. Evans Lloyd (London: Ackermann and Co., 1843).

Wilson, E.F., "Report on the Sarcee Indians," in "Report on the North-Western Tribes of Canada," *Report of the Fifty-Eighth Meeting of the British Association for the Advancement of Science Held at Bath in September 1888* (London: John Murray, 1889).

Wissler, Clark, and Duvall, D.C., "Mythology of the Blackfoot Indians," *Anthropological Papers of the American Museum of Natural History*, vol. 2 (New York: Order of Trustees, 1909).

Woldt, Adrian, *Captain Jacobsen's Reise an der Nordwestküste, 1881–1883* (Leipzig: 1884).

Wonderly, Anthony, *Oneida Iroquois Folklore, Myth, and History* (Syracuse: Syracuse University Press, 2004).

Wright, Julia McNair, *Bricks from Babel: A Brief View of the Myths, Traditions and Religious Belief of Races* (New York: John B. Alden, 1885).

APPENDIX F

RECOMMENDED READING

The following is a partial list of books, all of which are highly recommended for further reading.

On Flood Legends

Deluge Story in Stone, by Byron Nelson
Flood Legends, by Charles Martin Jr.
The Sacred History of the World, by Sharon Turner
A Treatise on the Deluge, by Alexander Catcott
The Origin of Pagan Idolatry, by George Stanley Faber
"Flood Traditions of the World," by Arthur C. Custance, in *Symposium on Creation IV*

Geology, Archeology and Historical Evidences

Earth's Catastrophic Past, by Andrew Snelling
The Popular Handbook of Archaeology and the Bible, by Norman Geisler and Joseph Holden
Noah's Ark: A Feasibility Study, by John Woodmorappe
New Evidence that Demands a Verdict, by Josh McDowell
Biblical Archaeology: Discoveries that Support the Reliability of the Bible (volumes 1 and 2), by David E. Graves
Discovering the City of Sodom, by Stephen Collins
Patterns of Evidence: Exodus (book and DVD), by Tim Mahoney
The Lost Sea of the Exodus: A Modern Geographical Analysis, by Glen A. Fritz
"The Biblical Significance of Jabal Al Lawz," Ph. D. dissertation, by Charles A. Whittaker
Is Genesis History? Conference presentations and DVD
Carved in Stone: Geological Evidence of the Worldwide Flood by Timothy Clarey
The Genesis Flood, by Henry Morris
Evolution - The Greatest Deception in Modern History by Roger G. Gallop
The World's Oldest Alphabet by Douglas Petrovich

First Nations Ministry

Introduction to First Nations Ministry, by Cheryl Bear-Barnetson

One Church, Many Tribes, by Richard Twiss

That's What the Old Ones Say, by Joseph RiverWind

Bruchko, by Bruce Olsen

Biology, Paleontology, Creation, and Evolution

Evolution's Achilles Heels, edited by Robert Carter

Replacing Darwin, by Nathaniel Jeanson

Darwin's House of Cards, by Tom Bethell

Greatest Hoax on Earth: Refuting Dawkins on Evolution, by Jonathan Sarfati

Ultimate Proof of Creation: Resolving the Origins Debate, by Jason Lisle

In the Beginning, by Walt Brown

Darwin's Black Box, by Michael Behe

Icons of Evolution: Science or Myth? by Jonathan Wells

Signature in the Cell, by Stephen Meyer

BIBLICAL CONNECTIONS

Babel/Confusion of Languages

Acoma Pueblo
Ancient Sources
Arapaho
Bella Coola
Blackfoot
Cheyenne
Chiapaneco
Choctaw
Juruna
Kaska
Ohio Tradition
Ohlone
Paipai
Quiche
Skagit
Tahltan
Three Sisters Peak
Tlaxcalan
Tlingit
Toltec
Yukpa

Creation Stories

Alaska
Asurini
Blackfoot
Creek
Cuzco Tradition
Greenland
Iowa
Pima
Shawnee

Dinosaurs

Iroquois
Tahltan

Fire Stories Reminiscent of Noahic Flood

Mundurucu
Yuracare

Nephilim

Chaldean Source
Chumash
Cree
Cuzco Tradition
Hareskin
Iroquois Nations
Kootenay
Lakota and Taino
Mesaya
Montagnais
Netsilik Eskimo
Pawnee
Penobscot and Passamaquoddy
Sauk and Fox
Tahltan
Tlaxcalan
Toltec
Zapotec

Long Day of Joshua

Toltec

Post-Flood Migration

Bella Coola

Chiapaneco

Choctaw

Coastal Salish

Coos

Cowichan

Gros Ventres

Hareskin

Kaska

Kitanemuk

Kwakiutl

Mandan

Mutsun

Paipai

Pomo

Quileute

Tahltan

Toltec

Tonkawa

Tsimshian

Tunica

Prophecies of Christ

Cherokee

Lakota

Spokane and Salish

Taino

Rainbow

Cheyenne

Gros Ventres

Lakota

Western Cree

Yellowstone Valley Tradition

Raven/Dove/Olive Leaf

Apache

Arapaho

Cascade Mountains Tradition

Catawba

Chumash

Coastal Salish

Cochiti Pueblo

Cora

Cree

Creek

Dene

Inca

Iowa

Jacaltek

Lenape

Mandan

Mocoví

Mundurucu

Natchez

Other Alaska Traditions

Palikur

Potawatomi

Purepecha

Tehuelche

Tuskegee

Tzeltal

Urarina

Wajapi

Wukchumni

Yuracaré

Subterranean Fountains

Gros Ventres

Hopi

Lakota

Pawnee

APPENDIX H

INDEX BY TRIBE, NATION, OR LOCALE